Y0-BZJ-249

Become Jesus

The Diary of a Soul Touched by God

by

Marinus Scholtes

(1919-1941)

Translated by Joop Bekkers, Ph.D.

Edited with an Introduction and Afterword by
Adrian van Kaam, C.S.Sp., Ph.D.,
and
Susan Muto, Ph.D.

DORRANCE PUBLISHING CO., INC.
PITTSBURGH, PENNSYLVANIA

Imprimatur:	Most Reverend Donald William Wuerl Bishop of Pittsburgh April 6, 1998
Nihil Obstat:	Joseph J. Kleppner, S.T.L., Ph.D. Censor Liborum

ISBN # 0-8059-4330-7
Library of Congress Catalog Card Number 97-8595
Printed in the United States of America

Second Printing

For information or to order additional books, please write:
Dorrance Publishing Co., Inc.
643 Smithfield Street
Pittsburgh, Pennsylvania 15222
U.S.A.

or

Epiphany Association
947 Tropical Avenue
Pittsburgh, Pennsylvania 15216
U.S.A.

Dedication

This diary of Marinus Scholtes
is dedicated to
the 1936 pioneers in formative spirituality.
With Marinus in The Hague, Holland,
they prepared the way
for formation theology and its
auxiliary disciplines.

Contents

Acknowledgments

It has been our singular privilege to serve as the principle editors of the papers of Marinus Scholtes, aptly titled *Become Jesus: The Diary of a Soul Touched by God.*

Our thanks go first of all to the family of origin and the adopted Dutch Spiritan family of Marinus for granting to the Epiphany Association all rights to his writings in whatever form or language. The Board of Directors and the Members of the Corporation have in turn assumed all the necessary expenses involved in translating, editing, and publishing the papers herein. They do so in the recognition that Marinus Scholtes in 1935 in Holland was the co-originator with Adrian van Kaam of the prototype Epiphany Association and its then embryonic formation theology.

This work in its entirety could not have been accomplished without the help of several people, starting with our translator, Joop Bekkers, Ph.D., whose unfailing dedication to Rinus' thought and intention resulted in this excellent rendering.

The Dutch Province of the Holy Ghost Fathers cooperated in this venture by providing archival information as well as many of the illustrations and photographs found in this text.

It would have been impossible for us together to produce this work without the tireless, infinitely patient attention to draft upon draft of the diary offered by our administrative secretary, Mary Lou Perez. We owe her a profound debt of gratitude on all levels of production.

We thank also the president of the Board of Directors of the Epiphany Association, David Natali, M.D., for supporting the publication financially and for encouraging us to bring our dream of sharing Rinus with numberless readers to reality.

Last but not least, we are grateful for the partnership that exists between the Epiphany Association and Dorrance Publishing Co., Inc., leading to what we believe to be a splendid text.

Most of all we thank God for giving us Rinus, for the grace of his epiphanic vision, and for the challenge he offers to all believers to become Jesus. May the fruits of his efforts bear benefits and graces he himself could not have foreseen.

—Adrian van Kaam, C.S.Sp., Ph.D.
Susan Muto, Ph.D.

TRANSLATOR'S PREFACE

by Joop Bekkers, Ph.D.

To translate a work of this kind was a rewarding challenge for me, although it was not always an easy task. Yet I enjoyed doing it and was [eeply impressed, both by what I read and by what I translated.

Marinus "Rinus" Scholtes' recollection notebooks or diaries were written from 1935 to 1941. They deal with his spiritual formation, reformation, and transformation rather than being only a record of daily events. Of course, the two cannot be separated. The text speaks for itself, yet some explanation may be useful.

Rinus' diaries comprise his life from his fifteenth to his twenty-second year, when he died of consumption. These were his years in the Junior Seminary, the Novitiate, and the Senior Seminary. He lived in The Netherlands. He was born in 1919 in the village of Naaldwijk, a center of fruit and vegetable growing about ten miles from The Hague, the seat of the Dutch government. Some of his sisters and brothers are still alive. The family must have moved to The Hague when Rinus was fairly young, for he never refers to his native village.

When the diary opens, as can be seen in this full edition of his writings, Rinus is in the fourth year of the Junior Seminary of the Dutch province of the Spiritans at Weert, a small town in the southeast of the country. The bulk of his recollection notebooks, however, are written in his Novitiate year (1937-1938) at Gennep, another small town, about thirteen miles from Nijmegen and only three miles from the German border. That is where his profoundest spiritual experiences took place. At the end of that period in his life he took his temporal or first (three year) vows, in August of 1938. After that time, however, when the daily recollection notebook of the Novitiate was no longer required, most of his notes were written down on retreat days. At that time he was at the Senior Seminary studying philosophy and theology. The note taking ended about two months before his death. To these diaries a few notes have been added as well as a number of letters, most of them Rinus' own correspondence, and a few letters concerning him.

Contents

The first diary written at Weert is very short, and is clearly about a young man's first effort. It portrays the start of his spiritual growth. Added to this first part, before he starts the then prescribed recollection notebooks, kept by all novices after their morning meditation, he wrote a kind of allegory, titled *The Spiritual Life: A Novice's Allegory,* dealing with some six or seven weeks at the beginning of his Novitiate year in Gennep.[1] In this section he compares his life at the Novitiate with a child's stay at a sanatorium. The chief doctor is God the Father; his assistant, "Elder Brother," is Jesus; the nurses are the saints, etc. He may have been influenced by the *Story of a Soul* by St. Thérèse of Lisieux, which he had probably read. He did not keep up this allegory. However, it does contain some remarkable observations on his spiritual growth as well as an effort to relate it to the mystery of the Holy Trinity.

As mentioned before, the second and third part of this diary are in the form of the daily required reports on the prayer life of the novices written during an assigned time in the study room at the Novitiate. These deal with his spiritual growth through simple, daily events and tasks that were deeply meaningful to him. He mentions some other persons there, as well as some books he, along with all the other novices, was obliged to read, such as Rodriguez and Tanquerey's book on ascetical and mystical theology. On a few occasions he refers to the Flemish priest, Edward Poppe, who had promoted Eucharistic devotion, especially among children, and whom he admired a great deal.

His growth in the life of the spirit continued, becoming intense and profound, up to the point of his experiencing a kind of mystical marriage of his soul with Jesus, an expression of the intensity of his personal orientation toward the "Dear Lord." His devotion to Mary was equally deep and continuous. With this spiritual fervor he took his first religious vows at the end of his Novitiate.

1. Incidently, the house there has now been replaced by a new building. It was damaged in the winter of 1944-1945 when it lay in the front lines of combat for some four months. At present it is a facility for aged members of the Spiritan Congregation. Its former inhabitants had to be evacuated in December, 1933, when Gennep was flooded; it escaped a second flood in January, 1995.

He then started his studies of philosophy and theology at Gemert. The influence of these subjects is often noticeable. Gemert is a village in the southeast of the country, about twenty-five miles from the German border, and some thirteen miles from Eindhoven. The Senior Seminary was housed in an old castle, dating from the thirteenth century, built by the Teutonic Knights. It was bought by Father Christian Lütenbacher, a French Spiritan, who introduced the Congregation of the Spiritans into The Netherlands. Rinus mentions him as well as several other students and some priests at Gemert, citing as well some other significant books and writers. During the first half year at Gemert no notes were written down. He resumed writing in February 1939. Most of his notes were written only once a month on retreat days. His spiritual life keeps unfolding, though after his mystical marriage experience it was no longer clouded by the suffering of the dark night of the spirit at Gennep. Yet it still ran deep.

Rinus fell ill about two months before his death and stopped writing. The last part of his body of work consists of some personal notes and correspondence by Rinus and others as well as a graphic description of his death on February 1, 1941, followed by two informative and inspiring obituaries.

Besides the themes referred to already, the following should be highlighted:

1. *His devotion to Mary*. It is basically edifying and orthodox. Rinus did not like sentimental or pietistic ways of praying or living the faith. The fact that he considers himself Mary's "slave" does not change his basic "manly" stance. Today the same devotion might be phrased as becoming "Mary's fully dedicated servant or child." The main thing is that he lives this devotion inspired by the classical writing and teaching of St. Louis Marie de Montfort on the "slavery of Mary." It was to this ideal that Rinus adhered with all his heart.
2. *His seriousness*. Rinus' diaries were not meant as such to be humorous, yet in daily life he was cheerful and merry enough. He liked acting, and the fact that he was chosen to play the part of St. Nicholas speaks for itself. A less than lighthearted person could never carry that role!
3. *The Second World War*. What will not be found in Rinus' diary is any significant reference to the events leading to and occurring during the Second World War, which at that time was only beginning in Europe. He avoids doing so in full obedience to the spirit of detachment from absorption in political news during the Junior Seminary, Novitiate, and Senior Seminary. At that time, rightly or wrongly, reading newspapers and listening to the radio, for all these years of spiritual formation, were strictly forbidden. This lack of reference is due, moreover, to the fact that his diaries started out as his way of

reporting on prayer-related experiences in the recollection notebooks all novices had to use after meditation. The Novice Master collected these notebooks from time to time to see when and how the novices were progressing in their prayer life. These reports were obviously not meant to be interlaced with speculations on the war and its events. To protect "recollection-in-depth," the Novice Master would pencil out any political views in letters addressed to the novices. In remarkable fidelity to the inner way of recollection learned in the Novitiate, and supported by detachment from newspapers and radio news, he alludes to but does not dwell on the eventual outbreak of the war in 1939 and the then mobilization of the Dutch army. He refers only once or twice to some officers who used part of the seminary buildings as their quarters. In characteristic fashion he expresses his high opinion of the Christian religious life of an officer who once spoke to the students.

The fact is that on May 10, 1940, the Germans invaded The Netherlands. On that day or the following one, the Senior Seminary in Gemert was shelled when it came in the front line of fire. Rinus gives a graphic description of the seminarian's stay during the fire fight between the Dutch and German soldiers in the cellars of the original Teutonic castle. He relates that after the fight they were forced out of the cellars, detained before threatening machine guns, and finally released. In faithfulness to the seminary formation of that time, he chose not to contaminate his contemplative union with Jesus with prolonged speculation and emotional outbursts about the German occupation of the country when he was with his relatives in the summer of 1940.

The Translation Itself

Rinus' handwriting, in the prescribed recollection notebooks, especially in the oldest parts of these reports, was not always perfectly legible. This was partly due to the fact that he, along with the other novices, had only a limited amount of time available after Holy Mass to record their meditation and related prayer experiences. Later on he was permitted to add to his morning notes written accounts of contemplations during the day. He had to do so, especially when the dark nights of sense and spirit made it impossible for him to record the experiences of discursive meditation as asked for in the guidelines to the recollection reports.

I did try to keep to the original text as much as possible, though this entailed a real challenge. On the whole, Rinus wrote a non-literary, colloquial, but otherwise correct Dutch, never vulgar, with some occasional schoolboy slang. Like all other novices he had not the slightest idea that these simple recollection recordings would ever be read by anybody else than his Novice Master. Apart from an occasional wrong sentence structure or mixed metaphor, his grammar and style are excellent. There are some phrases and quotations in Latin. For some days when he was at the Novitiate, he wrote his notes in Latin but changed back into Dutch, so as to express his thoughts and feelings better.

Some difficulties in translating were caused by the nature of the Dutch language. It can be very colloquial due to the typically Dutch custom of linking ideas with small concrete things or everyday happenings in imaginative ways. Expressions like "go sit on the roof" (when you don't agree) or "long toes" (touchiness) need some explanation to foreigners. Further, some puns got lost in the course of translation.

Rinus often uses affectionate names for God or Jesus or Mary: Daddy, Mommy, Elder Brother, etc. Above all, when he had deep mystical experiences, he grappled with the language, trying to express what is inexpressible or coining new words. This is a phenomenon that is likely to occur in every language: strong experiences tend to break through the usual grammar or sentence structure. Then, to express all shades of modality or feeling, the Dutch uses lots of adjectives, adverbs, or interjections, whereas English is a "verb-language," that is, it uses all kinds of verbal constructions or auxiliary verbs. Although I have translated the texts into correct English as much as possible some "substratum" of the Dutch may still remain.

Rinus is sometimes inconsistent or even mistaken in indicating dates or days of the week. I have stuck to one system, indicating both dates and weekdays. In regard to his correspondence, the way to start a letter, the salutation of certainly a personal letter, is different in the two languages. I have for the most part maintained the writers' style. That was the rule of thumb I chose to follow throughout my translation. I also gratefully acknowledge the stylistic improvements provided by the editors of this inspiring work, my friends and colleagues, Professors Adrian van Kaam and Susan Muto, who helped enormously to "Americanize" my English and capture the boyish yet mature phrasing of Rinus Scholtes. To safeguard the objectivity of the translation, they mailed to me any American-English improvements for my critique, correction, and ultimate approval in service of the integrity of the original Dutch text.

Introduction

by

Adrian van Kaam, C.S.Sp., Ph.D.

When I met Rinus in 1932, I was twelve, and he was thirteen. Our first meeting took place at the Junior Seminary of the Congregation of the Holy Spirit in Weert. We were among two hundred-plus other seminarians. Rinus had already been a student there for more than two years. We came to this boarding school in the South of Holland from two neighboring parishes in The Hague. Being from the same city added to our affinity and the eventual spiritual partnership that was its finest fruit. Many extra opportunities for prolonged, leisurely contact and conversation were available to us during the long Christmas, Easter, and summer holidays with our families. The early growth of Rinus' life in Christ touched me deeply. He shared with me the spellbinding story of his graced journey. Our soul sharing continued from the beginning of the Junior Seminary to the end of Rinus' short life in our major seminary in Gemert. He called me to his death bed for a final farewell before he left this world for the next.

Epiphany's Origins

In 1936 Rinus and I felt inspired to start with lay friends in The Hague a small prayer, reading, and reflection group. We named it provisionally "Pioneers of Mary." It was the prototype of the future Epiphany Association I would co-found in Pittsburgh in 1979 with Dr. Susan Muto and a few like-minded friends.

Rinus with his mother, father, brothers, and sisters. Top row, third from left.

At that time in Holland, Rinus and I were still lay persons in the Church. Together with our spiritual friends, we felt somewhat ambiguous about the triumphalism, power, and startling proficiency of the emancipated Catholic population of Holland. They emerged from centuries of persecution with large, devout families capable, through their sheer numbers, of controlling votes and wielding political power. When the oppression ended, and spurred on by the advent of democracy, they strove valiantly to organize a Catholic political party, to found their own unions, press, social care institutions and legislation, hospitals, radio stations, seminaries, religious communities, and free-standing Catholic Schools and universities—all fully subsidized by the State. These and similar projects flourished beyond one's wildest dreams and expectations. In some measure these developments were desirable, but, over the course of time, the shadow side of their proliferation became clear.

Holland was fast gaining the fame of being one of the best organized provinces of the West-European Church. Everything "Catholic" was enjoying almost unmitigated success. While also rejoicing in this blooming and booming Catholicism, what made us feel ambivalent at times were sporadic signs of some decline in graced openness to divine guidance, to the Spirit's gifts of humility, inner surrender and peace, of presence to Christ hidden in the center of our personhood. Diminished also was a taste for and a familiarity with the formation wisdom of Holy Scripture and the Christian classics. Was there perhaps a silent gnawing away at the conviction that God alone is the source, the first cause, of any effectiveness in the salvation of persons and populations?

God allowed mighty kings and armies to destroy the autarchic, pride-filled independence of Israel the moment his chosen people put their trust more in their own machinations than in his salvific power. We feared for the future of our triumphant Catholic organizations. At some moments in our imagination there arose the spectacle of mere "I"-centered influences in the times ahead, of insufficient interior strength to resist the seductive power of human pride.

Enthusiastic as we were to pursue our vocation, we could foresee clergy and religious questioning theirs, and perhaps leaving their dioceses and congregations. Would there not come a time when the flood of priestly and religious vocations would dry up? When activistic organizations, with less commitment to contemplation, would collapse? When many faithful would leave the Church?

We were by no means certain that such developments would take place. We had no prophetic knowledge of what would later transpire. Still we felt inspired by the Spirit to begin a small association devoted to prayer, meditation, and reflection on classical formation wisdom. [2] Under the protection of Mary, the Mother of Jesus, our association might help to sustain our own fidelity if and when the "best laid plans of mice and men" would fail to materialize.

We called our association therefore the "Pioneers of Mary." We implored her to ask her son Jesus to evoke in us, and then through us in others, what is beyond words: the depths of the human heart, the mystery of God's presence hidden in the recesses of our soul.

Dutch Catholic institutions should not be diminished or neglected. They should be inspired anew by the humble inner riches bestowed since Baptism by the Holy Spirit. For us this work of the Spirit was reflected in the Epiphany of all epiphanies, the appearance of Jesus Christ, mirrored in the heart of the Virgin Mother of God.

From the start of our association, we felt that Holy Providence was preparing us for a wider mission and ministry in the area of ongoing, in depth formation of the laity without neglecting similar needs in the lives of clergy and religious. Our call, therefore, was to pioneer a prayerful awareness of the Epiphany of the Divine Formator of humanity: the Holy Spirit. The Holy Spirit formed Jesus with the consent of Mary's immaculate and courageous heart. She bore God's own son in her womb. Likewise the Divine Spirit forms Jesus in our soul and heart in and through the heart of Mary. The diary of Rinus witnesses to this process and its precious fruits. It exemplifies the meaning of living an epiphanic Christian presence in the world.

In the last weeks before his death and gentle passage to heaven, Rinus kept joyously repeating to me that the Holy Spirit disclosed to him the mysterious mission of his brief pilgrimage on earth. He felt that he would be empowered to spend his heaven in fostering the mission of the unfolding of our Epiphany inspirations. From on high he would accompany and bless its participants, benefactors, and their families.

His simple writings contain the basic principles of epiphanic formation in Christ. They are hidden as sparkling gems in the unspectacular everydayness of his love life with God.

---

[2] Editor's Note: Certain formation classics, especially the more ancient and medieval, were written in a world different from our own. At present we find ourselves in the midst of a transition in the history of human unfolding. Still classics have captured some enduring features of basic human and Christian formation. To ignore this wisdom would be irresponsible. Yet it would be equally imprudent to neglect contemporary insights from outside the Church compatible with Christianity. Therefore, when I initiated formation theology in the 1930s, I felt compelled almost at the same time to launch a prototheological formation anthropology sustained by a pretheological formation science. These disciplines could facilitate the attunement of this new approach to contemporary developments in the sciences, arts, and disciplines affecting human and Christian formation.

Aversion of Emotional Display

What struck me in his writings as well as in our intimate talks was his delicate childlike sensitivity. His heart mirrored the sensitivity of the heart of Jesus, whom he called affectionately his Elder Brother. This inner warmth raises a question. In his writings Rinus avows at times his aversion from feeling and sentiment. In some passages he almost *seems* to deny the gift of emotionality. He confesses to a displeasure with the public expression of feelings in southern cultures. Yet the few people who knew him as intimately as I and his three successive spiritual directors did, could never doubt the tenderness of his loving heart. Neither can readers of this diary escape this awareness, though there is a difference between inmost feelings and their public display.

Dutch Emotional Reticence

Like most of his countrymen and women, Rinus had imbibed the typical Dutch demeanor of a somewhat stolid reticence about one's deeper emotions. Public displays of feeling, acceptable in other cultures, were frowned upon by "solid citizens" (or burghers) of Holland. Especially upper and middle class residents of The Hague seemed inclined that way.

This absence of display does not necessarily mean that emotion itself is lacking in them. A particular Dutch person may have as much feeling capacity as some Frenchmen, Spaniards, or Italians. But early in life many Dutch children may absorb the national trait of curbing one's spontaneous display of feeling, especially in bodily expressions.

Only at certain occasions will such display between Dutchmen be tolerated. For example, on the soccer field, after making a spectacular goal or winning the match, mutual embraces, cordial touchings, and endearing back slapping between the elated Dutch players themselves as well as between them and excited fans are acceptable.

The usual characteristic of curbing such spontaneity made Rinus different from many other masters of formation such as Brother Lawrence of the Resurrection, St. Thérèse of Lisieux, Blessed Faustina of Poland, St. Catherine of Siena, St. John Bosco, St. Philip Neri, St. Louis Marie de Montfort, St. Benedict Labre, Blessed Jacques Laval, or Blessed Daniel Brottier, to name only a few.

Role of this Characteristic in Rinus' Formation

Rinus speaks candidly in his writings about his inclination toward spontaneous expressions of his feelings for some fellow novices and seminarians.

Grace enabled him to turn the customary Dutch reticence into a virtue that could serve his spiritual growth by transforming these feelings of attraction to his confrères. Our own soul friendship in Christ was so uplifting that it was encouraged by the three successive spiritual directors to whom we both went for guidance.

The fruits of our blessed relationship blossomed in our "Pioneers of Mary" association as well as in its spontaneous outgrowth in the future Epiphany Association.

Childlike Candor

One noticeable characteristic of Rinus, comparable to that of St. Thérèse of Lisieux, is his childlike candor and its expression in his prayer life and his writings. Like Thérèse, Rinus spent approximately nine years in the religious life, including the Junior Seminary, which at the same time counted as a Postulancy, the Novitiate, Senior Seminary, and the Scholasticate. At the end of that period he, too, died of tuberculosis, the same disease that took Thérèse herself. Unlike the saint, who wrote her *Story of a Soul* as a reminiscence of her entire life since childhood, Rinus kept a daily diary of each event and his inner response to it, over the same nine-year period. Because Rinus' reflections are day by day recollections, they offer the reader an intimate look into the life of this young man in love with God. What also makes him different from Thérèse is his external reticence—in relation to the community—about his deeper feelings. In his private writings his style of life is further set apart from hers by the boyish, colloquial expression of his own type of spiritual childhood, developed by him before he knew of her now famous "little way."

Bridal Mysticism

Rinus distinguishes himself from Edward Poppe, a Flemish priest, whose process of beatification is in progress and whose writings Rinus admired, by his far earlier mystical ascent and by his "bridal mysticism."

Other male mystics before him lived a bridal approach to their mystic ascent. It seems less usual, however, in Rinus' contemporaries. The male mysticism of bridal love is based on the image of the soul (*anima*) as feminine and, hence the possibility of the soul's espoused love for God and of God for her. Rinus describes with characteristic candor his experiences of mystical betrothal and marriage, especially in his later diary entries.

Salvation of the Dying

Another unique feature is his unexpected, almost instantaneous inspiration to pray for the dying. During the Novitiate he starts a fervent life of prayer and sacrifice for God's merciful last invitation to repentance to sinners dying anywhere in the world. Rinus symbolizes the planetary outreach of this inspiration by literally naming different towns and countries, throughout the world. These hardened or despairing people may find themselves suddenly at the gate of eternity, and Rinus' prayers are waiting for them.

At that time this was a rather unusual devotion, especially in its bold, world-wide outreach. It even surprised me. Later, after Rinus' death, my reading of the diary of Blessed Sister Faustina Kowalska changed my mind. I was awed that this inspiration of God worked at the same time in these two chosen souls living in different countries, who were totally unaware of each other. Timewise their lives overlapped at least in part. Many pages in Faustina's diary testify to a similar participation in the final struggle of the dying anywhere in the world.

Rinus' Mission

Blessed Faustina had been made aware that her mission in time and eternity would be to spread the devotion to the Mercy of God in the Church and humanity. Rinus died young, like Thérèse and Faustina, from the same sickness, consumption, but it had already become clear to him that his mission would be to spread the awareness of the Epiphany of God's mercy, through the Epiphany apostolate, to the whole world.

The Pentecostal Epiphany, related to the birth of the Church, is the second great Epiphany of the Holy Spirit. The first one was his overshadowing of Mary, his formation of Christ in her womb. The second Pentecostal Epiphany reveals the Holy Spirit as the source of the infinitely merciful transformation of cosmos and humanity. The Spirit transforms us through the formation of Christ in our souls and hearts. Through him, in him, and with him the Spirit transforms us into living manifestations and mirrors of Jesus.

Publication and Promotion of Rinus' Writings

One of the ways to help Rinus in his mission is the publication and promotion of his writings, including his reflections, prayers, meditations, and resolutions.

An unexpected package from Holland arrived in Pittsburgh shortly before the death of Father Jan de Rooij, Rinus' last spiritual director in

Gemert. Its carefully bundled packet proved to be the thought-to-be-lost journals of Marinus Scholtes, accompanied by the terse message: "Now is the time."

Encouraged by Epiphany members I traveled to my Dutch Spiritan Province. There I met with a member of its administrative team, who assigned the right of publication of his writings to the Epiphany Association. I found in Holland an able translator in Dr. Joop Bekkers. He graciously agreed to do the basic translation from Dutch to English. This translation has been thoroughly re-edited by Dr. Susan Muto and me to adapt it to the typical American usage of English.

Reading Advice

Rinus has given us the treasure of himself. To receive his gift, you must read with a mind and heart prayerfully attentive to the Epiphany of Christ in your *own* life. No matter the life situation in which you find yourself, the Spirit always pursues you with an unfathomable love and mercy.

The life situation of Rinus is different from yours. You may feel uneasy with his style of expression or with the limited wisdom of the Novitiate and seminary programs of that period. But language and methods are always necessarily limited and somewhat time-bound. Each generation treasures its own preferences. Sometimes we smile about the customs of an earlier age. Similarly those who come after us will smile about our customs. But in the end none of this is crucial. What counts is that we allow ourselves to be touched by the miracle of grace breaking through such limitations century after century. In spite of all, grace can transfigure any struggling person through the sweet and painful embrace of the Beloved, who hides in the depths of our souls.

Read, therefore, in service of God's transformation of your own life. Rise above dated expressions, methods, and situations. Do not distract yourself during such moments of prayerful reflection by an anxious hunt for theological information no matter how necessary this may be at other times and in other settings. Read not too much or too fast. Read prayerfully, slowly, meditatively. Then quietly abide with what you have read. Be not dismayed by the repetition typical of a recollection notebook or daily log kept by all novices. The blessing of repetition is that it will gradually draw you into the dynamic stream of unfolding love between God and a young man of his choosing.

In the not so distant past many people were not able to flow with St. Thérèse's fascinating story of a soul. Even some first class writers could not resist the temptation to critique her bourgeois upbringing, her girlish and childish sentimentality, the glaring imperfections of the formation methods in her very human and somewhat fractured community. They all missed the point. The wonder is not the usual accumulation of such human frailties. The wonder is that grace so easily and thoroughly intervenes in the life story of chosen souls within any setting. It lifts the soul like a feather moved by a mighty wind to unexpected heights of wisdom and love.

My prayer is that Rinus' story of his simple yet profound quest for union with God will, under the guidance of grace, lead readers to the higher reaches of spiritual maturity.

Jesus,

let me be

an

Alter Christus

both

inwardly

and

outwardly.

I

The Junior Seminary

Weert, 1935

I
THE JUNIOR SEMINARY
WEERT, 1935

A RULE OF LIFE TO FURTHER THE LOVE OF JESUS AND MARY, written by Adrian van Kaam, in dialogue with his soul friend, Rinus Scholtes, in the Junior Seminary at Weert:

1. In the morning, directly after waking up, pray, "Dear Jesus, dear Mother Mary, I dedicate this whole day to both of you."
2. After getting up, kneel in front of the bed, pray the dedication to Jesus through Mary and three Hail Mary's in honor of the Immaculate Conception. Between every Hail Mary, say a short prayer: "By your Immaculate Conception, O Mary, purify my body and sanctify my soul."
3. During Holy Mass go to Communion, if possible every day.
4. After Holy Communion, tell Jesus what happened the day before. Lay open the needs of your soul to him. Offer him the mortifications, sacrifices, crosses, and troubles of the previous day. Discuss the coming day with Jesus.
5. Now the day really begins. Attend to the following items:
    a) Do at least five mortifications in honor of Jesus' five wounds of the Cross and on Saturday do seven, in honor of the Seven Sorrows of Mary.
    b) Do one good act of neighborly love.

Weert, Junior Seminary.

c) Wear a penitential garment (a rough garment, directly on the body). The white penitent's garment must *always* be worn whereas the penitential girdle need only be worn three days or three nights a week.[3]
d) Pay attention the whole day to not being self-indulgent. Don't baby your body. It weakens and sensualizes you. Be as chaste and pure and clean as possible the whole day and night.
e) Be kind and cordial during the day. Try always to be cheerful in *any* circumstance. Always say *Gaudete in Jesu et Maria* [Be joyful in Jesus and Mary]. During prayer, when there is time left over, say the Small Office, or part of it, of the Blessed Mother.
f) Eat moderately at breakfast and also during the other meals.
g) Say the Stations of the Cross in the chapel after the four o'clock small meal *(goûter)*, except on Sundays. On Fridays this can be done during morning recreation.
h) Survey the day, at night in your cell, in front of the crucifix: What was good or bad? After a sincere act of contrition and three Hail Mary's in honor of the Immaculate Conception, go to bed. Try never to use more than two blankets. Roll up the sleeves of your pajamas as far as the elbows. Keep your arms above the bed-clothes at night. When the lights go out, begin your meditation, after which you can go to sleep.

Friday, April 5.

First Friday of the Month. Today I decided to keep a diary.[4] I started it four times, but I stopped. I now have a lot of difficulties in almost every

---

3 The so-called "penitential girdle" was a modest wiry chain. Somewhat later, after our dedication as "slaves of Mary," meaning as her "consecrated servants," we replaced it with a smaller wiry model in accordance with the recommendations of de Montfort, the initiator of this devotion. Later again we dropped all such extraordinary penances. We did so in the spirit of the second founder of the Spiritans, the Venerable Father Francis Libermann. In that regard he was an early predecessor of St. Thérèse of Lisieux. Francis opposed all unusual or extraordinary penances. He counselled the gentle but firm way of everyday fidelity to one's daily task and making small sacrifices.

4 Rinus began this diary in the fourth class of his Junior Seminary at the age of sixteen. In a boyish yet honest fashion, Rinus records periodically what was happening in his inner and outer life. Here we see the seeds for later, much deeper recollections. Commingled with these entries will be letters written within the designated time span.

Rinus' Confessor, Father Hendrikus Berkers.

aspect of my life. Therefore, tonight, I went to see Father Berkers, my guide and Confessor. This morning, during a fairly good Holy Communion, I saw, as it were, two crosses: one was a beautiful, gilded crucifix; the other a small, rough, black, wooden one. I also saw a Franciscan habit next to a cassock with the cincture of our Fathers. I chose the small cross and the cassock at the advice of my guide. If Jesus wants me to become a Franciscan, he will give me a clear sign.

✠

I asked Father Berkers what I would have to do to become holy. Father said it was not so difficult: keep the rules and the commandments well. I will try.

✠

Saturday, April 6.
I made a good confession. I asked Father Berkers what I would have to do to become holy. Father said it was not so difficult: Keep the rules and the commandments *well*. I will try. Tonight I put two links around my arms to remind myself, in no uncertain terms, that I am and forever will be a fully consecrated child of Mary. For the rest, the day went well.

Sunday, April 7.
Last night I made two tighter links to wear around my arms as a sign of my consecration to Mary. The links have little tips. I will wear them as often as possible.[5] This day was only so-so. I am still a bit too thoughtless. I trust my own strength too much—like when the walk was canceled because of the rain and we had to study. I wanted to study hard, but I got a headache. At night I asked Mary to direct my brain and then I studied well for two hours.

Monday, April 8.
This morning Holy Communion was not as good as usual. I need to try harder. Since December 1, 1934, I have received Communion every day.

---

5 Such extraordinary mortifications happened only in this first phase of Rinus' spiritual journey. He soon found out that Libermann's way was the ordinary path of offering everyday small "love sacrifices" in keeping with the hidden life of Jesus of Nazareth.

I hope I don't fall into a rut. Today Mary and Henny [6] have been a great help with my two interim exams. The success is Mary's not mine.

Tuesday, April 9.
This morning my Communion was good, but the day itself could have been better. I also went to see Father Berkers today. "You should keep calm and at peace," my Confessor said. I then said to myself, "Do better, Rinus."

Wednesday, April 10.
I have not buttoned up my coat all winter, nor worn a vest nor gloves nor a scarf. I can bear cold well by now. But this morning I put on my vest again, for I must also be able to bear heat, even though this is hard for me. I will wear my vest all summer. Today I thought I was choking—and this is only the beginning! Stick it out! Tonight, while playing the harmonium, I gave in to sad thoughts about Henny. That's not good. My Confessor advised me against it, "so don't do it again!"

Thursday, April 11.
I had a tremendous headache all day long. I did not feel well. This morning I left my Holy Communion to Mary, my Directress. I was only able to say a few words, yet I believe that such an arid Communion is better than a sweet one. I don't care much for the latter. Starting tomorrow I will neither drink water nor take salt, for I am almost addicted to them. It won't be easy. But it is all for Mary![7]

Friday, April 12.
This morning I read in Vroeman's [an older fellow's] *Guldenboek* [*The Golden Book*] about Blessed Marinus, who was the brother of John of Damascus and who was also fully consecrated to Mary. So I do have a patron saint! I have now put my study under Mary's protection. I will do so solemnly after doing my Stations of the Cross. I prayed this morning from *The Golden Book*. That takes a whole morning period of recreation, and that's good. Mary was also a great help during my interim exam in religion. In Latin I scored 73 out of 100 points and that's fine. It's Mary's work! Thanks so much, my Directress.

---

6 Henny, Rinus' little sister, also died in childhood from the same disease that later took him, tuberculosis.

7 The attempt to diminish water intake was another example of "extraordinary mortification" and certainly not advisable. At that time there was little awareness of the present medical directive to drink ample water everyday.

Saturday, April 13.
When I got up this morning, I renewed my dedication. Yesterday I promised Jesus and Mary two extra chaplets. This morning, during meditation, Father Superior talked about Mary, our Directress.[8] He also said that this dedication [in accordance with the writing of St. Louis Marie de Montfort] may only be made after consulting him and with the permission of one's Confessor. If it's that important, then I've done far too little as yet. For I think it's so simple. Holy Communion and Holy Mass went fairly well today. Mary helped me to pass the whole day as her day.

NOTE FROM ADRIAN VAN KAAM TO RINUS

(Undated but probably May, 1935)

Ave Maria
On Friday, May 31, I'm going to dedicate myself to Mary. Tomorrow I'll organize some kind of retreat for myself. If you have anything edifying to say, please write it on a notepad and bring it to me. I also hope you will offer your Holy Communion for me next Friday. Pray then that your friend may become a good servant of Mary.

As ever in friendship, in Christ,
Adrian

P.S. Please keep this note to yourself.

Sunday, May 12.
I saved one and a half guilders for *The Golden Book*. Holy Communion this morning could have been better. But it is the first day of a new term. I had real inner struggles over these last holidays. I've heard and seen a lot that will trouble me this term.

Wednesday, May 15.
This year so far I received Holy Communion every day except on Good Friday. But I can't say I've made that much progress. Until now I used

8 In the Junior Seminary, it was a daily custom that the superior or the prefect give a ten to fifteen minute meditation for all the students in the large study hall before Holy Mass.

to think, "I won't do what I don't like to do." It was by good luck that I wanted to do what was prescribed by the rules of the seminary. When this was not the case, I bungled my work. That will have to change too! There's still a lot to be done! Jesus and Mary, my Directress, help me.

Thursday, May 16.
My study, prayers, etc. again went fairly well. I must try to persevere in this way.

Friday, May 17.
Holy Communion was not so good. The Stations of the Cross went better. I want to do them every Friday, and take a half hour for them. This night I fell asleep easily.

Saturday, May 18.
Before the afternoon things left me indifferent. My head was still full of dreams that were neither bad nor brave as a boy's should be, but in the afternoon things went better, and I made a good confession again.

Sunday, May 19.
I had another slack day. I also went to the Franciscans.[9] Tomorrow I will pass all of my recreation time in the chapel and think again about what to do or what not to do. Bless that boy for whom I feel a more particular affection. It's really difficult, for both his "outside" and his "inside" appeal to me.[10] Which of the two is more important? In other words, what should I do? Flee or bear with it or give in to it? Holy Spirit, help me tomorrow. [Later on in his diary, Rinus reviewed what he had written previously and wrote a few asides. For example, on January 25, 1938, he wrote, "That's a laugh!!!"]

---

9 The main monastery of the Franciscans was in Weert, the same town where Rinus' Junior Seminary was located.

10 As we shall see in these honest diary entries, Rinus invented a subtle distinction between surface attraction to others and a deeper attraction that could lead to soul-friendship. If the surface attraction was not deepened to soul attraction, it was called "particular friendship" of a kind that did not foster Christian character and personality formation.

Rinus, Age 14.

Rinus' Junior Seminary class. He is in the first row, second from the left.

Monday, May 20.

I was rather indifferent in class. This should not happen again. Yesterday I decided: 1) When the students leave the study, I'll remain in my place and I won't push my way forward; 2) I won't cough; 3) I'll pray the Stations of the Cross during morning recreation between my two classes. Furthermore, I'll stick to my own ways. I won't change them, no matter whether that boy is present or not. *Jesus, help me.*

Tuesday, May 21.

We visited "Circus Roberti."[11] I forgot to do the Stations of the Cross this morning. I'll remember to do them tomorrow. I'm still weak. Any other person who got the same graces would be much holier and better than I.

Wednesday, May 22.

I kept my word fairly well. Things are starting to go a little better. But I don't want to miss any chance I get to play the harmonium.

Thursday, May 23.

Things were again less good than yesterday. Twice I went to see Father Berkers, but, unfortunately, he was not in. I should restrain myself more and be less noisy, for it seems other boys are bothered by it and even have difficulty with it. There was one who himself warned me not to do it.

Friday, May 24.

Today was still worthless. Until after the Stations of the Cross, things were not up to par. I dedicated the day to Henny's honor. I won't and I shall not sin. *Jesus help me to become holy.*

[Later, the same day]. Today went fine, most of the day, except I yielded too much to my sinful inclinations.

---

11 The Junior Seminary not only organized in-house entertainments but also occasional outings. For example, when a circus came to town, all the seminarians went with the superior and the faculty.

Saturday, May 25.
Today was the same as yesterday, but after Chapter[12] I had to kneel in the refectory for having talked in the study. Now I have seen what a bungler I was. I was as miffed and indifferent as a cat. There's still a lot to be done before I become better and more reliable. At night, before going to bed, things were not that good either.

Sunday, May 26.
Today was a day of adoration and prayer for the needs of the world. I was rather distracted at the time. After Vespers I stayed with Father Berkers for more than an hour. We talked about everything, but my character still needs a lot of improvement. I should also try to go against my "inclination" [see Note 10] by either fleeing from it or by simply accepting it as it is, for the good I see in it only appears that way.

Monday, May 27.
This morning I made good resolutions, but I did not have a particularly good day after all. It must become better!

Tuesday, May 28.
Today was worthless! The trouble is, when I fall back into my old ways of everyday living, things do not go well. Come on!

---

12 A Chapter in religious life meant originally that the monks or nuns in a monastery would come together with the Abbot or Abbess who would point out the public faults or mistakes of the community. After that, individual religious would accuse themselves, as an act of humility and reconciliation, of violations of the community rule. The "Chapter" in the Junior Seminary at Weert was an adaption of this monastic practice. The superior or the prefect of the students would address the two hundred plus young men in the study hall about public infractions of the house rule. The "Chapter" Rinus mentions here probably had to do with the light punishment of kneeling in the rectory during the public reading of a spiritual book or the Bible by a student lector. Such little humiliations were a common practice when students were caught breaking the rules of the house.

Wednesday, May 29.
I received my own copy of *The Golden Book*. It is to be my "daily companion." If Mary helps me, I'll again make a good start. I wrote a little sermon today for Adrian van Kaam! Jesus, help me.[13]

Thursday, May 30. The Feast of Mary's Assumption.
I worked fairly well today, but I could do better. I got a reply from Adrian. Tomorrow, he said, we ought to start again to really work at our spiritual life. He thinks the time has come.

LETTER FROM ADRIAN VAN KAAM TO RINUS SCHOLTES

Weert, May 30, 1935

Ave Maria
Dear Friend;

[I was] really touched by your wonderful letter. I feel urged to reply with a few words, the truth of which I feel deep in my soul.

On May 31, 1935, not only you but I will also be Mary's consecrated servant. I know and feel our time has come. Formerly we were wont to say, "Our time hasn't come yet." But now I say, listen well, "Tomorrow our time will have come." By Holy Providence and through the Holy Virgin and Mother of God, Mary, and in accordance with God's irrevocable decree, it has come to pass that two poor souls were raised from the mud and dust of sin. Both were educated especially for what was to follow. The older was the first to be given the sure way to God's plans for him. Then God, and Mary, through the older one, gave the younger one the same way. And when they reach that way together, God can begin with his plans. Tomorrow we will, both of us, be on that way—the way to being consecrated servants of the Holy Virgin.

Tomorrow our preparation will be finished. Tomorrow we must be ready, tomorrow we must act. From tomorrow on we must live like saints, as de Montfort predicted. Therefore, from tomorrow on don't worry any more. Put everything in the hands of your Directress, your Mother. Be prepared to give up all your possessions at the first beck and call. Tomorrow the days of our holy actions will begin, believe me. Tomorrow your work will begin in everything: in your letters, in your example, in your struggle, in your sacrifices, and especially in your conversations and writings. Don't think that God will not realize his plans from tomorrow on. Before Easter comes again, that is, the term after Easter, you will have been obliged to act already. It may be in the holidays, or during the term, only God knows. But know only this, tomorrow our time will have come. From Friday on we must live like saints.

---

13 At the time of our Junior Seminary, we often exchanged notes to one another to encourage ourselves as soul-friends on our spiritual journey.

Remember, maybe you'll notice it in Holy Communion; maybe you won't. From Friday May 31, onwards!

Your friend, Adrian

P.S. One understands this or one doesn't. Explanation is impossible.

Friday, May 31.
Today Adrian van Kaam made his dedication. Now we are both consecrated to Mary. May she, our good Directress, assist us to become holy.

Saturday, June 1.
Today was fine. I am strengthening my will in every way, for all my willpower is up to now not worth a dime. *Mary, help me.*

Sunday, June 2.
Today was a flop. What a dud I am. Such a child like me is of little use to Mary, or so I think. She first has to teach him the most elementary virtues and qualities. It's a good thing I have such a good Mother and Directress. Otherwise I might just as well forget it, dud that I am! I had some enthusiastic thoughts during the day, but now only sad ones! What am I to do? Mary, help me, for I am sinking again. [Aside, added later, on January 25, 1938: Sap, pride!]

Monday, June 3.
The same old song. At the start, the day went fairly well. But I'm still unstable in my resolution and I have to fight my effeminate affection for a boy in first Latin [first year of classical studies] as much as possible.[14]

Tuesday, June 4.
There's no reason to complain today. Many things went wrong, of course, but if I go on slowly like this, I will have some good times. If only I could practice more willpower and firmness. Those are my weak spots.

---

14 Rinus was the eldest of nine children. He showed care and affection for the younger ones in his family. Missing them so much, it was natural that he felt attracted to their counterparts in the earliest year of the seminary.

A photo of Rinus' family. He is in the top row, center.

Wednesday, June 5.
I received Holy Communion as if it were my last, and I spent the day likewise. The Father "Visitator"[15] showed slides of the Missions. He also taught us a song and the Sign of the Cross in Swahili. This afternoon my study did not go too well.

Thursday, June 6.
An uneventful day without much devotion. I just flowed with things as they were. I saw my weak side again, for my difficulties have not disappeared by any means yet. I may reason, "It's no use for you to look at such a boy," but yet I do! This must change!

Friday, June 7.
First Friday. Today went by fairly well. My Holy Communion was not worth much because I do not like sung Masses. And it drives away my good mood to sing again after Holy Communion. As regards that inclination, it's going a bit better now. Jesus and Mary, please help me, then I'll persevere.

Saturday, June 8.
I passed the day in honor of Henny, but all the merits go to Mary to whom my life is fully consecrated. It is like a writer who dedicates his book to somebody like Henny while the profits go to the publisher, in this case to Mary. The day went well. I was also given two great charges.[16] I hope I'll fulfill them well. I intend to take them as seriously as I can, if only Mary will help me!

Sunday, June 9. Pentecost Sunday.
I prayed again ardently for the gifts of the Holy Spirit, especially for strength. The day went by fairly well. The weather was stifling; I can't take it too well, yet I'm making some strides. I keep playing on the sport fields, no matter how hot it is. [Aside written January 25, 1938: That's, I believe, the only resolution you carried out!]

Monday, June 10.
Today my devotion was less fervent again. Yet I am convinced that I have received strength. I hope to use it well. Today Father Henri Strick [the Novice Master visiting the Junior Seminary] gave a fine conference about the Missions.

---

15 From time to time a visitor is sent to the seminary from the Motherhouse of the congregation to inspect the state of the house.

16 Each student receives special work functions for which he is responsible. These occupations are called "charges."

Tuesday, June 11.
I beat the drum and I liked it. That went along well. It's good recreation and good muscle training.

Wednesday, June 12.
We had the afternoon off. The day itself was okay.

Thursday, June 13.
I worked on stage props. It's something I like to do. My diligence in studying was all right, but my devotion was not worth much.

Friday, June 14.
I saw Father Berkers for an hour. We talked about soberness and ardor. I hope my dislike of emotional noisy Frenchmen has somewhat diminished, for it is even an obstacle to studying French with pleasure.[17]

Saturday, June 15.
I again made a good confession. It was an excellent refreshment! The day went fairly well, too, but I should not want everything all at once. [Aside, later: Aha!]

Sunday, June 16.
This was not a particularly good day. I had a splitting headache, so almost everything went wrong.

Monday, June 17.
Today there was a revue, because tomorrow will be Father Superior's birthday. I acted the part of a sailor. Father Superior was given a clock.

Tuesday, June 18.
It's Father Superior's birthday today. In my Holy Communion this morning I particularly commended him to Mary. We saw a film, and [we enjoyed the usual] all-day feast.

Wednesday, June 19.
Things went a bit better once again. I made the resolution to pray well tomorrow, on Corpus Christi, but today my difficulties were great.

---

17 Dutch people are not given to much emotional self-expression. They tend to be more reserved in that regard than the populations of southern countries. As a typical Dutch boy of that time, Rinus felt some uneasiness with the emotional expressiveness of these cultures.

Thursday, June 20.
I noticed I was making progress with prayer before the Blessed Sacrament. It also says in my prayer book in the chapter, *Before the Most Holy Sacrament,* "One cannot stay there for an hour without becoming holier."

Friday, June 21.
We had our Olympiad.[18] I was ill when I went to bed tonight.

Saturday, June 22.
Today was no good. Against my better judgment I drank like a horse so that I did not sleep all night. This has to change!

Sunday, June 23.
Another hot day. This morning there was a procession with the Blessed Sacrament through the town. I mumbled three rosaries along the way, but I do not believe any of them went too well. Darn it! I can't stand the heat at all.

Monday, June 24.
Today was a little better. This way I shall slowly go forward; then it may be possible to get somewhere.

Tuesday, June 25.
There was no reason for complaints today. Everything was pretty good except that I could not study that much. This always happens before exams. Drinking water was okay. I drank once too much, yet I am moving in the right direction.

Wednesday, June 26.
I had a good Holy Communion. Mary and Henny were there, too. We three held a little "Chapter," and we said: "On Thursday, at the exam, I shall get 75 marks out of 100." [Aside, written on January 25, 1938: I think I did get those 75 marks, for I remember something like that.] But then, I'll do my utmost on Thursday night, after confession. I must and I shall and I want to become holy.

Thursday, June 27.
We had Latin exams. I did not do well. I'll just wait and see the results. I did not have much of a chance to pray either.

---

18 Every year the Fathers and teachers in charge of the seminary organized Olympic-like competitions with gifts for the winners they had collected for them on many shopping expeditions.

Friday, June 28.
We played volleyball against the "Rhetorica" [the sixth and final year of classical education]. We lost 2-1. I had another chance to curb my pride after all the praise I got. My Holy Communion was nothing special.

Saturday, June 29.
Drinking water goes somewhat better. I still drink a lot but not so greedily. Go on that way!

Sunday, June 30.
My study did not go well today. As a matter of fact I did not spend much time on it. Tonight there was also [the yearly] Sacred Heart Procession in town. It was better for me than last time.

Monday, July 1.
We had rice and plums today. My day went fairly well, except for the evening study. I also spoke to Father Berkers for ten minutes. I should not be pessimistic nor worry about my problems. *Jesus and Mary, help me*.

Tuesday, July 2.
I was asked to do penance and mortification for a fallen boy. When I went to the showers I took a cold one. Then I prayed to Mary and knelt down in front of my bed.

Wednesday, July 3.
I joined the choir. It's a choir for four voices. I'm first bass. I also became "second chief" at table.[19] May Mary help me, through her intercession, to do these things well. The fruit: Everything for her!!

Thursday, July 4.
Today went by fairly well. I must go on that way. Be calm and quiet at table. I'm getting more used to this job bit by bit. Tonight I also prayed a good part of the rosary. That's the way to do it. Stick it out!

---

19 Each table in the dining room had an appointed chief and an underchief or second chief. They took care that each student received at least equal helpings of food and maintained desirable table manners.

1935 (16)

Maandag 1 Juli

Vandaag hebben we rijst met pruimen gehad.
De dag was tamelijk goed behalve de avondstudie.
Ik ben ook 10 minuten bij Pater Berkers geweest. Ik
mag niet pessimistisch zijn, ook proberen ook mij
[illegible]! Jesus Maria helpt mij

Dinsdag 2 Juli.

Vandaag vroeg [illegible] mij om boete en verzoening te
doen voor een gevallen jongen. Ik ben 's avonds in de
[illegible] geweest en ik heb een [illegible] genomen. Daarna heb
ik 't kruisje van Maria [illegible] voor mijn bed.

Woensdag 3 Juli

Vandaag ben ik op 't koor gekomen, bij 't [illegible]
mannenkoor als 1ste bas. Ik ben ook vandaag [illegible]
geworden aan tafel. Help Maria mij door haar voor-
spraak en hulp om die dingen goed te doen. [illegible]
alles, in voor haar!!

Donderdag 4 Juli

De dag vandaag ging wel. [illegible]
tafel [illegible]
komen. Vanavond heb ik ook [illegible]
Zo moet ik 't maar doen [illegible]

Vrijdag 5 Juli 1935

A handwriting sample from July, 1935.

The dining room of the Junior Seminary at Weert where Rinus served as "second chief" at one of the tables.

Friday, July 5.
First Friday in July. I got up and attended Mass. Then my study before the classes went fine, but things were not good in the study after the class. I spoke badly about another student before saying the Rosary with the community. You will pay for this, brother Mule! I also joined the choir. If only everything would go well! *Jesus and Mary, help me.*

Saturday, July 6.
I was at the playground early this morning, and I started the day in the right way. But it could have been better. Tonight there was a film for the *Rhetorica*. [The Latin name for the sixth and last year of the classical gymnasium program.]

Sunday, July 7.
We celebrated the ceremony of the reception of the cassock of the congregation [the students of the graduating class of the seminary]. It was the fourth time I've seen it, but still it touched me. It is to be hoped I will see it only once more [before I receive it]! I also sang in the choir for the first time, and I was a prompter for the chorus. My devotion was good. There was no study [hour].

Monday, July 8.
The novices[20] came today, and the St. Antonius Brass-Band also came to play. We had to do a composition for exams this morning. I started the day rightly, but at night, while the band was playing, I had problems again. But I saw it was useless [to dwell on them].

Tuesday, July 9.
My devotion and my diligence at study were not worth anything! It should be better again. *Jesus and Mary, help me.*

Wednesday, July 10.
I did not have a good Holy Communion this morning. I was too distracted. Tonight I went to see Father Berkers. I mentioned the name of a boy in our year who, in my opinion, might cause trouble for the other boys. [Aside, added January 25,1938: That boy is now a novice here. Yet I think I was not wrong, not yet]. We also had our first "SOOS" "Student Society" night.[21] It was wonderful!

---

20 Each year the former students, who were in the last months of their Novitiate, came back for a day's visit to the Junior Seminary.

21 The fifth and sixth year students of the Junior Seminary were allowed to come together for literary and academic presentations by their fellow students in special evening sessions. At the end of the fourth year, before entering the fifth, they would have their first "SOOS" evening.

Weert, Juniorate sports field where Rinus loved to play soccer as many days as he could.

Thursday, July 11.
Holy communion was good. It was a fine morning, except for the study for the third class hour of the day. This afternoon I studied really hard. I made 33 reprints [of photos] together with Mr. Kooiman [another student]. I am going to do the Stations of the Cross in two parts, for this morning I have to do my charges.

✠

I also want to become holy according to the three degrees given in my religion book: 1) the state of sanctifying grace; 2) the envangelical counsels of perfection; and 3) the heroic (hidden) practice of virtue, in spite of all difficulties. May God help me.

✠

Friday, July 12.
An undeserved remark was made against my friend, Adrian van Kaam, but he accepted it well, without answering back. I should follow his example. We had an exam in "free translation." I did fairly well. This morning Holy Communion was not as it should be. I should pay more attention to this! For that has been one of the main points in my daily fare for half a year. I also want to become holy according to the three degrees given in my religion book: 1) the state of sanctifying grace; 2) the evangelical counsels of perfection; and 3) the heroic (hidden) practice of virtue, in spite of all difficulties. *May God help me.*

Saturday, July 13.
Today wasn't bad; it went mostly as usual. I should be less drowsy.

Sunday, July 14.
After Holy Communion I was thinking about everything, except Jesus. I also forgot to think of Mary. This should not happen again, Brother Mule!

Monday, July 15.
I had to get down on my knees without deserving this punishment. It was a little disgrace, but I notice that I am learning to bear this. *Jesus, help me.*

Tuesday, July 16.
We had a French exam. I also served Mass for the second time, which is a great help for me. If only I can go on this way!

Wednesday, July 17.

We had a general history exam. I did fairly well, but I doubt if I got as many good marks as last time. Well, that doesn't matter much, as long as my inner life is good.

Thursday, July 18.

I was given a footbath by Father Cosmos Bohemen [a German Language teacher, who also served as infirmarian in the Junior Seminary] for my perspiring feet. I hope it helps. I also had the chance to talk for a while with a certain boy on the junior playground. I should be more careful and reserved. [Aside later: The same old song. It hasn't finished yet, only it's another person now.]

Friday, July 19.

Today we practiced a German song, conducted by a German refugee.[22] I also pinned a picture of Henny under my sweater. It was also my last turn to serve Mass with Father Berkers.

Saturday, July 20.

Another exam, fortunately. One more week and I'll be home, promoted to the fifth year. Today I had those despondent feelings about not making the next grade. But Father Berkers told me to dismiss them because there was no reason at all for them. And even if there were a reason, it would not help to worry. Thank God, only one more week.

I am toughening up my body. Let me now also toughen up my spirit, which is even more in need of being well ordered.

22 The Junior Seminary gave room and board to a German, probably a Jewish gentleman, who had escaped from Nazi Germany. Later, after Germany had occupied The Netherlands, the seminary concealed among its students a Dutch Jewish boy, the son of the Dutch novelist, Herman de Man.

Weert. One of the rows of private "chambrets" for each individual student. At night Rinus prayed a lot in his sleeping room.

Friday, September 20 [after the recess in August].
The new year, my fifth year, has started now, with a good retreat, the best I have had so far. The school year started well too. I'm still "second chief" on the Himalaya floor,[23] and I'm one of the students selected for the small study room of the fifth year, a sign they have confidence in me. Let me not disappoint them! Today we had apologetics class for the first time. Father Superior said something about "particular friendship." It is quite natural for me to have those feelings, but I should fight them unconditionally, even if I do not see any danger. For I am deceiving myself. If it just remains like this and nothing more, it would be okay. But now I say, and may Christ help me with his grace, it's over! Even if it weren't wrong, in that case it's a little sacrifice. I am toughening up my body. Let me now also toughen up my spirit, which is even more in need of being well ordered. Jesus, Mary, my Directress, and Henny, be my strength and power.

✠

I have to make the most of what little talent God has given me, and I have to gain at least 100 percent. But I cannot do so myself.

✠

Friday, October 4. First Friday.
I started the day well with Holy Communion. Moreover, things went really well in general. I have to make the most of what little talent God has given me, and I have to gain at least 100 percent. But I cannot do so myself. Mary, my directress and Mother, help me. When I receive Holy Communion in the morning, I also receive the Holy Family in me: God the Father, God the Holy Spirit, and God the Son. I also let Mary receive Jesus in my name. Maybe the time has come when, through Mary, the Holy Spirit will form people who will do much good. [There is war again: Italy against Abyssinia.]

Monday, October 28.
Today after Holy Communion I began to make "four crowns:" the first five days for Jesus; secondly, three days for . . . .[24] [Translator's Note: Manuscript breaks off].

---

23 The Himalaya sleeping rooms were in the attic above the large sleeping room complex, hence its name.

24 The "crowns" to which Rinus refers are probably a means of devotion, mindful of the "rosary ring" used then and still in use by many today. The form of the ring, a combination of a circle with small spikes, looks indeed like a "crown of thorns."

II

Transition To The Novitiate

1935-1936

II
TRANSITION TO THE NOVITIATE 1935-1936

✠

The worse fault of mine—the one that hinders my progress—is my fickleness. I blow to and fro with almost every wind . . . I am not patient.

✠

December 3, 1935. A Reflection on Self-Knowledge.
Having looked deeply into my inner life, I will write down what I found there. In comparison to the many graces I have received I achieved pitifully little. Jesus and Mary cannot be blamed. I myself, meaning my bad inclinations and my unruly passions, are the cause. Sometimes a great part of the good things I do gets lost because of the show I make of them and also because of my selfish motives.

The worse fault of mine—the one that hinders my progress—is fickleness. I blow to and fro with almost every wind. Even the exceptions confirm this fault. Even if I have not been fickle, I still think I have done something great. Further, I want so much to become holy, but it has to happen fast! That is also wrong. I am not *patient*. Much also happens *only* in my inner life. Good and bad things. Usually, I cannot find words for it, for if I try to put it in words, it, so to say, slips away. I have likewise some good insights into the characters of the boys around me. But I cannot put all that I see into words.

I detect in myself another significant fault. I have no "middle way." To me it is either all or nothing. For example, if nothing succeeds in one study period, then I sometimes do nothing all day long. But if the first period goes well, then things start to flow again for me. I am inwardly sensitive, even if I don't outwardly show my feelings. It is so with many things. On the outside I look different from what I am inwardly, be it good or bad. This is only a "small list" of my bad points, for to be honest, I must confess, often with shame and anger, that I feel almost all the vices at work in me. [Editor's Note: For the year 1936 there is no notebook by Rinus as such. This type of reflection seems to have been replaced by many conversations and the spiritual correspondence which follows. Of course, some may have been lost over the years.]

LETTER OF RINUS TO ADRIAN

March 14, 1936

Ave Maria
Dear Friend:

At present we have started our studies on a good note, haven't we? We will both get the "prix-general" (general prize) for three reasons: 1) our zeal in study will be stirred up by giving whatever we can to [better] the results of our learning; 2) we strengthen our will (even if we don't get the prize; one should always try to reach more than one can expect); 3) our parents! (I won't say more.) The prize itself is not my real aim either! It's a kind of battle-cry to stir up our zeal to give the best we can! Who knows, we really may get it!

I say, Adrian, do you know that parable in the Gospel about the widow and the unjust judge? Even if he didn't want to give her what she wanted, he did so all the same to get rid of her nagging! So we've got to nag! Its no good to say after a time: "If Our Lord doesn't want to give it to me, let him keep it!" As if we had deserved to be heard by our prayer! No, the truth is, we really should nag!

Adrian, I've also been walking around with a plan (it's only a plan, mind you! Nothing has happened yet) to give H. The Golden Book. *Or to show it to him now and then only for a moment! Do think impartially about it; in your circumstances you can do this better than I. But now I'll tell you what I will do after Holy Communion. Do you remember the three boys (the ones with the blue-bordered award document on their desks)? Behind them stood a lot of boys. They, too, were pioneers of*

Mary. But maybe those good feelings of real friendship (a kind of triumvirate) also with H. are all inordinate affections! Still, as regards such affections themselves, I have not had any temptations yet. But that may be a trick of the devil! Would you think about it quietly, and let me know your answer. I will obey!!! For me, you will speak God's word on that matter. Judge me very indifferently! Not as you think I would like to hear—neither the opposite! But respond as if H. and Rinus are two strangers to you. Think of it after receiving Holy Communion.

For the rest, no more news.

Your friend, Rinus

LETTER FROM MR. ADRIAAN LANGELAAN TO ADRIAN VAN KAAM

Mundus Christo per Mariam

The Hague, May 22, 1936

To my friend and pioneer of Mary, Adrian:

I received your letter and have done what you asked. Fortunately, I managed to finish things in time. Like you, I'm already preparing for June 17, the feast of Mary, our Directress. It is then that we shall consecrate ourselves as pioneers of our dear Mother Mary. Then we shall be united in a special way in our League of Marian pioneers. We will cooperate with the task Jesus has assigned to Mary as his co-helper and coredeemer.

I'm sure she will bless our plans!

Keep praying for us and give kind regards to Rinus.

Your friend, Adriaan Langelaan[25]

✠

> *When I think about it, I can reduce everything to pride, vanity, and false humility. Together with the devil they will be my great enemies.*

✠

[25] Mr. Adriaan Langelaan was a leading lay person in our prototype Epiphany Association. He belonged from the start to the "Pioneers of Mary," the group started by Rinus and me in 1936 during our yearly Christmas, Easter, and summer holidays in The Hague.

LETTER FROM RINUS TO ADRIAN

Weert, June 3, 1936

Dear Friend:

Your words yesterday made a deep impression on me. There are things I can better write down than say.

Last night in bed, when I was going over everything in regards to the deep motive of my action, I found that pride is my main vice. When I think about it, I can reduce everything to pride, vanity, and false humility. Together with the devil they will be my great enemies. Help me to fight them, Adrian.

Last night I was proud to have a friend like you. On the other hand, I felt ashamed that I still had cooperated so little . . . . I would ask you now: Will you, knowing what kind of person I am, still remain my friend? Will you keep me as your first pioneer of Mary? I beg you . . . do so! I don't doubt you, you know, but sometimes I feel so miserable, and then I cling to [the thought]: Here on earth, too, I've got a friend's heart beating for me.

Also, as regards your words about the spiritual life, I must confess that you, having cooperated with God's and Mary's help, have gotten along much further than I. But I'm not sad about that, for that would be pride again! But I feel so unworthy to be with you. Neither would I like you to distance yourself from me, Adrian! We fight for a splendid ideal! Mundus Christo per Mariam!

Yet I'm not totally poor! My love of Mary has increased. I feel much happier in my servanthood. Yet, as you say, the spiritual life is more than that! I'm not energetic enough in my resolutions. For example, when I made the intention to avoid H., to ignore him totally, another voice said, "You sin against fraternal love." *I waver all the time between the two. I have not yet got that holy equanimity that makes me behave normally to everyone and control myself completely, not by a long shot, even if it may seem so outwardly!*

Adrian, I often think about our agreement (three points) and then I compare myself with Comollo, Don Bosco's friend. He went to heaven and became the support of Don Bosco with his foundation. If it's God's will and he takes me soon, I am prepared though I am by no means perfect yet! But when it comes time for me to die, you may safely take from me whatever you need. Also my Prayer Book, yes. At the moment I don't remember anything, so...let's make a deal. If you would like to have something from me, it must, of course, remain reasonable so you won't take my whole wardrobe, my clothes, etc., but some special object you like, for instance, a rosary or some books etc. you may safely take them. I'm serious!

Adrian, I also know your inclination.[26] *You've got to fight hard as well! I really pray much for you! You've got to fight harder against the flesh, and I against the spirit! I believe you can go against your inclination with mortifications of a physical nature, with natural means, (for example, when you are thirsty, don't drink, out of love of God, etc.) Next I think it helps to assert as a young man, the rights of your nature and to love the most beautiful creature God has made, his Holy Mother, your Directress. Fall in love, as it were, show her small attentions, receive in exchange her thanks, her smile, etc. just like every boy does here on earth, according to his nature.*

Sisters engage themselves as brides to Jesus. Why shouldn't we engage ourselves to Mary? You should imagine you love a queen. You don't hide it from her, but neither do you dare to tell it to her. Now with small attentions try to attract her attention and thus to win her love. And what a love you will receive! No earthly sensual love, but God's love, using Mary's love as a link in between!

I don't know whether it's a good means. You must have a spiritual life to see through something like that with holy wisdom. But now I'm speaking from my heart. At Pentecost I begged God, the Holy Spirit, for the gift of wisdom and reason. Is it perhaps divine wisdom that I use now? I don't know.

Well, Adrian, I've poured out my heart here in writing. I could not do it so quietly in speaking. You know, I won't forget our promise when it comes time for me to die. You won't either, I'm sure.

With cordial regards, Your friend Rinus
Mundus Christo per Mariam (M.C.P.M.)
How wonderful! (The world to Christ through Mary.)" [27]

---

[26] God had graced both of us with an unusual spiritual friendship. We were soul-mates, a relationship wholeheartedly approved of by the Confessor and spiritual director we both shared, Father Berkers, C.S.Sp. In the light of this inspiring friendship, we both had become sensitive to any attraction to an intimate friendship with others that would be less based on the inspiring motives with which we were blessed. This sensitivity made us acutely aware of any lower spiritual or mainly self-centered attraction to other persons.

[27] This is the motto or maxim we tried to live by with our lay pioneers of Mary in The Hague. Its epiphanic orientation was expressed in the words, "The world to Christ," meaning to make our world or our whole formation field an epiphanic reflection of Christ's presence. Mary would be an inspiring light (an "epiphany") of Christian character and personality formation.

LETTER FROM ADRIAAN LANGELAAN TO ADRIAN VAN KAAM

M.C.P.M.

The Hague, October 29, 1936

Dear Friend and fellow-Marian Pioneer:

You've made me so happy, Adrian, and, with you and Rinus, I rejoice at the "great news" you told me in your last letter.

Before I go on, I should first like to thank you for your postcard. I received it on the second day of my exam. I highly appreciate your interest in my concerns. It was a difficult and heavy exam. I also had the bad luck of making some blunders and am very curious about the result. I can expect to receive it between St. Nicholas Day and Christmas. I've not got any study to do now, at least not for the time being, so I can pay attention to our association and to myself again. This has become quite necessary. What a wonderful thought of yours, Adrian, to send me that fine book about the inner life. Many thanks.[28] *I promise to do my best to follow your good advice.*

More than in other years, I'm looking forward to a wonderful Christmas season! How's the study going? Persevere under all circumstances, Adrian! As you asked, I've enclosed this letter with the laundry [which your parents sent to you].

As you will notice I'm writing even worse this time than on other occasions. It's because I've had rheumatic pains in my right hand for some days. Thus I have difficulty in putting my big heavy fountain-pen on paper.

Adrian, give Rinus my regards. Also thank him for his interest in my exam.

Kind regards, also from Marie [his wife], and from my family. Don't let us stop praying for each other. Then we will certainly reach our goal with the blessing of the Holy Virgin Mary.

So I end again with a pioneer's greeting. So long!

Your friend and fellow-Marian pioneer, in Christo,
Adriaan Langelaan and Marie

---

[28] The book referred to is Dom Jean-Baptiste Chautard's classical work, *The Soul of the Apostolate*. From the start, the "epiphanic" or formation theology we were pursuing was based on prayerful reflections on Dutch translations of classics written by the masters or on Dutch originals of works by such writers as Gerhard Groote, Thomas á Kempis, and the Dutch "Beguines." Works we also profited from were Dutch renditions of the writings of John of the Cross, Teresa of Avila, Thérèse of Lisieux, Francis Libermann, Francis de Sales, Don Bosco, Bernard of Clairvaux, Jan Ruysbroeck, and the above-mentioned masters. This commitment to reclaiming the classics continues today in our Epiphany Association.

✠

I want to do anything I'm asked to do . . .

✠

LETTER FROM RINUS TO ADRIAN

M.C.P.M.

December 7, 1936

My dear friend Adrian:

I feel compelled to write to you about something. I do not understand lately what is happening to me. I want to become holy, just like you. I want it fervently. But there's something that stops me. I don't see or I don't want to see what that obstacle is. It's as if I sometimes feel a kind of brake on me. You know almost all my problems. I only wish that you could look inside of me, observe the circumstances, and show me the way impartially. That's it exactly. I'm partial or in favor of my own self. I don't know how far that goes, for there are arguments on both sides. Either this or that? Also your words, Sancto est omnia praesens *[Everything is present for the saint], struck me. I'd like so much to change.* Ego volo nunc sanctus esse, aeternum nunc *[I want to be holy now, an eternal now]. In this way we imitate God, as it were, in conformity, not congruence.*

Tomorrow, I feel we can receive many graces and blessings again for Mary's work. I promise to pray much for it. Now I'd like to ask you, urgently so, [for a sincere friend's prayer is powerful] if you, Adrian, would ask Jesus through Mary, our leader, for generosity in my life. I'm not generous enough. I want to have or keep behind something of all that I give to Jesus. The same with H. Also with us, Mary's pioneers.

Therefore, Adrian, I ask you to check on me and to pay attention to me, especially on this point. What I propose seriously now, with God's grace through Mary, but then as firmly as possible is the following: 1) I want to do anything I'm asked to do (directly or indirectly, of course, with reasonable requests); in other words, if they need me more or less, I'm willing to help, no more. So no obtrusiveness in regard to unasked-for services that may perhaps put annoying obligations on my confrères; 2) I won't seek out [occasions] to see certain fellows any more. Let them look for me! Don't think this is pride; it's the most radical means against H. (and that without creating the kind of tension that could lead to over-reaction). Well, at least you know now my greatest problem.

Your friend, Rinus

LETTER FROM RINUS TO ADRIAN

Mundus Christo per Mariam

December 21, 1936

Dear Friend in Jesus and Mary:

Whatever there is to be forgiven, I readily forgive with all my heart. It's my duty and besides the pot can't blame the kettle for turning black! I want to ask you to do the same for me. You know enough about me: I do a lot of bragging, at least outwardly [as if I were] a great pot, but inwardly [I'm] a small one. I don't want to say much about it. I haven't got the time for it. I pray much for you, you know that. And for the work of Mary, too! How wonderful it will be at Christmas; then we can receive much from God again through Mary!

I have to say, if you throw about Latin texts, you shouldn't translate them, certainly not to a boy who has studied Latin two years longer than you! That's a bit offensive, don't you agree?

Well, Adrian, let's try together to make both ends meet this year and not to lose our heads.

Let's pray for one another and for our protegés in Jesus and Mary.

Your friend, Rinus

III
The Diary of My Novitiate
Part One
Gennep, 1937

III
THE DIARY OF MY NOVITIATE
PART ONE
GENNEP, 1937

✠

My whole spiritual life can be summed up in two words: Mary and Jesus.

✠

Monday, March 22. (Editor's Note: These two entries were written in Weert in 1937 at the end of the Juniorate just prior to Rinus' entrance in the Novitiate.)

Today my friend [Adrian] told me he had taken up his diary again. Now I, too, am going to start again. I have turned over the pages of the last two years. How I had to laugh at what I wrote then! I have changed a lot since the last day I kept up this diary! I made one resolution after another. I over strained myself a lot. Fortunately, things are different now. My whole spiritual life can be summed up in two words: *Mary* and *Jesus*. The devotion of being consecrated to Mary as her servant, thanks be to God, has begun to grow like a tree of life. It is still a young tree, but it has brought forth some good fruits already. I don't know how I can thank Mary enough for this. I no longer make resolutions.

Instead I do everything in God through Mary. Holy Communion is the high point of my day and of my spiritual life. Tomorrow I shall see what my scribbles look like; this is written in darkness.

Wednesday, March 24, Holy Week.
Yesterday I made my Easter confession, and this morning I had a good Holy Communion. I notice with great joy that my Holy Communions get better and better, especially since [the start of] this term. I do not mean more emotional, but really better. I get more support out of them, especially because I invoke Mary's special presence. Thus I have the *real* Holy Family together in my Holy Communion: Jesus really present in flesh and blood in the shape of bread; God the Holy Spirit, who lives in me, his temple; and Mary, my Directress.

The Spiritual Life: A Novice's Allegory (Undated) [29]

You are small still, so very small. I like that! For if you do anything wrong, Mommy [Mary] won't be so angry. I have an amazing Mother! She has never beaten me, though sometimes I deserved it. She is so concerned, so mild. I would never want to disappoint her. I also have an Elder Brother [Jesus]. He can do anything. It is nice to play with him. And he can also help me when they [temptations] attack me, for he is very strong! Just as clever, big, and firm as Father is. I am a weak child, Mother keeps saying, a child of many cares. I have now been ailing for six weeks, and Mother told me to go to a sanatorium for the rest of my life.[30] But she herself as well as Father and Elder Brother will go there with me, so that they can better help me.

---

29 Due to his Christian character and personality formation in the Junior Seminary, Rinus began to be graced with the gift of a "second Christian childhood," a "second innocence." This gift of grace goes beyond childishness. Rinus' expressions of this transformative experience are original and daring, as this allegory reveals. Other people may express this experience in their own, more reserved way, but such is the way Rinus responded to God's call at this time. One could compare this aspect of his unfolding spiritual life with a similar attitude found in the autobiography of St. Thérèse of Lisieux.

30 "Sanatorium" in this allegory stands for the religious life and especially for the Novitiate which Rinus was just beginning. By the same token, readers may find the following allusions helpful. Rinus uses the term "nurses" to refer to the spiritual caregivers he needs, such as Mary and the saints. "Medicines" stand for the inner and outer deprivations which will heal the felt weakness of his soul and heart. Among them cod-liver oil represents the bitter experiences of aridity and his failure in discursive meditation. Rinus copes with them by describing metaphorically his struggle against his inner resistance to

I have got even more nurses, yes I do! One of them is always with me, seeing to it that nothing happens to me. Father told him to do so. They also give me many strong medicines. They sometimes don't taste good, oh no! But Mother says they are good for me. And still I sometimes don't drink them, like that cod-liver oil. Mother was sad then, for my sake, because I would remain weak. I am going to write down everything I experience here in this sanatorium. I will also record if I am growing well or if my health is declining.

Wednesday, September 8.
Mother's Birthday. This morning I drank my cod-liver oil like a good boy. I did not like it, but neither did I show it. Especially the last mouthfuls tasted nasty. But it's mainly because I had just gotten up and had not eaten when I had to take this oil. But I said first respectfully my morning-prayer, with Mother, to Father. This morning I was most intimately together with my Elder Brother. I may be *so* almost every morning. Today I asked him to give Mother the little present I bought. She prefers it this way, I think.

I played today, and it was wonderful. I also got a piece of candy. How nice and sweet it was! But Mother says I shouldn't think that my Elder Brother, Father, and she do not love me when I don't get sweets.[31] I only got them because it was Mother's birthday. I am now getting my good night kiss from Mother, Father, and Elder Brother. They are making the sign of the Cross on my forehead, so I can get up tomorrow with fresh courage and do my best.

---

these new experiences. When in the midst of this battle he is granted some spiritual consolation, he compares that with getting a piece of candy or other interior sweets. He takes also refuge in the caring patronage of his patron saints. He expresses his trusting intimacy and familiarity with them by calling them uncles and aunts.

He calls Jesus himself not only his Elder Brother but also his personal physician, who guides the whole alternating process of spiritual consolation and aridity. In his allegory the Novice Master becomes the director of this sanatorium of the soul. He directs him by advising him to take healing spiritual medications, which refer allegorically to the usual strengthening ascetic disciplines.

31 The Novitiate formation in this phase of Rinus' life began to be marked by aridity and the impossibility of discursive meditation. It seems safe to say that Rinus was drawn by grace into a dark night of sense and spirit. The average novice, not yet being there, had to be initiated, as did all beginning novices, in discursive meditation. That is why Rinus struggled to do what grace made impossible for him: the prescribed routine of meditating point by point.

The Novitiate at Gennep.

Friday, September 10.
How happy I am to be here! Mother, if only you knew how much I am moving ahead, as long as I remain your humble child and don't start boasting. Father has been so good [to me] again. He is the best doctor I know. He *can* cure me in this sanatorium, if only I am obedient and drink my medicine. On the one hand, I'm glad I'm so weak and sickly, Elder Brother. For then Mother shows her good care and love much more than at other times. I like to live on the diet Father wills for me. I'll be moderate and careful so that I don't get dirty. For I am such a bungler, Mom. Even if there is no place in the whole sanatorium to get dirty, even then I manage to do so when I do not stay close to you and my Elder Brother.

Dear Elder Brother, will you please help me again to drink my cod-liver oil in the morning before I come to you? I do not need any lumps of sugar with it. I should only drink all this oil, which is so good for me. Then I will soon grow and become strong. Thank you very much, Father, for the nice sweets you just gave me. I'll take a long time to suck them and play like a good child. Thanks a lot!

Saturday, September 11.
This morning the cod-liver oil did not taste so nasty. It was just great that I came with Mother to my Elder Brother. Or better that my Elder Brother came to me. Just before that Mother had been there already to see if everything was in order and to do some last minute dusting. Today I played wonderfully with my other brothers. Yet I must be careful not to leave a brother alone in a corner because I do not like him as much as the others. Neither should I play with brothers I like too much. For then it may happen that I leave Elder Brother alone so that I can play with another brother because he is so likeable. But I should not do so at all. I experienced this once before I entered the sanatorium. It weakens me too much—and I want to grow strong and healthy and big. Mom says I'm really improving!

Sunday, September 12.
This morning I drank really bitter oil, without scrunching my face. I know it's good for me, even though I don't feel it. I overcame myself twice today: once at table, and the other time when I played a lot and walked with a brother whom I don't really like. But this is nothing compared with what Elder Brother has done for me and is still doing. If I do as Elder Brother does, Mother says I'll be a strong fellow later. And that's what I want, isn't it! To be a strong stalwart man. Then I'll be able to do something for Father, too. I have also got a sweet aunt (Mother says I'd better say "Uncle" and "Aunt" to grown-ups I like) called Teresa [of Avila]. She, too, was in a sanatorium, Mom says. She came out of there so strong and healthy that she is now a great woman

whom Father, Elder Brother, and, for that matter, everybody likes very much. I have also got a nice Godfather. His name is John Bosco. Mom said I was allowed to choose a good guardian when I entered the sanatorium. I chose him because he likes children and really knows how to get along with them. He never beats us when we break something at play.[32]

Monday, September 13.
This morning the cod-liver oil tasted sweet. Father had added a lot of sugar. Also, as the day went on, I had a bit of licorice I chewed all morning. I finished it in the afternoon, and then I was naughty again. Mother wants me to be calm and quiet. That's the best way to get cured in this sanatorium. But I was not quiet at all. I regret that very much. At night we made up again with a little kiss. I promised Father and Elder Brother to behave better and not to grieve Mother again. I asked for pills to last the whole week. Mother gave me ten of them today. All those pills are meant to help me fight my great disease that must be healed by the time I leave the sanatorium! If I use the medicine properly, I will be healed. Mother says so. And Mother knows best! Elder Brother, how much I love you! I would like to eat you up! And I may do so every morning.

Tuesday, September 14.
I even like my cod-liver oil now, because Mother has added sugar. And this morning I was so happy when Elder Brother came to me. I was allowed to ask for whatever I wanted! Already when I got up I asked Don Bosco for the pills. He did not give me as many as Mother does, but they are of another, stronger kind. I got four, and two of them were meant directly for my head-disease (not the disease *in* my head!). For the rest, I played nicely with my little brothers, and I showed Father once more how much I love him. I feel as if I am really on the way, if only I stay with Father, Mother, and Elder Brother, eat well, and follow their advice. Mother says I sometimes have flushed cheeks. (I'm also anemic, so I have to take iron.) But she knows that this is only possible when I think of Father, Elder Brother, and her. For whenever I think of him I become warm with love. It makes the blood rush to my cheeks.

---

32 Each novice got to choose the name of a saint when he entered the Novitiate. Rinus chose St. John Bosco as his religious name. Later so did I. Bosco's dedication to the spiritual formation of young people attracted both Rinus and me because of our life call within "the call" to priesthood to serve the formation of lay Christians in the prototypical Epiphany Association we started in Holland.

Wednesday, September 15.
Ah, Mother remembers today her Seven Sorrows. I have consoled her, I really have! She then smiled sweetly at me. I've had many sweets today. But Elder Brother always says, "Take care not to cry when you don't get sweets any more. It's not fun and games every day." But I won't do this, Elder Brother. Even when you give me a pill that doesn't taste nice, I'll swallow it as well as I can, because I love you and know that anything, really anything, you give me is good for me.

Saturday, September 18.
At the weekly cleaning day I got many sweets, and I helped Mother a lot mopping up floors. The more I do for Father the more I love him and he loves me. So I have had a truly happy day today. Thanks so much, Elder Brother.

Saturday, September 25.
At the medical examination of the past week, it was clear that I had moved a few steps forward but also a few back. My doctor says that some of my wounds are getting better. Only now and then do they still itch. However, I may no longer scratch them at all so as to keep them from opening up again. My head-disease has not improved that much. It has come to a standstill, and that, says Elder Brother, who assisted me at the examination, is going backwards. For Elder Brother is always there when the doctor examines me. This kind doctor always gives me mild admonitions and wholesome medicines. Elder Brother says he is rightly called my personal physician, because he has been taking care of me all my life. But then I was too small to realize this. But he made me promise to listen carefully to Mother this week. She will once more impress on my heart what I have to do to give myself rest so as to let the biggest wound I have, my disease, be healed. For that reason Mom told me not to play so roughly any more, not to eat so much. That is not good for the stomach. Everything in moderation!

Sunday, September 26.
We are moving along slowly, Father says. I do feel myself growing stronger—I mean *less weak,* for I still fall quite often. I do not always get away with only dirty hands. They could be washed soon enough by Mom with a little water. But sometimes my clothes also get torn, and I feel upset for a long time, until the tear is mended. Mother, Love!

Monday, October 4.
I had a good healthy day. The director of the sanatorium [Rinus' Novice Master] told me about many really good remedies when I went to see

him for direction:[33] 1) I was allowed to have friends to play with but ought never to treat the boys as if they were "girl friends." "Boys with boys," Mother always says. 2) I should not boast so much when playing or working. I don't mean anything bad by it, the director says, but then I should not boast as if I really meant it. For the rest, it's wonderful here. Next time he will give me direction about other things, and I should especially be still at the appropriate time.[34] Then I may be healed much sooner. And I am willing to do whatever it takes to get healed. Often I am not aware of this need as much as Mother and Elder Brother are. They literally will do anything for me; I only need to swallow [the medicine]. Gradually it's not so hard for me to take my cod-liver oil. Getting on with my friends goes a bit better now. Only my bragging annoys them.[35] And Father doesn't like braggarts either. When I think I can take the oil by myself—get the bottle, uncork it, and pour it on a spoon—he lets me bungle, and spill everything. When I go to him again, kiss him, and tell him I regret my pigheadedness, my good Father takes the bottle again, pours the oil on the spoon, and I only have to swallow it. Sometimes, though not always, Mother or Elder Brother add a lump of sugar or something like it. And this happens not only with the oil in the morning but also with other things. I love my dear Father very, very much, and my dearest Mother, my dear Elder Brother, my friends, my three godfathers, Aunt Teresa, truly, all of them.

---

33 To each novice there is assigned a regular hour of direction by the Novice Master. Knowing in advance his hour of direction, the novice is asked to prepare himself prayerfully and thoughtfully for that hour. He does so by having at hand a so-called "direction sheet" with the appropriate questions regarding the state of his spiritual and communal life. Sample questions might be: How am I doing in my prayer life, especially in my meditation? What about my life of mortification? My spiritual reading? My relations with the other "fraters" (novices) in the community? My faithfulness to my charges? My growing understanding of the religious life, its vows and obligations? The novice brings his answers to these and other questions to the master for shared consideration of his progress or need for improvement.

34 When Rinus was in the Novitiate, the rule of silence was quite strict. During the day there were only two periods—one, the recreation period, directly after lunch, the other after the evening meal—when the novices were permitted to converse with one another. During the rest of the day one could only presume permission to speak, for example, when mandated by necessary practical, work-related demands, in an emergency, or when the request to speak was justified by the necessity to express brotherly support.

35 In various entries of the diary, Rinus confesses to boasting and bragging. From the obituary, added at the end of this book, written by an anonymous

✠

It seemed as if my heart was just under my skin, so big did it seem to be through that love wound.

✠

Thursday, October 7.

My Jesus, now that I am writing this I think something has changed in me all of a sudden. When I was with you again this morning, Elder Brother, when we were very close together, and when Father, who is everywhere at the same time, looked at me with great love, especially because you were with me, then I suddenly felt wounded in the middle of my heart. It seemed as if my heart was just under my skin, so big did it seem to be due to that love wound.[36] Now I love them all even more: You, Father, Mary, my dearest, the Mother of all my little brothers and friends, I love everyone.

---

classmate of his, we know he did not feel that appreciated or accepted by his classmates. His inclination to boasting and arguing may have been caused by an unconscious need to break through this wall of felt rejection. This lack of popularity may have been due to the profound inner graces he was receiving—graces which set him apart from his classmates. The cumulative effect of such inner movements of grace may have made him act somewhat differently from others, who experienced that difference, at least implicitly. We find something of the same reticence in the diary of Blessed Faustina Kolwaska of Poland. What also may not have enhanced his "melting" into the group was his somewhat stiff, reserved, slightly fastidious background as a native of The Hague. This, too, made him different from many boys from the more lively, outgoing, and easy going rural South of the country.

36 The sudden love wound in the middle of his heart, which Rinus experienced completely unexpectedly, would have been less of a surprise to him had he been aware that the same gift was given to other Christians whose formation was shaped by the Divine Lover in extraordinary ways. Such elevations belong to the way of Christian mysticism, especially in its early stages.

137-'38 (35) 2³

Donderdag 7 October
Mijn Jezus, nu ik dit schrijf is er geloof ik iets in mij veranderd
zo maar ineens. Toen ik vanmorgen weer met Jou, Grote Broer
te samen was, heel dicht bij elkaar, en toen Vader, die overal te
gelijk is mij met veel liefde bezag, vooral omdat Jij bij me was
toen ben ik ineens gewond, midden in mijn hart. 't Leek wel
of mijn hartje vlak onder mijn vel zat, zo fijn leek 't me worden van die liefste wond. Nu houd ik nog veel meer van
allemaal. van Vader, van Jou, van Maria, mijn liefste Moeder
van al mijn broertjes en vriendjes, ik houd van iedereen.
Vrijdag 8 October
Wat is er nu toch kleine Rinus. Waar ben je toch onge-
rust over, net of er iets is dat niet goed is? Ja mijn Grote
Broer en mijn liefste Moe, iets zit me dwars. Ik ben nu
hier al 6 weken in dit Sanatorium, en ik leef al een lange
tijd op dieet, maar dat volg ik soms niet helemaal precies.
Enfin dat is 't niet, want daar heb ik Meester iedere keer vergif-
fenis voor gekust, en Vader en U trouwens ook. Maar ik twij-
fel of ik als ik dat dieet volg zoals ik dat nu zo goed mogelijk
doe, of ik dan wel echt genezen zal, en U plezier doe.
En of dit sanatorium waarin ik niet veel leer op school
en niet hard hoef te werken, eigelijk geen verloren tijd is.
Ook pieker ik wat of wel echt goed en lief met mijn vriendje
speel. Kortom is dit nu 't goede sanatoriumleven wat ik
hier leid?

A handwriting sample from October, 1937.

Friday, October 8.

Now, what is it, little Rinus. What are you worried about? What is it that's not quite right? Yes, my Elder Brother and my dearest Mother, something is bothering me. I have been at this sanatorium for six weeks, and for even longer than that I have been on a diet. Though I do not follow it exactly, that is not the problem, for every time [I fall] I kiss Mother to ask forgiveness, and Father and you, too, for that matter. But I doubt, if I follow the diet as I do now—as well as possible—whether I will really be healed and please you. And I wonder if this sanatorium, where I don't learn as much as at school and needn't work hard, is not really lost time.[37] I also worry whether I really play well and nicely with my friends. In short, is life in this sanatorium the right life for me now?

The answer is: the diet was composed by experienced doctors, who know the right medicine for healing. So, Rinus, you should follow it *completely*. Your mood doesn't detract from its effect. And if you cooperate well, if you trust the diet, then it works faster. So whether you are, on the one hand, glad, cheerful, and in high spirits or, on the other hand, downcast and sad (which you should never be), as long as you follow the diet, you are sure to be healed. So look at your diet chart. Do not pay attention to your good or bad moods. Just do [the best you can], and it will always be good. I, your Elder Brother, together with Father, have prescribed this diet. You know we are very skilled doctors. So you must please us by allowing yourself to be healed completely by following this prescription. Moreover, we sometimes apply special treatments to you, like [giving you a] massage or rubbing [your head] whether it hurts or not. Let us do the work. It's for your own good.

When all is said and done, [there is no need] to complain about it so much. Besides, a year of life in the sanatorium is *never* wasted, even if you would not have any classes at all. For the healthier you get now, the better you'll be able to work in later life. That's clear, isn't it? Then, too, the very fact that you are worrying about the state of your sanatorium life and about [making] the right contacts with your fellow patients is a sign of good will. And more than "good will" the doctor doesn't ask of you. For if a patient wills to be healed, then he is received by the doctor and the rest is done by him. The patient only has to allow himself to be operated upon. Now, dear boy, that permission you have given us more than once, even many times a day, for six weeks. But if a moment later you forget the sanatorium, then you think you have not given consent.

---

37 In this passage Rinus may be alluding to his experience of the basic difference between an informational and a formational approach to learning. Both are necessary. Each includes in some measure the other. Yet, as in Rinus' case, it seems that at certain moments one is called to give preferential focus to one of the two without totally neglecting or depreciating the other. Rinus seems to have preferred from early life to focus on the lived experience of Christian formation while always being sufficiently informed by the doctrinal faith tradition of the Church.

Look, when a doctor, after having obtained consent, is going to treat a patient, it is not necessary for the patient to keep on thinking actively, over and over again, "Yes, I have given him permission." Of course not, as long as he does not chase the doctor away by actively *refusing* consent, the latter quietly goes on with his treatment. And when the patient says occasionally, "Go ahead, Doctor," all the better. But the doctor won't really stop if you do not keep saying so. He would stop, of course, were you to say, "I don't will [the treatment] any more!" But this must be said with full and free consent. For if a doctor is operating and the patient says in his pain, "stop it," the doctor won't listen, because he knows the patient will be glad after this treatment and thank him for carrying on.

Well, Rinus, take all this to heart. We are at work on you even if you do not think of us for a while. Every now and then you say, "Go ahead, Father and Jesus." Then it's good. Persevere!

Out of gratitude I am now kissing cordially the picture [I have] of Elder Brother.

Saturday, October 9.
My dear Jesus, my dear Elder Brother, what game shall we play today to enjoy ourselves? You know, don't you, that today I should give Mother something. What will it be? I really don't know, for I have already given everything. Have I kept a top or a marble for myself? I know [what I'll do]. Today is Saturday, and this afternoon I'm going to help Mother with her work. I may clean the corridor. I will do this out of love for her as well and as quietly as I can.

Tuesday, October 12.
Mother told me some more about our Father, and Elder Brother confirms it.[38] Let me see if I remember [it though] I can't [quite] understand it. I may say it all wrongly. Elder Brother says that I'll grasp it when I have grown up. But ah! I'm still so little. Father is without beginning. He has never been made, so Father is God. In sacred books (Elder Brother says that everything written in them is true), it says that God created the souls of people (including my own little soul) in his image and likeness. My soul is a spirit like God is a spirit. My soul has reason and free will like God does. But my soul, reason, and free will are limited, whereas God is infinite in everything.

---

38 This entry and others in the notebooks reveal a certain enlightenment about the Trinitarian mystery. Such illuminations are difficult to express for a young novice not yet schooled in informational theology. Therefore, they make for difficult reading that contrasts with the childlike simplicity of the usual expression of Rinus' experiences before and after such passages.

So far I think this is not so difficult, Mother. But now the next step: God has two factors in his being, reason and free will, which from all eternity are in God and these are also infinite. For example, justice proceeds from reason and the will, for I see with my reason that something is just. I am thus informed on that point. And now I *will* also that justice. In this way all qualities originate in God. Therefore, we can also say, for instance, that God is love. For reason and free will are necessary to bring forth love. These qualities are borne by a personality—in the spirit of God.

So whether I say God is infinite love, or justice, or mercy, it is the same as saying: God is an infinite spirit, with infinite reason and infinite free will. But these qualities of cooperation among spirit, reason, and free will are outward, at least, that's how we poor people living in a world of matter express it. But Father's infinite reason also works from all eternity in an everlasting Now (so he is now working in me, too), and he understands and sees his own infinity with infinite clearness. He understands himself in one idea. This idea is infinite, because both his active impelling reason and its object are infinite. This is, as it were, the personified divine reason. It is the second person of the Most Holy Trinity, my Elder Brother, Jesus Christ, who is in everything equal to the Father.

The second person, too, is spirit like the Father, gifted with the same attributes of reason and free will. He, too, sees and understands the Father. Love goes out to what is most beautiful and wills to possess it or to unite itself with it. For the love which Father and Son feel for one another is infinite because of the infinite depth of both. For Father and Son will with an infinite *will* to unite with one another, and, from this, arises an infinite Love, which is God the Holy Spirit. This Person, too, is spirit with reason and free will. He, too, sees, knows, and loves the Father and Son in an infinite way.

And this Divinity, one God in three Persons, resides in me through sanctifying grace. How wonderful! Father not only resides in me but also works in me. God loves me, poor dud that I am. God is my friend. Thus in a certain sense my form is like God's form. I may begin to think and act as God thinks and acts. How beautiful this is! And how seldom do I think of this! My only great Father, too dear for words, and my very greatest and strongest and most lovable Elder Brother, I love you so much, in spite of how little I am. I allow myself to be healed completely by your specialist's hands. Heal me, whatever method you use. It doesn't matter. Cut me as you see fit, wherever necessary. Break all my resistance. I surrender to you, sweet Daddy.

Wednesday, October 20.[39]

My dear Mom, during our walk I seriously erred in brotherly love. Forgive me, I won't do it again, out of love for you. But now I want to write down something harmless that happened last week during the [weekly] walk [outside the Novitiate]. It caused an enormous upheaval in me. We are forbidden to accept and eat food during a walk. The novice with whom I was walking—and with whom I get along with so well—was given some apples by his family. We went on and took a side path in order to eat the apples at our leisure. My other fellow novice did not want an apple. And I? I would have rather he had not been given them at all. I do not even care for apples that much. But after some hesitation I accepted them. Why? 1) I knew quite well it was forbidden; 2) I knew it would be a humiliation for me to accept them, certainly in the presence of another novice, who did not take them himself. These were reasons *not* to accept them, especially because the "apple"-novice added that he did not mind if we did not want to eat them. But that was only a mere conventional polite remark. So I took the apple and ate it. Yet I realized fully what I was doing: 1) it would certainly have hurt my fellow-novice, who would have to keep the three apples which, after all, he had been given and had accepted for us; 2) he would not have got much pleasure if he had eaten them alone; 3) to show him that it would have been better not to take them, it was sufficient to refuse *one* apple; a second refusal might have caused bitterness and unrest; 4) it was an exercise in humility in the presence of two other novices. But this small fact has left a great impression on me. For it was a *voluntary* fault, which I do not make very often, thank God! I saw that it was just that [kind of fault] by the [guilty] mood it effected. I could now let my trust in Jesus take over. In a church on the way I prayed with more fervor, though my humiliated nature would have preferred to pretend indifference. On the whole, I am thankful to Jesus for this humiliation and for this proof that I behave now a bit differently with respect to public humiliations.

---

39 This entry discloses the refinement of the loving conscience of souls touched deeply by the Lord. Grace makes them feel far more sensitive about the slightest voluntary venial sin they may commit. It is the overflow of love from God and for God that pains the soul so deeply about the smallest offense. The very thought of offending this infinite Love saddens the privileged soul immensely. This sensitivity may help to explain the length and depth of this simple story about an apple Rinus accepted and ate despite the Novitiate's rule against accepting gifts from people when making the weekly walk outside the Novitiate.

Tuesday, October 26.
My dear Daddy, how is my healing going? Do I keep my diet well? The year still has a long way to go. In fact, I will stay here under your treatment for at least forty-two weeks more, that is, of course, if it pleases you. I enjoy this health resort more and more. Every day, indeed every hour, I love you and Mother and Elder Brother more. I am his little friend. We always go and play nicely. Sometimes he takes me with him on his bike in a child's saddle and we cycle through the surroundings. Then he lets me see how beautifully Father has made everything, and how many people would like to harm Father if he weren't so strong. And then I keep saying all the time only one thing: Dear Jesus, when I, too, am big and strong I will tell all people how good Father and you are. [Editor's Note: This Novitiate recollection in "allegorical" form ends on the date shown, October 26, 1937. Rinus evidently kept simultaneously another Novitiate recollection notebook or diary beginning a few months earlier on August 29, 1937. This document follows.]

IV
The Diary of My Novitiate
Part Two
Gennep, 1937

IV
THE DIARY OF MY NOVITIATE
PART TWO
GENNEP, 1937

Sunday, August 29.
I meditated precious little! I am not well-versed in this trade, not by a long shot. I'll do better tomorrow. What little meditation I did was divided as follows: I was looking for practical cases in which my main vice comes clearly to the fore . . . But then I didn't go any further.

Monday, August 30.
Things were a little better today, maybe because I had made more, much clearer notes. Today the retreat started. I like that. I hope now, with Jesus' help, to get into my stride at once. But I don't want to study during the retreat. Today my meditation was also better because I followed a cleaner line and because I feel good. "Practice makes perfect." Well, old boy, tomorrow do even better! I have become reconciled to the idea that I am really a "frater".[40] But how happy I do feel here! How

40 The title "frater" is used in religious priest communities in the Netherlands for members who are neither lay brothers nor ordained priests but who prepare themselves for ordination, either as novices or as vowed religious students in the Senior Seminary.

Rinus' Novitiate class of 1937. His Novice Master, Father Strick, is in the first row, center, and Rinus is in the second row, fourth from the left.

much better it is than I expected. This morning I got the idea of doing a singing meditation, that is, I prepare the night before by ticking off various songs and hymns. [Aside: There are eight meditations a day for three days of retreat.] Of course, I mean singing inwardly, but then following the rhythm in my thoughts so that, as it were, I am singing in a dance, and singing everything to God, like a child. For this meditating profoundly about death, heaven, and hell, means nothing to me. Well, just try, old boy. *Qui cantat bis orat, qui saltat etiam bis orat.* ["One who sings prays twice, one who dances, also prays twice."]

Same Monday.
[This practice] went a bit better. I hope still to learn it. Also singing inwardly, or rather making inner music, is not singing alone. To prepare my meditation, I'll also write down some titles of appropriate pieces of music. I wonder if I am not too stiff and too fastidious in the eyes of the other boys. I think I am overly anxious about my cassock. I'll try to do differently, with God's help. I have not been able to find ejaculatory prayers yet.

✠

[It helps to say] as an ejaculatory prayer: Jesus, Love.

✠

Tuesday, August 31.
It goes better, thanks to Father Gijsen's [the former Novice Master, now a teacher and Confessor] good lessons about meditation. I meditated again on the Garden of Golgotha. [Editor's Note: Rinus probably meant the Garden of Gethsemane.] The practical example given to me while talking with Jesus was to be more recollected today, to be in chapel or in my room more often, to make sure I am not distracted. [It helps to say] as an ejaculatory prayer: *Jesus, Love.* I also noticed that at first I had a wrong idea about meditation. What I now regard as meditation seems much easier to me. It can go on all day, so to say. I only hope I now have the right idea.

Wednesday, September 1.
[Written in Latin] Today my meditation was mediocre. Yesterday Jesus gave me sweetness. Today he did not give me this [feeling]. But I am not angry with him. I know it's better [this way]. Sweetness is the prize, or a stimulant for a start. But often, Jesus, I do not feel much sweetness, though my meditation is not bad. I sense your presence, Lord, here in the Novitiate. I feel as if I am completely in your presence. All day long your eye follows me. Thank you so much for having

brought me here. My pride is my greatest vice. Yesterday I was humiliated four times by others (who did not realize they did so!) Thanks, Jesus. I have brought you my intention (while thinking about this) to be still during the day, to walk, act, and talk quietly. Jesus, how quietly you accepted your cross!

Thursday, September 2.
[Written in Latin and Dutch] I do not know how to express my love for Jesus. *Amo te*, [Latin]; *ich liebe Sie* [German]; *Je vous aime, mon Jésus* [French]; *ik houd van U* [Dutch]; I love you, [English]. I am so glad about this. If only I could please you or would not grieve you. Otherwise I have nothing to ask you but love, love, and love again. Divine Most Holy Trinity, you own my body and soul completely. You shimmer through me, I know and feel this! Thank you, God. This morning I did not enjoy a "felt" meditation. It doesn't matter! I'm glad about it, for now God in his grace allows me to fend for myself: to put, as it were, the food in my mouth and then to swallow. It is different when the Lord gives me thoughts filled with feelings. All I have to do then is swallow. In either case, God be praised. [Whatever way] he thinks is good.

This morning my meditation was about nothing else but love. It is my intention to give more and more love today to God, to the saints, to my fellowmen, to my family.

Friday, September 3.
This morning I did Jesus a favor: I bore my sleep and absent-mindedness, my dullness and even my boredom with patience. I was somewhat ill this morning, too. I had slept only six hours. So my resistance was caused by the condition of my body and not by that of my soul. I cannot force what the body resists. Thus, when I am sleepy, I cannot compel my body not to feel sleepy. Of course, I should not *yield* to sleepiness. But I cannot do anything about this condition itself, except to bear with it patiently! And I did so with God's help. I was even glad I had this experience, for I have pleased Jesus. Today there was adoration. Love, Jesus.

Saturday, September 4.
[Written in Latin] Meditation was no good. Any beginning is difficult. I hope I will learn to meditate well. It's so necessary; it's so good for the religious life.

Sunday, September 5.
The first half hour of my meditation was worthless, but, during the last fifteen minutes, it suddenly occurred to me that I trusted far too little in God. The proof of this is the fact that I always sit and plan how well

I will do things *tomorrow*, while I, with such thoughts in my mind, do less well today. Another proof: I have a kind of mistrust, or rather an unrest, about whether I will last out this year. If I have confidence, I'll leave it all to Jesus. He has given me my vocation. He will, therefore, pave the way to [its fulfillment], if only I cooperate. *Resolution*: To continue my inner prayer, fully confident in the Holy Trinity who animates me.

Monday, September 6.
I was absent-minded most of the time, yet I know that all is good. The only resolution I made was to make a fresh start. I know that I am going to change here. I've gotten over my half-heartedness. I have not been impatient since I entered the Novitiate. I firmly believe that St. Teresa [of Avila], together with Mary, my Mother, has seen to this. The foundations are there, so go on calmly, Rinus, with God's help. Jesus, my love.

Tuesday, September 7.
My meditations, even now, are still not much. It's good to practice humility, though I still do so very seldom. I thought in my pride that Rinus Scholtes would be able to meditate at the flick of a finger, right away. But *Frater* Scholtes did not get away with that! Fortunately, I have not become impatient, which is more than I expected. But it cannot be done in any other way! If only I please God who lives in me, what do I care for feelings for or against [discursive] meditation. Jesus likes as much to see a sleeping child as a waking one, as long as the child is not lazy and falls asleep on purpose. When I am sluggish sometimes, I must remember that. How good God is! Tomorrow I'm going to meditate on the *same* subject. My God, my love. Calmness and diligence. For you![41]

---

41 As we shall see, Rinus' inability to engage in imaginative and discursive meditation while living in what he calls the love-will, often all day long, is a result of the dark nights in which he is being initiated by the Holy Spirit. Already toward the end of his Junior Seminary, Rinus had been gifted with the prayer of quiet. The average novice has to begin with discursive meditation. Especially in the initial period of training, a novice has to learn this step by step method. One of the reasons Rinus doubts at times if he will make it through the Novitiate is that he has had little or no success in following this prescribed style of meditation, try as he might to do so.

Wednesday, September 8.
Today on Mother's birthday my meditation was no better than yesterday. Yet I know it is good because I am not sleepy and distracted on purpose. I was less absent-minded during the third quarter of the hour. Then, with Jesus, I prepared for Holy Communion and Holy Mass. I promised Mother as a birthday present to guard my eyes well, today and tomorrow. I will try to make this a habit. It's great to know that Mother, of course, will also treat us. When Elder Brother brings in the money, Mother asks him to give me something, and then she adds to it from her own treasure-box. How immensely generous she is! I did not dare to ask for anything because it is not *my* birthday but Mother's. She knows well what to give me. I'll give her some more small gifts today!

Thursday, September 9.
Meditation went slightly better, meaning that I was less distracted. I asked myself if perhaps I took the initiative to make myself the choirmaster, and therefore put another novice in the wrong light in regard to his qualifications. I do not think I did so. I was tempted to do it, in fact, quite a lot. But Jesus did not want me to commit an offense against brotherly love. Yet, when I was told I was likely to be the choirmaster, I talked to others about him and put myself, as it were, in the foreground. But now I'm not going to think about this any more, for such was my resolution this morning.

Friday, September 10.
I am inching further ahead bit by bit. I was not nearly so sleepy [today] as yesterday. And I could pay attention more to my meditation. Thank you so much, dear Jesus. Of course, always go forward! I've asked myself whether or not I am still permeated by a sense of the high dignity of the priesthood, and if I really know how unworthy I am for that [call]. Furthermore, in every meditation I end with love, though somehow still without *feelings*. I'm almost inclined to believe that I love Jesus extraordinarily, that is to say, as I have never loved him up to now. But what of it? I am hardly willing to do anything for Jesus. And what little I do gives me a great deal of difficulty. Still with God's help I go forward, that's for sure. I've received a great deal of grace during these past fourteen days in the Novitiate. Who knows how much I have wasted! Please, forgive me, my God! I'll make the same resolution as yesterday: humility. Mother Mary, my Directress, help your poor consecrated servant and child. My Jesus, my love.

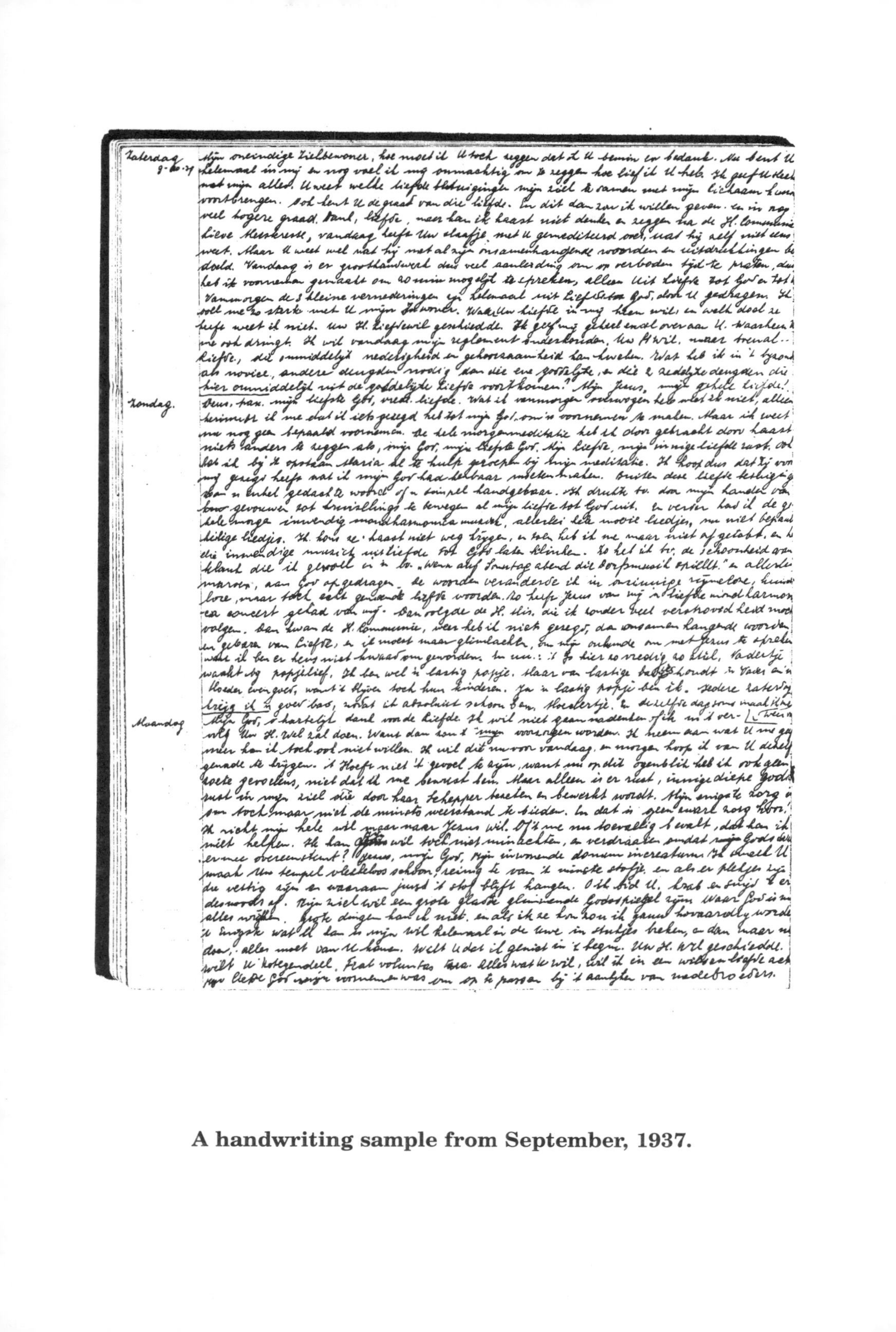

A handwriting sample from September, 1937.

Saturday, September 11.
Thanks to the grace of God my meditation went a little better. Yes, if you take Mary by the arm, you receive every grace. As a matter of fact I have not had a permanent subject [for discursive meditation]; I just give free rein to my love. Love always finds something in the Beloved to give even more love. My resolution was: stay more recollected and silent, especially during choir lessons, and try to be more cheerful, charitable, and pleasant during recreation.

Recreation is not meant for me only but for my fellow novices. When they have had a pleasant recreation (also through my own efforts), then it is good for me, too, even if I myself received nothing from it. I should ask for much more trust. Mary, my Mother, I am and remain your servant, a slave of love to Jesus and Mary. Do with me as you will.

✠

I am willing to give Jesus as much as I can.

✠

Sunday, September 12.
After sunshine some rain will fall. One cannot always experience spiritual consolations. That would not be good for me. All things considered, I have not meditated on much of anything. I only prayed to Jesus. Yet I felt as if my prayers were full of love or, rather, I knew myself to be filled with love, despite feeling completely arid. I turned this [spiritual aridity] into a small sacrifice to Jesus. Of course, it was in reaction to yesterday's exuberant feelings that I now experienced such dryness. I am really willing to give Jesus as much as I can, though, and even more. I want to be more recollected today. I also have an official rule now, with my spare time well organized! Jesus, help me. St. John Bosco, I beg you, obtain for me the virtues and know-how to live my apostolate and my life as you did (even if mine only looks similar to yours), either here [at home], or better still, in the missions.

Monday, September 13.
My meditation slightly improved. I was less distracted. I could not stick that well to the subject, yet I said a lot to God and asked for much. Ah! God in my soul, I feel my love of you and my neighbor growing, almost every day. Where it will lead I don't know. I'll only let myself be guided by the love, grace, and promptings of God, the Holy Spirit. I don't care where I arrive, it's all the same, it's all good. My Jesus, the pains in my stomach that I had this morning are also for you and borne out of love for you. I wanted to give you much more.

As regards brotherly love, I made the resolution to stay calm. I am much too agitated and domineering during recreation. I want to play ping-pong every time, and with a particular novice, because it's such a nice game then. But in that case I am being selfish. I will play ping-pong with whoever asks me, directly or indirectly—even with those who are no good at it. Ah! Jesus. Likewise, because I love you, I play the mouth-organ for the sake of my fellow novices. That's why I ask you to make my music agreeable. Oh! Love.

Tuesday, September 14.
Jesus, my God, my All. What do you want of me? Sooner or later my heart will burst out of its chest for love of you. But I won't be afraid and anxious about what will happen to me. You do much work, God the Holy Spirit, just go ahead [and keep doing it]. I want to go all the way with you. I really won't be afraid. Please, do as you wish.

My meditation went fairly well. Don Bosco began early. I was on my knees at a quarter to six. Never mind, it's good for me. The first fifteen minutes when I spoke to God were the best. I think I do much better when I look at something, for example, a crucifix. But that may only be due to lack of exercise and love. Yes, to a lack of love! My God, I think of you far too little. Ah! Help me to love you more and more! Please do so, my God. You are almighty. I now have, as it were, a taste of your love. I won't stop before I am satiated. It won't be soon! Let me again be charitable to the other novices.

Wednesday, September 15.
During meditation I can hardly do anything else then shake off sleep and distractions. I don't speak so much to God actually. And when I do it's almost always about love and not about my gratitude to God. I forget everything, such as interceding for myself and others. Even after Holy Communion, I forget to do that. I don't do anything else but give Jesus love. Then I express this by silly movements, for instance, a simple gesture that is nothing special, such as crossing my arms when they were first folded, or something similar. This [gesture] represents embracing Jesus. So instead of flinging my arms around Jesus' neck, as if he were standing in front of me in bodily form, I do so in a spiritual way. And by this external movement I express what I would do if Jesus were standing there. So that movement is the same expression of love. It's as if someone were clenching his fist against somebody else, who is not even present. It is like a lover who, full of desire, stretches his arms toward his Beloved. He neither notices nor suspects anything of that motion, but with Jesus it is much more effective. He knows everything. He accepts this gesture as if it were a real embrace.

Today I dried Mary's tears and silently contemplated her sorrows. I gave her seven gifts, the seventh, which she really has already (for I am her fully consecrated servant with all that I have). But I was still attached to these other things, meaning that, had I not given myself already totally to her, I would give her these things now. They were my wristwatch, my cincture, my fountain pen, tennis racket, mouth organ, and the pleasant feelings I experience when I'm in the company of a certain novice. (I gave her this last thing already now, because it is not yet soiled, although I know from experience that this still so-called "supernatural feeling" can degenerate into a merely self-centered love. That's why I gave it to her apart from the rest.) Mother, how lovable you have been to bring me near to Jesus.

Thursday, September 16.
Today I tried to meditate on God, the Holy Spirit, but [the results] were not all that great immediately. I was often distracted. But God, the Holy Spirit, is so good. He wants to inspire me in a special way all day long, especially during recreation. Then I have the most difficulty: 1) to practice brotherly love; I am far too selfish; 2) to keep inner peace; sometimes I am much too elated and, at other times, I am far too silent. I feel like a poor wretch who means well and yet is always left on his own. Especially at such moments, inclinations to particular, that is, to selfish [exclusive] affectionate friendships, arise. Away with them! This is easier said than done. It's especially on this point that I must follow the inspiration of God, the Holy Spirit. In spite of everything, I know I love God, and I feel this love growing.

Friday, September 17.
I tried again to speak to God, the Holy Spirit, but I was often distracted. I must watch for these as yet harmless and sometimes even salutary reflections and daydreams. They only gratify my feelings and may end up in sensuality or even temptations. Away with them, Rinus! Today is Friday, which means commemorating Jesus' death on the Cross, and making small, special mortifications nobody sees: not fasting or eating less, even though it is an Ember Day. The quantity needn't be less, Rinus, but you may mortify yourself as regards the quality. For instance, take dessert like the other novices do, but swallow it without tasting it, or take away its nice taste with a mouthful of coffee. Nobody will notice. And then again practice brotherly love, but don't let it degenerate into sisterly love!! We are all young men of at least eighteen here, so we need not all be so tender and soft. Of course, there is no need to swear. But there is no need either to talk softly in a sing-song way when you want to do something with another novice. Be good and charitable but not soft and girlish. God. Love.

Saturday, September 18.
Things were not so good. Partly [it was] my own fault, partly my condition. I forgot to ask God *permission* to meditate, in other words, for the grace [for it]. I thought such things happen spontaneously, but this thought must be nipped in the bud! It is one of the biggest impediments to God's grace and strong help. Well! How should I, who need God's grace and help more than other people, as I am so much weaker than they are, even dare to think that I can pray, remain pure, and be humble without God's grace? Forgive me, Jesus dear. Perhaps I did not dismiss this thought soon enough.

Sunday, September 19.
Today my meditation showed some improvement; it was actually quite good when I compare it with other days. But, thanks to God's goodness, I myself was better prepared [to meditate]. Yesterday he inspired me to pray much more and well before every work. For example, when I visited the Blessed Sacrament after dinner, I asked for the grace to enjoy a good and cordial recreation; thereafter, I enjoyed the recreation so as to obtain grace for saying the Office well. Thus I move from one request for grace to the next, and I keep asking for more grace. I hope I no longer believe that I, by myself alone, can manage. I am also firmly convinced that I do not bore God with this eternal asking and beseeching. On the contrary, Father Berkers impressed [the opposite] strongly on me. My resolutions for today were: 1) to keep silence better, especially during choir practice; and 2) to speak slower and more clearly during recreation, for I cause my fellow novices trouble if they can't understand me well. Jesus, please give me this grace. I'll keep bothering you. Oh, my God, my love is growing. Thank you!

Monday, September 20.
From midnight on I asked Jesus [in tune with] my breathing and heartbeat for the grace of making a good meditation. I did my best; after all, feelings do not make for a good meditation as such. All things considered, my meditation was not bad. But love, my God, I still love so little in my practice of the daily rules. Be that as it may, I am glad you keep me humble and small through my shortcomings. Puffed-up frogs are neither beautiful nor lovable. In their grossness they are rather pitiful. Jesus, you love a sweet little child, who does nothing but express its feelings by crying and croaking. I cannot help it that I write and speak and act from love.

My Jesus, sometimes I can't pray at all. I mean [I can't] arrange my thoughts. I can only look at your image or close my eyes and just love you with a laughing face. What will happen along the way, I leave to you, my God.

Mary, my Mother, what can I say or do to thank you for having brought me so close to Jesus through the "slavery of love." My resolution for today is to keep my eyes more cast down or raised up during periods of silence, for that is at times necessary for my inner peace. I must direct all my love to God, not to my fellow novices, but only to God. In God, with God, through God. Jesus, help me.

Tuesday, September 21.
My Jesus! I can hardly say or write anything about love. I want to be quite still again, very very quiet; I look at your crucifix, I look at you without saying a word or doing anything. [I want] only to love you—then there are times again when I say the strangest things to you. I talk to you and laugh with you and kiss your crucifix. One way or the other, I always feel my love growing. I get almost afraid because, except for short intervals of an hour or so, this [love] has been growing for the thirty-four and a half weeks that I have been in this place of love. I hardly care for feelings. Whether I am feeling it or not, I *know* my love is in you, to you, with you, and for you. The only thing that sometimes bothers me is the question of how I, as the miserable, weak person I am, can express my greatest possible gratitude [to you]? And not only to you—for in truth I thank you most of all—but ah! my God [what about] the Holy Spirit? I think so seldom of him. I am going to do so more often, and, above all, love him more. Neither do I know how to thank my dear Mother. For I owe my whole spiritual unfolding, and especially my love, to her, that is, to my consecration in love to her, my Directress. Together with God, the Holy Spirit, she has formed me—and I have allowed her and him calmly to form me for all four years. And now, yes, I would almost say I see the results. But I'm afraid of becoming proud. Jesus, you are my confidence and my love. Yes, I am getting thirstier and thirstier. I am drunk with love. Today's resolution was again to guard my eyes much more—-either to cast them down more often or to raise them up. Jesus, God, the Holy Spirit. Ah! Love!

Wednesday, September 22.
My God, the Holy Spirit, thank you cordially. I had thought meditation would not go so smoothly, but it was much better than I expected. I feel full, but there is room for much more. Much more love, O! Jesus. Sometimes I hold my heart to keep it from exploding. But what is *my* love in comparison with that of the saints? And how great must Mary's love have been! How was she able to keep her heart in her chest!

Ah!, Mother, give me something of your almost immeasurable love. With a little love from your bottomless heart, my thimble of a heart will be filled to the brim. And you'd better keep filling it. For in this thimble are holes. They let love seep through to other vessels driven by the pressure of your supply. My God, how great must your love then be? I have plunged into it, and I almost feel dizzy. O my! What I'm saying is foolish, I know, but I have to say something to express my love.

Today I made a resolution to make [an evening] meditation from now (already begun at half past seven) until half past nine. Then with a wink of love and a sigh I will sleep until tomorrow. My God, I am so weak. If you let me go for a split second, if you withhold your grace, I would plunge into the deepest abyss of sin. Be careful my good Jesus. Don't trust too much in my fine deeds and words, when you help me with your grace. Do not think, please, that I am strong and can do anything for a change *without* grace. My Jesus, I am so weak that I would deny you at once. Should the greatest, yes, the very greatest sinner who lives on earth and who is now dying this very moment, receive from God the grace he has given me in his incomprehensible goodness, that sinner would be a *great* saint in heaven at his death if only he cooperates. And I, who receive so much grace day after day, remain as tepid as always—and I even offend you. My God, your holy will be done. It pleases you to see me extremely weak. My rule is your holy will.

Thursday, September 23.
Ah! My Jesus, I knew my confidence in you was not in vain. Last night you wanted to play hide-and-seek, and I was to find you. Only now and then did you say something to direct my way, but I could not find you. All at once, after Holy Communion, you could not hide your countenance and you laughed, and I found you again, and now I am again close to you.

My meditation was fruitful. With God's help I repulsed two attacks by the enemy. The devil thought he could catch me easily and draw me away from you, but every trick of his had only the opposite effect: my love for Jesus increased. Because I show acts of love, my soul becomes more beautiful through new grace. The few dimes I earn [in this way] are added up and put into Mother's treasure box. So! Devil, don't you know I am Jesus' and Mary's consecrated servant? I guess you've found that out by now! You are strong enough when I'm alone, but my Protectors trample on you, don't they? My God, my resolution is to watch over my eyes, so that my inner prayer is not disturbed. Jesus. Love.

Friday, September 24.
My crucified Jesus, there were many distractions today, but I fought them well. I think I had a good meditation. Its preparation went better than usual. But I'm still so awfully weak. I have so little love when I compare myself with the other novices. And yet I know my love is growing because I'm able to give others much love, for the sake of love itself—for God is love. Thus God and love equal each other perfectly; they are equal; they are one and the same. God *is* love.

Last night I was also allowed to give others much love. My Jesus, I would like to call out to you, solely out of love for you, and to the first person whom I meet: "What would you like to have from me, for the love of God? How many litres of blood? How many square inches of my skin? How much of my strength must be at your service?" I'd like to feed the whole world with my blood for love of you—and, should that blood be as hot with love as it is inside me, dear God, what love would then be given to you?

To get a sinner out of hell, I would be willing to suffer the worst pains of hell, if only I were still allowed to love and see you. I would be willing to suffer the punishment of all those damned in hell and of all the souls in purgatory, provided they would be allowed to go straight to heaven and to love you more and more forever. My God, how I should love you then, for suffering purifies love! And, if I were to suffer the pains of hell, I would do so out of love for you. I would even redeem the devils from hell to take them to heaven. Then they would love you. My God, even that wouldn't be enough. I would like to create beings, always new beings, so as to make them love you. But alas, how foolish I am. None of this could even begin to represent the tiniest flicker of your love [in me].

My Jesus, we cannot repay your love. Let us, therefore, humbly confess our impotence and silently [allow the] shower of your benefits [to descend] upon us. Only a quiet sigh, an expression of impotent gratitude, should be our answer. My God, I tremble to think that there are beings on earth who hate you. Hate, how could that be possible? Could I change their hatred into love! Oh Jesus, my great Love. I love you above everything!

Saturday, September 25.

Today I meditated on your little house in Nazareth. I almost made a fool of myself. I entered there when St. Joseph was busy doing carpentry work. Instead of introducing myself as one always does to strangers, I flung my arms around his neck and started talking like anything. Of course, it didn't occur to me that St. Joseph could not speak Dutch! But he didn't think my embrace was that strange, I believe, for he did not push me away. It may be an Eastern custom. But I thought, if *he* doesn't think I'm crazy, he, the spouse, then Mary and Jesus won't do so either. As I was speaking a bit more to St. Joseph, the door opened and Jesus came in. He was a sturdy boy with *red* hair, about four years of age. I left St. Joseph right away, and lifted Jesus up, and, yes, I dared to kiss my God's face directly. I said only: "Jesus, Love." But then I came to my senses, and I thought, what will St. Joseph think of me for having acted so boldly? I looked at him, and he was smiling. Then I was almost frantic with happiness. I walked into the living room to [see] Mary. I don't remember what I said to her, but I reclined close to her heart, and she to mine. After this expression of love, we had a talk in the living room. Mary spoke a little Latin, so did St. Joseph. Fortunately, a Roman customer happened to enter the shop, and we asked him to be our interpreter and to tell who I was and where I was living. Then he left, and I looked at the happy family, and hardly said a word. I only smiled and spoke about Love. Then I flung myself upon the ground, which is a sign of slavery in the East I believe, and I asked my Directress about today's task. She gave me the workaday directions I would fulfill well out of love for her.

Sunday, September 26.
Today I was more distracted than usual, yet I made a good preparation [for meditation] the very moment I got up. I also [did so] in the garden by the cross and the statue of Mary [on the grounds of the Novitiate]. But, due to these distractions, I see I don't yet love you enough, not by a long shot. Would that I could love you like the least saint! But I am too often distracted. My thoughts roam everywhere. If only I could suddenly see that we are supposed to meditate in chapel and that Jesus is present there, I wouldn't go on with that thought, or I would at least take Jesus with me on my ramblings. But, even so, I am not distracted voluntarily. Since I do not *will* [these distractions] I do no evil. I'm sure of this, but if I loved Jesus more I would *always* think of him, and I would feel uncomfortable immediately if I were thinking of something else. But I'm not angry at all about what is lacking in my love. I simply let God, the Holy Spirit, work [in me]. What he wants of me he can have, without reservation. Even if I don't know now what that might be, I'd want it in advance.

My good Jesus, only out of love for you will I take up my rule of life, my little cross, that is slowly but surely going to weigh me down. But the more pressure [I feel], the more love I receive from you. My unspoken resolution for today is to exhaust myself, so to speak, [for you] and to show love toward God, Jesus, the Holy Spirit, my Mother Mary, St. Joseph, my three patron saints, and my fellow novices. Jesus, thanks to your pressure and grace, I am starting to love more and more in a supernatural way. But it is not enough, not by a long shot! Much, much more love. My God and my All. My Love, my Everything!

The cross in the park behind the Novitiate where Rinus went for prayer.

The statue of Mary on the grounds of Rinus' Novitiate.

Monday, September 27.
Today I was rather distracted. Yet I was full of love for everything related to God. At this moment I'm still meditating on the same truth as this morning. God is dwelling in us. That's so beautiful, isn't it! After Holy Communion the whole Godhead inhabits us. The Holy Trinity permeates us with the soul, body, and blood of Jesus Christ. What little faith I have if I still remain lukewarm! But let me start again with fresh courage.

Today I again made the resolution to carry out my love of God as well and insofar as possible in everything, above all, in relation to my fellow novices. If I had the power to be omnipresent, I would preach the love of God to anybody I touched or saw. If only everybody who read this got the same power, how soon the world would be on fire with love for you, my God.

Tuesday, September 28.
Quiet and rest. I had a really quieting meditation. I felt like a large deep lake with the inviolate, undisturbed silence of nature reigning. The Spirit of God hovered over the water. God is in the water; God permeates the water. O most Holy Trinity, present here in me, I feel you being drawn deeper and deeper into my inmost self, gradually deeper, without thrusting or wrenching. I hope I may not in the least freely resist this gift to my soul received from you. I don't think my soul resists you, my dearest, dearest God. As to what the body wants, and as regards the involuntary (and sometimes voluntary) weak spots—ah! You know I am extremely, extremely weak. And what of my faults. It is as if I am running swiftly down a [long] corridor. I meet you, Jesus, and in my haste I bump against your arm. You look back, astonished. But when you see that I still walk on steadily, and that I hadn't even noticed my rudeness, you don't mind it so much anymore—especially when I fling my arms around your neck afterwards and beg your forgiveness. You kiss away my guilt, both for all my unnoticed acts of rudeness, and for those I committed rather on purpose.

My good Jesus, if you wish me to tell you now, already in advance, that I shall never again offend you, then you would have to let me die this minute. But I'd almost dare to say, even you, with all your grace and all your power can't prevent me from offending you. So weak am I. Ah, Jesus. I'm sad too about my own weakness. For I don't want to offend you. I love you far too much to fail to do your holy will in the least [respect]. But I am so weak. Yes, Jesus, today I will think often of God's presence.

Wednesday, September 29.
I was again rather distracted during meditation, but not of my own free will. I also dismissed a serious impure temptation directly, out of love

for God. I don't really need any feelings to know or to make my love of God stronger. My resolution was to almost exhaust myself in more and better "love-attentions" (they needn't be great acts) toward my fellow novices out of love for God. I also know now that even if I were in the middle of Paris, for example, I would still do for all these strangers services of love out of love for God, who is the God of *all* people. But my Jesus, this will [of mine] is not your will [now for me]. At least, you don't want me at present to translate this desire into action. For you say: "No, my little Rinus, you'll stay here within the four walls today and prepare yourself well so as to be able to give much love later on. Here you've got the other novices to practice on."

Yes, my God, the easiest contacts for love are my fellow novices. But it's sometimes difficult for me. For they all carry God in them. They've all got sanctifying grace and their beautiful vocation. All follow you generously in a much better way than I do. For I firmly believe they experience many more difficulties. But look how calmly, cheerfully, fervently, and religiously they go through their time of probation here. How much I can learn from them and follow their example. O my God! Suppose for a moment that each of them would receive the grace I receive from you and use so little [of]. They would burn with love for you, dear God. I wager they would already be on the third [unitive] way long before this or in seventh heaven! My Jesus, make me holy.

✠

What joy! My Jesus, my great love!

✠

Thursday, September 30.

Today I had great difficulty again in meditating. It's still not easy to remain fervent when you've got no feelings. My Jesus seems to hide from me, but I smile, for when I want to make him appear again, all I need to do is to laugh out loud and say that I know where he's hiding. And then Jesus comes out. But no matter how arid my meditation was, my acts of love, the movements of my will toward God and in God, go on all the same. I experience even more love toward God than yesterday. Today I feel strengthened and exhorted to fulfill these two resolutions: 1) to pay strict attention to brotherly love, that is, it should be fervent and cordial, but it shouldn't degenerate into sisterly love, for in that case God is not my object but I'm only seeking myself; 2) to do everything in a quiet way: not to slam the doors or fling plates; also to walk as quietly and gently as possible.

I got this hint from yesterday's spiritual reading (of St. Francis of Sales). He also said that he would speak during periods of silence for the sake of brotherly love. I intend to do the same, but . . . it should exclusively be for the benefit of one's fellows. For if I seek myself herein, then it's an imperfection.

Say another novice asks me what we are supposed to do now, or something like that, when [the information] has been put on the bulletin-board in the study. Then I can quietly answer him. Or, for that matter, if somebody asks [me] if I've got a good book on the life of a saint, I can freely say yes or no, and if necessary, offer some further explanation. But I need not turn this talk into a recreation! Do I express myself clpearly this way, my Jesus?

Tomorrow it will be First Friday. Millions of people will offer reparation for their own and other people's faults. There will be adoration, too. What joy! My Jesus, my great love!

Friday, October 1.

This morning my meditation went better than usual. I followed the Stations of the Cross with Jesus and his Holy Mother. I continued them during Holy Mass, adapting them to the liturgy. I'm glad I am again fastened to my cross (my rule of life.) Out of love for God, I won't try to tear myself loose from it. It won't work, and it will only hurt more afterwards. Ah! My Jesus, my love of the cross has grown. Thank you so much for that. But: *numquam satis est*, no, Jesus, it's never enough. Always more love. Forgive me for this expression, dearest God. But I would almost say: the more love and grace you give to me, the more I can give away. For I do not want to keep anything for myself. So it's to your own advantage and, of course, [especially, to mine]. But that's silly talk, isn't it, Jesus?

Ah! my dearest Mother and Directress, only now have I seen and understood how much you must have suffered when you followed the first way of the cross. I saw you standing there among the other people who were quiet for your sake and kept staring at you. But you didn't even notice. Your eyes were directed only to Jesus, to him alone. Yes, and now and then to me as well, for now I, too, walk with you.

Saturday, October 2.

My God, your love fulfills all my desires, but also everything for which my soul longs. For everything is included. My meditation was without feeling, but I think it was good because I fought against distractions and concentrated on you, my good God. My resolutions do not vary much. It's not necessary either. I try to get into the habit of keeping these resolutions. If I concentrate again and again on brotherly love during recreation, and in union with Jesus, and on pleasing my brothers, then I will end up doing so spontaneously. The same goes for recollection. If I keep paying attention to inner calm, as well as to outward quiet and composure, it will become a habit at last.

Ah, Jesus, today I also made a resolution to think more of my Guardian Angel, especially during the month of October. He is so good, my Angel, protecting me always and whispering to me all [I need to know]. I do not listen enough. My God, how miserable, cold, and weak I must be: 1) You, in my soul; 2) every morning Jesus Christ bodily present in me; 3) being a consecrated servant and *protégé* of my Directress and Mother; 4) having a Holy Guardian Angel willing to do anything for me; 5) along with three holy patron saints, who are interested in me and put in a good word for me; 6) and a little sister in heaven [Henny]. And *even* then I still sin.

Sunday, October 3.

I have tried to meditate on the virtues of St. Thérèse of the Child Jesus: humility, simplicity, confidence in God. But I cannot say I was successful. And that, in spite of the fact that we had been allowed to sleep half an hour longer. I have again resolved to avoid any kind of boasting, especially during recreation. And also: whatever you do (Rinus), do it slowly and well.

My Jesus, thanks from all my heart for your grace. Fortunately, the sacrament works *ex opere operato* (by its own strength); otherwise I would not have received much grace. My Jesus, shame on me! Imagine treating such a worthy gift that way! It's not mere routine work, you know that! But it's for lack of faith and conviction and, above all else, of love . . . I have far too little faith and love. But, my dearest Jesus, you do not mind my being so weak. (I'm telling this to St. Thérèse, whose dying we commemorate today.) Your will be done. It's fine that I remain weak. The only thing I worry about, dear God, is whether I cooperate well—I never do—*but* I worry whether I don't put obstacles in the way of your love and action. Help me!

Monday, October 4.

My Jesus, with you I meditated upon the use of time. I hope I used my time well this morning. My Jesus, I lack a lot in this respect. Actually I have been wasting less time since the fourth year of my Junior Seminary.[42] So, for more than three years [including this year] I have made minimal progress. But with your help I can do much better. I have been wasting time, more or less consciously, for more than fifteen years. Fifteen years is a long time, my God. But in a while I shall put all the faults of my age, especially those pertaining to the waste of time

[42] This classical "gymnasium" education took six years.

during the first fifteen years, as well as the three and a half later years, into a parcel glued with spiritual (imaginary) tears of repentance. I give you this, kiss your crucifix, promise to behave better, smile at you, and ask for grace for the future. Ah! [my meditation] is nearly complete with a movement of the will. Then I move again with fresh, divine courage—always doing better. So my resolution is: to get as much as possible out of my time. (Prayer is the best way of using time, not nervous agitation, activity, and restlessness.) Prayer plus action means using time doubly well. Therefore, inner union with God. Next to that especially, humility. As for me that's the pivot on which everything hinges.

Ah, dearest indweller in my soul, help me. God, the Holy Spirit, enlighten my mind to make me see all I have to do. But, above all, don't let me lose my recollectedness. This is most necessary for union with God, and also for the best and most productive use of my time. It is so peaceful and quiet here in my soul. "Mommy dear is waking near her little boy." I should like to apply this beautiful song about St. Thérèse to myself. Dear little Mother, come to my small, weak soul . . . My Holy Guardian Angel, ah! How often I shall thank you in heaven for your protection . . . My Holy Patron Saints, St. Marinus, St. Paul, and St. John Bosco, I say the same to you. Later I hope to thank you more than I could ever say for your protection, example, and inspiration. . . . My God, what am I to say to you to put into words my gratitude. If I don't know what to say now, what then later?

Tuesday, October 5.

My meditation was not particularly good today. There were many distractions. That is nothing. But I was so absorbed in them that it did not occur to me to dismiss them. Only a few times did I suddenly think: "Oh yes, I've got time now to speak to Jesus."

My God, dwelling in me, you must surely intend something for me, in spite of the distractions I experienced in prayer. For I did not have any sweet feelings this morning. Yet you gave me such quiet and love after Holy Communion. I feel everything in my soul from the first to the last part to be in deep quiet. And, my Beloved, I myself, poor weak child that I am, cannot fathom [how], but I [somehow] know the cause. For, in all this dryness, I still found a moment to call Mary into my heart, after Holy Communion. So she supplements the little I say to Jesus and even much more what I do not say.

Today, I decided, at least for the time being, not to make more than three resolutions about the things in which I fail the most. Therefore, I want to try to create good habits by repeated resolutions: The first is to avoid all boasting in words and deeds, especially during recreation. (I really don't mean all that I say. I do not want to boast when I act like a boy from The Hague;[43] I just want to say something.) The second is to keep recollected. (Above all I should try to do outwardly what is going on within me.) For inwardly I am much calmer than I appear outwardly, though sometimes it's the other way around! Jesus! [Help me!]. The third is [to show] humility in everything, literally in everything. (My God, you who reside in me because of sanctifying grace, you would not even like to live in me if I were proud. Ah! Make me humble.)

Saturday, October 9.
Infinite Guest of my soul, how am I to tell you that I love you and thank you. Now you are wholly in me, and still I feel powerless to say how much I love you. Lord, I give you everything. You know what signs of love my soul, together with my body, can pass on. You also know the measure of my love. And this is what I would like to give you, to an even greater degree. "Thanks, Love." I can hardly think and say more after Holy Communion.

Dear Directress, today your little servant meditated with you about what he doesn't even know himself. But you know what he means with all his incoherent words and signs. Today there's a lot of manual labor to do, and many occasions to talk during periods of silence. Therefore, I resolve to talk as little as possible, only for the love of God and for you. This morning you carried [with me], for the love of God, three small humiliations. I feel so strong with you dwelling in me. Where your love in me wants to go and for what purpose, I don't know.

God, your holy love will be done. I surrender to you totally, wherever you lead me. I want to observe my rule of life today, but, above all [I want] to love your holy will. Such [love] can nurse humility and obedience. What other special virtues do I need, as a novice, besides the ones that come forth directly from divine love? My Jesus, my whole love!

Sunday, October 10.
Deus, pax [God, peace]. My dearest God, peace and love. I do not know what I meditated on this morning. I only remember saying something to my God in the form of a resolution. But what [it] was specifically I can't say. Indeed, I spent the whole morning meditation hardly saying anything else than "My God, my dearest God." "My Love, my intimate Love, [my soul's] rest." When I got up I also invoked Mary's help for my meditation. So I hope she said in my place what I should have made known to my God—besides this expression of love by a single thought, a word, or a simple gesture of my hands.

43 The Hague, residence of the Dutch queen, seat of government, workplace of ambassadors, and civil servants is sometimes imagined, rightly or wrongly, to instill a certain civic pride in its residents. True or not, others may explain this as "grandstanding."

For example, I expressed all my love of God by moving my hands from a folded to a crossways position. Further I made internal mouth-organ music all morning, singing all kinds of nice songs, though not exactly sacred music! I could hardly get them out of my mind. Then I stopped wearying myself and made that same inner musical sound out of love for God. Thus I dedicate to God the beauty of sound I experience, for instance in "Wenn auf Sonntagabend die Dorfsmusik spielt" [When Village Music Is Played on a Sunday Night], and all kinds of marches. I changed the words into senseless, rhymeless, and artless, yet genuine, words of love. In this way I gave Jesus a loving concert on the mouth-organ. Next came Holy Mass, which I could follow without much distraction. Then there was Holy Communion. Again I said nothing but incoherent words. I made gestures of love. I kept smiling all the time about my inability to speak with Jesus, but really I did not get upset about it. And now it's so peaceful and quiet here. Daddy is watching over his dear little child. I am a troublesome boy, I admit. But a father and mother love troublesome children just as much, for they remain their children after all. Every Saturday I get bathed so well in forgiveness that I am absolutely clean, dear Mom.[44] And sometimes I get dirty the same day . . . .

Monday, October 11.

My God, thanks with all my heart for your love. I won't bother about things like whether I will do your will in the future, for in that case it would become *my* preoccupation. Instead I will take in stride whatever you give. I can't desire more, can I? I want this for today. And tomorrow I hope to get the same grace from you. It needn't be *feelings*, for at this moment I haven't got any sweet feelings either, at least none that I'm aware of. There is only quiet, intimate, deep, divine quiet in my soul, which is being possessed by you. My only worry is not to offer the least resistance. And that's no heavy worry, really it isn't. I direct my whole will to Jesus' will. Whether I do so to please myself or not is something I can do nothing about. I can't despise and twist my own spontaneous will because God's will happens to be in harmony with it, can I?

Jesus, my God, my *donum increatum* [uncreated gift] living in me! I beg you to keep your temple spotlessly clean, to purify it from the least speck of dust. When there are greasy spots to which the dust [that I am] sticks, I pray you, to scratch and cut them off as needed. My soul wants to be a large smooth shining mirror of God. Where God is [first], everything else secondary should give way. I can't achieve great things.

44 It was Dutch custom in the old days that children were put in a bathtub, bathed, and scrubbed spotlessly clean every Saturday night. Confessions by analogy had a similar effect on Rinus.

If I could, I would soon be proud. The only thing I can do is to break my own will [my willfulness] to pieces within your will. Then I may begin to act in consonance with you. Everything should come from you. Is it your will that I begin to enjoy doing your will? Your holy will be done. Do you want the opposite? *Fiat voluntas tua* [your will be done]. Everything you want, I want with an act of will and love. My dear God, my resolution was to be careful [to look only at you] when looking at the other novices.

Tuesday, October 12.
My Jesus, I've come to the end of an emotional day. Tonight [during the evening conference] the Novice Master said something about sinning in conversations. That's something we should pay more attention to. As regards my past life, I'd rather not talk about it now. Often I knew there was something wrong. But I begged for forgiveness long ago. On this occasion I want to make up for everything in an act of love-will to Jesus. Above all, I want to be careful, during evening recreation, about talks that can harm brotherly love. In the afternoon [recreation] I am usually too busy playing to talk that much, but in the evening my dry, smug-faced personality often comes to the fore.

Today we had manual labor in the afternoon. I kept relatively silent until we received permission to talk. (That permission came fairly soon, fortunately.) But during choir practice it went wrong. Ah! I'm not upset about it. I know how extremely weak I am. I have "willed" forgiveness from Jesus again, and, although I have no sweet feelings, I know *everything* is good again with my God. My love, make me humble and let me give love.

Wednesday, October 13.
Deus, amor [God, love]. My God, how great is your love for people, that you stoop down to work in my most ungrateful soul and to image yourself in me? Ah, my God, if you were, for example, an angel and I did not love you so much, I would say: "Please, stop it, there is no credit to be gained by it. My soul is formed only slowly and spoils everything soon again! Exert your masterly influence upon other souls. They are cut out of much better cloth [than I]. They allow themselves to be led in a more docile, more intimate way. How many masterpieces you could have made if you had shaped other people's souls with the same number of blows you've dealt to mine. I say "masterpieces!" But fortunately he who is at work on me is God himself. He knows everything from all eternity, and I love him so intimately. I do know, if I do not now surrender wholly to him, my guilt is much greater than if I resisted an angel. Yet I implore you, my God, for the sake of my small but huge love for you [the love] which you have raised in me, please stay! I dare to say, make me love you and love creatures for your sake ever more. You are

On the right hand side of this photo is Father Strick, Rinus' beloved Novice Master.

obliged to make my soul larger and more refined, for the way it is now, it cannot possibly contain more [love]. Your holy will be done. I do not beg that my small will, surrendered to you, must always be *by nature* in accordance with yours. "Ah, Love, my only love is you, the infinitely powerful God who lives in me." The resolution of my meditation is really to penetrate more and more into Jesus' love. I also want to be calmer and more recollected so as to hear better his inner intimations.

Thursday, October 14.

My God, Jesus, my God, the Holy Spirit, you are my intimate profound love. I did not meditate much. Only for about fifteen minutes could I say I was not distracted in my thoughts. I hardly said anything to Jesus after Holy Communion. As for my Holy Mass it consisted of only a few acts of will during the main parts. And yet . . . how much love I feel and know for my God. I now feel so strengthened by him that I would do what I did in my dream last night. [It went like this: I thought there was a Chapter presided over by our Provincial Superior. During it, it was said that I had done something wrong. I forget what. In any case it was a fault with regard to particular friendship that I had *not* committed. I heard my serious fault severely reprimanded in public. In the end I was sent home.] Everything [though in a dream] seemed to be happening in actuality. Yet I kept smiling and thinking it was God's will. My heart broke with grief, but my will merged completely into God's. I even remained glad and internally quiet. Yes, my God, I should like it [to be] this way: whatever happens, may your holy love-will be done in me. Now I only appear to exist. You have my whole being in your possession. Keep it, my God. *Amor divisivus est* [Love is diffusive]. May I diffuse my love for you among all creatures, only and exclusively for love of you. Last night, in spite of my melancholy mood, I had and I also contributed to a cozy and cheerful recreation. But, to tell the truth, I had fervently implored God's help in chapel for this [favor]. Oh, Jesus, let me say my sweetest words to your heart. Let me put my purest joy in the silent power of love. My God, I am not worthy of being full of you, of being allowed to think and act as you do. But here, too, . . . not my will but yours be done. Anything, really anything you want to make of me, is fine with me, my dearest Love.

Friday, October 15.

It is so peaceful and quiet here. Mom is sitting up with her dear little child. My God, I only know two words: Love . . . Thanks. How good you are to such a poor lamb like me. Again, I hardly know what to say after Holy Communion. I feel overwhelmed. I can only send flashes of my will to you. I think, "What else can I do but will what God wills for me? I have not worried any further about what else I must do, as it pleases you to leave me as weak as I am now, so that I can only be kept alive by sweets. Your holy will be done, even though my natural pride rebels against it.

It also seemed right to offer you a small thing, my electrical device, which I had exchanged for pictures at the end of the last year [in the Junior Seminary].[45] But I haven't got the photographs yet, and I probably won't get them, especially if I don't say anything. I won't say anything, out of love for you. In this way I can practice parting with something.

Oh, my crucified Jesus, today is your day. This morning I asked you for some little thorns to be pressed into me like grains of incense in the Easter candle. Whether it's your holy will that I feel them or not—you know everything, really everything. Whatever you will, I will. My God, I feel the need to tell you that I love you and that I will your operation *quidquid id est* [no matter what it is] with all my heart. Love, always more love. I had resolved during a distracted meditation to be more careful with my words, thus, not violating charity involuntarily. I often do so without even being aware of it. At other times I do it with no bad intention. This has to stop too, for it might grieve God and injure my neighbor's honor, whoever he is, [whether he is] known or unknown to those [who are] listening. Further, I must articulate everything distinctly. I often talk indistinctly because of my agitation, which, to be sure, only shows on the outside, for you are within me my God. Further, [I must] avoid swear words. The Novice Master said yesterday we shouldn't say words like "Be damned!" Jesus, Mary, Joseph, help me!

Saturday, October 16.

Dear God, you may hide yourself and pretend to be angry. I know everything is really good. You love me more and more. And I am quite willing to bear that small penance (of having been totally distracted from morning until now). Now I will force you to give me a sweet look. For I read in Rodriguez[46] that you had said to a saint, Gertrude I believe, that God looks affectionately at her and at everybody, yes, everybody, who looks up at the Cross with repentance and love. So if you give me the grace to behold your Cross lovingly (I can't do so without your grace), then obviously you must look at me [with eyes] full of love.

Dear Mother Mary, I leave the rest to you. It's your day. You must order me to do whatever you want. For today we have manual labor again. How much I must have changed! I see, with your help and assistance, that I behave differently now from what I used to do, in both my

45 The device Rinus speaks of here was then a popular boy's toy. It emitted a small electrical shock, testing a person's stamina before he dropped it.

46 A Spanish spiritual writer on religious life whose words we novices were obliged to read daily.

melancholy and my numb moods. It's God's work in me through your hands. I let myself be kneaded [today] as well as yesterday. Everything today is for you, my love.

Sunday, October 17.
Oh God, my rest, my eternal Sabbath, my infinite deep still lake. My God is my soul, my everything. Thank you with all my heart for allowing me to be fused with you. Rinus is gone. God thinks, acts, and uses me as an instrument only. My good God. I am a strange kind of instrument, am I not? Hardly have you cleaned it well when it's dirty again and not so fit to be used anymore. And there's always a chance of the handle coming loose. Then you'll have to strike [me, your] hammer really hard on the ground to make it useful again.

Ah, my God, throw that thing away! I am not worthy of your care. If you cleaned and used any other instrument than me, without any exception, with as much care, you would be able to use it as you wished. Why am I resisting? [I guess] you dare not strike so hard with me because you are afraid the whole thing will fall apart. Your holy will be done. The worse the instruments are (I mean the worse their condition) an artist uses to create a work of art, the better the artist's greatness will show. He created such a beautiful product with such bad materials. All things considered, I beg you, use me for anything you want. I'll do my best as much as possible and leave the rest to you. For you will be glorified more because the work of art is so beautiful while I, poor instrument, am so bad. Give me your love and your strength, and let me do whatever you will. I know for sure that it will be good. Ah! dear God.

Monday, October 18.
My God, thank you so much for allowing me to take part in Holy Mass and Holy Communion. Oh, love, how my love is going to grow! For a quarter of an hour, I did not exist anymore. I had been completely absorbed, as it were, by the Godhead. Thanks, my God. With you I feel strong enough to start a new day of love. And, no matter how I bungle, your love is always ready to forgive me again. Forgiveness, in the sense of pardoning faults, is given to me—and, as the word, *vergif* (in Dutch) also means "poisoning," I deserve this for all my infidelity. But the love stays.

My Jesus, how great and, above all, how deep is your love. I love you from the bottom of my heart. I don't mean like "At heart he is a good fellow, he just doesn't show it." No, my dear Jesus, I do all I can to show you how intimately I love you. But I, by myself alone, feel powerless. I can't express myself strongly enough. You operate in me, and, whatever you will for me, is fine with me. I hope to be a patient instrument—both an instrument and a work of art combined.

Today I want to do everything, really everything, in and for your love. That was my resolution this morning. It seems vague, but it is clearly defined because I only need to keep one idea in my head: Love. Let me be careful that people, even my fellow-novices, don't carry away part of my love for you. I love them all, that's true, but only out of love of you. For the rest I will do everything as well as I can with your strength and grace but especially with your love and [I will] not pay attention to my feelings.

Tuesday, October 19.
Jesus, my rest, my peace, my love. Dear God in me, I am full. I can't do or think or say anything without love flowing out of me. I am boiling over. It's all your work. What you will, Rinus wills too.

My God, during meditation I did not say much. I have hardly been anything but distracted—and you willed it. Everything you will, I willed, I will, and I shall will it. Thus I have put my past, present, and future will into one act of the will and given it to you. Anything you want.

My Daddy, I kiss you for your forgiveness of all the sins of my past life up to this moment, whether voluntary or involuntary. I kiss you for forgiveness for all the acts that could have been better if I had used your grace to the full. I beg your forgiveness for all grace, which I could have merited and used, but which I lost by unwillingness or through insufficient cooperation on my part.

My Daddy, I want to express all this in a perfect kiss of repentance and love. I also beg your forgiveness for whatever will go wrong in the future, which I don't want now. But you know how weak your little child is. He's so weak that he has been fed almost all of these eight weeks with sweets. He thought if he did not feel or taste anything that Father was away for a moment. My Father, my Mother, my Elder Brother, and my other uncles and aunts, I want to be your child, your brother and your nephew even if you don't always indulge me when you come.

Wednesday, October 20.
This morning when I got up I dedicated the first hours [of the day] to God by kissing the crucifix. I was distracted while dressing and during morning prayer. I had a stomach ache for the first fifteen minutes of meditation. I had to go to the washroom. The next fifteen minutes I had to calm down by dedicating to God the humiliation of having to leave during meditation. During the last fifteen minutes I was dozing off. I followed Holy Mass only half-heartedly. I was so glad I could receive Holy Communion, but afterwards I hardly knew what to do with my soul's guest. Fortunately, I had called Mother beforehand. So I have been distracted all morning. I feel absolutely nothing. Yet I know I love

Jesus very much, and that my soul is quite pure through the fervent acts of love I made, though my feelings were cold. I feel strengthened, or rather I don't *feel* but I know myself to be strengthened so as to pass the day in God's love. Obviously I made no resolution this morning. Yet I want to do everything in love again. Everything in God, with God, for God, and through God, with Mary as my mediator. Then I may be able to save souls. Today I will go for my [hour of] "direction."

My dear Jesus, let me please say what you will that I say. I don't dare to say everything as yet because I think I boast or that I am afraid of doing so. I'm so weak and yet so strong through you. Which of these two things should I put forward? Or which is prominent? I really don't know. My God, the Holy Spirit, I'll say what you prompt me to say.

Thursday, October 21.

My dear God, really present in me by your indwelling as Father and Friend. I almost cannot describe your love for me. It is thus not I who write, but you in me. I no longer make my bed, but you do so in me. So also it is you who eat and pray and sing in me. When I walk, reading Rodriguez, I'm doing so in outward appearance only. In reality it's you who live in me. How little do I realize this! How tiny my love is in comparison to the great graces I receive from you unceasingly so as to do everything in your love. And I use so little [of what you give]. I'm unworthy of it. If, for example, you would give [these graces] to the novice next to me, he couldn't think of, or love anything else but you. He would be absorbed in you all day. The heat of his love would be beyond bearing. He would do the most troublesome job with a cheerful face and accomplish everything. He would love everybody without exception, simply and solely for yourself. And I hardly do anything with the same grace. I'm thoughtless and cold. I seek myself in jobs and in my fellow novices.

I can only say one word to defend myself against all these accusations: "Love"—in an act of the will. Your will be done. It pleases you to see me small and weak. I also use a [special] gesture to draw me closer to your breast, in spite of my horrible tepidity and infidelity, and to kiss you for your forgiveness with a smile, right in the middle of your Holy Face. I'm glad I have got the audacity to do so. For thus I force you to forgive me. Ah! Don't be angry at that expression, my dear Father, and my dear Elder Brother. I always regret that I fall. I never want to grieve you. Everything for love's sake!

Friday, October 22.

Many thanks for the new stream of grace you released in me today. Last night I bungled again. That's why I was sad this morning because I may have offended my Father, even by a voluntary venial sin. I am so weak and so extremely delicate. But does this make my love and confidence less? On the contrary, surely not. Isn't a weak child incapable of anything? Isn't he much more devoted to his guardian because he can't do without him at all? Absolutely. Therefore, I know that my mirror of God is now quite clean again and even more beautiful than yesterday. For I put Elder Brother in charge today within my person. Now everything is absolutely clean. I love you so much, my Daddy. You should know how much I'm willing to give to you. In a word, everything. Just say what you want and, with your support, I'll do it. The least movement today until the stroke of midnight is dedicated to you. I move out of love for you, for by moving I glorify the Creator and Preserver of my existence. All out of love for you.

My dear Elder Brother, many thanks for having cleaned my little temple completely. I know you don't like half-hearted work. I'm going to look like you, for everybody can now see we're brothers together. We walk, act, and think in the same way. Of course, you on a large and I on a small scale. But that's why the uncles and aunts take great pleasure in the little man that is imitating his Elder Brother. I write crazy things, Mom, I know. But it's your fault, dear! You have taken me to the furnace; now I'm going to be burnt. I beg you, pull me even closer to the furnace of love. If I had to burn up with love and be scattered in black ashes, it would not matter. My dearest Mother, how am I to thank you for your mediation. I want to do my servant's duty as well as possible.

Saturday, October 23.

Heart of Mary, motherly heart so burning with love, so brimming over with love, so good and full of love. I find it hard to imagine all the poems I should write to tell you how I love you. Today, at Elder Brother's visit I was allowed to sit between him and you, so that I heard all you had to tell Jesus.

Dear Mother, didn't I surprise you today through my Brother? It was just like my being at home in the old days while the children were being dressed or undressed. Then, as I recall, my Dad would dress me, and I would go to Mom, wearing something over me—so as to hide the fact that I was already dressed. Then I would ask, "Mother, will you dress me please?" And Mom would say, "Come here, my boy." Then I would take off my overalls and enjoy the greatest fun if she pretended to be "surprised." Then Mom would give me a cordial kiss. It was the same today.

This morning in the garden I asked my Brother to wash me beforehand—for my Mother, Mary, does so always. She asks Father for the soap. But today Jesus had already washed me. He is as good at it as Father. And I was clean, completely clean. All [of me] was love. Not a spot or even a fleck of dust was left on my soul: *Tota pulchra es et macula non est in te, anima mea!* [My soul, you are wholly beautiful and there is no speck of dirt in you!] That's how I did my meditation. And then I called to Mother at Holy Communion. How glad she was to see her child looking so clean. That's the way mothers are when a son does something. They [like it but they] always think it could stand some improvement, especially since such washing is a "woman's job." So it is with Mary. She took a cloth and tried to polish [to a brighter shine] my inner mirror. But to no avail! There was not a speck of dirt on the cloth. Jesus had done a good job. (Today I will take another "bath" during Holy Confession.) I could see how glad Mother was because of my cleanliness. Then Jesus entered. He pretended his dear Mother had worked so well, but I gave away the secret. My Jesus, I can hardly hold back . . . O my God!

Sunday, October 24.

My God in whom my soul indwells, what do I do with my love now? Where's the fuel which I, with my little flame of affection, must enkindle out of love for you? Yes, it truly must be very sparse, this fuel of mine, for the blaze is so small. One doesn't set fire to a tree with a little match, only to straw and paper, if there isn't too much wind. But where can one find more inflammable matter than in my fellow novices in this house of love? "My God," I can hardly say anything else except, "My God, my love, my God, my whole will, my God, everything."

Today I made a resolution to fight the devil in my thoughts of pride. It's a wonderful means. With God's inspiration, the [resolution process] started with temptations of impurity. I, strengthened by God, my dear Mother and my other protectors, challenged the devil when he appeared with his temptations. "Go ahead, cause me even much more trouble," I said "Get even more devils to join you; give me even worse fantasies; all you accomplish is to make me show my love of God even more, for I will not give in." And then he slunk away, with his tail between his legs, for the devil certainly does not want me to trust God more fervently and to love him more. That's why he takes off quickly.

Monday, October 25.

Many thanks for the fresh new strength you gave me unaware at the stroke of midnight, until a quarter past four, and from that time until this moment. I did not have a "felt" meditation today, yet it was quite a good one. I made two resolutions that don't get in each other's way: one for the whole day, one for the recreation, namely, to be more vigilant throughout the day, especially with my eyes. Let me cast down my "blue watchers." Then I won't have so many distractions; neither can I see on the faces of the others any approval or disapproval of what I do. Still, during recreation I should not hold my tongue; I should then also look freely and openly at my fellow novices. That's why I have again resolved for those two hours to avoid every semblance of boasting. I certainly should not show any impatience, for instance, when the game is not going too well. And also, in everything: love, a child's love of parents and family. What Father does is always good. What Elder Brother does is law, and what Mother asks I do. I should listen well to the promptings of God, the Holy Spirit, and follow them. Therefore, the quiet I experience now must remain. That's why I should have love, intimate divine love.

Ah, Daddy, every time I love you more, I know it, and I am grateful to you for it. But *numquam satis est* [it's never enough]. Love *and* love *and* gratitude. My Elder Brother, this morning when we were together, you dusted me off again. I also feel the gift of innocence coming back partially and gradually. If only you are glorified in this way.

Tuesday, October 26.

Love, my Father, love, my Mother, love, my Elder Brother, love, my God, the Holy Spirit. Love. Many thanks for your fire in me. *Amor diffusivus est* [Love is self-diffusing]. This makes me feel a vehement urge to pour out all my love for others. This morning I made the same resolutions as yesterday, thus vigilance, especially with the eyes, during periods of silence; no boasting during recreation; even if I don't mean to be proud I should still control myself.

Mom, I wrested something from my Father, I really *wrested* it, for I used Elder Brother as bait. At the Consecration, during the Community Mass, I asked Father (while I, as it were, raised Jesus himself at the elevation) to grant one more last irresistible flash of love to a poor sinner on his death-bed in The Hague—so that this poor human being must surely love God and thus repent. I asked for him or her the same love and grace you give me so often. I know for sure that this grace would set a much greater fire to *every* other soul than to mine. So this was the first. At Holy Communion I asked the same for a dying person in London, and at the Consecration, during the second Holy Mass, for a poor female sinner in Paris. Oh, what a delightful day. Three more souls [are] with God. They'll be in purgatory by now, I think. At first I did not dare to ask for any sign that they were saved. I know for sure that it is so. But, upon thinking for a moment, I asked for three great humiliations today, if only they did not involve voluntary sins. For, if Mother Mary agrees, I may be able to help them sooner to get into heaven. But not my will but hers be done.

Wednesday, October 27.

My Jesus, I love you with all my heart in and through everything. Last night I forgot to wind up the alarm.[47] It was my fault this morning that

47 Rinus was appointed to wake up all the novices.

everything began fifteen minutes later. Of course, I was a bit confused by that shortened meditation. I'm also sorry I upset everything. Yet, in spite of all that, I was glad, for it is precisely in such happenings that I see how much more I love you [these days]. I was a bit distracted, but I was not angry with myself at all, nor snappy at everything. I certainly loved you as much. Even now, I know and feel I have received much love and grace to do everything in fervent love of you. Everything, without any exception. Many thanks for that grace. My Father, my All, my Love.

Thursday, October 28.
Please, my dear God dwelling in me, bear the folly of my love. I don't remember whatever I said to you nor for what I asked. I wanted to set a love-fire burning in all people, at least the 150,000, or so, who will die today, all of them without exception. [I wanted] not a crumb of sin or punishment to be left [in them] so that they would go straight to heaven, to love you eternally, forever, and without end. To love you forever. Yes, I had wanted to do so, my love. You know everything. You also know that my desire was genuine. But I was not worthy to ask this [favor of you]. That's why I first dedicated and then concealed myself completely and tactfully in the bread and wine at the offertory. Then, at the consecration, I suddenly came out of the bread and wine, smiling, for left there was not bread and wine but Jesus Christ. So my Father was bound to see me in the chalice, dripping, as it were, with [the blood of] Jesus. Then I asked for the final irresistible *coup de grace* of love, grace for a dying sinner in Brussels. At the moment of Holy Communion, when Jesus could not escape from me, I forced him to help another sinner, a woman in New York, into heaven with his last ray of love. I say forced, for "*all* you ask you will receive," literally all. So . . . [there are] two more souls who can, and even must, *love* you in all eternity, for they can no longer turn their steps to illusory goods.

Friday, October 29.
My dear God, I have scooped up three [more souls]. At the oblation of the bread, I put all the wrong things of my whole life [on the plate] with the host. Because the priest prays about *Immaculatam Hostiam* [Immaculate Host], my Daddy could not but destroy everything in me that in any way or in the least respect was or is against his love-will. At the oblation of the wine I again crept secretly into the chalice. I was a bit nervous. Wouldn't Father think me irreverent? But what I did was done to save a soul, so I took the risk. I remained really quiet. In the meantime, I signaled Mother to join Father at the moment when I would pose my bold question. For it was only a question. I did not ask for the sake of merit, nor did I rely on anything [of my own]. But, then,

I haven't got anything. It was nothing else but a question put to his Almighty Lord by a confident yet poor soul.

Thus came the moment of holy consecration. At the transubstantiation I was bound to be discovered again. When the priest raised the chalice with Jesus Christ's flesh and blood, I again asked for the salvation of a dying sinner in Berlin. That was number six. At the moment of receiving Holy Communion, I asked for a poor sinful woman in Australia. During the second Holy Mass, at the consecration, I asked the same for a dying person in Rome. So, today three more souls, who otherwise might have been lost, are now able to love God eternally. Today my Guardian Angel will probably call for "recreation-with-smoking-permitted,"[48] because there is joy in heaven when poor sinners have been saved. Pray that my Holy Guardian Angel doesn't leave me alone, not for a moment. Yes, dear Daddy, please watch over Rinus, for he falls to the ground in no time. He may snatch souls away from the devil when he is with Jesus but only if Father protects him, and if he does not become proud, for if he does, the devil will snatch him!

Saturday, October 30.

My God, my Daddy, is it your wish to give the celestial residents recreation again? If not, you'll have to change the rules of heaven. For it says in them that there is joy whenever a sinner enters heaven. Today another three have arrived, perhaps not yet in heaven itself, but they are saved anyway. One from Moscow, one from Jerusalem, and one from Chicago—again three souls who will love you forever. If I could, I would ransack the whole of hell to let all those poor damned souls love you. But I am saying foolish things, for that would be against your justice. But I would like to set a fire of love to those three billion people who are living now, so that all of them would die from love of you. For whoever dies in this way comes into your kingdom of love. They all may, or rather would be bound to love you. And even then this would not be enough. I would like to change every particle of dust, every grain of sand, every drop of water into human beings—people created in your dear image, people with immortal souls. And then, dear Elder Brother, with your divine heart in my hands, I would change this whole innumerable multitude into a sea of love-fire, so that everyone

---

48 In the Novitiate at that time smoking was only allowed at certain periods of recreation. On the occasion of a special feast, novices could be surprised by a permission to enjoy a special "recreation-with-smoking." Rinus uses this earthly metaphor to express the angelic joy in heaven, spoken of by Jesus in the Gospel when a sinner converts.

of them consumed with love, would die and sing eternal praise to you in your heaven. And even then I would not yet be satisfied. Never are you loved enough, my Father. That's bad enough but even I do not love you as I ought. I am not willing to give you enough [of myself] in daily life. Thanks to your grace I should burn with an ardent love of God. But alas! I almost look like a fire-resistant block of stone. How I have resisted and how I still resist such a devouring fire of love! Change me into paper, my God, then burnt flakes of love will fly up to you.

✠

May your will be done completely without any resistance from my side.

✠

Sunday, October 31.

Today is the feast of Christ the King, a day of much grace. Now I have seen what you mean by grace. Last night I had to fight a heavy fight against [a temptation to] impurity. But I won magnificently, with the crucifix in my hand and on my heart, with your loving help and assistance, with the protection of my Guardian Angel and of my Directress. No, not I won, but God, in and through my body. That was the first grace, a crucial test of love.

The second came during meditation, another heavy attack. The devil used heavy guns. I am thankful to him for this, for my love of my King became stronger through this ordeal.

The third came after Holy Communion, when the devil tried to prevent me from asking for the salvation of a poor dying sinner in Peking. I said "tried." For I made my request, though I was not feeling anything. But that doesn't matter. Thus I begin this new day, quite full of love. My King, this morning at a quarter past four I declared my complete submission to you. Today I *trust* you entirely. May your will be done completely without any resistance from my side.

Tuesday, November 2.

How wonderful, my Father, there are again countless more souls who will praise you eternally in undisturbed happiness. I can safely venture to say—for it's not me who says so but only the little instrument [I am] in God's hand—that I, too, have helped many, just by asking. My Mother works with the merits of my acts—[she oversees] every least little motion made out of love for Father, Brother, and the Holy Spirit of love. Like a spoiled child I seize the chance to ask for just about everything. I ask and I receive. After all, Elder Brother himself said so: "Ask and you will receive." I have especially "abused"—in a holy way—my meditation, Holy Masses, and Holy Communion. And I know Father was pleased, for when I asked [his help] my confidence grew. Still I did not want to detract from Mary's ownership of me. Oh, how many souls will glorify you, my Father, from all over the world. I have presented every part of the world [to you]. And in a while there will be High Mass. So I keep moving, so I keep loving. My Father, love of you almost drives me crazy. I can hardly say anything to you without expressing my love in the maddest of ways, for instance, by fidgeting with my shoelace when it's not necessary, or by just removing a leaf from the road. Yet I know you like that. Please make my way a way of love.

Wednesday, November 3.

Dear Father, many cordial thanks again for your renewed grace. The only thing that still concerns me is that I perhaps resist my love-spirit. But I don't really know how else I can cooperate. I give you absolutely every authority to effect [your will] in me in whatever way you want. What else am I to do?

Today five more souls will love you through all eternity. At my request three souls, two males and a dying female sinner in Holland, have received your last irresistible *coup de grace* of love. Now they will be happy forever after their term in purgatory, not because I, but because Jesus asked for it, for I used him as a shield with Father. Never enough, never enough! I keep looking for matter to burn in your furnace of infinite love, my Father. In spite of my great coolness, I myself am totally permeated with matter that seems inflammable. Every movement, bending my writing fingers, the quiet in and out motion of my breathing, the regular beat of my heart, in a while the work in my room, dinner in the refectory—everything, everything, out of love for you. And still I feel powerless to express my love in any way at all [that matches yours for me]. I want to be a sponge soaking up God's will.

Tomorrow will mark the start of our retreat, a week of grace. Today I resolved—or rather it's an everlasting resolution—to give love, ever more love, to you, who are more than worthy of it. I have to improve my outer ways: being modest, and speaking articulately, to carry out in a *less* imperfect way the love that fills me. Still, it's the inner love that is and remains the main thing. If I consider everything in love—and so, in God, the rest will go well as a matter of course.

Thursday, November 4.
Meditation was quite arid and distracted. Holy Mass was the same, likewise my preparation for Holy Communion. What does it matter, if only I please Jesus? After Holy Communion I could again speak cordially with him, my Elder Brother. I know that I love him so much.

Also, at this moment, even though I am totally arid, I know I'm writing out of love for God. I also find repulsive all those thoughts of annoyance that rise so unexpectedly against my fellow novices. Although I feel these upsets and my nature agrees with them, my supernature abhors them. Yet I must go on calmly, I must go forward, in love.

Tonight the retreat begins. I'm asking you a favor, my Father: allow me to receive your Jesus, I beg you. How else can I hold out against the strong temptations I feel against the holy virtues? How can I expel those feelings of dislike for the religious life and for *Weltschmerz* [melancholy]? I know I appreciate your Divine Son far too little. But, I am so weak. If you don't want to welcome me [with ease], my Elder Brother, you will have to do so by force, for example, by unbearable pains [of longing] or in another way. Forgive my boldness. I only say this because I need Jesus so much. I want to become holy. My little will [wants to be] completely inside of yours. Everything is an act of love. I live on love. My Mother and Directress Mary, how good you are for having brought me so much closer to Jesus. *Per Mariam ad Jesum*: through Mary to Jesus.

Friday, November 5.
Dear Jesus, I'm so full. Now the great retreat has begun. As the Novice Master said yesterday, after general confession a whole new life begins, because the past nineteen years are totally crossed out. It seems to me the best thing not to make a general confession. I'll mention this to the Novice Master, for I am digging into the past in almost every confession. I am far too scrupulous when I am alone, but not now, for Elder Brother told me this morning that I was seeing the spiritual light of [a new] day. After Holy Communion my dear Father gave me the invaluable grace of a perfect, absolutely perfect, contrition. I was also given the grace to use this grace. I knew I spoke the truth when I said that I sincerely regretted *everything*, literally everything, that had been against God's holy will during my life of eighteen years, ten months and four days—because I had grieved my dear Father. Out of love for him, I wanted to be totally and absolutely unblemished so that he, in his work of mirroring in my soul, had not met nor would he meet the slightest resistance. My Creator may shine as much as he will through

his image in me. He can perform his eternal action of knowing and loving *ad intra,* i.e., inwardly.

Now I have come, as it were, from Mother's womb like a thrashing baby. All the time she fed me with the food she received from Father and Elder Brother. Now she may feed me again at her breast with God's milk, which she has first received and taken into herself, and thus passes on to her poor weak little child. Father and Elder Brother watch over my cradle, for I am a premature baby who has to live in an incubator; otherwise the fragile light of life will die [in me]. I must be *fed* extra [food] and strengthened. There must not be a spot of dirt on me, for that hurts [Daddy and Mother too much]. So weak am I.

Saturday, November 6.
My Father, fortunately I could nourish myself with your Son again. I was distracted during meditation. During the last fifteen minutes I asked forgiveness in case I was perhaps guilty of those distractions. Then came Holy Mass, during which I was completely arid, yet I was glad to suffer something for and with Elder Brother. At the Consecration I again plunged two faithful souls and one poor dying sinner from London into Jesus' furnace of love. If only I could throw myself into it. Now I asked Father again for them without any merit of my own. I was utterly arid, and my *nature* wanted even to leave the chapel. But no, I was still glad for Father's sake. Jesus and Mother were asleep, but then I arranged with Father to surprise them, for when Jesus awoke at Holy Communion I offered him the three souls: two in eternal glory, and one saved for eternity. I then told Mother for the umpteenth time that I did not ask in virtue of any meritorious work of my own, for that would be stealing. No, it was simply and solely a request at a moment when my dear Father *cannot* deny me anything, because I simply use as a connection his Divine Son, my Elder Brother, in whom Father takes all his delight.

Sunday, November 7.
My Daddy, how dear you are for letting yourself be loved so much by me. I feel unworthy even of direct sighs to you. But you want this yourself. My existence, as it is now, has been given to me by you. You knew from all eternity that I would waste, or not use enough, so much grace meant to make me holy. Every other existing creature, if it would have been given the same grace, would be unable to see, think, and love anything else but you, my Father. It is my firmest conviction that if the greatest sinner (man or woman) who is alive on earth could now change places with me in all things, I would be a worse beast than he is. He would faint from his craving for you: his ribs would break because his heart would be too vehemently brimming over with love of you, my God. He would enkindle his whole surroundings and make all of them

burn with love of you, my love. How [mysterious] are your dispensations! Still you have not done it in any other way.

My Father, my dearest Father, I won't ask why. I have no right to know. There are enough statues and works of art made of worse stone, of more simple building material, than I. Perhaps, indeed surely, it is best this way. Your holy will be done.

Today I was given permission to rescue four more souls for you and through you. Two are in your infinite love-furnace of happiness [heaven] and two have been plunged into your love-crucible [purgatory] to have the dross burnt out first, but they already cannot will anything but your will for all eternity.

Monday, November 8.

Love makes my heart swell red-hot in God's furnace. Love makes my blood grow warm and my breathing deeper. I must often keep my mouth open during meditation because not enough air can get through my nose. And these are only *natural* feelings that of their own accord are swept along with my will, which is no longer mine. This morning I clearly noticed that it is not my *nature* that is the cause of that tender love of my dear Father, for I was arid and distracted during the first half hour [of my meditation]. But again and again that fire entered, and I had to go along [with it], whether I wanted to or not.

I am only four days old, and Jesus begins already to intervene so deeply in me.[49] I need not do anything except his holy will, and he makes me do only this. I need but say "Yes, it's well and good in every way." Father now fills me with all kinds of consolations. Mother gives me milk. And when I receive Elder Brother, I am saturated, filled to the bursting point, and I must always put a white bib over my worldly shroud. Then I only need to consent to these frantic thoughts of love; I must dare to be bold.

Today I asked immediate redemption for five faithful souls, three from Russia, two from Japan. I told Father that Jesus was so thirsty he could hardly bear it. I asked, and consequently received. And also four poor dying sinners have now been confirmed in your infinite love forever. I only regret that I did not dare to be bolder. For how can I quench Jesus' thirst with nine souls? That's impossible, isn't it? I also regret my lack of confidence. I was quite without feeling after Holy Communion. I could not think or say anything else but "Jesus, your holy will [be done]." I love everything: you, and everything you love. Yes, always more!

49 The time alluded to here by Rinus is not clear. Perhaps he means the first four days of this traditional great retreat of conversion in the first semester of each Spiritan Novitiate.

Tuesday, November 9.
My dear Father, I am drunk when I write this, drunk with your love. And yet, I never think it's enough. I want to serve you so as to love you always and always more. Dear Father, dear Elder Brother, my Love Spirit, do intervene even more. I am frightened at the very thought of my possible resistance. Take no notice of my nature, I beg you. Rinus is willing but Scholtes still resists.

Today the angels and saints once more enjoy "recreation-with-smoking" because certainly eight more sinners have been saved for sure: two from France, one from Java, also five Russians—all faithful souls, who are now happy in heaven forever. And I, poor fellow, I am still subject to the laws of inertia. My soul wants to be detached from everything; I want to be all for you, but my body resists [this abandonment]. However, thanks to your grace, my resistance isn't as strong as it was. Even my body sometimes cooperates, though, in general it remains indifferent. That's how it should be. When my soul wants something, my body has to serve it. When my soul doesn't need my body for a while, it should remain indifferent to all creatures. My soul always wants more love. My Father, I know and understand well that I can't always have consolations. These are only a means, and they are your gift. But if I now say: everything you want, Rinus wants, too, then I mean *everything* unconditionally. Then I need not wonder anxiously whether I have the right disposition the moment I see this or that happening. I can't help [what I feel] anyway. If you help me so much when I'm quiet and in a good mood, how much more will you help me when I am tempted and vexed by all that goes against nature? I just think: If I fall, it's *my own* fault. With God's grace I abhor those words "my own fault." What I meant to say is that I *definitely* don't want that. [Is there any reason] why I should be afraid? Such an [excuse] would almost make you responsible were I, already now, or later, to fail you in some situations. That's foolish, isn't it. [It's as if I] doubt your infinite justice. But that's past already, Father. These are just temptations, my God.

Wednesday, November 10.
My Father, many thanks for allowing me once again to be united to your infinite only-begotten Word, who became man for us and who offers himself as food in the shape of bread. My dear Elder Brother, many thanks to you, too, for coming. You have again polished everything and adorned it with new grace. Make me grow forever in you as you keep growing in me. Many thanks to my Spirit of Love, too, for his inspirations and preparation in my place. For I was wearing my poor head out just trying to find a word, an expression, for my love. But that would mean satisfying myself, which I don't want to do. That's not what I have been created for. And also, dear Mom, many thanks for

your presence. I have nothing but one word: Love. In this love is contained your holy will [Father]. In it is all that I have to do or to omit.

My Father, today it occurred to me to advertise for you. It is too ridiculous to mention. Maybe I'm talking nonsense. But it seemed to me I would please you if I showed how happy life is after all when it is understood in your Love. So away with all wrinkled foreheads—as if our reason were big and deep enough [to contain you]. Away with profound meditations, away with severe fasting and hollow cheeks. Only joyous love, childlike love, always trusting in you under *all* circumstances. Frank, playful love, I think, pleases God most of all.

Why should we only tell our parents and friends about pleasant experiences and outings to make them laugh wholeheartedly and contagiously? Why not tell our Father about the same? Why do we give him only stiff formulas and official prayers—like speeches we do not mean.

Thursday, November 11.
Many thanks, my dear Father, my Elder Brother, my Spirit of Love, for allowing me to receive Jesus, my God and my all, in my body. You knew my infidelities. You knew I had deprived you of glory from all eternity—I a worm, who calls himself your friend and is glad to be so. I deprive you of glory. I am acting against the purpose for which I was created. And still the God of heaven and earth is willing to descend into me to strengthen me. You could have given me tremendous stomach cramps before Holy Communion; then I could not have received you. But you allowed me to be filled with [you] Jesus, pledge of grace and love. I am here now, satiated, inebriated with you, ready to begin a new day. Many thanks for your infinite strength. Everything, everything, and once again everything. Rinus is allowed to will all that you will—not of his own power but through your grace.

This morning I tried to meditate about death as realistically as possible. I imagined I had collapsed in chapel, that I had died, and I smiled with happiness at the thought. I imagined the particular judgment that would also take place in chapel, and I was full of love and confidence, notwithstanding all my sins. I placed my soul completely in God's hands, and I was not afraid at all.

How had this change come about? For example, two years ago I wasn't like that. The love of death has grown slowly, together with my love of God. My dearest, how can this be? By grace, by abundant grace. I am so full of the love of God. In spite of my unfathomable weakness and cowardice, I bear and would like to bear everything, out of love for him. How great, therefore, must God's grace have been! If I weren't so full of love, and if God weren't my Father but only my Creator and Lord, I would be horrified of death because of my sins. In proportion to the grace received, they are much greater than those of the worst sinner. Love have mercy on me, a poor sinner, please have mercy.

Friday, November 12.

My God, how can I give voice to my love and thanks? The creator of heaven and earth, God infinite in all, my Elder Brother, Jesus Christ, has deigned to come into me. Not so much because of me but because of his infinite being. God in Three Persons is present in me. I am possessed by God; I am no longer master of my own self. But I wanted this [loss of self], and, with God's help, I want it still. If I am being foolish now, I can no longer be held responsible. I am frantic with love. My God is urging me on irresistibly. And I agreed. I begged for it myself. It is all due to love. Yes, indeed, my body is tormented by it. The infinitely holy God does not tolerate any half-heartedness in me, not the tiniest fleck, not the least wrong attachment, no matter how small. Whenever I have done something wrong or not as perfectly as possible, whenever I have asserted myself, I am not at rest until I have asked for forgiveness with all my heart. Then I turn into myself so as to have God's love urge me on again. My body sighs under [the weight of this love]. It presses upon me worse than before, for my God is only beginning. But my soul is as happy as can be. It has let itself be wholly absorbed in God's being; it takes delight in God now, though it cannot yet fully express its love and its knowing of God, for it is still stuck in a perishable body. But the more that body cooperates, the better my soul will be able to express itself. Like my soul is superior to my body, so my God holds my body in his power absolutely. And what a loving power this is! And I owe all this, every bit of this absorption to my Mother Mary, for having dedicated myself as a consecrated servant of love to her. How glad I am for having done so.

Saturday, November 13.

End of the retreat. Back to practical life. It began today with a meditation without feeling and an arid Holy Communion. So Jesus likes to set about his work. He thinks, now you know how to love, so show it. *Deo Gratias*. And today I was allowed to do so. But, my dear God, I pray to you, don't expect too much of me yet. I am only now out of my incubator, and I still need strong food. But I know you do not put anybody—and surely not me—to a test beyond our strength. I have very little strength, *ergo* [thus], my temptations are not that great, and this is because grace is so abundant. So I am resigned quietly to the aridity of my Holy Communion. Whatever it may be like, you won't throw the eight souls who have been confirmed in your love forever out of heaven. That's for sure. Further, I have decided to shorten a bit the maxim I thought I had found yesterday. [I'll keep] the same idea, but express [it] in two words now: *Amor Dei* [Love of God], exactly the same as "*quid prodest: amor Dei?*"—"What doth it profit a man to gain the whole world and lose his soul . . . [to be without the love of God?"]. I ask myself [that question] now with every action; and I say "*Amor Dei*" at the prompting of your holy will. So when obedience or another exercise of your will comes to me, I say "*Amor Dei*!" In the subjective tense: it means an expression of *God's* love toward me. But when I act and ask myself, "*Amor Dei?*", then it's an objective tense, in other words, is it out of love for God that I do this or that or act in this or that way? For example, *Amor Dei?* [Is that the reason] I'm writing?

Sunday, November 14.
Father, my dear Father, let me serve you again with fresh courage. I love you so much, I am quite willing to bear aridity and distractions out of love for you, if only I could be sure that I am not guilty of these myself. Now you have forgiven me everything at Holy Communion. Yes, my Love, how infinitely good and sweet you are to me. I have moments of aridity during meditation, and no feelings at all during Holy Mass, yet you give me the strength and the grace to ask for souls at Holy Communion and at the Holy Consecration. I'm almost scared that I'll have to pay for my boldness one day. Just imagine, you, the almighty God, infinite in all, you have sworn, as it were, through your divine Son on earth that you'll give anything anyone will ask you for in his name. It's like what happened at Herod's feast. Herod had sworn he would give to his daughter anything she asked, and, though she abused [this favor] she got what she wanted because of his words and his oath.

Likewise, I boldly use your words. I hope I'm not abusing them. I am the greatest sinner (in proportion to the grace I have received). Still I ask you, infinite Father, to save seven souls in the name of Jesus Christ: three from purgatory during the Consecration of the bread; three dying sinners during that of the wine; and one at Holy Communion. Now, isn't that abusing my freedom to ask you for [such a favor]? You promised it, so I count on it, or rather, [I count on] Jesus' thirst for love. To crown it all I ask as a sinner, for I can't appeal to any good works (I've no right to claim any because they all belong to my Directress). So God is forced, as it were, to give me what I ask for, since all conditions have been fulfilled: 1) I rely on your words, for you are eternal truth, so I ask and receive; 2) and I petition you in the name of Jesus Christ—and at a moment when Jesus himself is the mediator and advocate in his own sacrifice of love. So Father has to respond, for it says nowhere that the petitioner must be perfect in some way or possess a certain spiritual rank.

Monday, November 15.
My Love, my Father, I now feel strongly the fruits of the retreat, for [by contrast] I have been absolutely distracted all morning. I meant well, but things did not go well. Yet what sustains me and makes me glad are all the strengthening graces [I receive] as well as the eight souls that quench Jesus' thirst for love somewhat. With your love and your divine

presence in me, my God, I'm again going to pass the day in your service like one possessed by you. Yes, I want to serve you with all my heart and soul. I don't care about feelings any more. I'm even glad for the dryness, for by now you want to give me a bit less baby food. But, dearest Father, don't rely too much on any outer strength of mine. You know that I am liable to do anything. I am so miserably weak that I wonder if ever before such a fragile creature existed. Outwardly, I look normal. But inwardly, it's almost incomprehensible that I—with such an abundance of grace—am still such a helpless and unfaithful person. Yet it pleases you to send me love and grace over and over again, while you know me better than I do myself. So you have not yet spat me out, because of disgust at my tepidity, you are willing to try once more with me. Thanks wholeheartedly, my dearest Father.

And what if you did not give me so much strength and grace? You could spit me out, for then I would be nothing. By myself I might use every occasion, any little bit of dust in me, to go against you. Infinite God, have mercy on me. I don't deserve your pity. For it is true, I am a poor, unhappy beggar. Yet I am still proud and insolent despite my destitution. Ah, Father, remember that no matter what, I am still in everything your child, created in your image and likeness. Your divine Son, my Elder Brother, Jesus Christ, died for me and merited everything for me. If you want to spit me out, he will show you [the depth] of his divine love [and mercy] for me. But, please, try once more with Rinus.

Tuesday, November 16.
My Father, cordial thanks for your grace. I would like to ask you to allow me to collapse and die at the very moment I am now writing. Then I would melt into your infinite Being. But I won't ask for anything you don't want. It's like St. Thérèse says "You give me grace to will to ask what you will (and to do so). You give (and do, of course give) yourself." I also feel so confident that I, in spite of my boldness, have pleased you by saving seven souls every morning and making them happy. I like very much to ask in this way, because by so doing any feeling of self-satisfaction and of conscious self-importance is excluded. You may give it to me—no you *must* give it [because of your promise] for "a man's word is his word." [By the way I'm not yet a man only a little child in the life of love.] If you give [me what I ask], you do it because of your own [infinite generosity] and absolutely not because you let yourself be mollified by the *person* who asks you. What only counts for you is your infinitely true word, and the one [Christ] who is used as a shield or a bridge by the poor sinful questioner. That's why I'm so glad. But, alas, what are fifteen souls that now turn from their sinful condition to love, by God's special grace, in comparison to the 150,000 or so people who die daily? And if, for four days a week, all those dying went straight to heaven, so about 600,000—what is that in proportion to Jesus' thirst for souls? And what does that little number of five do

every morning? And, on top of these, the three souls I beg [to be released] from purgatory daily? What's that in proportion to those countless souls still there? So there's no need for me at all to pride myself on those one hundred fifty or so souls I have made eternally happy with this new approach.

But, thanks be to God, Jesus has given me enough strength and grace not to be proud! Oh, if only I could ask for more. But Mary also acts with my works and merits. And she will really not be satisfied with seven or eight a day. Not that my works are worth saving even one person! Not at all. But when a child gives his Mother his few saved pennies he also thinks it's quite a lot, for it *may* really be quite a lot for him! But in order to buy something for Father, Mother must add almost everything. Yet, she likes doing this. She looks at the love.

Wednesday, November 17.
Dearest Elder Brother. What comforting things you just told me when I came here from my room. My meditation, Holy Masses, and partly my words of thanks were all without feeling. It did not matter. I'm not praying for my own pleasure but to give Jesus reparation. Whenever I felt arid, I always had the unconscious feeling that it was my fault. Then, on the staircase, Jesus comforted me. He said that, through the grace of Holy Communion this morning, combined with the little bud of repentant love, I could, with his grace, cleanse my whole soul. My soul is even more beautiful now than after my baptism. In God I have been allowed to merit something extra. Mary has adorned my soul. And, in the light of the general amnesty Elder Brother granted me, Mary did not want to stay behind. She has forgiven me all punishment by means of some indulgences from her own treasury. Whatever I earn or can earn goes to her. It's her property. Surely if I were to die this moment, I would go to heaven.

Oh, my Father, it's all due to your goodness. I haven't done a single thing [to merit] this. I have only been bound to love and serve you under your irresistible impulse of grace and love. I won't resist that impulse at all. Yes, [grant me] even more, even much, much more.

This morning I also had the inexplicable boldness to ask for [the salvation of] one more soul. Thus again there are fourteen souls happy forever. How the angels and saints will celebrate today! Recreation with smoking and festive pudding with dessert topping. I'm only kidding! In heaven joy is spiritual.

Friday, November 19.
My intimate Beloved, my God dwelling in me, you, my infinite All, you, my only love, my only happiness. You my ruler and loving sovereign. You, my beloved eternal Creator necessarily in awe of your own being. You who cannot stand the least division. You have wounded my heart. You usurp me totally. I like to be forced, urged, and driven by my

Creator, my almighty God. You, dearest Father, you my "All Father." I feel so wholly absorbed in you that I cannot for the slightest moment disobey my daily rule without you compelling me to obey it again. Everything for you, literally everything. You don't want or tolerate the least deviation. My body sometimes groans and sighs: "If only I were free, and not drawn so much by God, who won't allow me the least fault." But my soul is completely lost in you; out of its own free will it has surrendered itself unconditionally and as completely as possible to you. It doesn't want to withdraw anything of that.

My love, my beloved Father. This morning under your irresistible urging of grace, I began to do everything in love immediately upon waking up. As a matter of fact this has become a habit of late. I did everything in love, though I really had no consolation during meditation or Holy Mass. I had to keep my wits about me so as not to fly off everywhere in my imagination. But, after Holy Communion, I united myself with Jesus completely and disappeared totally. I elevated my God on my tongue. I dedicated him to my Creator. Once again I reminded him of the words of the Gospel, "Whatever you ask in my name, my Father will give you." So I asked in Jesus' name, at a moment when my dear Father could not deny me anything. He took delight in what I used as a shield and advocate, namely, his own divine mind, as powerful, as infinitely great and true as God the Spirit himself.

Saturday, November 20.
My dear Elder Brother, cordial thanks for your many graces and for your love. Today is Saturday. I have hardly asked Mother for anything. Yet I have not forgotten her on purpose. It's just that I feel absorbed by you more and more. Sometimes I am impelled irresistibly to do this or that good work or some small mortification. I'd like to give more. I have surrendered to your divine love-will. I do not want to take back anything, no matter what the consequences of this surrender may be. Spirit of Love, wholehearted thanks for everything. I may enter into your congregation, wear your cassock, be dedicated in a special way to you. I love my cassock, my cincture, my collar, and everything that reminds me of my dedication to you. I love my cassock, even though it often disturbs and bothers my nature, since my maturing body feels imprisoned [in it]. My body is sufficiently well-fed, even over-fed. I now feel that my blood is strong enough to fight any possible treacherous diseases. I won't fast, no, but a bit less [food] won't harm me.[50]

---

50 Because of the death of his little sister Henny from tuberculosis, Rinus was strongly commanded to nourish himself well and to avoid fasting. The Novice Master himself as a young priest had caught this illness and spent a long time in a sanatorium before his recuperation. In spite of this care, Rinus still succumbed.

My Love, my infinitely dear Father, I'm still trying to find a way to express my inner feelings of love and surrender to your holy will. If I knew I could love and will [fully] at this moment, I would like to do it. But I must allow you to act. You yourself must extend and expand my personhood to enable it to contain more love. Father dear, cut, fell, prune, and chisel me wherever necessary. Don't pay attention to my sometimes groaning body. My soul agrees to everything, everything you want. *Fiat voluntas tua* [Your will be done] everywhere, as long as and as strongly as you wish, in a totally unlimited way. Today I was allowed to save six more souls from purgatory and nine from eternal death. Thanks!

Sunday, November 21.
My dearest God and Father, you, my only final goal, my only good, my only love. My thirst keeps growing under the flood of your irresistible grace. My confidence keeps growing in spite of my sins and faults. They are always greater still because I have received so much more grace. I am weakness personified. Yet, I, that poor weakling have been able to glorify you today, my Father. This morning we had two Holy Masses. Soon we will have, if you please, another Holy Mass, so in total three Consecrations and Holy Communions. In other words, there are four moments when my Beloved cannot deny me anything because Jesus Christ, the mediator, pleases my Father. Therefore, there's not the slightest reason to pride myself on the number of souls [who have been saved]. Besides, my dear Father will see to it himself, since I am dry as dust at those moments, except perhaps at Holy Communion. My Father makes me feel how powerless I really am. When I do ask, I glorify my Creator in the face of all creation. For the whole of hell, purgatory, and especially heaven are really and truly witnesses to the effect of my petition. The devils gnash with fury when another prey escapes. In purgatory they are glad about everybody who enters, because, after all, one is certain there of eternal happiness in spite of the pains. In heaven there is a feast. Jesus has said so himself. So billions of beings know what has happened. Only now they [the demons] will wonder who is so bold as to ask for such things and to receive them.

Monday, November 22 (On the same).
They are gazing down at all those billions of immense celestial bodies until they arrive at one of the smallest, our little globe. Then they turn up their noses. Can that creature that has asked for such profound favors and received them exist on such a small planet? They still do not see it, for of the five continents of the world, they must pick the smallest: Europe. They turn up their noses even more, those inhabitants of hell. How magnificent a creature he or she must be to live on such a minute part of an already minute planet. Still they don't find the bold

petitioner. Of all those countries in Europe they must again select one of the smallest, The Netherlands. Here and there the devils growl fiercely. How has such a creature dared to ask for superterrestrial things! All [damned] creatures now turn to The Netherlands. Still they don't find the petitioner. Holland has so many towns and villages. In one of the smallest, Gennep, there that audacious petitioner lives. The devils howl with great humiliation. How dare such a lowly creature ask for such a great thing! Furiously they want to rush at him. Still they do not see him. Even Gennep is too large to entertain such a poor little mouse as he is. There are a number of houses in Gennep. The petitioner is in one of them. The devils rage with fury against one who wheedles so many souls out of their clutches by his clumsy beseeching. Full of rage they direct their eyes to the Novitiate. At last, among all the people there they find one of the youngest, in fact, the weakest, as regards powers of soul; he who, in proportion to the greatness of the grace and strength he has received from God, commits even greater sins than the proudest devil in hell or the poorest outcast among people. And that tiny being, that weakling, ventured to ask God, whom he dares to call his Father, for the salvation of about nine souls a day, simply and solely relying on his weakness and on the infallible word of Jesus Christ that "anything you *ask* the Father in my name he will *give* you."

What a terrible howl must break loose in hell, when that creature dares to ask such a favor! If he were able to see with his physical eyes the greatness of a soul, of even the poorest one expiring in the state of grace, he would die of beholding the resemblance of that creature to God. Likewise the opposite is true of a soul dying in the state of mortal sin.

And yet that weak insignificant worm dares to require from God, his Father, the fulfillment of his promises to the word of Jesus Christ to give, just like that, a *coup de grace* of love to dying, sinful women and men. Yes, there I stand. What am I to answer to their contempt? God is infinitely great. So the distance between him and us *always* remains infinite. Yet Jesus did not say that *only* holy souls were allowed to ask the Father for everything in his name. Jesus did not say anything about the petitioner—only about the petition: *how* it must be asked. And if I do so, the conditions of the petition have been met. Thus the granting of the request is infallibly sure. Please Father, many, many more [souls]!

Tuesday, November 23.

My Father, I am completely full of you, yet I beg for more. I can never love you enough since you always love me more than I could ever love you. I willingly admit my powerlessness. I willingly admit my absolute dependence on you. I willingly admit my state of being absorbed by love. When I'm writing here, it is not I who am writing but my God, my dearest Father in me. When I look out of my eyes, it is not my soul that is shining but the Divine Being who has absorbed, as it were, my whole soul. Even though your union with me is more intimate than that of my body and soul, still the former union can be split, the latter can't (unless my nature changes). Alas, my Father, if you let loose of me for one moment only, [if you withhold] your powerful grace, I tremble to think how deep I would fall. Thus I beg you, don't let me go. I'm tepid, I'm inattentive, Father dear, I know. I am weak. Please remember that. Have you forgotten all the sins of my former life? You do see, don't you, that I'm capable of the worst. What is to happen to me if you diminish your grace? Please, Father, don't diminish [it]! The older I get, the further I penetrate into your love, the more grace I need. I'm too proud, but fortunately this is only the case with my body. [Pride] cannot conquer the soul any more, as long as you keep it wholly in your power. So I beg you, intervene even more profoundly, always more deeply, in me. Let me, at your choosing, be frantic with love. Love, Father, love. Your holy will, in literally everything!!

Wednesday, November 24.
Father, give me the words to express all you have done to me this morning. How infinitely dear you are. Daddy, I want so much to call you my dear Father. I tried to meditate on the *Our Father*. But I haven't finished one *Our Father* in forty-five minutes, although I was not particularly distracted. I had no consoling feelings. But that's something I'm getting used to; it doesn't bother me any more. But with the *Our Father* I got as far as *your will be done* everywhere. I feel and know so well, my God that therein lies the core and impetus for my whole life and being: your holy will. Will-power [the power of your will in me] and love are the same to me, covering each other completely. Your holy will is your love, and my love is your holy will. Hence my key question is: *Amor Dei?* It's just the same as the conformity of my will to God's will. How richly adorned I was when I left the chapel and still am now, thanks be to God's grace. For if that was lacking for one moment I would be like a pig walking around in the mud. I sometimes feel as if my body and my imagination were trying to loosen my soul from God. But my soul doesn't want this. It clings even more intimately to the bosom of God, its Father! Clutch me more and more! I am possessed by you, my Father.

Today, at two Holy Masses and one Holy Communion, I could give Jesus fifteen more souls to quench his love thirst a little. But what are fifteen compared to the 150,000 or so who die daily! Father, my heart bleeds when I consider that so many do not know, or do not even want to know, your love. If I lived more in your love, I could do much more for you. When Jesus, my dear Elder Brother, touched my tongue at Holy Communion I first gave him a small refreshment. For Jesus was so thirsty, so thirsty for souls. Therefore, with the Creator of heaven and earth on my tongue, I asked my Father in me, in his name, to give three dying sinful women the *coup de grace* of love, so that they could hardly refuse [it], so that they will enter eternity with the words, "Love . . . Repentance . . . Salvation!" [on their lips]. I was like a poor beggar who could give a thirsty King nothing but water. But Jesus is refreshed by it, that much I know. But how much more, would I like to refresh my Father in and through Jesus.

Friday, November 26.
Crucified Jesus, my elder Brother, what thoughts must have run through your mind in the Garden of Olives? You, the all-knowing God, saw all the sins of your creatures in one flash. For many your suffering would be fruitless; it could possibly even effect to serve their ruin. You also saw my sins. How dare I call myself your brother, child of the same Father, the adopted war-orphan that still dares to offend you? I receive much more grace from Father than other people—and proportionately I commit much worse things than the most miserable of sinners. Yet I always want to return to you. You see my impoverished will. You see my total surrender as a love-victim. You see me as a person who has surrendered to your infinitely holy will, under the pressure of your grace, one who is possessed by God. And yet I still commit faults. You have probably felt more grief about me than about other sinners. Yet I have also been allowed to quench somewhat your love-thirst. Fifteen souls are eternally happy: six [released] from purgatory and nine dying sinners. But, think again, how minuscule is nine compared with the 150,000 dying daily! Why can't I ask for all 150,000? As my total surrender to your holy will is growing, so grows my trust in you; thus the more I shall receive as a consequence. Still, there's a feast in heaven now, even for those nine souls.

Dear Father, if only I might make this love strategy known to everybody, particularly to my fellow novices. As they are all much holier than I, they will ask for more. You can't deny [your children] anything, for you are eternal truth. You never break [your] word [once it is] given. So if you say, "I shall give something," I would be a villain and an ungrateful creature if I said, "I'm not so sure about that."

How narrow-minded we are when we compare God's goodness with people's goodness. It would be like saying, "If you keep asking the richest multimillionaire, he may answer one day, "Now stop it, for you will only end up being ungrateful for my gifts." You may say you regret it, but after a while you'll ask the same again anyway. Father dear, I trust completely in you. I don't want to reason in this way as if I were *only* human. I want everything you want. [I want] love, all your love. I surrender myself totally to your will. So you are to do what you want. Don't tolerate the least resistance, Father.

Saturday, November 27.
My God, my Father, now I know what you mean. You want to fill me up with so many favors and graces that I don't even have room enough to say, "Thank you." I won't worry, therefore, if I am filled up to the brim and still don't know how to express my love and thanks. Gratefulness without words is even greater. Among people it could be compared to a poor, loving mother with her children. She is helped on all sides. So much good is done for her that she does not know how to say thanks. Just the look in her tearful eyes every time she faces a new good deed is more than enough. Can there be anyone who says, "Woman, you are an ungrateful human being; we give you all kinds of things and you don't even say, 'Thank you.'" No, when they [her benefactors] look at her, they know her gratitude. So it is even more with my soul. She cannot say a word of thanks to her Creator and dearest Father. The only word she can speak is silence. She lets herself be filled with graces and good deeds and then keeps quiet. My God fathoms my heart and innards. My Father also knows how grateful I am, even if I do not express it in so many words. Still my will does it. I only say one brief phrase: "I will it, Father." You know what is implied in that act of will: everything, everything, up to the smallest thing that you are willing.

Father, I'll keep saying, *Nunc coepi* [Now I've begun], for that's what the Novice Master advised. All I do is of no value (measured by human, material standards). A supernatural organism is strengthened with virtues and gifts and put into operation by actual grace. All of this I have received from Father. Into Mary's hands, I place these merits, that much I know. But I owe this to you, Father dear, not at all to myself. The only thing I do is to resist. I make little progress in virtue and holiness—and this in spite of the fact that I haven't got anything else to do but to let myself be treated by you. I myself do not need to do anything about myself. I only need to unite my will to yours.

Sunday, November 28
This morning I could again show that I love Father, even when I feel nothing. During meditation I received the program for Advent: 1) to get into the habit to use more often my maxim, *Amor Dei?*; 2) to try to interpret anything wrong that I might see in my fellow novices in a good light; but first I should try to avoid seeing as much as possible. Instead I should keep recollected and not let my eyes roam everywhere. Those were the only spiritual fruits of my meditation. The rest of the time it was only, "Father, I won't give in; I don't want this temptation." Then again, "Father, I love you, even if I don't feel anything. I love you even if my thoughts go in every direction." Then again I chased the devil away by reminding him of his pride.

Holy Mass was not much better. I *felt* cold, but I *knew* myself capable of everything out of love for God. Today I even dared to ask for more souls than yesterday. And there will be a High Mass later so I can ask for more and more. I want to do everything for you, Father. I feel heavily charged electrically, with [transcendent] will power. As soon as your holy will gets in the least in touch with my mind, a spark springs forth and there is contact.

Today the Ecclesial Year has also begun. This morning I said again, *Nunc coepi* [Now I've begun], always *now*. Do not think about what may happen twenty years from now, how I may live my priesthood at that time. No, do not think of that. Only now: *Amor Dei?*

I must make a holy Novitiate, or rather, make the present one holy. Always *now*, always again, everything out of love for God, my Father. *Now,* repentance of everything in the past that was against God's holy will. *Now,* a great resolution of the will, but, above all, at this moment, [yes] to the action of God's love-will. Father, please help me!

Monday, November 29.

Holy, holy, holy is God in his whole being, all holy, all thinking, all willing. I should look up new words to glorify God's greatness and power. How glorious that I may serve and glorify God, for the length of eternity. How tremendously sublime for a human being that he is able and allowed to please God by his tiny mortifications. What greatness, to be able to please God, and to do so for all eternity.

Gloriously infinite Father, this morning I was completely rapt in contemplating your infinite being. And all that greatness is happening in me. I was standing, so to speak, right in front of it. How I thank you for the reasoning power you have given me. How I thank you for your own revelation about yourself. Now I can easily direct my reason to the infinite Truth itself. That truth is also in me by virtue of God's presence.

Dear Father, I should like for a whole day to describe the impressions of my meditations one after the other. But I know that my natural reason, which I received from you, would be incapable of going so deeply. Thus the only solution that remains [for me] is [the memory] that you have illumined me. You have allowed me to be absorbed in you totally for half an hour. *You illumined me*. You let my reason just look at you, see you, and partly see into you. How powerful you are, and how coherently your whole being is constituted. How wonderful that I may know you so as to love and to glorify you for the whole of eternity.

Why, oh why, am I not dead yet? Then I could already delight in you; then I could already praise you, sing of your attributes, adore your Being, and, above all, love you totally and undividedly in myself. But in this life you are also in me; you "grab me" tighter and tighter. [You give me] much more love!

✠

What do all these failures matter?

✠

Tuesday, November 30.
I tried as much as I could, dear Father, and I did not succeed. So I leave everything to you. It's better that way, if only you are glorified. You must grow in me, and I must fade, slowly but surely.

Dear Father, I have now received much more from my aunts than in former years, for St. Nicholas' day. Why? I know. It's because I wear a cassock. In other words, they don't do this so much for me personally (for I always remain Rinus Scholtes with or without a cassock), but they honor you by honoring me more when I wear the garb marking my surrender to you. I like that. You can never be honored enough, and I can never be disdained enough. Neither have I the right to refuse the honor rendered to you, as if it were my property! Even if that honor were given to me personally, then I would still not have the right to [refuse it], because that honor is Mary's. If they honor the servant, they honor the owner who provides for him, who gives him commands, and who completely possesses him, alive or dead. Alas, my guilt is even greater when I'm *looking for* that honor, because I like it so much and I am so proud. You do know that, my Father, don't you? Therefore, give your child much strength to endure everything well, both honor and contempt. Everything for your Holy Being. Everything to honor and adore you. Everything according to your holy will.

Father dear, what does all this aridity, all these tiny, ridiculously minuscule humiliations (so painful for my nature) matter? Everything for you! What do all those feelings of distrust in your forgiving nature matter, after my repeated falls and after so many good resolutions and graces? What do all these failures matter—the things I had begun out of love for you, with the best will in the world? Everything for you, everything in you, everything through you. I feel as if I am permeated by you. Or better I know this to be the case because feeling is so fickle. Reason, however, is your own sanctuary. No other being than you or those to whom you grant this power can enter there.

Wednesday, December 1.
Father, dear, the [informational] "theological" question about action *ad extra* or *ad intra* [outward or inward] of Jesus Christ's Incarnation and of his presence in the Most Holy Sacrament, is a mystery this puny human reason of mine cannot fathom, yet I could lose myself completely in these mysteries. Then my reason becomes like a little boy standing in the splendid grand hall of a palace, full of adornments. He

can do nothing but gaze in silence and say, "Ah! how beautiful." The only thoughts I had were: One cannot say that, for example, God, the Holy Spirit, became incarnate, or that God, the Father, is present in the shape of bread, at the Consecration. But, of course, where the Son is, there also are the Father and the Holy Spirit. So it is not a mere action *ad extra,* I think. Enough now! Let me stop [this kind of] reasoning, for I may only be "ranting heresy," and that's not my intention at all.[51] I believe everything the Holy Church believes. Nor did I do this to "checkmate" St. Thomas.

Dearest Father, I feel myself longing more and more for the Cross. At first I find that Cross only in small things. I'm so glad for them, because in them I see that you keep working on me. I would really like to die because already [my soul sees] that nothing here [on earth], in and by itself, is worth living for. My soul only longs for you. *Sed fiat voluntas tua* [but your will be done]. I'd like to become old, if that's what you want. I'd like to die now, if that's what you want. I'd also like to go back to the world, if this should be your holy will. I would go to another congregation, wherever or whenever, but only if it's your will. Then, too, I also want to be silent in my room because it's your will. I want to do my chores well, because that's your will, to begin [the prescribed daily readings of] Rodriguez in time, because that also is your holy will. [I want] to be humble, not to talk about myself again [to others], because you don't want this. Father, dear, do not forget my weakness. Without you I am an animal; with you, an angel.

Thursday, December 2.

Daddy, many thanks for all your graces. I have only been awake for two and a half hours, and already I have been flooded with graces. My soul is growing more and more beautiful. It's looking more like you than ever before. I may increasingly will and think as you will and think. And, then, what about that empty logbook with a clean criminal record! How much grace [it represents]. Still, this wasn't enough for you. For today I again used my "infallible" power over you, by demanding, as it were (this means, by asking in a very sweet way), redemption for six souls in purgatory, and the grace of final perseverance for twelve dying sinners in the name of Jesus Christ. But what are twelve, compared, after all, with the 150,000 who will die today. And what would all those 150,000 people be compared to Jesus' unquenchable love-thirst for souls. That's why I should not pride myself in regard to all those souls saved. But I may ask for more!

---

51 For Rinus, as for most spiritual writers, the consonant empirical formation of their life in Christ is the focus of their primary theological attention. They refer to the faith of the Church as expressed in its doctrinal catechesis. They are not informational-innovative theologians, but they do prepare the way for a systematic formation theology by sharing their experiences of Christian formation so vividly.

Whenever I enter a church or a chapel, I may ask Jesus, and thus in his name the Almighty Father who is in me, for one soul from purgatory and for the grace of final perseverance for one dying soul. And I may also increase the number of those for whom I ask during Holy Mass. For if the grace for salvation is given anytime it must be during the Holy Sacrifice of the Mass. But once more I just *ask* for them. Any merits of my whole day, of the entire condition of my soul, anything that gives to the least of my acts a supernatural value, and every other merit, all belong to my Directress without reservation. I do nothing else than simply *ask*. For a servant [of Mary] on earth is also permitted to ask for something with impunity. So, sweet Mom, I do not withdraw in the least my [condition of] consecrated servanthood; on the contrary, if I had one more body and soul, you would get these, too. My whole life is for you, my Directress.

Friday, December 3.

I began this morning by surrendering my whole being to Father. That's gradually becoming a habit. I do it almost automatically, even if I'm still half asleep. But my whole meditation was without feeling. Distractions [arose] because I must play Saint Nicholas. After all, I didn't make myself Saint Nicholas. So, I'm not responsible in this respect, dear Father. But from this I do see that I've not grown enough in "holy indifference," far from it.

How necessary it is that there be holy priests, indeed deeply holy ones. The holier the priest, the more fervent the people. So to inspire people to holiness the priest must be holy "to the third power." Fortunately, I need not take care of this matter myself. Father operates in me and I consent. Father and I have made a deal: Father looks at his work, that is, at the good achieved in me and through me, and so Father forgives and thus forgets what is bad. I, poor wretch, look at my work, that is, at my sin; I don't look at the good things around me that have been done through me, for that's not my work. I only think of my sins and of my [stubborn] resistance to my Father's work in me. Then I shall surely not become proud, not in the least! Neither shall I be discouraged. That would be sheer foolishness! For who is stronger? The devil plus the world plus my own piggish body plus all my bungling of God's work plus all my sins and omissions plus all my proud feelings. In a word, would my minus sign be larger than the plus sign of the infinite God? It would represent a new kind of pride to say this! Whatever you want, Father—yes!

Saturday, December 4.

Many thanks, dearest. You make me feel embarrassed about my part, namely, [all I do] to hinder [your good work] while regretting all the bad [work] in me. You have your side, namely, all that is good. Why, then, do I want sometimes to meddle in your work? That's when the only thing I do is to mess things up. But often—as often as I ask and even the times when I don't—you take over my work. I've hardly got anything to do. Fortunately, I cannot spoil much either. Now everything is clean again. You have purified and washed me clean completely. Again a little piece of the old Rinus has been deadened. Or, rather, he has been totally benumbed. If the new Rinus wants to operate, then the old Rinus wakes up in a flash, and we're in for it. There will be the devil to pay. But, as long as I have a doctor as competent as my dear Father, or a woman doctor like Mary, with a few nurses like my Holy Guardian Angel, St. Paul, St. Marinus, St. John Bosco, and a nurse who also takes a keen interest in my illness, like St. Thérèse of the Child Jesus, then [I'll be fine]. They are all operating on the old Rinus and healing him in the hermetically sealed operating room of silence and recollection. Having put him to sleep completely with the chloroform of love, the operation goes well. They cut and heal the old Rinus. The poor patient's health keeps improving. And should he complain of pain now and then, don't take notice of that, Father.

Sunday, December 5.
Actually, there's no need [for me] to write down a recollection, for my meditation and Holy Mass and Holy Communion were completely arid and distracted. The only thing that I like so much, the only thing that enables me to see that Father's work in me keeps going on, is that I'm not really sad or angry about it. On the contrary, I am glad to have the opportunity to show Daddy that I love him for his own sake and not because of sweet feelings. In spite of all my distractions, I'm full of God's will. I still want everything you want, in the smallest detail. And so I go on again.

I received my Jesus in Holy Communion. I did not use fancy words. That's absolutely unnecessary. Honestly, though, that St. Nicholas [event] is running through my head. I am to play him tomorrow. I keep thinking about what to say. At the end of Holy Communion, when I was lost in distractions again, I could not keep from suddenly smiling. Jesus asked why. I said I was thinking how comical it would be if I, as Saint Nicholas, would lose half my beard tomorrow night, so that there would be a child's face on one side and the venerable face of the good old Saint on the other. Then Jesus could not help smiling, too. He, my good Elder Brother, will help me tomorrow.

Monday, December 6.
Peace, quiet, God. There is rest in my soul again. Today my Father celebrated Saint Nicholas day. I could ask what I wanted, even for material things. I asked first for a new empty logbook. Mother, too, must pay a lot from her treasure box. If I were to die this moment, I would go

straight to heaven, without [having to go] to purgatory. I know that with moral certitude! But Father cannot expect *absolute* certainty from me, for that can only come from him, the eternal Truth. I'm so glad again. Everything is good. Father looks at Rinus with pleasure. But, then, you look with pleasure on your own work, for all that has been achieved, Daddy, is your work; whatever is wrong with it is my work. Yet I will not succumb to sadness, for I am deeply convinced that I am still too weak to go as far as Father would want, even were I able to. I have surrendered to him as well as I can again today.

Tuesday, December 7.
Love, love of sacrifice, love of will, to be willing to do everything for you—to want this firmly, to regret everything you have had to bear from me, even the least thing that was against your holy will, and not to want anything else. A firm resolution to will everything you will. [What a disappointment], then, to be so very distracted both during meditation and Holy Mass [and again] at Holy Communion to be without any feeling at all. I was as cold as ice. Now and then the most intense and disgusting temptations ran through my imagination. They even allured the "lower animal" in me, so that my body found a certain pleasure in them but my will did not consent. With a funny joke, I chased the devil away by humiliating him at his worst. I bore that temptation willingly out of love for God, fighting it [mightily]. All these things taken together are great graces of God, and I received [them] this morning.

Many thanks, dearest Father. I know, though I don't feel it, that this is your way [with me]. You made me a match for all the devils of hell. Father, once again, many thanks. I cannot thank you enough. I want to fight again for you in the spirit of that poem about Flanders: "Standing right in front of you and fighting for you tooth and nail."

Father dear, I have received much strength again. Whatever the cost to my own nature, I won't look back. I will trust in you alone. You restore all the wrong tracks I make when I show repentance. I would be proud and ungrateful were I to believe that everything was not clean again until I felt this. No, old boy, that [thought] isn't good for anything You have received Holy Communion. You have asked for God's forgiveness. [Your words were] sincerely meant even if you felt completely arid. You should trust in God. Yes, that is my fondest wish.

Wednesday, December 8.
The Feast of Mother's Immaculate Conception. This is a feast for her children, for her consecrated servants, and so it is a feast for me, too. Father has cleansed me beautifully and hung festive graces on me. Today I cannot commit any sin, not the least one either of impurity or otherwise, provided I cooperate with God's grace. I asked for that grace

in the name of Jesus Christ, and so [I asked] "infallibly." I was also allowed to suffer a little this morning. With the best will in the world, I could hardly say anything to Father and Mother. My soul was flowing over with love, but my body did not cooperate. It doesn't really matter, does it Daddy? If only you are glorified, I don't care about the rest. Yet I know you are strengthening me. I've become cleaner than I was before Holy Communion. At this moment, too, my writing is supernatural. I am doing my recollection [report] because it's God's holy will. I'm doing this out of love for him alone. I also resign myself to my chores. That's God's will, too, so I must want to do it. Strength comes from on high, if I beg for it. That is why, before every exertion of my small "authority," I should turn inward and have God act in me.[52]

Thursday, December 9.
Now it has begun, dear Father. Many thanks for your renewed gift in me, for purity [of heart] in everything. It's now a moral certitude for me that if I died this moment I would go straight to heaven, thanks to God's infinite goodness. Today after Holy Communion I meditated again on God's infinite Trinity. Father, dear, how profoundly impenetrable you are. Many thanks for your teaching. I begin to grasp [its truth] more and more insofar as it is granted to my natural reason to understand such great things. What I can do is to resolve to permeate everything more strongly with love.

Friday, December 10.
This morning I meditated on the infinite triune being of my dearest Father. I had a foretaste of heaven. Already I find delight in dissolving my puny reason completely in the contemplation of God's infinite being. Father dear, you allow me to penetrate deeper and deeper! Many thanks! I'm not worthy of [this favor], I know. Yet you have permitted me to respond in this way. So I resolve to love you again with more love. [I resolve] to love everything out of love of you alone. All my work, my chores, I do everything out of love of you. I need also to be more careful during evening recreation, not to get attached too much to a *frater quidem* [a certain novice]. Be careful!

Saturday, December 11.
Dearest Father, many thanks again for your abundant grace and blessings. I'm happy, my soul is happy here, even if my nature and body sometimes rebel vehemently against the stresses of the Novitiate and

52 The "small authority" Rinus speaks about refers to his job as leader of manual labor. This position entailed the authority to tell the other novices what to do or to correct them when they did not do their jobs well.

even more against the pressures you exercise on me yourself. But, dearest, don't pay attention to my body; it is corruptible anyway. My soul has surrendered to you. It lets itself be treated completely by you. How resistant my body and my lower nature often feel, for example, when some point of the rule, even the least or the most important, must be practiced and my body does not want to do so. For instance, when I am busy preparing music, and the bell rings to announce that within five minutes the reading of Tanquerey's book on the spiritual life, or something like that, is to begin. Then I *must* stop, whether I like it or not. This "I," which in this case is my body-I, resists, but my soul finds it good that God steps in so firmly. For it is Father himself, who exercises that pressure. When the bell rings, it is he who says, "Rinus, my boy, it's time for this or that." Father does not even permit me to finish a half-written word without a feeling of reproach![53]

Much stronger than that is the pressure I feel when I have been offensive or unpleasant to some other novice involuntarily, on a whim. Then I'm completely upset. I do not quiet down until I have made up for it. Take Friday afternoon. I first had to apologize, or else you wouldn't stop reproaching me. It's the same when I speak without any necessity at times of silence. Again and again I feel you saying in me, "It's not allowed. Don't! It's against my holy will." Then I may once more ask forgiveness. Father is satisfied with that. What dislike my body feels under such a yoke, one so heavy for its nature that it doesn't allow me to fling off this harness. Yet my soul is so glad with God. Many thanks, Father.

Sunday, December 12.

Dearest, I am quite willing to bear the humiliation of being distracted all the time during meditation, Holy Mass, and Holy Communion out of love for you. I started out well this morning by surrendering to you—I'd almost say wholly and utterly—with a feeling of "let-things-happen-as-they-may." I have surrendered to God. I can't calculate the consequences.

In spite of all the distractions I feel, I really love you more than I can say Father. Everything, everything out of (I hope) pure love for you. The resolution I made today was to be careful not to get overly attached to a certain novice. Now I'm still free, notwithstanding all the temptations and feelings [I have]. Thanks be to God's grace and strength, neither have I been tempted yet to pat someone on the head or to use silly words of endearment and softheartedness. But who will guarantee the future for me? That's why I request, "not to play chess with this person any

53 Unfortunately for us, that may be the reason why certain words or sentences in Rinus' diary remain incomplete.

more unless he asks me." After all, I should have brotherly love for all.[54] So if he asks me I won't refuse, for, the truth is, I'm not harsh by nature.

Monday, December 13.

My almighty Love. You have been so undeservedly good to Rinus. Yesterday he was allowed to read about Stanislaus Kostka, the patron saint of the Novitiate. This holy young man received many extraordinary graces, such as no distractions during prayer (just like St. Aloysius); he also cooperated with your grace in a wonderful way.

I feel full of energy, [fully ready to obey] God's will. I only beg you for actual grace that makes me burst out in love-acts for you, my most dear Father [and Father] of all. How beautiful you've again made my soul, even before Holy Communion. And then afterwards, what a treasure of graces my Elder Brother brings me? Mother, too, with such sweetness, takes something from her treasure box and pays the fine on my record. Now I can earn as much [grace] as possible. This means if Father dear urges me to do something by his grace, or if I may do God's holy will with [the help of] other graces, or if my soul puts no impediment of sin or punishment in the way, then I can earn much more for Mother. I also continue to ask for [the release] of souls from purgatory and for abundant graces for final perseverance for poor dying sinners. I cling to Jesus' words: "*All* that you ask the Father in my name he will give you." True, somebody may come and say that one can only be heard infallibly if one asks something for *oneself*. But I stick to Jesus' words. Father also knows I ask nothing for myself, at least not directly, save for the grace never to offend him, never, I repeat, never again to

54 Rinus' words "brotherly love for all" indicate clearly one of the chief purposes of the warnings in religious community life against "particular friendships" as distinguished from "spiritual friendships." Caution against particular or inordinate, exclusive, emotional attachments was rooted in a concern for "brotherly love for all." The exclusive selection of one or a few brothers or sisters over and above others could lead to the splintering of a religious community into small cliques of men or women attached exclusively to one another by bonds of particular friendship. Added to this for Rinus, as a chosen soul, was the pain of the pressure of grace, the grace to suffer for God's sake the loneliness of detachment from any particular friendship in one's community. Jesus revealed the same to Blessed Faustina Kowalska, whose life was in part contemporary with that of Rinus. She writes in her diary: "At that moment the Lord gave me to know how jealous he is of my heart. 'Even among the sisters you will feel lonely. Know then that I want you to unite yourself more closely to me. I am concerned about every beat of your heart. Every stirring of your love is reflected in my Heart. I thirst for your love.'" [*Divine Mercy In My Soul: The Dairy of Sister M. Faustina Kowalska* (Stockbridge, MA: Marian Press, 1987, No. 1542)].

sin! The rest doesn't concern me—whether I die young or old, whether I'm ill or not, whether I become a priest or not. Everything that God wills, only that [do I will]. I'm a poor beggar, a fully consecrated servant of Mary's. I have nothing to contribute but the begged-for gifts and graces I always receive from my great Benefactor, my own intimately beloved Father.

Ah, Father, you always give [out of your abundance], over and over again. I need not knock on anybody else's door but yours. If only all beggars knew this address! I would like to tell [it] to everybody and not keep it selfishly for myself. Such a good Father gives to every supplicant. Why don't people ask you for much more, dearest Father?

✠

Love makes my soul vibrate. Love makes my soul tremble.

✠

Tuesday, December 14.

Love makes my soul vibrate. Love makes my soul tremble. Love fills my whole being with acts and desires of love. All because I love you, my only love. Father, I say [love] always more. It begins already when I get up. I like to get out of bed and then to wash myself out of love. If it were daytime always, then I would serve you [in this way] always. Even now I serve you by doing your holy will, also when I sleep. Daddy, dear Daddy, I carry you everywhere! All my outer acts must come from the inside. When I have attended to the inmost source and cause of all things, then everything falls into place. I need not [be the chief attendant] of my inner life. I only need to will with full [trust] that you look after it [for me]. The effects of this inner care, I mean [what I do] outwardly, must be done in tune with this principle. I must will to do what you will. The strength and success or anything [that comes from this] is under your care. Daddy, you've got to do almost everything. I only need to consent. It's true, wherever I go I carry my skeleton with me. But thanks to God's grace I've also carried you inside me for eighteen years, ten months and fourteen days. I beg you Father, grant me the grace I need to keep doing this. If you don't strengthen me by your grace, I will fall and keep falling. With you, and with you only, can I withstand those severe temptations. Everything out of love.

Wednesday, December 15.

I'm dripping wet. I feel soaked through with you, dearest Father. Your strength, your grace, vibrate through my being. I am *paratus ad omnia quae vis* [prepared for anything you wish]. I feel and know myself to be strong with your grace—not because of my own strength, but only because of you: in you, through you, for you, dearest Father.

This morning I was not distracted, thanks to your grace. With the best will in the world, I could not say exactly what I talked to you about, whether I asked for anything or whether you told me to do or to omit anything. I don't know.

I only had two severe temptations, which I think were straight from the devil. When I turned to you to mock the devil [he's no match for you], he was gone. It's great to feel a strength within myself that is not my own. It prompts me to unconditional, generous holiness. I'd like to have the strength reserved for God alone.

My love, you must act. I am your servant, and I hope a willing instrument. Daddy, dear Daddy, how powerful you are, how sweet and good. If only all people knew this, they would burn with love—with a pure love of will and action—for you. They would all love you much better than I do. I'm still weak in spite of all the graces you give me. I'm still the least as regards virtue and holiness in the whole Novitiate.

Jesus, I don't say this because the saints have said so but because it is so. The saints were *really* humble. They were holier than their *confrères*, but they said they were the least. I'm not holier than my fellow novices. I'm really so weak that I take all of them as examples for my life, each of them uniquely dearest Father.

Thursday, December 16.
Father dear, out of love for you, out of ever stronger and more fervent love for you, I took the "vow" of chastity today. It will last until Thursday at midnight. I did so out of love for you. I also asked for special graces for twenty dying people, especially abundant grace for perseverance to the end.

Dearest, I also asked you to make my external behavior more gentle. But I did not ask it as a question with an infallibly right [answer]. It's far from sure that this is your holy will. Nonetheless I made a firm resolution to give orders in a calmer way. Please help me.

You've charged me with the tasks of workleader and of choirmaster. You know how unpleasant and troublesome this is for my nature. My body must bend to your holy will. If it doesn't want to bend, then it must break. You're the boss. [I must do] everything out of love for you, Daddy. I feel and know myself to be strong again through Holy Communion. Your holy will, everywhere!

Friday, December 17.
My Father, my Creator, my Redeemer, many thanks for your grace. He who has surrendered to you is the better for this. He who has fallen into your loving arms does not need to be afraid of anything. Urged on by your love, I have taken the vow of chastity for three days more, until

next Sunday at midnight. I am also praying for the [grace of] fidelity to make anything I do count for the worship of God. For your glory is more important than anything. I've noticed that I ask nothing anymore for myself at Holy Communion. I always ask for graces for others, for the redemption of faithful souls. Your love must be victorious.

Daddy dear, I now vow for one day that whatever I have to do, I will do out of honor and love for you. This vow I must follow, but, because of my weakness, I must add a few things: If somebody addresses me [during the hours of silence], I'll answer. I believe this is one thing I need to do. For example, if I'm carrying a bucket of water and the bell rings to prompt me to follow your holy will, I won't let the bucket fall. After all, I'm your child, am I not?

You know well what I want and mean by this vow, don't you, Daddy? It's to show you that I love you, that your love intoxicates me. Never [is my love sufficient], Dearest, never [is it] enough. Please Father, am I allowed to take these vows? Isn't it against my consecration as a servant [of Mary out] of love? Isn't it against prudence? I don't think so. I have God's honor in mind, and that suffices for everything. Further, I rely on your strength, not on my weakness. Besides, I take these [private] vows for short periods, not because I don't love you more but to be prudent in view of my weakness.

Saturday, December 18.
Dearest Father, you have filled me to the full with grace. Many thanks. You are so good to a poor wretch like me. Thanks for your goodness, dearest. Saturday is Mother's day. Today I renewed the vow of chastity, also the vow to follow the Novitiate rules. That doesn't seem so dangerous to me either. For the measures are equal: sin against the one is sin against the other. With your indispensable strength and the power of grace, I hope to fulfill that vow well and to keep it. I have your honor in mind, dearest Father. I rely on your help. Today I made the resolution to keep smiling, or rather to try to keep smiling!

Sunday, December 19.
Thanks, thanks, many thanks. These are almost the only words I can utter, dearest Father, for all your gifts, and, above all, for your love. I burn with love of you. If it pleases you so much when I burn from love for your will, when I obey your holy will in the way you help me to obey it now, when I put nothing in the way of your work in my soul, then I can beg you for more, ever more.

Daddy, today I made three vows, for one day only, out of love for you: 1) to be chaste; 2) to keep the Novitiate rules; 3) to say the Stations of the Cross. This is to show you how much I love you. I do these things, urged on by your grace. With you I know myself to be strong! Mother Mary, everything for you. I'm your fully consecrated servant.

Monday, December 20.
Father, many thanks. You overload me with blessings. I did "penance" last night and this morning. I bet the holy hermits are convulsed with laughter when they hear of my "acts of penance." But that doesn't discourage me at all. I have a broad back. If I please you in this way, then a small sacrifice, made out of love, will please you much more than the severest whipping of a Desert Father if it would be done by him, for instance, to avoid going to hell. The love of God is on a much higher scale than the hope of reward; the latter is again higher than the fear of punishment.

Jesus, my dearest, you have intoxicated me. I should like to cry out in turn: "Love, Thanks, Penance!" Please, I beg you, help that poor wretch who calls himself your little brother. He is such an ungrateful sort of man, no wonder you have been working on him. If you were to let me loose, your work would fall to pieces—and so would I.

Daddy, suppose you were to give me a little less grace during the temptation that sometimes pervades me totally. Then I would fall. Now I always implore your grace. With each victory I grow stronger. Without your power I would collapse flat on my face. Help your poor little brother! Today I was allowed to renew the vow of chastity, until Monday at midnight. Yesterday I was "on direction," and I talked about this [vow].[55] Please help me, Father.

Tuesday, December 21.
Dearest Jesus, dearest Elder Brother, how strong I am when I am with you and in you. What a power I have over the heart of Almighty God, my Father, when I speak in your name, my Jesus. Today, out of love for you, I asked again for the grace of final perseverance for five more souls. I know if I grow in love and holiness, I may ask for many more. Imagine how many souls were saved by St. Thérèse of the Child Jesus! [The number] will only be known at the Last Judgment. Ah, how shameful it would be if I turned up there with a measly 500. I might have saved many more. I might have been God's instrument to obtain more grace for poor souls if only I had been much holier, if only I had cooperated more with the grace of God. The answer to a prayer is always equal to one's trust. The holier one is, the more [abundant] is one's trust in God. When I, for instance, with God's grace and out of

---

55 Part of the Novitiate's rule includes the obligation to visit one's Novice Master at a regularly scheduled time to discuss one's fidelity to the rule and one's general progress in the life of prayer and perfection. Rinus obviously wanted to talk about the vow of chastity. This being "on direction" in the Novitiate is to be distinguished from private spiritual direction with one's Confessor. It is up to the Novice, however, to freely disclose to the Novice Master questions he may also discuss with his Confessor.

love for Jesus, ask for five souls, it is not necessary that the grace be exactly given to persons dying at that very hour, nor for this moment! One hundred years before my request, God may have granted a soul abundant graces to persevere to the end because Father knew that I would ask for [this favor], urged on by his grace. There exists no time for God. We see at once how silly a number "five" is when we consider there have been and will be billions of people [who die]. How dare somebody say "five" is far too large a number. No, I say. If I were a saint, I would ask for that grace for a million souls at a time. I regret, more than I can say, that I am not holier. Then I would ask for many more souls, with even greater confidence!

How many souls has Mom taken to heaven! If only I were allowed to count mine with hers, since I'm consecrated to her. Then on Judgment Day her glory and renown would become even greater, even if a trivial number like mine were added to her fabulous capital. Mom, help your poor servant. He is so weak.

Wednesday, December 22.

Many thanks, dearest Father. In spite of all the disgust I feel about the world and about life because I long so much for you, I'm always glad to be allowed to work another day for you. Every moment I grow in sanctifying grace and, therefore, in the love of God. I never have enough love. For this reason I'd like to live until the end of the world so as to receive more and more love from you. Still things are best the way you want them.

Daddy, I'm homesick for you. Why am I not yet firmly united with you for all eternity? I promise you, I'll do my best in heaven. I'll sing a lot for you, for I love you so much. I'll sing a song of love. I'll link my timid singing to the choir of those who love you much more. I will be happy to love you without end. How delightful are the things awaiting me. Death, you are welcome.

Thursday, December 23.

Daddy, haven't I lived long enough yet? Why am I not with you forever? Should I, such a weak and brittle creature, be exposed even longer to the risk of losing you? Why am I not yet collapsing while writing this? Why am I not dying of heart failure? Should that happen, I would tumble into your infinitely loving arms. I could never leave you again.

One thing is for sure. Those seven hours I slept last night took me seven hours nearer to death, and four additional hours have passed since I started writing this. Oh happy last hour! There will come an hour, a quarter of an hour, a minute, a second that will be my last. And then, wonder of wonders, then I may love and praise my God, my Father, eternally, without end, without any danger of ever losing him. Then I'll be allowed to see Mother and offer her my services. Then I may address Jesus Christ, my dear Elder Brother, and be happy with him. [Can't you see] I'm dying of homesickness for this everlasting love. Daddy, how long yet?

Friday, December 24. Christmas Eve.
[I] stayed awake until half past two. The Novice Master did not allow me to fast, so I won't do so. How wonderful, Daddy, I may serve you now for twenty uninterrupted hours on end with my reason and active will! Remember, I also need more graces to do so. This morning I received more than I deserve. Many thanks. With you I feel as strong as a lion. United with you, I want to overcome all temptations, yet again and again that cowardly barking dog comes back. Besides [the devil's] horrible impure temptations, he also starts expressing blasphemous thoughts. That wretch dared to say he was equal to God. What a laugh! I make fun of him. What nerve! How could such a dirty dog, such a filthy pig, think himself to be God's equal? With all his great intelligence, he must be stark raving mad to think for one single moment that he could be equal to the almighty, infinitely holy, entirely good and loving God, who is my dearest Father.

Father, how did the dirty beast dare to think so? Now he is my mortal enemy. United with you I want to thwart him and his adherents (my flesh and the world) wherever I can. But you must help me, Father, or else I'll lose. Holy Guardian Angel, gird on your shield more firmly. This is getting serious. This [battle is fought] out of love for God. Certainly no one would dare to measure himself against that infinitely perfect being. It's too absurd for words, isn't it. Mom, help your child and poor servant.

✠

I've never had such a fruitful Christmas.

✠

Sunday, December 26.
As regards feelings, I have never experienced so cold a Christmas. Everything was cold, no loving emotions, no "poetry", no crying of a new baby. Yet I believe I've never had such a fruitful Christmas. With God's help, I made a good preparation. Feelings do not matter. I really didn't mind being so cold at Christmas. If you keep helping me out, I'll remain victorious, but without you, I can't make it. Dear Father, the struggle is sometimes more than I can bear. The images are so expressive and clear, and my lower nature finds them so pleasant. I don't want this because you don't [want it for me]. Whatever you will, I will

also. I only beg you for your indispensable support. Then I can stand safe against a whole hell full of beasts. Dear Mother, help me.

Wednesday, December 29.

Meditating doesn't progress as it used to. It feels as if my head is in a straight-jacket during times of prayer. I sit in chapel. I'm quite aware of God's presence. I can say with full conviction that I love him above everything. I'm willing to do anything, literally anything, he wants me to do, but for the rest—nothing, not during all those forty-five minutes. No particular resolutions, no feelings, nothing, only the same [basic resolution]. Father, I love you. I want to do whatever you want me to do. So, after all, my prayer is not so bad. I've been told so more than once. Well, I let Father act in me. The purification must be complete and penetrate me deeply. Many thanks, my God.

V
The Diary of My Novitiate
Part Three
Gennep, 1938

V
THE DIARY OF MY NOVITIATE
PART THREE
GENNEP, 1938

Friday, January 7.
On this first Friday of the month and in this New Year, I received much grace from Jesus at the adoration. I also bungled a lot by being really uncordial and grievous toward another novice, who had to give a singing lesson, simply because in my opinion, that lesson took too much time. During the lesson itself things went fairly well. I grumbled a bit to myself, but I took part in the singing. Then at table I vented all my spleen in a sarcastic remark: "And then an hour's singing lesson to sing yourself to sleep." I was amazed at myself. There was so much dislike implied in that one sentence. It affected my confrère even though he tried to laugh it off. I was bewildered myself, yet [I allowed this unkindness] to last through the whole of our dinner. After that my annoyance died down [mainly nerves I think], but meanwhile I had hurt my fellow novice. Forgive me, Jesus.

Sunday, January 9.
Today I again received many graces from you, dear Lord. And yet I ask many more. I asked for some "Don Bosco graces," among them the method of sanctification [he practiced]. Father, I asked for this [favor] in Jesus' name, and so I received it. Many thanks. Let me use [these

The Novitiate at Gennep.

graces] well. I can't profit from them without new graces. Be merciful to me, poor weakling [that I am]. Mother Mary, assist me. The struggle is so severe sometimes. I want everything God wants, whatever it may be.

Monday, January 10.
A day of recollection at the beginning of the second trimester. Now I don't take the slightest notice of [the date], for there isn't so much difference here between holidays or ordinary Novitiate days. I hope to make good use of the grace of this day and of that renewed stimulus by means of special new graces given by God. Also the preparation for my birthday has begun! At the same time I celebrate the anniversary of the patron saint of my religious life, St. John Bosco, who died exactly on January 31. So I was born on the date he died. I already pray for many graces on that day, especially from my patron saint. He has to show that he, a mighty advocate with God, feels some liking for a cool Dutchman. On earth Don Bosco was also good for poor sinners, so I trust he won't forget me either. Or else I'll tell Mother. Then she will tell Jesus, and then Don Bosco won't have heard the end of it, for Jesus loves me infinitely! I'm consecrated to Mary. I'm her beloved child because I'm so extremely weak. So don't quarrel with me, for I am not alone, isn't that true, Father?

Dearest God, tonight I heard a splendid conference about you. I like to hear talks devoted to you. I like to hear you praised and honored. My Father, my Creator, my God, my only ultimate goal, my trust, my holiest, my most intimate love, my everything, my redemption, my Novitiate, my priesthood, my apostolic life, my will—all is you and you only. I love you so very much, Father. Believe in my love in spite of all my wretchedness and weakness. I'm like a little ant who says to a human being: "I love you, I want to be trampled underfoot for you." I have polished a grain of sand for you. Don't you find it beautiful? The receiver can't help but smile, though he doesn't get any heavier or better, thanks to a mere grain of sand. To an infinitely higher degree this is the case with me. I am a worm compared to God, the Father [of the whole world].

Tuesday, January 11.
Dearest Jesus, many thanks for the increase in "Don Bosco grace," which you again granted me this morning. I pray to you now for a new grace, simply said, to use the other grace well.

Dearest Father, I can't tell you how happy I am with you. Yet I keep begging you for more grace since I am so incomparably weak and lax. I would like to choose to do not the easiest but the most difficult things out of love for you.

Mother Mary, many thanks for having brought me so close to Jesus. Dearest Jesus, many thanks for having brought me so near to God my Father. I just wish I were able to express my gratitude in a way that approaches its depth, but I can't. My beggar's silence is my only song of thanks to my dearest God and Creator.

Wednesday, January 12.
Father dear, today I could fully repay you for all you've done for me. It was through the Holy Sacrifice of the Mass, by dedicating to you Jesus Christ as a sacrifice of petition, thanks, atonement, and adoration. My dear Father, you have now been fully repaid by Jesus, your divine Son, for all my horrible sins and ingratitudes. I was also able through Jesus to adore you fully. During meditation you allowed me to keep my mind on what I was doing. Hence, I hope to have gathered much fruit today.

Furthermore, I begged for the renewal and strengthening of the "Don Bosco grace" I received from you. Show me how to use it well, dearest Father.

My Mother, everything to God through you. I am and remain your consecrated servant. My dearest Jesus, my possession, my sacrifice to God, give me the grace to show you my love and gratitude today by little attentions. Never let me be separated from you.

✠

I don't exist anymore.

✠

Thursday, January 13.
My God and Father, I'd almost dare to say, you had nothing left to ask of me this morning after Holy Communion. I offered you *Jesus* as a sacrifice of thanksgiving (for everything), of pleading (for all graces), of atonement (for all sins and whatever goes against your holy will), and as a sacrifice of adoration (self-annihilation), so that all my sins were repaid by Jesus' pleading. All my asking for graces, for the present and the future, in short, for my whole life, was upheld by Jesus' own asking. All my expressions of gratitude were complete. I would almost dare to say I've given God as much as he has given me, not the least of which is my self-annihilation. I don't exist any more. So God, my dearest Father, has been satisfied and repaid by his own gift, his Son, Jesus Christ. Now it is I who should thank Jesus. In this case, too, my personal prayer is worthless. For this reason I had to renew my consecration to Mary. She is my *mediatrix* [an intermediary or intercessor] with

her divine Son. So Jesus is satisfied, too. And as for my gratitude to Mother: for this I take the saints as mediators, especially Don Bosco, who loved her so much. In this way, all of my life is a hierarchic ascent to God.

Again, my dearest Father, my own prayer, my own fulfillment of duty, in short, all my little doings serve to show my good will. I hardly expect anything in return. I only pray in and through you. For Holy Mass and Holy Communion are the center of my day. The day has only ten hours [in it] to render thanks, and again ten hours to prepare for the next Holy Sacrifice of the Mass. Therefore, I can forget those small mortifications. They are really nothing; they don't mean anything. I do them only to show you my good will. You always see my good intentions, yet I rely on you so little, my God. But I want to be better, Dearest.

Guess what? At her deathbed Mrs. Gosschalk [a Jewish acquaintance of the family] was given many graces for final perseverance because two days before her death I made Jesus ask for abundant grace for her. It appears as if she used it well!

[Translator's Note: For about two weeks Rinus wrote down his notes in Latin, because practicing Latin might come in handy for his studies the following year. At that period of time all class readings and lectures as well as all examinations in the Senior Seminary were in Latin. In these notes (part of which are barely legible) he wrote in the same way as before. He also mentioned in passing the anniversary of his grandmother's death, January 24.]

Wednesday, January 26.

Sweet Mom, I'll write in Dutch again because my love can't control itself. How good a "switchboard operator" you have been again this morning. Good service, really [the best]. What do I owe you? Faithful service as a servant fully consecrated to you, right, Mom? I'll think things over for a while before I have to or want to say something to a fellow novice. I'll ask for your approval or advice, especially during manual labor. I'll also make it a habit always to smile, though this isn't easy, my dear Directress. It is easier during prayer and Holy Mass and after Holy Communion, but sometimes I forget during recreation. Don't you think it's strange, Daddy, that a consecrated servant like me [now put in charge of the manual labor of his fellow novices] must play the supervisor over others, who are not [slaves of Mary] but free people? Just think, you live in all these novices; and all of them would be better than I am if they were in my circumstances and received my graces.

My Elder Brother, I'm really a useless instrument. You could see that again yesterday during the walk.[56] The first part went fairly well. I just listened. But in the later part my old self surfaced and I talked about my relatives. Last night was worse. I even started to quarrel. Of what use I am to you? Don't you see I'm just a self-opinionated sort of man! But I'm not as bad as that, am I, Daddy? Today I'll start again. United with you, with your grace, I may wear the habit of the Congregation. I'm so grateful for their willingness to try me out for almost six months now. I'm not worthy of being here among all these holy novices.

Thursday, January 27.
Mom, my sweet Mom, why do I still love you so little? Why do I do so little for you while you do everything for me. I am in living communion with your divine Son, my Elder Brother Jesus. He was in your own immaculate, spiritual womb with his whole Mystical Body. Thus I am fed by you. I am growing through the work and food [you supply] by your own pleading.

Dearest Father, many thanks for everything. I have been allowed to say thank you because of your own goodness in me, for you have given your divine Son to your people. See, the Holy Church (to which I belong) also gives him back to you as a sacrifice of thanksgiving, atonement, supplication, and adoration. In the same way we offer ourselves.

Daddy, dear, don't refuse the little dirty box that contains such an infinitely pure and beautiful diamond. Of course, you could ask yourself: What am I to do with that all too dusty box? But what is the box going to do if you don't accept it? You do accept it, don't you? I am yours, dear Lord. Have pity on my weakness.

I repeat, and will keep on repeating, that without your grace I'm no more than an animal. Without your grace I would be a worse sinner than the worst one who ever existed or will exist. If he were to take my place, you would see, dearest Father, how holy he would be. He really would not waste any grace unlike me, poor little worm of worms. Yet you have shown your willingness to try me out. Many thanks! With Jesus, with Mary, under the abundant rain of grace, something can be made of me. Alas, dear Jesus, I'm an ungrateful instrument. You've experienced that enough already, haven't you? Be patient with me, Daddy.

---

56 Once a week the novices were sent out in groups of three for a long afternoon walk outside the Novitiate. One novice was in charge of setting up a list of names comprising the groups of three, which was then submitted to the Novice Master.

Friday, January 28.

Love, my God, how great is your love. Meditation was completely and totally distracted and full of devilish attacks. I've taken it from God's hand and fought it as well as I could with his help. Holy Mass was the same or even worse. I accepted this aridity as my punishment. It wasn't until the Consecration, when suddenly—with the total self-sacrifice by Jesus in Mary to God, our heavenly Father—that a kind of twitch overtook my mouth. I couldn't help it. I think it was a smile, but I'm not sure. This has happened more often and lasted longer of late, especially since the novena in preparation for my birthday. I believe it's the active grace which St. Joseph (in his great sanctity and humility), and St. John Bosco (in his way of sanctity, love, and gentleness) are asking for me. I will be given [these gifts] in full strength on my birthday. Remember, it falls on the dying day as well as the feast day of my patron saint in religious life, Don Bosco himself.

I'm happy now, even as I'm writing this down. My face is bent in a peculiar way. It's not a natural feeling. My head is filled to the bursting point. My prayer has been without the least imagination for quite some time. But whatever happens, I don't really care. Yesterday the Novice Master said during my direction hour: "As long as your life leads to an ever greater tendency toward and practice of perfection, it's one of the surest signs you are on the right way." So I have my Father to steer me and to work in me as he wants. I remain a poor little wretch, a small cell in Jesus' Mystical Body, born within the womb of his Mother. Many thanks for everything, Father.

Saturday, January 29.

Two more days and then I hope—or rather I know for sure—I'll receive in all its plenitude the grace St. Joseph and St. John Bosco have asked for me. Mom had better prepare her little consecrated servant well in these last days. I badly need her assistance. How sweet she is to me. Today I may again serve the infinite Creator, my dear Father. I can only do what he wants because I am a member of Jesus' own body. What would a small cell of a body do *outside* that body? With the body I render all honor and glory through our head, Jesus Christ, to the Father: *Omnis honor et gloria, per Ipsum et cum Ipso et in Ipso* [All honor and glory by Him and with Him and through Him, our Head, Jesus Christ]. Besides, a child in the womb must of necessity go where its Mother goes. And his Mother is the most perfect being God ever created, so that dear Mother will go wherever God wants her. There's really nothing left for me [to do] but to show my good will . . . and I show it by yielding to Father's grace. He urges me to do my duties as perfectly as possible, for Father doesn't tolerate cowardice. Further, I must make some small sacrifice now and

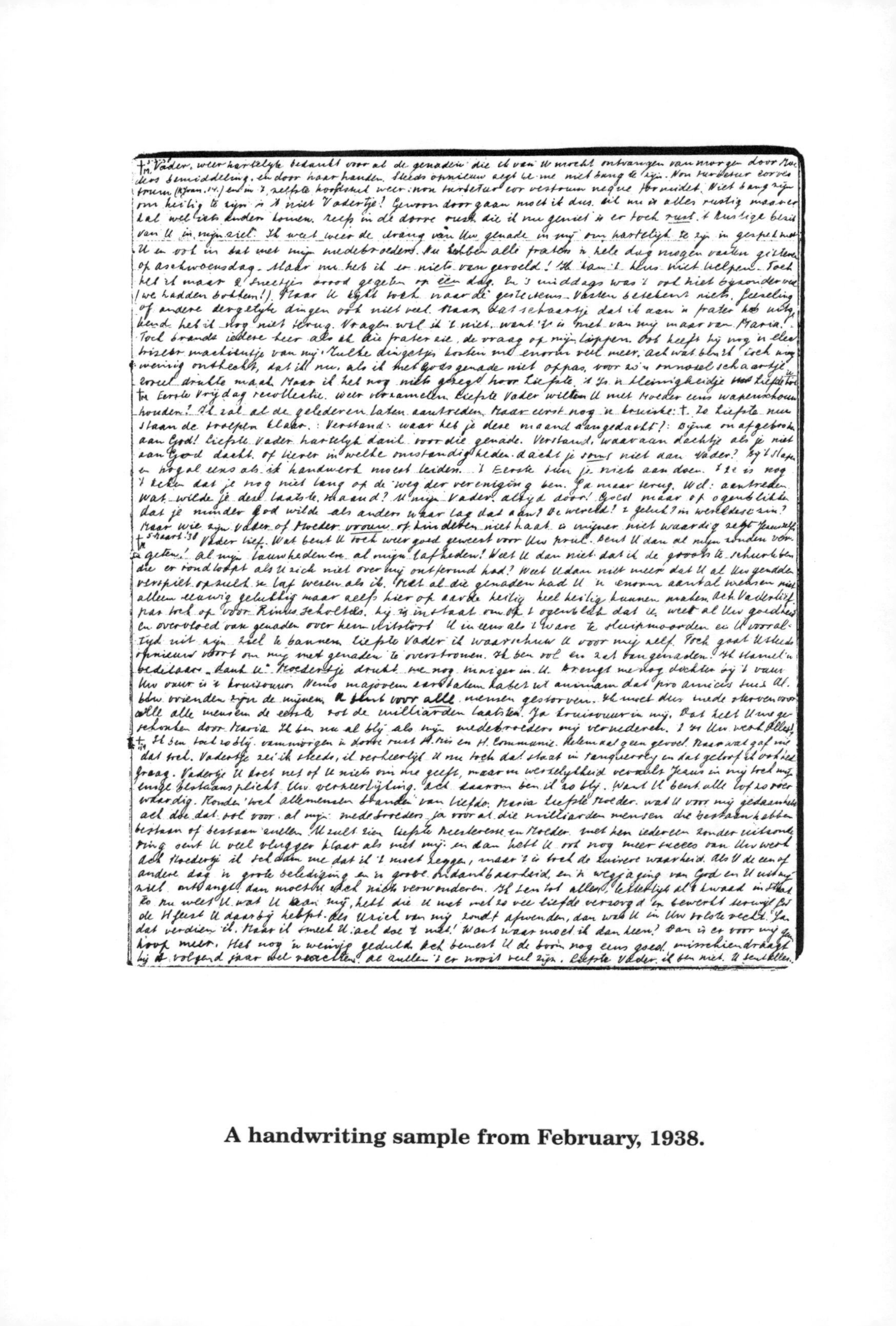

A handwriting sample from February, 1938.

then, urged on by his grace. The only thing [he asks] is that I remain wholly pliable so as to receive all promptings from God. Mother Mary has made me pliable by bringing me so close to my Elder Brother, the *fornax ardens caritatis* [the burning furnace of love]. Whenever the wax tends to get somewhat hard, Mother puts it closer to the fire. Therefore, all the acts of cowardice I commit so abundantly—and about which, with God's grace, I may repent every time—are an occasion for her to bring me closer to the fire. Many thanks, sweet dearest.

[Translator's Note: Again Rinus wrote down his notes in Latin for several days. On January 31 he thanked St. John Bosco for all the graces received on his nineteenth birthday (without going into detail). His notes are written in the same way as before and need not be translated to follow his journaling.]

Thursday, February 10.
Father, I'm going to write in Dutch again. Then I can better express myself in love. This morning I tried to meditate on death, but I did not get far. I began by reading yesterday's notebook, but then I closed it. From that point on, you grasped me firmly. You haven't let go yet. How much I longed for death during those few minutes!

Dearest Father, you've seen for yourself that I can't say anything any more. I must let you speak. Father, if you grasp my soul and speak to me inwardly, then I am deeply happy. I'd like most of all to be alone at such moments, for I am afraid that it may become noticeable [to the other novices]. I'm smiling, and I can't help it, yet I'm completely motionless. I should let go of the fear of what people will think. Help me, Mother dear? It's my pride. I believe I can't bear it when others look at me and perhaps begin to snicker. But from now on I will say—with God firmly in my soul—I surrender myself wholly. Father Gijsen[57] allows me to do so. "It is good," he said. So I don't care what my fellow novices might think. I'm also quite happy, dear Daddy, that you are willing to speak to me inwardly all day long the way you did this morning. I only have to keep inner silence and allow you to do as you like.

Mom, many thanks for drawing me even closer to the fire. How immensely good you are to me! In heaven I'll be allowed to see you, to thank and serve and love you, forever.

---

57 Father Gijsen, the former Novice Master, now retired but still available for teaching a course on Tanquery, was Rinus' Confessor in the Novitiate.

Friday, February 11.
Dearest God, I've asked for the Cross. You thought it would be good for my salvation so you've given it to me. I'm glad, although my nature is quite upset. You need to knead, press, cut, and purify me. Perhaps, then, something good can still be made of me! I know myself to be in safe, caring hands. Later I'll thank you for a whole eternity for all the little crosses I was allowed to receive.

Dearest Mom, what Father wants you want too, and thus so do I. I'm your consecrated servant. If I remain very still and sensitive to all the impressions of grace [I receive], I'll become a better and better servant. Then I can serve you as I ought.

Holy Guardian Angel, what a difficult job you had this night. You had to chase a lot of devils away, didn't you? But dreams mean nothing. I only see in them more clearly how weak I am without God. I need his help more than ever to avoid all signs of particular friendships. I have to smile now when I think of that dream. The devil shows his cards in so many ways. Don't you agree my good dear Archangel Michael? Or are you one of Michael's relatives? I'll find out later when we can see and admire one another in heaven.

Dear Holy Angel, how nice that will be. You know what it is to behold God without a veil, face to face. I'm sure you have taken, are taking, and will take up and use every obstacle to help me attain the highest possible place in heaven. Just knowing I'm in such safe hands makes it easier for me to surrender myself wholly to Father.

The whole point is to be transformed into another Christ.

Saturday, February 12.
My dearest Creator, this morning I again checked up on my hopes and dreams, namely, to do missionary work sometime in the future. Prayer [is the answer], and once again, prayer. By praying I hope to net some souls for you. By fasting and penance I hope to get them to church and confession. Above all, I should welcome everyone with love. And especially [I need to do] everything through Mary for Jesus.

Mom, [you are] the same sweet Mom at this [and every] moment. Will you then help the servant consecrated to you? I'd like to become a Don Bosco for Bagamoyo [in East Africa]. What lofty desires I have. What must be done now to fulfill them? That's the question. The whole point is to be transformed into another Christ. The better this transformation succeeds, the better will be everything God demands of me. At present a sublime woman artist, together with a divine artist, is at work on my image. If it was up to them (Mary and the Holy Spirit) everything would be excellent. Their aesthetic implements are as fine as can be. Thus good artists, good results. Now the truth comes out. Is the "direct object" [of their efforts], Rinus, good? Is there no impediment on his side? Isn't he too active? Then [the risk is there] that the greater part won't succeed either. Since I am the direct object [of their "artistic work"] I should be "passive" in two senses: 1) have everything done to me; 2) be ready and willing to undergo *suffering*, for instance, the abandonment which, as Rodriguez says, is the greatest cross.

Ah, Father dear, help me to have a good Novitiate. Mom may have a great plan in mind for me. I have made myself available for everything. So anything God wants may follow.

Mom, the day before yesterday I experienced moral suffering. Now I'm having physical pain. I'm well aware that the former is much more violent than the latter—which I did not want to believe in the past. Help your poor weak child. He is so small. Your will is good, utterly good.

✠

You consoled me with your inward speaking.

✠

Sunday, February 13.

Dearest Father, you are unchangeable. You were so good to me yesterday. You consoled me with your inward speaking. You are still the same today. Indeed, you are even more my All for me. With the help of your grace, and the means of grace (Holy Mass, Holy Communion, Holy Confession), I hope to grow and grow every day in your love. Intervene in me at deeper and deeper levels. Don't spare me, dearest Father. You know I don't belong to myself but to your daughter, my dear Mother Mary.

Dear Daddy, the tenderest names aren't tender enough to express my humble love for you. How, then, is it possible for you to express your infinite love for people? You have found the only, the most perfect means, namely, yourself. You are infinite. You want to express this boundless love. Whatever you want will happen in perfect accord with your holy will. For you are almighty. Hence the expression of your love could only be yourself in the Holy Eucharist. In my case things are totally different. I hope to love you much more for all the being I have received from you so far. It is more than [my heart] can hold. I would like to love you with all the non-being in me, that is, to love you with and through yourself. I can do so thanks to your infinite goodness. [It still amazes me] that you give yourself [so freely and fully] to me in Holy Communion and at Holy Mass. There, on two fronts, [I experience] an infinite declaration of love as [mutually] given: by God who gives himself—who is infinite love itself—and by man who gives back the God he himself has received.

Monday, February 14.
Mom, aridity doesn't matter. This morning I merited a lot [of it] again, through Jesus' grace; for *I* can't say anything to him [by my own power alone]. Mom, you are so sweet to me. Presently we'll go to Holy Mass again, myself and my Directress? More saints may accompany us, St. Joseph, your virginal, beloved spouse, who has become my boss since my birthday. (St. Joseph, feel free to ask something of your little servant too, that silly, naive servant of Mary.) Next, my Holy Guardian Angel, that good detective who must guard me like a millionaire's son. Then I won't be kidnapped and robbed of my wealth by "mad Harry," who thought he was equal to God. That's a laugh! You dope, you thought you were equal to God! You must be raving mad! You are a match for me when I'm alone—but now, with God and all those patron saints at my side, don't even try! And what about all those other saints, especially John Bosco. Mom, I'm sorry to say I have a bone to pick with St. Paul, the patron saint of my confirmation. For I've got an idea that he just lets me stew in my own juice. I'd like to ask him something, if you don't mind.

St. Paul, would you please use your mighty [powers of] intercession with God to cure me of my speech defect, only, that is, if it's God's will! For I don't pronounce words correctly! I'm often simply babbling because I think more quickly than I can speak. Would you please render me that favor in eight days' time? I'll do my best to cooperate with that grace. When I've received it from you, I'll invoke you more frequently and speak of you [to others], just as I now try to make St. John Bosco known everywhere. On your part you must keep your word, St. Paul, that is, of course, only if it's God's holy will.

Tuesday, February 15.
Dearest Father, believe me, it's not applesauce every day. Just because you make me do and say everything, it doesn't mean that it's easier for Rinus. It isn't. But nothing [deters me]. Mom, make my soul more receptive from hour to hour, so much so that it becomes sensitive to the least prompting of God's grace.

Dear Holy Spirit, with your seven gifts! Many thanks again for your quiet activity [in me]. Sweet Mom, what else can I do? Please tell me? I still have to improve a lot. It's especially hard for me when, for instance, as the leader of manual labor, I've got to do some chore during the day which has to be interrupted by a spiritual exercise. It's difficult then to dismiss that work completely from my mind. Often, when I say the rosary, I end up talking to you about that task instead of praying. I know that's not really right, is it, Mom?

My crucified Jesus, another effect of the work of the Holy Spirit, in cooperation with my Directress, is a heightened love of the Cross. I fall asleep with my crucifix pressed to my breast or to my lips, just like a little child goes to sleep with a doll. So, Mother, when temptations or melancholy or *Weltschmerz*-like sentiments come over me,[58] I hold the crucifix tightly again and say: "Yes, Jesus, I too must suffer, and suffer a lot. I know, you can safely nail me to your Cross. I'm so glad when I'm given a small cross [to bear] during the day. I can't bear heavy ones yet, my Jesus."

Wednesday, February 16.
I was cold today. Father did not say much. It really doesn't matter. God's holy will be done. It may be a punishment for what I did yesterday. Yet I'm so quiet and happy now. I know that God is unchangeable. My dearest Father is still in me. He still loves me. It's fine, dearest Father. You have already comforted me so much. I have to suffer something once in a while. Yet I can now imagine that suffering like this is the greatest [gift] of all for a soul, as Rodriguez confirms in his second book. Now mine is not so bad yet. But if Father sends [me the grace of experiencing] real abandonment by him, it will surely be a heavy cross to bear.

Mom, I'm not afraid because you are still holding me. I know everything is for my own good. Thus, I quite willingly submit to the divine will.

Dearest Father, what if everything came upon me at once, both being abandoned by people (that's not so bad) and the feeling of being abandoned by God (that's very bad!)? Why entertain these fixed ideas? For you are united with a soul [who feels abandoned] even more intimately than otherwise. Suppose that you really left a soul or rather that you were driven away by mortal sin? Then the soul would be left in a quite different state! Daddy, help me please.

Friday, February 18.
Dearest Mother, this morning I was allowed to suffer a small [cross] during meditation. Severe, uncommonly sneaky temptations, that I could not possibly drive out, [rose up from within] and so I endured them. I kept saying; "Daddy, you know I don't want these [thoughts], for you don't want me to want them." Strangely enough, everything was quiet and calm inside. It doesn't matter at all that I had no consolations today.

---

58 The term *Weltschmerz* refers to a literary period beginning with the German writer *Werther* and, therefore, also called "Wertherism." It spread, only for that period, to many other countries, among them the Netherlands, where the writer Rhynvis Feit, was one of its protagonists. *Weltschmerz* represents in this overly melancholic and darkly emotional literature a view of the world [*Welt*] that wallows in the tearful somber sentiments that Werther sees, experiences, and describes.

Mom, when up to now I have mentioned consolations I only meant internal divine consolations. They happen when God takes possession of my body too, directly, perceptibly, as it were. Then I sometimes sit motionless for half an hour or longer, neither stirring nor getting tired. My soul only needs to listen to God. I am completely inactive both inwardly and outwardly. My soul enjoys God's presence. All I do is simply listen. That's what I'll call consolations in the future. What I used to have, felt sensations and imaginations, has been over now for a long time. In fact, my imagination is no longer of any use in prayer, though the devil uses it fairly often for temptations. But, poor dope, he can't get to my soul in that way. Only its surface "ripples." For the rest, everything is quiet. So today, for a change I was left more alone. Now I well know that it only *seems* to be so, for in reality I can't fight any temptations without God's help and grace.

✠

Melt me so as to bring out the form you want.

✠

Saturday, February 19.
Daddy, today I've hardly said anything to you. Only my ideal of becoming a holy priest has gathered strength. Your little victim-servant agrees to everything. He is surrendered to your divine will. Dear Directress, help me or else I can't do anything. I'm completely in your spiritual womb. Form me to what God, the Holy Spirit, wants and for as long as you like. Melt me so as to bring out the form you want.

Sunday, February 20.
Dearest Father, as a matter of fact I don't need to write any recollection report now. I've done nothing else during these forty-five minutes than bear the pain in my stomach out of love for you. After meditation I had to leave. I could not help it. Holy Mass and Holy Communion were arid, too. Whether it was my own fault or not, in either case I have to go on cheerfully. I'm awfully glad that you've shown in this way that you accept your victim and do not repudiate him. Many thanks, dearest Father. Now I feel stronger, able to bear more suffering. Help me in my weakness.

Dearest Mother, many thanks, too, for an increase of will-power as regards purity. I had a first beginning of it last night. Many thanks. I'm awfully happy about that, dear Mom.

[Translator's Note: From here on in his notes, Rinus puts a cross ✠ and an M for (Mary) before every date, and sometimes at the end of his entries.]

Monday, February 21.

Today I was allowed to renew my victim-sacrifice during Holy Mass and at Holy Communion. Jesus again made me feel something of what that is going to mean. My nature shrinks back, it's true. But my supernature has persevered with God's grace. Once more I renew my victim-sacrifice or rather not I but Jesus in me, and my dear Directress. I am her consecrated servant, though a servant full of lumps and bumps, the very worst she's got. Now Mom has been busy cutting out those warts and tumors, those faults and my cowardice, for five years. [She works on me] together with her divine bridegroom. [Their operation] hurts her consecrated servant, of course. But up to now he has often been anaesthetized in God's love. Mary also began [to cut away] some little warts. She wanted to start with the big one I've got on my back, I mean a lack of confidence that always compels me to look at the world to calculate whether I can still go on in this way and not care about what other people think. But she has not been able to get rid of it entirely. As that old wart on my back shrunk with each painful amputation, so there grew an even bigger tumor in my chest every time I began to puff myself up with pride and self-centeredness.

Now one day Daddy came to my Directress, Mary. He asked whether she had a victim for a good cause. Then, strengthened by Mother's encouragement, I offered myself. What that "good cause" was I didn't know, though she, my Directress, did. Thus I became your sacrificial offering to the Father. Now I'll be handled in a tougher way. I know it's because a victim-sacrifice with warts, tumors, and lame legs isn't worth anything. Still you gilded me, like those sacrificial bulls of old. You put ribbons in my hair like they did for that traitor from Greece, who also played the part of a sacrifice at Troy [an allusion, of course, to Homer's *Odyssey*]. Even though I become successful, I know it's only external, for I remain a victim. Dearest, I'm so glad I may be your sacrificial offering.

Tuesday, February 22.

Dearest Father, once more I could offer you, through Mary's hands at Holy Communion, a few small crosses. Daddy, I just don't know how to express myself fully enough at the Consecration and Holy Communion. I know *I* must move out [of the way]. Holy Mass is for *all* people, for those of the Old [as well as the New] Testament. When the words of the Consecration are pronounced, I say: "Father, *everything* (that is all people) for *everything* (your sacrifice of adoration); *everything* (Jesus Christ, God and Man) for *everything* (all the evil that was or is or will be committed by *all* people in *all* places at *all* times—your sacrifice of atonement); *everything* (I beg you, in *all* my prayers for *all* people) for *everything* your sacrifice of supplication; *everything* (thanking you) for *everything* (what you have given—your sacrifice of thanksgiving). So, in other words, Daddy, everything for everything, or all for everything, or everything for all. Through Jesus Christ, in him, for him, and with him, and in and through and for Mary, everything is included in whatever can be asked for or given by you.

Do you remember, dearest Father, that in the beginning of the Novitiate I prayed for only five souls at a time, then gradually for more. But, for a considerable time now, it is not *I* who have prayed any more, but Jesus in me who has begged for anything that is possible. Nothing, no prayer of mine, is said any more for myself in my Holy Communion or Holy Mass. Everything [is offered] for the world.

Wednesday, February 23.

Dearest Mom, this morning Father van Mierlo's [a Spiritan priest] mother died. He came back with Our Lord [in the Eucharist he had carried to her sick bed] and told us then about her departure. I think it was too late for her to receive Holy Communion before her death.

Dearest Father, give this young priest and also his family strength and courage to endure this loss. Many thanks for the grace you gave this woman in her last hour, for on the previous night she did receive the Sacrament of the Sick. I'm not worried about her soul at all. A priest's mother is privileged in your good book. As a reward for the sacrifice and the suffering she endured for her son for twelve years, she was allowed [before her death] to see her award on earth, namely, her son at the altar. *Requiescat in pace* [May she rest in peace]. Alas, I am still on earth.

Dearest Father, whenever I see a person preceding me into eternity I envy him or her. When will my time come? Your holy will be done, my Lord. If you want me to wait a little longer, to do something for you, it's fine with me. But I beg you, be careful with me, for I'm not to be relied upon wholly yet. I may be good now and full of ideals. I may love you with all my heart. But don't rely on that, Dearest. I'm still so weak.

Thursday, February 24.

Dearest Mom, I have another small cross to bear that you may offer the Father through Jesus. Fortunately, you offer it and thus it gains some value. If I had to do it myself, I'd best forget about it. Yet Father is in me, even if I don't notice it. He was so perceptible in me yesterday (which is not the case now) and the day before yesterday. Then he is also with me today, for God is unchangeable. With the help of his grace, I have been allowed to remain in his love, and hence not to commit any sin. Even though I do not see or feel Father's presence, I'm not worried at all. I simply smile at this. How can an infinite God hide himself in a small body like mine, not quite six feet tall, and certainly not six feet wide! Presently, during the Holy Sacrifice of the Mass, I'll ask Mother to help me renew my dedication, both as a victim-sacrifice united with Jesus, and as a consecrated servant [of Mary]. Then everything will be fine again. Further, I'll renew my trust in the power of prayer. If I ask, for instance, in Jesus' name, at the Holy Consecration for abundant grace for perseverance for *all* dying people, I'm sure they will receive it. For Jesus doesn't say, "Ask for yourself and you'll receive," but "*ask*" without any restriction. Don't you agree, Jesus?

Friday, February 25.
Dearest Father, I think what is happening to me is good, but I'm not worthy of being drawn to you. My soul yearns for full union with you, that union you have often allowed me [to taste briefly]. It was then as if I were possessed by God, as if you had entered my whole reason and will. Now Father, whatever you do to me is well and good, for I know you are unchangeable. I'll wait and meanwhile do your will as well as possible. I'm not anxious now, for inside me everything is peaceful. Do you remember how heavy the storm was yesterday after those severe temptations suddenly arose again. I smile at them now. I cling to you through Mary. I dedicate everything to you. I beg for your grace. I let the devil rage lasciviously. With you [at my side], he is not able to harm me.

Dearest Mother, in a moment I will again celebrate the love sacrifice of the Mass. My poor self doesn't come to the fore in prayers and other situations any more, thanks to your work in me. Together with the Holy Spirit, you are always at work on my soul, on my whole person, to turn me into a good image of Jesus. I came to know Jesus on the Cross, abandoned by everything and everybody, even [in his humanity] by his heavenly Father. I want to be worked on in this way. That's what I want to become [another Christ]. But much patience on your part is necessary, my Love Spirit. For you know the kind of person you are dealing with. I rely on you. I won't be afraid. Everything you want is good. Your holy will [be done] in *everything*.

Saturday, February 26.
Father dear, I can't write anything, for I don't know what you said to me this morning. I had temptations, distractions, and all that, yet inwardly I was deeply calm. Now and then I said something like "Dearest Father, I love you," or "How immensely good you are," or "I accept with love the little crosses you want for me, nothing more." Even at this moment, while I'm writing, my soul is in deep, unspeakable rest. It is in union with God. My reason and will are directed toward him. He holds them while on my part I just wait. I'm not worthy of your speaking to me. I'm waiting and yet I'm happy.

Dearest Mother Mary, I slept wonderfully last night. I always keep the crucifix near me at bedtime. Then I take it up spontaneously. When I awaken I kiss it and say at once that I want to suffer, out of love, everything that Jesus and the Father want me to suffer that day. I then offer before the crucifix my dedication as a consecrated servant and also as a victim-sacrifice. I can't possibly give more because I have not received more. Take everything, Father.

Sunday, February 27.
Dearest Father, I'm happy still. In spite of all the temptations, distractions, and sleepiness I feel during my meditation, Holy Mass, Holy Communion, and adoration, I am still profoundly happy. You are there in my deepest being. I have a feeling that I can't get to that place myself, so deep are you in my soul. The only thing that remains is the truth that you are present in me. I sense and know your presence in an unfeeling way.

I'm speaking nonsense, aren't I? I can't say how it is, except that you are there. I was again permitted to let Mom offer you a few small crosses, I mean the pain in my stomach and all those stains on my Sunday cassock that are so hard to remove, the ones caused by carpentry work. I must smile now when I think of how annoyed I used to be about this kind of thing. Now I laugh about it.

Dear Daddy, think of the many graces you have poured on me lately! I'm so happy, so deeply at peace, in joy despite aridity. Everything [in my life] may turn upside down, but I am still, all the time now, near to you.

Dearest Mother, today your servant must stand sentry, that is, be on duty at the Blessed Sacrament. Beforehand I offer you all the consolations [or none] received in my prayer. I don't pray for myself but for you and all people.

Monday, February 28.
Dearest Father, you have seen again how weak and little I am. I bear that humiliation out of love for you. Today I was allowed to make the same consecration through Mary as yesterday. I sacrifice by way of reparation all the consolations I usually experience at the adoration of the Blessed Sacrament. I also want to bear with a smile today all inner sadness and darkness. Help me in this resolution through the power of your grace.

Dearest Father, I'm glad I may show you my love. No matter how arid I am, today I want only to pray. I do not want to do anything else because I don't feel anything. Mom, help me, for in this darkness I bump against everything. I also want to be kind toward all the other novices. Above all, I've got to be especially careful about those feelings of natural resentment I now experience against that confrère of mine. I may be in for trouble here because of particular friendships. Yesterday he humiliated me. I felt grieved, and hence resentful. But, dearest Father, everything remained on a natural level; my "supernature" remained undisturbed, though I admit I gave in to resentful thoughts by neglecting a brotherly service I usually render. I must be careful that my resentment does not turn into a greater affective attachment. Thanks be to God, I'm not alone. Mother is with me. God is in me.

Tuesday, March 1.
St. Joseph, now I should keep my promise, too. You know you gave me on my birthday the great grace of holiness for which I asked. Now it seems to me that this grace is that of uninterrupted rest in God, whether the rest is arid or sweet. It alternates, but it is mostly the arid one (also today). Before my birthday I also had that rest, but at intervals. Now for a month (especially for the past week) this grace has become more and more continuous, deeper and deeper. Now I want to thank you, too, by invoking and honoring you more. Whenever I think about you, I admire most your purity. You are joined to Mary in matrimony, to the most beautiful woman that ever existed or will ever be. I believe it was Dionysius who said, "If I didn't know that Christ was God, I would have adored Mary." You always remained a carpenter, quiet and in the background. People thought you had a son, but you knew better. There was nothing [human] of you in him. You only worked and suffered for him, nothing more. How holy you really are!

Thursday, March 3.
Father, many thanks again for all the graces I received from you through Mother's mediation and through her hands. Over and over you tell me not to be afraid. *Non turbetur cor vestrum* (Jn:14), "Let not your heart be troubled," and again in the same chapter of John, *Non turbetur cor vestrum neque formidet,* [Neither let it be afraid]. Don't be afraid to be holy, that's the message isn't it, Daddy? I just have to go on. Everything is quiet now, but some [other disturbance] will come. Even in the arid rest I now enjoy, there is still rest. It is a quiet possession of you in my soul. I know again the urging of your grace in me to be cordial when talking to you and also to the other novices. Yesterday all the novices were permitted to fast for the whole day. It was Ash Wednesday. But I didn't suffer anything from it! I really can't help it. I only ate two slices of bread for one whole day. In the afternoon the fare was not all that much either (we had smoked red herring), but you look at my inner self. Fasting doesn't mean anything. Whipping or other similar things don't mean much either. But, take those scissors I lent another novice who has not yet returned them. I won't ask for them, for they aren't mine but Mary's. Yet whenever I see that novice I'm burning to ask him. He has also got a small electric [testing] machine of mine. Such small things are enormously more difficult for me to handle [than fasting]. Ah, how undetached I am that I should make so much fuss about such silly scissors. I should be more careful [about such things]. But, with God's grace, I haven't said anything yet. Dearest, it's a trifle, but [I keep silent] out of love for you.

Friday, March 4.
First Friday, Recollection Day. Rally the troops! Dearest Father, will you hold an inspection with Mother? I'll line up the ranks. But first I'll

make the Sign of the Cross. Dearest, now the troops are mustered: Reason, what did you think about this month? Almost uninterruptedly, of God. Father, many thanks for this grace.

Reason, what were you thinking about when you did *not* think of God—or rather, in what circumstances did you *sometimes* fail to think of Father? During sleep and fairly often when I had to supervise the manual labor [of my fellow novices]. You can't help the former [Rinus], but the latter is a sign that you're not yet, not by a long shot, on the road to union. Fall back!

Will, come forward please. What did you will this last month? You, my Father, all the time! Good, but what was the reason that you willed God less at some moments than at others? The world? Happiness (in a worldly sense)? "But he who does not hate Father or mother, wife or children is not worthy of me," Jesus said.

Saturday, March 5.
Father dear, how good you've been to your bungler again. Have you forgotten all my sins? All my tepidity and my cowardice? Don't you know that I would be the greatest villain who walks [the earth] had you not commiserated with me? Don't you wonder why you are wasting all your graces on such a cowardly being like me? With all those graces you could have made an enormous number of people not only eternally happy but even holy, really holy, here on earth. Father dear, do be careful about a certain Rinus Scholtes. He is liable to slay you at once, as it were, and to banish you forever from his soul, precisely at the moment you are again pouring all your goodness, the abundance of your grace, into him.

My dear Father, I warn you about myself. Yet you continue to flood me with graces without measure. I am utterly full and satiated with grace. I am stammering like a beggar, "Thank you." Mother presses me even more intimately close to you. She takes me ever nearer to the fire. Your fire is the fire of the Cross. *Nemo majorem caritatem habet ut animam dat pro amicis suis* ["There is no greater love than this: that someone should lay down his life for his friends."] All your friends are mine. You have died for all people. So I have to die with you for all of them, from the first billions to the last. Yes, the fire of the Cross is in me. You have given it to me through Mary. I'm glad, therefore, when the other novices humiliate me. It's your work in everything.

Sunday, March 6.
I'm so happy. This morning during Holy Mass and Holy Communion I was in arid rest. I had no feeling at all. But what did that matter. Daddy, I said continually, "I glorify you now." I believe that is also in Tanquerey. I'm glad I believe it.

Daddy, act just as if you don't care for me at all, though, in reality, Jesus fulfills in me my only reason for being: your glorification. That's why I'm so glad. For you are more than worthy of all praise. I wish all people could burn with love.

Mary, dearest Mother, what you have done for me, please do for all my fellow novices, and for all those billions of people who have existed, exist now, or will exist. You'll see, dearest Directress and Mother, that you'll finish much sooner with all of them than with me and that your work will be more effective.

Mom, I'm ashamed to say it, but it's the truth. If one day you receive a great insult, gross ingratitude, and the expulsion of God and you from my soul, you should not be amazed. I'm liable to do anything, literally every evil. Now you know of what use I am to you—I for whom you care [so tenderly] and work on with so much love, with God and the Holy Spirit helping you. If you were to turn away from me, it would be within your full right. Yes, I would deserve it. But I beg you, please don't [go away]! For where would I turn then! There'd be no hope for me any more. Be a little more patient with me. Fertilize the tree once again. Maybe it will bear fruit next year, if there will be [a next year]. Dearest Father, I am nothing; you are everything.

Monday, March 7.
Father dear, it's becoming more and more an established practice [of mine], at the first moment of consciousness when I wake up, to think of you, to talk to you, to renew my consecration and good will through Mary. It happens naturally. I'm happy about this [special] grace. Furthermore, I experienced that arid rest and the pain in my stomach during meditation. I did nothing else for those forty-five minutes than try to bear with that stomach pain out of love. Yet I was glad when meditation was over because I had such a need to go. What a little boy I am! How the Desert Fathers would laugh if they heard about my "mortification." Don't you agree, Father?

✠

I am in repose.

✠

Tuesday, March 8.
Actually I needn't write, dearest Father, because neither you nor I have said anything [to one another] for these forty-five minutes. I knew myself [as I was] in you and [as] you [were] in me. I was also aware that

I glorified you increasingly (or, as it says in Tanquerey, before the "prayer of quiet" comes the "prayer of simplicity"). Glorifying you is the only reason why I must and may exist. So the purpose of my existence is realized. That's enough, isn't it! The fact that it is not so pleasant for my nature matters less now. Nature cannot give orders here.

Presently I will be attending Holy Mass. How happy I am about this. A reparation of infinite value will be rendered to the Father. Then I can be absorbed in the Mystical Body of Christ. If only I were allowed to be a small member close to the neck of his body. Then I would be quite near my Mother and Directress.

Didn't St. Bernard say that Mary was the neck of the Mystical Body through which everything comes to us from the Head? Father dear, this morning I could smile through all that aridity, for everything is quiet deep within me. I am in repose. I sleep as it were, on the breast of the Father. At some distance away, Mother stands and looks with a smile of joy. She is so glad that her consecrated servant, her child, her sacrificial-victim, which she has formed through so many graces and so much care, may rest on Father's breast.

Wednesday, March 9.

Dearest Father, it's only a trifle. Accept it, an hour's worth of pain in my stomach and that certain humiliation. [Accept it] not for me because I did it, for that isn't true, but to show my good will, the will Mother formed in me with so much care. Now, I go on again, as I usually do.

Daddy, do you remember [what happened] last night? Something strange. Lately I often find myself smiling during prayer. But then suddenly I started laughing. I couldn't do anything about it. I was so happy all at once. It seemed to me my mind had expanded along with my forehead. I'd be inclined to almost say that the surface of my imagination (like a white screen waiting for the film on which images would appear) was suddenly as tall as it was wide. I saw nothing but light, soft, deep-yellow light. A moment later it was gone. It may have lasted for only a minute. I'm glad about it, although I have neither seen nor known what it was. I do remember at the time feeling an unusually great love for God and for the Cross. Daddy, [grant me the grace] of a humble surrender, as it is said in Tanquerey. Whatever may happen to me, it's as nothing. I have ceded the right of disposal of my little all; it is now God's through Mary's hands. So be humble. Surrender completely. *Non turbetur cor vestrum*.

Thursday, March 10.

Actually, Father, I need not write anything for I cannot remember our talking together about anything, at least not after Holy Communion.

Yet the [gift of inner] rest was more intimate than at other times. I am happy. If I now ask myself why this is so, I have no other answer than: "Because you are in me and I am in you; because, especially of late I may glorify you over and over again." Every morning when I get up, it comes into my head directly that I may glorify you again. Also during Holy Mass and at the Consecration I beg nothing else but: "Dearest Father, in the name of Jesus Christ, my Lord and my God, give all people of all times the grace to glorify you as perfectly as possible." I also pray for this and for nothing else after Holy Communion. Once I have said this, there is nothing left to say. Parents, family members, authorities, anything else I used to mention explicitly, none of that comes to my mind at the moment [as specifics] to be prayed for. Actually I do nothing else than rest, always and in everything [in you].

Friday, March 11.
Mom, today is Friday, the day of the Cross. Need I say more? You know that everything you want is what Father wants, too, not because you want it but because he does. That I must suffer, I accept gladly, whether inwardly or outwardly. Even if Father makes that rest in my soul more arid and desolate than it is now, it would be for the best. Anything Father wants is good, isn't it, Mom?

I'm writing now while smiling. I'm going to make my bed with a smile, and on and on. My face remains the same as during prayer. My inner repose doesn't change either. Whether I'm in chapel or at recreation (although the latter is still a weak spot) that wordless conversation still goes on. It's not really a conversation. I'm glad I may glorify you. I'm even much gladder that this glorification flows on, as it were. It is a quality that keeps operating in my soul, thanks to the inner form you gave me through Mother.

Therefore, I am immensely happy. Thanks to your grace, Daddy, my soul is as unstained as yesterday; it is even more beautiful, for you say yourself that love keeps on increasing. Then so does the beauty of the soul, isn't that right?

Saturday, March 12.
Father, many thanks for your exhortations and advice. Over and over you repeat in me, *non turbetur cor vestrum:* [Be not afraid to be holy, even if it is seen by others]. You glorify me in this way; you are for me a means to give grace to your fellow novices, to your fellowmen. With my Mother as your intermediary, you are powerful."

Daddy dear, I don't want to be afraid. By nature I'm scared, especially about what people may think. The only thing that's helped me so far was to keep a good disposition. That's another gift [I received] from you. When I commit myself to do something twice (like a good deed) it's hardly any trouble any more, for soon it becomes a habit. There are now some habits in my daily life like this that I don't even pay attention to, though initially they cost me a lot of trouble, for instance, prayer at table (in my Junior Seminary) in Weert.

Daddy, if only you are glorified as perfectly as possible by all people who existed, exist now, or will exist. My prayer is for *all* people without any limit in time. How wonderful [to know] that you are inexhaustible and almighty! I ask without limits through Mary, through Jesus, to you and for you because I ask for your glorification. Yes, I know you as you are. Accept me as your sacrificial victim.

Sunday, March 13.
Mother, you certainly offered Father that pain in my stomach at the Consecration? It's nothing, I know, but you can always decorate these unmentionable trifles of mine so nicely that they please Father. It reminds me of a St. Nicholas' feast day. Then, for example, a red herring was disguised in such a way that at first glance people could not see it was a herring. [As I recall] it had been decorated with ordinary potatoes. Father enjoys being offered something, not because he cares for a cold herring or an ordinary potato (my bungled work), but because my Mother has disguised these things so nicely. She puts a ribbon on them here or there and cleans them with particular care. Even if you throw away that potato, I don't mind it, dearest Daddy, provided you have been glorified by it. Even if it's just for one moment, that's good enough for me. Everything must glorify you, even if it is only through her love or because of Mother's intervention.

Monday, March 14.
Father dear, this morning during meditation, I actually thought: "How are things with me? Are they either arid or is the rest sweet?" I'm arid without feelings of devotion. That doesn't matter. I haven't had them for a long time. And my muddled imaginations don't matter either. They stay outside. Neither do feelings of vexation or getting annoyed with confrères matter. My will isn't in them.

Do you remember, Father, what I told you a few days ago? It was that all these thoughts are nothing before my will consents to them *expressly*. If I were to say freely to all those thoughts, "Yes, actually it is like that; he's as bad as I think," [that would be wrong]. But as long as I don't will this, I haven't consented to *anything*. It's just like a patient saying to a doctor who had to operate upon him without anaesthesia, "Doctor, I want you to amputate that leg." And if, because of the pain, I might say during the operation, "Stop it," he must *still* go on, for I want to get rid of that leg. It is the same with temptations.

But to return to the point I was trying to make: you see, Daddy, those little things might be a cross, if you did not let me repose on your Fatherly breast. But that rest is much deeper than the weight of the little cross of aridity. Now I don't know whether I have an arid rest or a sweet one. But that matters less. I leave it to you. You do with me just as you like. Really you must not look at me [at what I may feel].

Tuesday, March 15.
Father dear, things are going well again. That worry and distraction the first moment, when I became choir master, are over. Last night I dedicated everything to you through Mary. Now you are choirmaster for three months, so all will be well. You yourself know best how we should sing in your honor to please you. Now that it is your will that I do this for the next three months, the same theme wells up again: *Non turbetur cor vestrum* [Don't be afraid to do your job as well as you can.]

Daddy, I thank you most cordially through Mary for all the help you've given me as a supervisor of manual labor. Anything that is or was good [about what I did] there is *your* work. All the bungled things that came in between are my work. Whenever I lost "inwardness" and tried to do something without you, things went wrong. I must do the same about singing. I keep reposing very intimately on your breast.

Wednesday, March 16.
Father, last night I suddenly found a solution for the question that has worried me for so long. I thought, now I'm happy, yet arid and full of temptations. Everything seems at times to work against me. Failures that used to upset me (for example, breaking the toilet), things that would have discouraged and saddened me formerly, [don't any longer]. I'm resting happily on Father's breast in spite of all those things. What's the cause?

Last night the solution came from the thoughts of our second founder, Father Francis Libermann: "Who is united with Jesus (I prefer: 'Father,' and then I mean the whole Godhead) *always* lives happily, even if he is at Calvary, if only he likes to be there."

Yes, Daddy, that fits in, for whenever I have temptations I start smiling with happiness, because I may glorify you even more, but *through* Mary. So it is with aridity. When I feel it, I start smiling almost spontaneously to thank you. So I'm at ease now. Thus the knife cuts both ways: Mary has both formed me by letting me be with her at Calvary, and she has united me with Father. From this arises my state of happiness.

Thursday, March 17.
I'll be short today, Daddy, for I still have to say my Office, and besides, what am I to write of forty-five minutes of aridity? Still I was allowed to repose on your breast. Dear Mother, it really doesn't matter, aridity or no aridity. If only Daddy is glorified, that's all.

Friday March 18.
Dearest Father, this morning I was allowed to rest uninterruptedly again [on your breast]. The moment I got out of bed, I felt as if a flood of graces washed upon me [to help me] to serve you as well as possible today. I haven't got much else to write down, for my rest is arid. You and I hardly say a word. And what you say is so deep that I can only take it in with my reason and not express it in words. Thus you told me this morning how to behave as a choir-master so as not to disturb in the least my recollection or this rest. My soul has taken it all in, but I can't really write it down. With your grace I'll just try to do so.

Dearest Mother, yesterday again you could gather some of the earnings of this servant consecrated to you. They were the merits of small mortifications. Once again I say with all my heart: [I am your] servant and victim.

Saturday, March 19.
Now at last I've arrived at the conclusion as to why the state of my soul *is* arid rest. To be sure, I am in aridity, notwithstanding the deep peace and repose in God, which always makes me happy, however dry I may feel [inwardly]. Today was the feast of St. Joseph. I've hardly thought about him. What did I think of then? I don't know myself. Now and again I said: "Father, if only I glorify you," but for the rest there was nothing. Yet I'm happy. I'm not afraid at all. I have a Mother and Directress, who has led me up to now. She will also take me further, I hope and trust. I can rely on her.

Sunday, March 20.
Dearest Father, many thanks for your help and instruction. I went to see the Novice Master last night after evening prayer. I asked his advice about spiritual books. I disliked almost all of them, with some exceptions, for example, the life of St. Thérèse of Lisieux of the Child Jesus and that of Edward Poppe[59], but even then only as regards the last period of their lives.

---

59 Edward Poppe (1890-1924) was born on December 18, 1890 at Temse in the Flemish-speaking part of Belgium. He died on June 10, 1924 at Moerzeke. He was a priest at Ghent (1916-18) and then served as rector of a convent at Moerzeke. At the same time he was a spiritual director of seminarians in military service. His spirituality had a strongly eucharistic orientation. He took part in the "Eucharistic Crusade" a movement starting with the Norbertine Fathers in Belgium, to put the Communion decrees of Pius X more into practice, especially with children. His book of prayers, *Bij de Kindervriend* [*With the Children's Friend*] was considered a masterwork of pedagogic adaptation in his days. The process of his beatification has been started. More biographies were written of him after 1941, the year Rinus died. He may have read one of the earlier biographies as well as some works by Poppe himself.

I also asked [my Novice Master] how to behave in times of temptation. Here I must not remain passive. He thought this a bit risky, and thus you think the same. He talked for half an hour, all the while reassuring me that I needn't be afraid, not of the devil either. Neither, then, do you want me to fear him.

Last night, dear Father, I was allowed to glorify you through Mary and Jesus. I suffered a little out of love for you. I stayed awake until two. I was sick and had to go to the bathroom. At last, around 2:45 A.M., I fell asleep. Again I had to thank you on my knees, you, Father dear, and Mom, too. I used to become impatient and melancholy under such circumstances. Now I remained quietly united with you. I must admit you have changed my soul very much in a short time. Daddy dear, many thanks. Yet you can't rely on me at all.

Tuesday, March 22.
Mom, I really don't know what to write now. I wanted to ask Father this morning what to do to be faithful during the prayer of quiet, for the great St. Teresa [of Avila] says there are many who reach this [stage of prayer] but few who go on. Yet God wants them to go on. If they do not, then it's the fault of these souls themselves. It is they who place some obstacles in the way of the promptings of the Holy Spirit.

Therefore, sweet Mom, I've come to remind you that I'm a servant wholly consecrated to you. I am your unconditional property with all my faculties, including my will. Use them, I beg you. *Compel* me to follow God's promptings. I'm glad when you do so. You are fully entitled to do it.

Mom, you will do this for Rinus, won't you? You always say, and Father does too, that you love me so much. I beg both of you, to force me, as it were, to holiness. You can do me a great favor. Father will be the more glorified by greater holiness. So you see, all that is good shall return to you, Father dear. Please do so, I beg you, *sed fiat voluntas sancta tua* [but only your holy will be done].

Wednesday, March 23.
Dear Father, how thankful I am to you for making me suffer a little this morning. How concerned you are for me. Yesterday you again made me experience that mysterious "I don't know what" twice. It was a very profound insight while I see nothing. It was an unusually vehement love, both in the natural and in the supernatural [spheres]. It was especially a desire for suffering, for the Cross. Then I could not control my features. It seemed as if I were smiling fervently and gladly. My mouth twisted even more than usual. For these last few weeks there has been something quite unusual in the lines about my mouth. They are caused by your love and the repose that makes me so deeply happy. Twice that happiness came upon me last night, twice that heavy gust of love. Its

duration was only for a moment, but how long it lasted I don't know either. The happiness was so intense. Everything in me, my senses—in other words my soul and body—shared in that joy. I could imagine the happiness of heaven in this way; only the deep beholding that is now dark is then full of light, full of God himself who gives himself to be enjoyed. This morning Daddy showed me again I can do nothing on my own.

Thursday, March 24.
Dearest, if only you are glorified it doesn't matter if I am arid and feel as if I have not glorified you. I should be willing to suffer a little, too. The truth is, I suffer and enjoy myself simultaneously. On the one hand, I suffer from my aridity because I'd like so much to glorify you with Mother. On the other hand, I enjoy you in the undisturbed, though arid, repose in which my soul is and remains plunged.

Dearest Mother, those merits I was allowed to receive this morning, by virtue of that little drop of suffering, are yours. Do with them what you will. I haven't got any special intentions any more, not even for my parents. I can only beg for grace for them so that they may glorify God as perfectly as possible. What you want to do with your consecrated servant's merits is all the same to me. You already do everything to promote God's honor, to assure that he is glorified everywhere and always, by everybody. What more useful things can be done with my small good works and mortifications than what you want to do with them? For your will was fully enclosed in God's will, already during your life, and even more so after your death.

Friday, March 25.
I have not done much more than laugh and rest for ninety minutes. Father doesn't desire more. I was also allowed to receive many graces today, I don't doubt that for a second. They were surely not felt consolations. That's way in the past by now. This morning I renewed the two dedications of consecrated servanthood and sacrificial victim. I'm also as morally certain as one can be that through God's grace my soul is now in an absolutely unstained state. It wouldn't even surprise me that, if I were allowed to die now, I would not have to go to purgatory. Unfortunately, this state doesn't last long, for in a few hours there may be stains on my soul again. Yet, many thanks for this grace, dearest Father, because it gives me even more joy and trust in you. Still I shouldn't rely too much on it (I mean on this state of soul), for I might get peevish and discouraged if it changes again. So I just say, "Don't say anything." After all, if Daddy works in me and if I repose in him, if I don't own a thing and have yielded everything to Mary, why should I worry? I must keep saying, here and now (*hic et nunc*). I should glorify God always. Neither the past nor the future interest me. *Now*, Father

dear. Then I will never be worried about the future or the past, nor [will I] be hurt in self-love. I'll always glorify you *now*. It seems to me this will never cause [me] to worry, Daddy.

Sunday, March 27.
How it grieves me that I'm still so preoccupied with singing in spite of all my efforts and my repeated utterances that I leave everything to you. [Why fuss], especially since you gave me such a good idea about [how to conduct] the choir practice and about [how to give] a good performance? It's true, you want me to be the choir master. Otherwise the Novice Master would not have given me the job. I also may apply all my talent to raise the [quality of] the Gregorian Chant to as high a level as possible. But I do so and will only do so to promote your honor! Now I'm afraid I'm going to put myself into the foreground since time and again I'm preoccupied with the singing.

"Look at that," you will say. "That tiny tot has received everything from me. At first, he devotes himself to the task I have set before him, to my greater honor. That little being who literally cannot do anything, now prides himself on his imaginary success as if everything has been achieved by his power. Quickly, stick a pin through that swollen little frog." If you think this, you are perfectly right, Father. Shall we make a deal: if things turn out well, I accept that you will send me a proportionate humiliation to keep me in balance. If, on the other hand, everything goes wrong, then I'll think, *Daddy shows me what a nothing I am on my own, so what right do I have to be proud when things go well again.* Above all, let me stay recollected and reposed in you. Feelings don't count, and certainly not contemptuous feelings about the likes of me. I should be a realist in the true sense of the word. But, then, I'm still your child.

Realistically, God lives in me and I in God. God is in my confrères as well. They all act and move by him and for him. It's completely clear! Furthermore, there's an eternity [that awaits us]. All people who have existed before us will either praise or curse you forever. It's true, isn't it! At Holy Communion Jesus Christ, God and man, comes to my being in the shape of bread. Again [this is] as true as anything can be true. Ah, Father!

Monday, March 28.
Infinitely dear Father, I'll only surrender and not resist. Whatever you want, do it. *Non turbetur cor vestrum*. Take me, if it pleases you. Press my deformed, small, imperfect soul to your heart. Do it now. I must confess I'm immensely happy at the very thought of my unfathomable unworthiness. Wickedness makes me hesitate somewhat to let myself be immersed by you in your Love and your Reason. In a word, let me be plunged into your being and come forth again, shining with new

grace and terrifying to the devils. [Let me be] a joy to my Mom and all my holy patron saints and my Holy Guardian Angel as well. That my dearest Father wants to unite so intimately with me is the fruit of their labor. I can do nothing but stammer a word of thanks to so much love and devotion on the part of my God and my holy patrons. I stand before them embarrassed by the depth of my weakness. All those saints don't even seem to pay attention to it. They ask just as if I, too, belong to their race. How wrong they are! I defy St. Francis of Assisi, St. Thérèse of the Child Jesus, and indeed all the other saints, who wrote that they were among the worst sinners. I challenge all of them together. They would not have dared to write that they were the worst sinners if they had known me as I am. In proportion to all the graces God has granted to me, I believe they would not have dared to say such a thing [of themselves]. If they had, I would say, "You don't know me. You think of me as much better than I am."

Tuesday, March 29.
Love's rest, intimate love's rest. Daddy, the fruit I was allowed to gather from your imprint of love the night before yesterday is more love for my brothers. I now see so many good things in my confrères that I'm ashamed when I remember my judgments of the past and of not so long ago either. This morning after Holy Communion I could see all their good qualities, one by one, beginning with the Fathers. And not just "he *may* be . . . ," but with plain facts from daily life. Likewise with all the novices. I'm really glad about this, Father dear, for "you will know the tree by its fruits." Now I'm not worried either about self-deception when you visit me.

Dearest Mother, again I'm standing before you inundated with new graces. Each Holy Communion grants me tremendous blessings—every time more in proportion to what I already received. For example, always 30 percent more. That 30 percent is added to the capital, so the 30 percent of the next day increases even more, and so on. Also during the day even more grace is added. The Stewardess [Mary] of my estate knows a thing or two about "finances"! I'm only a rich man's crazy son, who hasn't the remotest idea of what my Father owns. He leaves everything to his Stewardess, but that's the most sensible thing he could do.

Wednesday, March 30.
Most dearest Father, many thanks for the new graces. This morning you consoled me. I was sad that you were so much blasphemed and insulted. Then you explained to me quietly how everything fits together. Among other things the devil can't offend you any more because he is bound to [hate you]. So *free will* isn't there any more [for him]. With all his eternal hatred of you, he does nothing else than [paradoxically] glorify your justice. So there is a huge difference between his

blasphemy and the voluntary blasphemy of man. [Human blasphemy] would make God die if he were mortal. It is, therefore, an infinite offense to his Majesty. This is totally different from the much more vehement but compelled blasphemy by Satan. Therewith, he does not offend you but glorify you. You mock him. This is also Satan's great fury and powerlessness. He is bound to glorify you through the blasphemies his condition involves inevitably.

If the matter is considered from that angle, it alters the situation somewhat. For Satan disseminates his hatred of God (which is a glorification of God's justice) among people. They commit real blasphemy by accepting his hatred of God. Therefore, if in Russia young people are brought up so systematically without God, under the influence of the devil, there will be a great many cases in which people have little or no guilt. You always know how to draw good out of evil, so I'm not afraid for the salvation of many Russians. Prayer and the grace of final perseverance are assured for them, too, aren't they, Father?

Thursday, March 31.
Dearest, you make me more and more at home with a life of intimate union with you. It's becoming a need. Every morning I'm so glad again to be at your service. I want to serve you with the help of your grace to the best of my ability. In other words, I will to do your holy will.

Daddy, I always forget those small mortifications I do during the day. You always ignore my daily failings, but I don't. The more favors and graces you grant, the more I'll remind you of them. I keep saying: "Father, do be careful, for I'm certainly not to be relied on. I can betray you in a moment. I'm capable of every evil. Be merciful to me and keep me from falling." I'll go on saying that, Father.

Friday, April 1.
Dear Father, may I thank you again for a new grace of which I was not yet aware. Perhaps it was another outcome of your March 27 visit. Then I received the grace of appreciation of my brothers. It has become easy for me to see their good qualities. This grace may now work for me in the opposite direction. For this morning after Holy Communion I was serious when I longed to be despised. Formerly I meant that, as a Christian and a clergyperson, I would be considered mad by the world due to my "ridiculous" way of dressing and living. Now I long to be looked down upon by my brothers. I long to be known by all of them just the way I am. What contempt and dislike of me would there then be!

This morning I was able to apply this new grace immediately to those little crosses. They are pinpricks, compared to the mortifications of the Desert Fathers. Today, adoration of the exposed Blessed Sacrament! My Father told me to make more sacrifices. Dearest, if you help me, I'm willing to try. Obedience above all! I remain united with you inwardly through everything. I want to beg for this grace of yours once more today.

Saturday, April 2.
Mary, dearest Mother, is it safe to let me walk about with such treasures? You'd better keep a sharp lookout. The servant consecrated to you doesn't do anything with those graces. For he is so lazy.

Dear Daddy, again my love of you and of all my neighbors has increased, thanks to your visit yesterday afternoon. I can't control myself. I must write about my love.

Mother, protect my weak hand. Most dearest Daddy, you in me, but, above all, I in you. I love you. I don't know how to express what my love is. But you know everything. You understand. You want the love of my reason and of my love-will in one movement of my soul.

Dearest Father, I'm beginning to will and reason as you like me to do. I'm most grateful for this [grace]. My dearest, my most dearest Father, what do you want from Rinus? Sacrifices? Also those that I feel physically? Then give me . . . your grace. I'm willing to try. Pain? Suffering? You're welcome! *Fiat voluntas tua* [Your will, not mine, be done]. I accept everything with love and supernatural joy. You must give me the grace [I need]. Otherwise I can do nothing. Contempt? You're welcome. Also out of love for you. Here my nature is most reluctant, but the love of being despised has arrived at last. It is a choice grace in spite of my reluctance.

Sunday, April 3.
Today I received only Holy Communion (there was no early Mass), for Father Superior is not home. There will be a High Mass presently. Now I have eaten a little lamb [the Body of Christ], already slaughtered for my sake, as Edward Poppe would say (although I do not agree completely with that thought). The holy hosts were consecrated during [an earlier] Sacrifice of the Mass. One might say, in a way of speaking, that the lamb is three days old. Before and during Holy Communion, I also united myself with all the Holy Masses that were being said [anywhere]. That's a good thing to do, isn't it, Father dear? Mom, don't leave me in a lurch, even if your goal has been attained to some degree, I mean the goal of bringing me nearer to God. I'm not to be relied on in anything.

If only I could make others love you as I love you.

✠

Monday, April 4.
Father dear, now you've seen again how weak, and how little recollected I am, when something special happens, and especially when it is soon to happen. You suggested to me yesterday (the idea is not mine but yours) to offer Brother Winoc [the cook of the Novitiate] a live chicken tomorrow. Now, when I think of it, I begin to smile every time.[60] Father dear, now you should also make the bird start cackling. Please do! That's much funnier, isn't it? Your holy will be done. If it fails completely, I really don't care at all, at least not for myself. I only think it would be a shame if all those good fathers, brothers, and novices would not enjoy themselves. For the idea is yours. So it will be your fault if it fails. But no more concern about that! Everything will be fine. Your ideas aren't the worst, are they Father? If it fails you can surely blame me. [I'm the one] who's wrong, my Love. My growing love!

What grace, Father dear! I cannot possibly control myself any longer. It must flow out from me. If I only could make others love you as I love you. If only you would will that, Father, you would see every human being serving and glorifying you more than I am doing now. It's really true, Father. Remember not only am I so weak: I'm also not to be relied on very much either.

Tuesday, April 5.
Today I was again permitted to suffer a little for you. That's good! You are being glorified as perfectly as possible. I only need to cling to your holy will, to do so faithfully and leave the rest to you. Let all people despise me; they'll never [be able to despise me] enough. Only you can reprimand me as I deserve, for you know everything. If all people knew what you know of me, dearest Father, they would spit into my insolent, hypocritical face. All their hatred of me would tend to your glorification, since they hate in me what you hate in me. What else but my sins?

---

60 This incident with the live chicken offers another interesting example of how Rinus tried to be pleasing and entertaining to his confrères. What he may not have realized was the unavoidable impression he made on them that he was somehow different from them in spite of all his love-inspired attempts to come across as "a regular guy." His self-accusations in his diary about sometimes "boasting" to be interesting during recreation may come from the same predicament: an almost desperate attempt to break through this invisible wall of experiences, seemingly different from those of others. An example I personally remember is a trick meant to amuse an audience. He had taught himself to put a shaving blade in his mouth and to hold it between his teeth without cutting himself.

Wednesday, April 6.
Mother, this morning for your sake I fought against distractions and especially against temptations of impurity. Many thanks, Daddy, for the victory I gained with your help and grace. Foolish devil, you do see, don't you, that your attacks only result in victory for me as long as I'm united with such a loving Almighty God and Father. And, after each victory, more merits (all of which are for Mother, of course); more sanctifying grace (especially the deepening guidance of the Holy Spirit and his seven gifts); more will power and strengthening (more actual grace for the next battle).

My deeply beloved God, possessed by me. It has become such a habit and a need of mine to pray always (that is, to speak to you) that I also do this when I'm distracted. The distraction consists really in changing the subject [of my thoughts], just like people first talk about spiritual matters but imperceptibly slip into temporal and profane subjects. They keep conversing, even if they have wandered from their former subject, that's all. Is that bad, Father?

Thursday, April 7.
Dear Daddy, this morning you let me have a look into your Being. Now light was shed especially on the Holy Spirit. I see that you wanted to teach me this [truth] in another, more elevated way. Although, thanks to your elucidation, I understand more about it than I did prior to this morning, yet I do not sense the same "dark" clarity here. [I know] this sounds contradictory, yet I must put it this way. You gave me [that kind of clarity] about the Word, the Second Person of the Most Holy Trinity. Let me leave this topic now because I much more love you than I know you, [intellectually speaking].

Dearest, most dearest Love. Yesterday you put your seal under that "blood contract" between us. You granted me your love-imprinting gifts. These enable me to fulfill [my part of the] contract as perfectly as possible.

Mom, my dear, good Mom, what do you want from your consecrated servant? Everything God wants. What does Father want? Everything he tells me through the [ecclesial] authorities. So [I must] obey everybody who has [legitimate authority] over me, no matter how much or how little. As a matter of fact this [principle] applies to all people. They are God's children. I am his (and consequently also his children's) attending servant.

Friday, April 8.
I really don't know what you spoke to me about this morning, Dearest. I only know that you did speak. Maybe I'll find out [what you said] later during the day. For you haven't spoken lately without giving me the grace [to grasp] what you are telling me. My Father, I'm always trying

to find new words to express my love for you and, especially, new mortifications. The thirst to suffer for you keeps increasing. It's all the work of grace. I hope to cooperate well. I want to do what you impel me to do, but, more importantly, I [want you] to make me do whatever you want, to get rid of whatever you want me to discard. Above all, [I must] remain wholly receptive, out of love for you.

I don't know any more what to write. I feel such a great urge welling up in me toward you. It is still vague. It only gets more clearly defined insofar as you seize me. Life truly will become a cross to me after some time. I say beforehand that I am willing to bear it gladly out of love for you. Your holy will be done. If you want me to go on living, even for a long time, I say, "Fine, excellent" to that. You can will nothing but your own glorification. That's what I will too, urged on by your grace. In this regard, you and I are in exact conformity, aren't we Father? Make me more and more fit to glorify you.

Saturday, April 9.
This morning I [prayed] without feeling, but I don't care, if only you are glorified. I'm not going to pray to obtain consolations (even if they offer the purest joy and peace on earth). If it pleases you to give me again the [gift of] infused contemplation, thank you, Dearest. If not, that's fine with me, too. I won't love you any less for it, for Rinus is worth nothing.

Last night I talked about humility with my confrères. They also told me (more people say so) that I have a natural affinity for philosophy. Whatever may be true of that [observation], it left me completely cold. I was in exactly the same mood as last night when they humiliated me. Yes, I was also glad then. My gift for philosophy is God's work. By saying this, they glorified God. I was glad when it was said later on that I wasn't a good choir master and that I was inconsistent. That's what *I* am. I'm even worse than they told me. It seemed best to accept everything without saying anything. Dearest Daddy, many thanks for the grace of granting me this [humiliation]. Help me more and more.

Sunday, April 10.
My all! I feel "drunk" just by thinking of you. Every time I make a mistake, you are always at once willing to forgive me, if only I go on! I coyly return the favor. Whenever I do something wrong, I do penance at once, with the help of your grace. When you ask me about that, I don't know any more what to say. You just seem to ignore my sins. How good you are!

Monday, April 11.
To show me once more what a nothing I am, you let me wander distractedly in my imagination. So be it. Also in aridity you are glorified.

If only that happens, then for the rest, nothing matters. Yet you did not make [the aridity] last for [the whole] forty-five minute [meditation]. New thoughts arose based on what you let me know yesterday. [I pondered] the place of the devils and the damned in relation to you. What is the real difference between their state and that of the blessed! This question came up. And you were so good as to help me. I believe that the devil, too, with his reason and will is completely pervaded by your spirit, reason, and will (for you are omnipresent), [but the devil is utterly self-centered]. By contrast, the blessed, with their spirit and its attributes, lose themselves completely in you. They forget themselves since they see even more infinitely present in you what they see in themselves. How great must be their happiness to praise you, infinitely, eternally. When, Father, [shall their beatific vision] be mine?

Tuesday, April 12.
Again I must accuse myself to you of weakness, dear Daddy! Last night the Novice Master summed up a list of defects that are incompatible with religious life. I discovered I had *all* of them in me, up to the very last one: vanity; lust for power; pride; over sensitivity; suspiciousness; reticence; using little [attention-getting] tricks; sensuality (for instance, thinking of nice food); being filled with trite worries. These are only a few. I would have stood up at once to say that I was unfit for the religious life. But the Novice Master added, "This means, of course, if they are not fought against, in other words, if God's grace is not in us." Thanks to Father's goodness, he *is* there with his grace to improve me. But this [truth] gives even clearer proof that everything comes from him. I am nothing; God is all.

Wednesday, April 13.
Fortunately, I am one day nearer to death, dear Daddy. You have told me so much about heaven already. You've given me so much to enjoy of yourself, [so many reasons] to glorify you lately, that I almost get homesick. Once again I repeat, "I'll wait as long as you wish." I only want your own glorification. . . . Even if I had nothing else in heaven but your love, and even if you had only a small portion of my love, the glory of heaven would be the same. Even if I suffered unbearable pains, I would still be content. And, if I knew besides, that this promoted your honor, I would suffer eagerly.

Father dear, tonight we chant the Matins and Lauds of the Holy Week. Be glorified in everything. Even if the music doesn't always sound so good, I don't mind it so much now. My only goal is your honor, not the [satisfied] feeling I get when everything goes right. You do completely as you think fair. Don't take notice of me.

Dearest Jesus, my Elder Brother, I hope I may again receive you presently in Holy Communion. Do you mind if I say hardly anything besides "Dearest Jesus. You are my Mediator. You must glorify the Father for my sake, not only *for mine* but for *all* of humanity." Then I swallow you and say, "Dearest Jesus, I give you to the Father *in* me." Mother is there, too, with her spiritual presence. What else am I to do? Jesus is glorified infinitely, and so is Father by their mutual relations in me. Mother is as happy as can be, too.

Thursday, April 14.
Dearest Father, although you told me not to mention my great ingratitude, I can't help but repeat it all the same. The whole of last night I told rather "unsavory" jokes—to put it mildly—and I heard them told. Is that any language for a novice? For somebody who wants to become holy? Father, you saw that I regretted it. I also did some penance for it with the help of your grace. You tell me not to dwell on it any more, or else self-love becomes an issue. So I'll stay mum about it.

Thursday, April 21.
Many thanks, dearest Father. My letter was sent to Father Berkers. I told him everything. [I wrote to him that] I was permitted to make some small sacrifices and was advised to say many prayers and also that I tried to do all things in such a way as to glorify God the most. If only *that* happens, I can leave the rest to you. The reply [of Father Berkers] is [for me] your voice. I'll obey. Make me holy, as holy as you desire me to be. Saints can glorify you much more perfectly than less holy people could.

Please Daddy, Rinus likes this growing intimacy with you so much. Mother helps me, I feel sure. Jesus also gives me more and more strength and graces in Holy Communion and Holy Mass. Everything on your side is ready. If only you will now grant me an abundance of actual graces, I hope to cooperate better than ever. [The grace] has to come from you. I only wait for the movements of your holy will. Use your superior power over me. I have surrendered completely to you once and for all. Suffering grief for you is a delightful suffering because I love you so deeply. All this is not my work but yours, Daddy.

Friday, May 6.
My only Father, this morning after Holy Communion you gave me much to think about for my sermonette on the evening of Mary. To say what you prompt me to say, I need as much grace as you dare to give me. I'm only nineteen! I stand there without prestige or dignity. I stand there with all my faults and bad examples. In a word, the person who delivers the sermon stands in complete contrast to the words he speaks. I do not say my words but yours. With the help of your grace, I'll make many sacrifices to prepare for it. I'll pray a lot to give you the chance

to pour out graces on my fellow novices. Believe me, I'm not asking for success!

Even if I get stuck in the middle of my speech, even if it is most miserable as regards diction, attitude, and form, if you are glorified by it, [that is enough]. If only one thought of one listener went to you [because of it] or if one new resolution would be made, then what is said would be far beyond the level of speech. Grace is unspeakably high above those natural impulses that are roused by a glowing speech. If only I might be the instrument to [be used by you] to grant others your grace! I'm sure, Father dear, the sermon will bear fruit because the soil [in which it is planted] is much better than the rock-garden that is my [contribution].

Dearest, most dearest Mother, I'm so glad I may speak of you and show you my servile and childlike love. I'm firmly convinced I can't do this on my own. I'm even less capable of making my words bear fruit. (After all, the aim of my sermonette is to increase Father's external glory.)[61]

✠

I yearn to be more, and more an incarnation of Jesus Christ.

✠

Saturday, May 7.

Jesus, my Lord and my God, this morning I could offer you nothing at all but good will. That gift, too, I had first received from you. I was aware, both during meditation and the Holy Sacrifice of the Mass and at Holy Communion, that I'd like to do *everything* God, my Father, present in me, wants me to do. I didn't know what else to say. Yet I do not grieve at all. Though it is painful at times, I long to be more and more intensely holy and always holier. I yearn to be more and more an incarnation of Jesus Christ. Many thanks for the grace to be able to experience that gift, dear Father! Yes, I love you (I still *will* you). Yes, I want to do everything, and anything for you, if only you are glorified. All is quiet in me. Sleep on, dearest Father. You've made me rest in you so often.

---

61 In the formation theology Rinus helped to initiate, Father's inner glory is distinguished from the unfolding epiphany of his external glory. We cannot add or subtract anything of the eternal glory that God is. We are called, however, to share co-formatively in the unfolding epiphany of his glory in the realms of creation, redemption, and transformation by the Holy Spirit.

Nothing, *nihil, nichts, rien, niets*, but your holy will be done. I feel that by your grace I'd like to do everything you will or want me to do. For the rest I only beg *adveniat regnum tuum* [Your kingdom come]. You are everything; I am nothing. Even now I'm still smiling. I don't meditate any more for *my* own pleasure, do I? Dear Daddy, it's good that way, so good. With your help, [show me the way] to greater holiness today. Please, Dearest, help me.

Tuesday, May 10.
My dearest Father, many thanks for all your graces. This morning you invited me again to fly, as it were, higher and higher on the way to holiness. It has now become a burning thirst, a yearning, a craving for intimate union beyond words with you. Here I identify in my mind's eye with Edward Poppe. This morning you asked me, "What is this interest of yours in him?" To tell the truth, Dearest, he speaks my Dutch language. He is of the same ethnic background. In terms of our character, we have a lot in common. He was tall (so the idea that saints are always slightly shrunk, little men is wrong). He had the same problems I have (at feasts and parties, for instance, he had to overcome his fear of what people would think of him). He didn't smoke or drink alcohol. We have more points in common, but I must say that (in one sense) I am ahead of him; I mean that you seem to have given your great gifts sooner to me than to him. He began this abandoned way when he was already a priest, at least I think so.

How ashamed I am to stand in his company. With more gifts, and with the same dear Father who guides me, *I yield* fewer results. But I won't despair. With Mary, my Directress [I'll go on] to battle!

Wednesday May 11.
Dearest Father, how you torment me through this feeling of homesickness for you! It grows stronger every day. The worst thing is, Mother is joining in it, too. She makes me more and more thirsty for you, my own dear everything, for you the final end of my desire. You, my most dearest Father. If you allow me to come to you now, I promise to be very quiet in heaven, to remain unnoticed. I'll possess you for eternity and I'll glorify you forever. *Sed non mea voluntas sed tua fiat* [Not my will but yours be done].

Mother, perhaps I'll be permitted to be at your court as your youngest, least important, and most useless servant. Maybe? Yes? Yes. I'm content with the least place, if only Father and Mother are glorified and honored as much as they deserve. If only my most dearest Father is adored by all creatures insofar as possible [I'm content]. Then all will be well. Even if I wasn't allowed to be [a member] of Mother's court, as a punishment for my wicked cowardice [on earth]; even if I could only see and greet her from a distance; even if she would not look at me at all, even then I would still love her.

Dearest Mommy, I thank Jesus for the love of you he has instilled in my heart. Yes, even if I am your child and even if you are my dearest Mother, I would still say to you, "I love you with a love that I have received, for, left on my own, I might not even believe in you!" Can't you see, Dearest, that my own self, my own nature, is materialistic? That by nature I might be a dyed-in-the-wool communist! Fortunately God has won me over totally.

Thursday, May 12.
Dearest Father, I surrender completely to you. What now happens to me, I don't know myself. I doubt [myself] in everything. Every time the thought occurs, in my imagination, that I've deceived my Father Confessor or my Novice Master, but, thanks to your grace, I reject it. Was everything a deception on my side (or just something that comes out of me spontaneously)? Yet when I said it or wrote it down, I had to claim it as my own insight. I thought in the presence of God and before my crucifix that what I had said or written was the truth. Thank God, I have not lost the [gift of] high and deep rest [in God]. Although everything is turned upside down in the lower part of my soul and in my human nature, [I'm at rest]. Perhaps [these thoughts] are trials given by you to both punish [and teach] me. No doubt I deserved punishment for not cooperating with grace. Had I cooperated, I would not be so homesick now. Neither would I have that gnawing, painful longing for you, my one good and ultimate aim. Who can satisfy [this homesickness]? Only he who is my final aim itself, hence only you, my dearest Daddy.

Friday, May 13.
Last night it was read [in the refectory] about Father Doyle [a Jesuit chaplain known for his practice of ejaculatory prayer] that he noted down all his good deeds every day. I want to do the same, out of love for you. I'll start tonight, [I'll do it] but only for *one* day, one ordinary day. I hope to go through it as if it were any other day. So tonight I'll start to write down everything!

Dearest Mother, yesterday I heard the news that Ben [Rinus' brother] had been taken to the hospital for his appendicitis. Is it selfish of me to say that [I care] but that also in a way his condition does not concern me personally since I said at once, "Your holy will be done, my Father?" Then I remained as quiet and cheerful as before. Is not [this holy equanimity, this absolute trust] a grace I received from God through Mary's mediation? I really don't know. I like Ben very much, and after Jantje [their youngest brother] he most likes me, I know. Why is it, then, that I would like, perhaps selfishly, to consider only my own physical suffering as something painful? You know, don't you, that I'm capable of enduring anything [for your sake]? So I also dare to say to you: "Give me his pain, if that is your will." Even if I had to be operated upon, I think I would still say now, *Fiat voluntas tua* [Your will be done], my God. What if that really happened? All things considered, I'm not so sure. If only you are glorified as perfectly as possible, all will be well. I also surrender to you that feeling of homesickness for you. If you leave me in aridity, that, too, is good, Father.

Saturday May 14.
It's really nothing, Father dear, but I could do nothing at all this morning. Except I love you. Through your grace I will whatever you want or might want from me. Help me also to be more generous during the day. I can't ask for more, can I, Mother? Perhaps I'm also to blame for this aridity. I thought I could practice on the organ, but now I see I was absolutely wrong. Tinkering with one's hands does not yet make for a decent accompaniment! I'll leave the matter to Mother. For the rest everything is good. God is all; man is nothing—and Frater Scholtes is even less than nothing—*nihil nihilorum* [nothing of all nothings.] Through his sins he wallows in negatives. Father, [help me] please!

Sunday, May 15.
Today is a day of glory for my Mother and my Directress. The whole deanery [of the town of Gennep where the Novitiate was located] will be dedicated to her. Most dearest Mom, it's never enough [to honor you], not even if everybody adorned their [feet] with small blue-and-white or yellow-and-white flags. "His Most Reverend Excellency," Frater Scholtes, will also add luster to the procession today by his [loyal] presence.

Woe is to me, dearest Father! I was late this morning. I had to go down on my knees. Hardly had I knelt down when you got to me again. Not so intensely as those twelve times of [sensing] your certain presence. Yet you united yourself with me. You are waiting for me everywhere. I'd almost think you were in love with me. Don't you remember how often I offended you yesterday? I could not even make a few small sacrifices for you, such as not drinking water after manual labor and physical exercise! And, then, what gluttony [in me] when I did drink! Out of love for you I also tied my hands to the bed with little ropes so that I would be obliged to sleep with my hands *above* the blanket. Yes indeed! Frater Scholtes, that "brave" Frater Scholtes, got scared. After sighing in handcuffs for forty-five minutes, he broke them and fell asleep as usual. A pasteboard knight, don't you think so, dear Mom?

Monday, May 16.
Yesterday the whole deanery was dedicated to Mary. I also had to walk in the procession. Thanks be to you, Father, I could remain united with

Jesus and Mary. Otherwise I would not have known how to keep a straight face. There were so many "young daughters" [a Catholic youth group]. For safety's sake I refrained from looking up when we (the clergy) had to walk between a double line of the Catholic young women from the organization, who gave the Roman salute. You never know, I'm such a funny clown. Well, it's over now. Yesterday I also found by experience that the way of St. Thérèse—to eat out of love, whatever comes at table—doesn't always work for me. I have to learn to award myself in nothing and to mortify myself in everything. Dearest, if only you would help me.

Tuesday, May 17.
It's still on the quiet side inside me. My feelings meant nothing. I slept badly. All that was of no avail! Father gave me grace to serve him anyway. I *want* him and I possess him, that is a fact. No feeling is necessary in this regard. Presently, I may attend another Holy Mass and perhaps receive Holy Communion. How glad I am about that. Out of love, out of deeply willed love for my Father, I beg him in Jesus Christ's name for abundant graces to keep smiling all the time.

I don't show my inner joy because I'm afraid of what people will think. Every time Mother exhorts me not to be afraid. *Non turbetur cor vestrum neque formidet. Creditis in Deo, et hic credite*. [You believe in God, believe also in this.] A ton of grace is needed [to overcome fear]. Sacrifice, yes, I am a sacrifice of love. I feel more and more that my Father has accepted me.

Wednesday May 18 (On the same).
But it's only because I've offered myself through and in Mary. I'm so glad I'm allowed to suffer, and to suffer a lot. Yes! I am and have been [suffering] a great deal lately. Yet I'm so quiet, so intimately united with Father. My nature suffers much, indeed very much. Yet I really don't care at all, Dearest. Everything that is your holy will I accept with pleasure. I won't ask for anything, neither for more nor less suffering. Ask for nothing, refuse nothing.

Dearest, yes I want and can do so only by the power of your will. It's because I'm possessed by you. Just as formerly people possessed by the devil were thrown into water or fire by him—and they could do nothing about it—likewise you throw me into suffering and self-denial. You press so urgently that I can't resist any longer without becoming unhappy. Yet this [urgency to love] doesn't cause any scrupulosity, for you are and remain an infinitely merciful God and a dearest Father for your child. I remain the nought, the nothing, that should be much more distrusted as he receives more gifts of grace from you. You can still expect ingratitude and unfaithfulness from me. My heart shrinks as I say so, but I'd better warn you beforehand. After your giving me enough good things for a whole lifetime, after living in me without interruption and dying for me, I'm still liable to turn my back on you and to deny you. Alas, it's true!

Thursday, May 19.
This morning I haven't got anything to write down because there isn't anything. I want everything God wants. I was allowed to do some small mortifications, and beyond these, there was nothing. But what does it matter? In the highest point of the will, everything is engulfed in Father. This is such a grace. Furthermore, I feel exhorted to cooperate well with grace today. That's all. It will do. Everything out of love for you!

Friday, May 20.
Tomorrow I may go on a pilgrimage to Heijen [a town quite a distance from the Novitiate] in honor of Mary. There's a Lourdes grotto there. The intention of our pilgrimage is to obtain the grace of a good retreat. O love, O love, I can't write sensibly about love any more!

Mother, what have you been up to with me? From where have I received that fire? I would like to do all the acts of penance of the saints out of love for Jesus and my dear Daddy. Alas, I'm powerless, but no, love isn't powerless. I might give myself [credit for] pinpricks, but never for great things. Love must supply what is lacking in my will or my consent.

Father, you are dear beyond words! As I'm writing this, my nature is cold, both inwardly and outwardly—nothing, absolutely nothing, no feeling. Yet I feel my *will* glowing with love. Everything, everything, absolutely everything you want, your sacrificial victim wants too, dearest Father. This isn't mine but Mary's work. She has branded the servant consecrated to her. It is a way of punishing him for all his cowardice and faithlessness. [He has] indeed been thrown, with hands and feet tied, into God's love-furnace. Now I must glow whether I like it or not. Many thanks, Mother. It isn't time yet for Holy Mass and Holy Communion! Then Father will be glorified perfectly. How I enjoy being present at Holy Mass. God is glorified perfectly in Jesus Christ. Amen!

Saturday, May 21.
This morning we went on pilgrimage. It was the ideal weather for it! Bleak and wet! I also saw the Novice Master at my usual direction time. He asked me about my way of meditating, and so on. "I may continue as usual," he said. Many thanks, dearest Father. Now, [I can] go forward filled with courage, of course, with your help. Otherwise I needn't try!

Deeply beloved, most dearest Father. My all, "my breath," as my Novice Master said so well. My homesickness, my final aim, my most

Dearest. Everything, O Eternal Being. I don't know how to express my love. I love you as much as a limited being like me can love you. I take delight in being tormented, as it were, in being squeezed dry by your love. The tiniest little fiber that still clings to my creaturehood, I must cut out! You are my tormentor, but what a loving, deeply tender tormentor [you are]! You want everything. Everything, literally everything, also my faults, and beforehand any bad thing I might do.

Ah, Dearest, do take everything. It has been yours for a long time anyway. Squeeze me. Press me. I'm glad to be touched under your hands through Mary. Shouldn't I be thanking her [all of the time]? She has shown me the shortest way to the Father. Dearest Mother, now you see what you've done: You've made a human soul drunk with love for her God. Many thanks for this! And yet how spiritual is that intoxication. My body, yes, my body and my natural feelings are so wholly and differently disposed.

Thursday, May 26. Ascension of Jesus.
Tonight [there will] probably be adoration with exposition of the Blessed Sacrament. I am really happy about this, since there will be more [chances] for thoughts and feelings of love to come up for you. If I consider everything, all the movements of nature and and grace in me, then I see there's a vast difference between the two. My will (absorbed, as it were, by you) is full of your holy will. My nature draws me to creatures, to a girl, in this case with a strong natural urge. The reasoning [power] of the soul has also been absorbed by you. It still hurts occasionally, but that is caused by its feeling out of its element, I think. Anyway, it's always only for a moment, Dearest.

Friday, May 27.
My most beloved Bridegroom-to-be, many thanks for your grace tonight. My turn to pray [before the Blessed Sacrament] was from 3:30 to 4:30 A.M. After that time we all were allowed to pray in our rooms for half an hour. I thought that wouldn't be easy, but you see, Rinus, it always goes well when Jesus helps. Dearest, we did not say much to each other. Fiancées don't do that either when [they are] dreaming in the moonlight, do they? Yet beforehand I had sacrificed all pleasure and happiness to you. Indeed, I need not repeat this to you any more. I haven't had consolations or feelings (in the physical senses) for a long time now. But I was allowed to suffer a little last night as I fell sleep. It seemed I had a kind of death-struggle. My heart was beating like mad. I pressed my crucifix firmly to it to show Jesus that my love was for him alone. I was too weak even to [resist] drinking some water. I did something reasonable, so, in this sense, it is not without some merit. I could have glorified you more by *not* doing so. Anyway, that's the way I am: selfish.

During their time of engagement, the two engaged people get to know each other's characters better: I yours, you mine. I'd better say nothing. If I sum up my bad points, I'll still say less than the truth. Tonight I said to you: "Dearest, the more beautiful and fruitful you make me, the more glory you will have. The worse the material is from which a thing of beauty is made, the more its Maker is praised." That's as clear as the daylight. Likewise with me. How can I now say (also practically) that I *myself* act or do God's holy will?

Sunday, May 29.
Dearest, my deeply beloved All. Next week we will have a feast, our espousal festivity! How happy I am. Through all aridity and distractions, I have known that my soul's life is far *above* the life of the senses. It's becoming more and more so. For, just like St. Paul, "I discover in my body a fight against the spirit, another law. And I don't want (as a body) the good I must do but the evil that I, the higher soul, don't want." How glad I am whenever I think, for instance, "Now, at this moment while I'm writing, I glorify God more, or rather, God glorifies himself more through his wretched creature, as, for example, [he did] last night." Always sanctifying grace grows in a soul in the state of grace when it commits reasonable acts. How much more so when these acts glorify God more directly, for instance, by its obedience or by its resolution to serve God better? And so my life passes in ever growing love and glorification of God. O delightful life! Dearest bridegroom-to-be, my God! You award your own gifts, for I of myself haven't got anything. You glorify yourself through me!

Monday, May 30.
I can't say anything else. Love cannot be snared in a net of words. It keeps growing and increasing in me, against all the resistance of my body. I'm driven almost irresistibly by love to deny myself everything out of love for my Espoused. I surrender to it. *Caritas Christi urget me* [The love of Christ urges me on]. If only you are glorified more and more. . . .

Tuesday, May 31.
The last day of Mother's month. Tomorrow the month of my Beloved begins! Dearest Mother, how much I owe you, especially this month. You should not think I've forgotten you or love you less because my thoughts keep going to the Beloved of my heart. It's like the engagement period between people. Always his thoughts are with her, and hers with him; yet they still love their mothers as much, at least if they are loyal people!

Besides dearest Mother, you have attained your goal partly, for you wanted to marry your consecrated servant to your divine Son! So it's your greatest pleasure to see your servant always wrapped up in love of the Beloved. I'd like to do everything for him. Everything. But I'm as much of a nought as nineteen years ago, or an even worse bungler, for I have offended my dearest God so often. I was allowed to regret everything wholeheartedly through his grace. Now I may say with Mother, in all humility and truthfulness, *Tota pulchra es anima mea et macula non est in te* [You're quite beautiful, my soul, there's no stain on you], and *Magnificat anima mea Dominum, quia fecit mihi magna qui potens est* [My soul magnifies the greatness of my Lord, for he who is mighty has done great things for me]. Yes, I know so clearly that everything is his. If only you [Jesus] are glorified more and more. Dearest, you can do or not do with me as you wish.

✠

I want everything you want, really everything.

✠

Wednesday, June 1.
I don't know what to write today. I loved God and God loved me. All that God wants I want, too. For the rest I felt only aridity and distraction. That doesn't matter at all, does it? You remain my Dearest, don't you? In this way, Father, I can see that *every* meditation, even the most arid or sleepy one, is still a *good* one because every time I wanted to do better out of love for you. Throughout all the aridity I always knew that grace of good will in me. If, for instance, the Novice Master had come to me and had ordered me (in such an arid state) to do something my nature did not feel like doing at all, like scrubbing the reading room, I would have done it all the same, gladly and at once, out of love for my Beloved. And that's the main thing, isn't it, Dearest, that we do your holy will more and more?

Even now, while I was feeling utterly distracted and arid, I felt the love-will surge up in my breast. I'd like to do everything for you. I won't refuse any of my "habitual" mortifications, even if they go against the grain with me. I want to be cheerful again during recreation. In short, I want everything you want, really everything.

Many thanks for that grace, my Beloved. How I would like to thank you. You are really so good, and so sweet, in spite of all obstacles. Yes, your holy will be done! Until death! I want to sacrifice myself once more with you, in you, through you, and for you. (I'm also Mary's fully consecrated servant.) You use [my good] will, I know. Many thanks for that. All shall be well, won't it? If only your holy will be done. . . .

Friday, June 3.
Today is First Friday. My Dearest Bridegroom-to-be has gone to sleep in me. I've let him sleep quietly, notwithstanding the temptation to wake him because I felt so lonely. I'm so glad! For now you consider me almost your spouse.[62] You are no longer afraid I'll break away from you and cut off the proposal. Isn't it the same as what happens in the world? When he and she have known each other for a while, they really don't want to keep one another waiting too long, for fear their relationship will suffer. Nor will he act sleepily when he visits her, no matter how tired he feels. He does not want to risk her getting angry with him. But Jesus isn't afraid of that happening [with me]! What a great joy this is for me! God treats me as if he never wants me to go away from him! This makes me so very happy. I'm as happy when my soul speaks through my reluctant body. If I were to judge according to nature, if there were no God who strengthened me, then I could not stand it. I am here for two days more, and in those two days I could not have controlled myself as regards particular friendship, and so on!

Saturday, June 4.
Dearest, a great feast tomorrow! Whitsunday! My engagement feast. My most Dearest. Today was the vigil. I thought about it during my meditation. All is good. You were so busy yesterday! Did you rest well in my body? It doesn't matter. Your bride's heart beats more and more ardently for you and out of love of you.

O my Love, I asked several gifts from you already during my years at Weert. Yesterday I asked for them to an even greater degree! If there were fourteen gifts (although seven is quite a lot), I would ask for all of them. You are almighty, aren't you? Have you ever heard that a fiancée who is infinitely rich refused his bride seven simple gifts? That bride can glorify her Bridegroom much more immensely with those gifts, so freely [given] to her! Especially at the engagement banquet the Bridegroom-to-be is very generous! I'll let you invite the guests, Dearest! You understand more about these things than I do, don't you?

Sunday, June 5.
Whitsunday! The day of my spousal festivity! How long I have looked forward to this day! At last, now every habitant of heaven knows.

---

62 In classical European languages, the word soul, *anima* in Latin, is feminine. The age-old metaphors of bridal mysticism, for both men and women, are rooted in the perception of Christ as the Bridegroom or Spouse of the feminine soul. One of the possible preferred forms of the spiritual life, which the Holy Spirit may inspire in some people like Rinus, is that of bridal mysticism.

Everybody on earth to whom you want me to tell it may know that you are now espoused to me! It's beyond words what I'm experiencing now. I have asked my Bridegroom for a higher degree of the seven gifts of the Holy Spirit, as an engagement present, and I have received them all.

Ah, my Dearest! My love Spirit, my All! How am I to express my thanks! The soul, the weak soul of Frater Scholtes, is engaged to God, the infinitely eternal Being. How I long [to be] in that engagement bed, that is, in the bed of suffering. There my soul will, as it were, be fecundated by my Bridegroom to bring forth the fruits of his glory. Yes, I must be stretched on the Cross. I must suffer a lot, rather I may suffer a lot, for I love suffering so much because I so love you.

Tonight I must give my sermon in honor of Mother. Really, I can't [give it]. I haven't gotten any further than one and a half pages [of text]. Yet I'm not afraid at all! Now even less so than yesterday. I leave everything to him who fills my soul, to my Espoused. *Non turbetur cor vestrum*. Do not worry what you will say, for the Holy Spirit will tell you what to say. Please help me.

Monday, June 6.
My infinitely dear Fiancée, many thanks! I still don't understand how I had the nerve to say that introductory word [in my sermon] to Mary and ask for a blessing. I had not finished the writing of my speech at all. When I began to speak I didn't know how to finish it, even then. I could read everything on my paper in three or four minutes. But I hardly looked at the paper. Yes, it's true, you inspired me as to what to say. They say I spoke for more than ten minutes, but I don't even remember what I was supposed to have said. Yet everyone said it was splendid! Could one find a clearer example to show that these weren't mine but Jesus' words! I dedicated any success to your glorification beforehand. My only object is to glorify you, my dearest Bridegroom. I meant everything I said. That's true! But *what* I said I don't know. How strong the operation of your grace was yesterday. They praised me then (so: you in me, in other words, yourself for your own gifts). I don't know if what they said was true because I felt such equanimity about it all! How great a grace of yours that is. It made no difference at all to me, when a short time later some other novices blamed me for something "wicked," I didn't mind it at all. "It's good," I thought. Many thanks for that undeserved grace, my Beloved. I'm sure that I could not have borne this [cross] a year ago.

Tuesday, June 7.
How many graces the Holy Spirit has given me! An engaged person in this world could not have been more willing to do so much for her Bridegroom than your betrothed for you, my Dearest! Yet I know that it's not the many different ways [of expressing my love] that matter. No

outpouring, [however strong] could capture [the extent] of my love. It is deep and quiet. Yet my body has to express itself, too, if only to deprive nature of the chance of setting its heart on a girl in this world. How I had to smile yesterday! During the walk I was told they thought I had no feelings because I always go against "it" so much. If only they knew how sensitive I am. Others think that my prayer and work go along so easily, that I am filled with consolation because I've always adopted steady habits of prayer (at prayer times, etc.). How greatly mistaken they are! [Thank God] in my heart of hearts everything is still at rest.

Thursday, June 9.
Dearest, during the night there was a thunderstorm like no other I've known. Yet I was never so quiet as in this weather. [The lightning] was quite near. I'm firmly convinced that [it] struck in the neighborhood. But I held my crucifix to my breast and everything went well. These last few months I have slept with a crucifix, just as a little kid does with a teddy bear or a doll. Yet I know Father likes me to do this: 1) because of all the proofs of love rendered to him through the crucifix; 2) because I think of my Beloved at once in the morning, quite spontaneously. Most Dearest Being, you in me and I in you. I am totally united with you. I, your child and friend, even your betrothed by your grace. O My God! Yet, you can still not rely on me. On my own I'm the worst man who walks around.

Friday, June 10.
Beloved, I don't know if I'm guilty of this aridity [I feel]. The Novice Master said that I should ask myself about this. But really, Beloved, I won't do so: for then I may lose my confidence. I would feel that it certainly would be *my* fault every time. I wouldn't have a single good day in the Novitiate [were that the case], and perhaps not at Gemert either. Now, then, away with it![63]

Last night I was allowed to do the daily Stations of the Cross, as a penance. I could also make an act of perfect contrition so I went to sleep peacefully! Beloved, it's true, my nature is as cold as ice. If it has a *feeling* of love, it's certainly more for the world than for you. And yet, if now and then my soul expresses itself, for example, in my room or in bed, the body joins in! Actually, it isn't like that now. At this moment I must force my body not to look so gloomy. It really doesn't matter at

63 As is clear from some passages in his writings, as well as from self-revelatory communications with his spiritual directors and his soul friend, Rinus' finely tuned conscience led him into occasional bouts with scrupulosity. He was warned to watch for the beginning of scrupulous thoughts and put an end to them immediately.

all! Everything shall be well! If you have been glorified a little more, then, as far as I'm concerned, all is good. Yes, *all*. Now I may attend Holy Mass again and receive Holy Communion. How much grace (how few feelings!) I hope to receive then, for [I want] to serve you more and more, my Dearest, to love you exceedingly. Many thanks.

Saturday, June 11.
Dearest, most dearest, Mother, I love you so very much. Since I am espoused to my God, I love you much more than before. It's just like the engagement time people experience. My thoughts, my whole being, are always with my Beloved whom I have been allowed to be with me for more than nineteen years, though without loving him as much [as he deserves]. Now, thanks to your cooperation, [Mother], and thanks above all to him, we have found each other. Now we are espoused. Now I'm his! Forever! And you yourself have done everything to make this happen. Dearest, most dearest, Mother. No, I don't doubt for a moment that you are truly happy, even if I don't think that often of only you any more. Yet I am and remain your fully consecrated servant. Any merits that arise have been much greater since my betrothal. They grow every moment through the graces and gifts of my Beloved. Still they are undisputably and unreservedly from you, never doubt that! There is nothing but profit in this for you. You deserve it, don't you agree, dearest Mother? This is the way to go, isn't it?

[Translator's Note: On Sunday June 12 Rinus wrote his notes in Latin on the same subjects as before.]

Monday, June 13.
In my "direction" time the Novice Master told me that he might subject me to some "humiliation."[64] But, if this [admonishment] is anything like what he said tonight, it won't be so bad. I hope to receive a stronger mortification next time. As it is, Dearest, I'm glad I may offer

64 Rinus refers here to a conference the Novice Master gave that night about aridity during meditation. He pointed out that one should ask oneself if perhaps this aridity is due to neglecting one's preparation, or of not living a life of recollection, or of not giving up certain attachments that hinder the workings of grace in the soul. The Novice Master was aware of the dark night of aridity given to Rinus by God. He also knew that Rinus' sensitive conscience could make him anxious about any possible guilt in regard to his aridity. Therefore, he had forewarned him during direction about this upcoming conference by telling him that he could expect some "humiliation," meaning a word of admonition. Because of the benign personality of this outstanding Master of Novices, the matter was handled in such a way that Rinus did not feel humiliated as he had expected.

you some anguish of soul everyday. For I can't deny that I'm in the "springtime of suffering." My nature sees itself opposed by my soul (which is to say by you, because you own my soul) as regards all its self-gratifications in thoughts and acts and in particular friendships. Though my nature suffers from it, it doesn't really mean anything, Dearest. Mind you! I'm glad to feel this way if it shows you something of my love. And [believe me] I feel this love growing! Time after time [I seek] more "habitual" mortifications. No sooner have I gained one more than your love asks for something else. Thus it is that I can write down mortifications that after some time have become a habit for me. They then give me much less trouble. *Semper crescendo* [Always better] with your help!

Tuesday, June 14.
How happy I am again! God has once more been glorified infinitely, just as my Dearest deserves, in an infinitely satisfying way. I was allowed to be wholly present [to him], to be joined with him at Holy Mass! Yes, my dearest Jesus, my greatest cross is now my powerlessness to express my gratitude and love for you, Bridegroom [of my soul]. You have made love and gratitude so deep and great in me that I could almost say: "I, too, love you with an infinite (that is, an unfathomable) love!" But I can't express it well. I feel [my love] running over on all sides, [gushing out] toward all my confrères. There is no limit to the extent [of this love]. If all two billion people on earth were holy, so holy that the whole world was burning with love of you, I would still not be content. Even if all people who lived before our days were *all* in the highest heaven, and could express an ineffable love of you, no, I would yet not be satisfied. All people coming after me should also enjoy this happiness. That being true, I'd wish all angels had remained loyal to God. On top of this I'd regret that there were no more spirits to sing praises to you and to love you.

Wednesday, June 15.
Beloved! Now that I know your answer through Father Berkers (that is, through his letter) I want to obey it with your grace:

1) Do nothing peculiar; therefore, I dropped habitual mortifications that were conspicuous . . . in any case I had been doing so already two days before I received Father Berkers' answer!
2) Duty: in and through everything. God's holy will be done in the rules of the Novitiate! Obedience! Without this the higher life of prayer is worth nothing. If there *is* obedience to *all* superiors and rules (to the constitutions, etc.), then this is the check-mark of approval of the life of prayer!
3) No judgment, even less, no condemnation.
4) Humility (in other words: truth).

5) Do or omit [whatever my superiors] tell me, even if I meet with failure and opposition. (Does Father Berkers know I've been a choir master?)
6) Help to build up the holiness of my fellow novices or my surroundings by prayer and example! What a beautiful task!

Thursday, June 16.
Dearest, intensely loved, Beloved. There was only Holy Communion this morning without a Holy Mass. It's a pity, but it was impossible [to celebrate Mass]. There are only two Fathers left in [the house].[65] Further, every bad thing I did yesterday has been both "forgiven and forgotten" by you! Thanks to your grace, I obeyed you. I did not stop doing my duty, in spite of discouragement and misfortune, faults or dissatisfactions. Therefore, I forgot all about yesterday's failures! With renewed zeal infused in me, Jesus urges me further and further along the road of holiness. How I like to be driven on [like this], I, his [future] soul bride. Yes, I know he wants to be with me in solitude! I must surrender to him: that's a [new] bride's duty! There will be new fruit then, perhaps new delight, in things spiritual! But, inevitably, suffering will follow, ever more suffering—to ripen the fruits so as to give birth to [more of] them. That will cause pain, but, yes, I'm quite willing to suffer. I suffer in him and through him. [All for] my Beloved! I love to suffer because I love him with a love that is becoming more and more deep and intense. Beloved, what creature can fathom my love? Yes, your Mother, my Mother-in-law, and dearest Directress—she will be able to see how deep or, better still, how shallow my little rivulet of love is compared with her ocean!

Friday, June 17.
Ah, my Beloved, outwardly I was cold during Holy Mass and meditation. Yet you know that through all this coldness I love you with my whole heart and soul. The will is what matters. That is enough, isn't it! With your help and your grace, I hope to be pushed along on the road to holiness! The more holiness, the more love and glorification I may render to you. That's what matters to me. Not pleasure or sweetness, not meriting greater happiness in heaven! No, it's love that attracts me to heaven, to express what I love!

Saturday, June 18.
Yes, indeed, it has been like this before! Distractions, dislikes, dryness! Yet, as I always do in these circumstances, I've asked myself, "Would you still be willing to do God's holy will? If you were asked this moment, let's say by the work leader in a haughty, *commanding* tone,

65 Probably the two Fathers had parish duties to fulfill in the churches of Gennep, easily accessible from the Novitiate.

for example, to scrub the toilets, would you still obey, even with pleasure, because it's God's holy will?" And I can still say by your grace, "Yes, with great pleasure, Dearest." Therefore, I'm not afraid of so much aridity! Then it can do me no harm, but, on the contrary, [much good]. Yesterday I bungled: I prayed my rosary carelessly. So it goes, brother!

Sunday, June 19.
Today it's your holy will that we go on a procession through town? We are also to sing a few songs. Please, Beloved, whatever your holy will is, I'll do it with pleasure (*super*naturally), but I can do literally nothing without your "domestic help." I'm cold and arid. The flesh is unwilling, but you know yourself that the will is still united with you. Everything is going well. Even if I have to squeeze these words out of my mouth, that doesn't matter!

1) God is unchangeable. If he still wants to be betrothed to me officially at Pentecost, he won't break this [relationship] off without reason.
2) No good can really arise from a natural imagination that is not well-grounded. (Were that the case, then my whole espousal would be nonsense, [a mere figment of my] imagination.) The means must be proportionate to the object. Otherwise [such merely natural imagination] would be haughty arrogance on my side, and God can never bless that.
3) It *has* been blessed. God has been glorified by [our espousal]. These are hard facts. Even *nature* (against which I now reason in the light of my *super*nature) must yield to them and accept them humbly. So my betrothal is real. God is unchangeable. So, as far as he is concerned, our espousal is still on!

Monday, June 20.
Dearest, I should not reason as I did recently, for then I can't sleep at night. [That's what happened again] yesterday. That's when I'm again imprudent. That's when, like yesterday, I keep tossing and turning in bed, so much so that I forget how to be still! Father Gijsen said that it's not a good idea to lie on your stomach face downwards, so I mustn't do so. I promised you then not to (although I hardly ever lie face downwards); yet I did so again last night! I regret it with all my heart. I also regret my imprudent touch. It was not meant at all to arouse unchaste emotions. Indeed, I seldom have them, and then only during sleep. Mostly I lie quietly. Needless to say, my self-love was humiliated, but that's not so bad. The worst thing is that in this matter God was less glorified.

Tuesday, June 21.
My most dearest Bridegroom. You have once more been infinitely honored. The holy sacrifice of the Mass becomes more and more meaningful to me. I'm really joyful in spite of all my misfortune! My heart beats faster and faster (in a spiritual sense) when the sacred Host and the chalice are raised to be adored. Then I [almost burst] with gladness. The Father, God himself, is immensely glorified. My Dearest, love flourishes against all odds, or better still, by virtue of these odds. Many thanks, my love.

Wednesday, June 22.
I sat sleepily in chapel this morning. Like a radio that is tuned low, so was the sound of my intimate conversation with my Beloved. My God and my All. It resonated from the deepest point of my soul to the lower part, but that doesn't matter! Now powers of grace are waiting under steam until God himself pulls the throttle. Then they are under full steam—[pulling] all for you! I have given complete consent to everything you might want of me. The rest I leave to you. It's necessary not to put any obstacles in the way! Yes, all my faults were forgiven yesterday. Everything is pure again! I'm ready to serve you, my Dearest. Help me please, for without you I'd sink away in the mud.

✠

I will to live united with you so that not I exist and act, but you.

✠

Thursday, June 23.
Dearest, I know I bungled again. [My life] is not that good yet. Still you give me your graces every time [I need them]. Many cordial thanks! I accept them gladly.

Dearest, through all the bad times my heart keeps moving toward you. Oh yes, you punish me severely for the least deviation. It's the clearest proof of how much you love me! By God's grace I'm already sorry for a little infringement of the rules, etc. It's as if I had committed a murder! Wholehearted thanks for that [sensitivity]. In the spirit of St. Thérèse, I say: "I'll gladly bear the feeling of regret and unease for acting against you. I do so out of love for you. If you keep sending your grace, every time anew, then everything will be restored." Yet my love is not less, Dearest, even if I bungle sometimes (often)! I want to love you, and the will to love *is* love. Well, then, I must love you very much, if it's only a matter of willing to. For I can't tell you how intensely I *will* to live united with you so that not I exist and act, but you.

Friday, June 24. Feast of the Sacred Heart.
I was half asleep during meditation and Holy Mass. What the Novice Master said is really true: To meditate well the body should be healthy too! Yet I was aware that in my heart of hearts both will and reason were united with God without interruption! So all is well. Do whatever you want with me. I am wholly receptive, and I'd like so much to remain that way. For, if the Holy Spirit acts in and through me, then my Beloved becomes the Eternal Being who is so infinitely dear to me in all his infinity. And he will be glorified much more.

Dearest, yesterday my greatest sorrow and regret was to have sinned against the rules and against charity. You were glorified less, and that's why I suffer so much. Last night, following several short acts of penance for reparation, I also made the Stations of the Cross. You let me know that everything was restored, because Jesus renders the Father eternal homage every morning. He also includes the homage of the members of his Body at the same time. Thus everything was provided for. All was settled this morning.

Saturday, June 25.
I did not speak aloud, but I believe I was again dozing off this morning. Yes, I do love God, and I tell him so again and again. I beg him especially for a spirit of inwardness, for a deeper inner life. I ask that you, my Dearest Beloved, act more, ever more deeply, in me. What else then? I'm sometimes sleepy, and, meanwhile, I'm also distracted in the bargain! Don't think for a minute that I believe that everything is as it should be.

Tomorrow I'll meditate in the "classical" style. I'll try to clarify a truth from all sides or to imagine some mystery. You see, Beloved, that's what I also find so strange. You know I used to have such a lively imagination to visualize you. I used to do so after Holy Communion, or at other times. But that changed in the final year [at Weert], if I remember well. I don't think I have had representations of you in my imagination during the whole Novitiate! There may have been some exception at the beginning. Once more I want your holy will completely. I beg you for that [gift].

Sunday, June 26.
Today I meditated on "apostolate in the neighborhood." It's in the little book *Mijn Ideaal* [*My Ideal*]. My dearest Directress and Mother Mary has taken me so close to the Eternal Being that I want to teach others that Mary is the way too! If my own experience may be of help here, then I'm quite willing to inform others about it. Though it sounds foolish enough, in this respect I'm not afraid at all of becoming proud. For what of "me" is included here after all? I'd rather say: "In spite of myself Mary has taken me close to Jesus first and through him to God!"

My dearest Bridegroom, my eternal All! How gladly I let my reason and will fall into your lovable infinity. In spite of darkness, I see a clarity that is beyond words for me. It may seem nonsense to say it, but it is true! Dear Mother, I want to show others your way. *Per Mariam ad Jesum* [Through Mary to Jesus].

Dearest Mother! You also know how much I love you. My dearest Love, my Bridegroom, your espoused bride makes herself available for everything. That's a bride's duty here among people: how much more so in the spiritual espousal and the [preparation] time for [mystical] marriage? My Beloved, I'm pining away with love, even though I have an infinite love to imbibe. My love-will comprises your whole being in all its infinity, yet I'm trying in vain to find something [of me] you did not yet have (as if that were possible), and then to give it to you, my love.

Wednesday, June 29.
Please, Beloved, help me, I'm becoming empty. Tonight there is Benediction (in polyphony), and I'm [sure] you can use me to sing you a worthy benediction. Please, Beloved, I know I do not deserve you due to my lack of recollection today. Yet I beg you to have mercy on me, your exhausted little bride. I'm craving for you, just like a girl throughout her busy work day longs to see her beloved in the evening, after all her work is done. I want to return to you completely, not to deviate in the least from your service. Dearest, just this once, forgive your little bride. Let Benediction proceed as well as possible in your honor. If only you are glorified, that will be enough for me! Please, Dearest!

Saturday, July 2.
My love, how you once again tease me! I did not know you were so jealous, so eager to keep a soul you've won after a long pursuit. I have surrendered to you unconditionally. I have even been allowed to be espoused to you. You don't tolerate it at all that I should turn away from you. And I don't want to either, mind you. With you and in you everything is as it should be. I love you more than myself. My Beloved, I'm stupefied with love, drunk with sweet sorrow. It's your fault if I'm a bit intoxicated! You are responsible for the incoherent utterances of love that well up from my being. Yes, it's your loving fault, my Beloved.

Sunday, July 3.
Pull me away, foolish eternal All filled with love. You make me literally giddy. My legs are so light, some time I'll fly. I'll fly away out of love, with love, with a love that hurts and yet [gives me] such sweet pain. My Beloved, press, squeeze, do whatever you like. I'm quite willing to be choir-master and bell-servant if it's your holy will. I renounce those feelings of annoyance and rebellion that arise occasionally. My love, my Beloved. What have you begun with me? This morning you punished

me for again slipping off the road a little. But now I am in love, drunk with love. I am mad with happiness, a painful happiness, though everything is for you, out of love for you. May you be glorified as perfectly as possible. Yes, I sing your praise eternally. I love you forever and ever and, without end, I tell you of my love.

Wednesday, July 6.
My Beloved, did you see me yesterday? I fell back again, even further behind, and that against my promise. How imprudent I was with the sense of touch! What if it had gone any further? What if I had chased God away from me by offending him infinitely? And yet, if this wasn't the case—thanks be to God a thousand times—then it was owing to his goodness only. But the worst was still to come!

Today, during the whole day, I did not behave well either! I looked into a newspaper during the walk and thereafter, instead of studying, I just played the *harmonium* for some time. It was meant as a boast; otherwise there would not have been any need to pull out all the stops. Yet I was also happy today because your punishment shot through my being like a purgatory. Yes, I suffered much, but I'm still happy. For, if you didn't love me you wouldn't punish me.

✠

Nothing at all may stand in the way of your grace.

✠

Saturday, July 9.
My Beloved, many thanks that I could receive the Sacrament of Confession again. *Ego te absolvo a peccatis tuis* [I absolve you from your sins]. So all my sins and shortcomings, both voluntary and semi-voluntary, don't exist any more. Many thanks also for the gift of faith. I don't doubt for a moment (neither in thought nor practice) that your [forgiveness] is true.

My Treasure, today I bungled again even after Confession! But, God be praised, there were no sins! Nothing, absolutely nothing at all may stand in the way of your work of grace! You must be able to do what your holy will [wants to do with me] without any restriction. Burn away what resists you, my Espoused. How sweet your holy will is, even if it is hard on my nature. Armed with your will, I know myself to be strong.

Dearest Mother Mary! If I say now a "Hail Mary," it pleases you infinitely more because the Holy Spirit greets you through me.

Sunday, July 10.
Today there is the ceremony of receiving the cassock at Weert! Dearest, it's now been more than a year ago since I was allowed to receive [my]

habit. I now wear your testimony around openly! I'm a Catholic and a religious. Anything done to me or against me is now done to Jesus or against him because my garb affects the opinion of those around me.

My Beloved, tonight I will play during Benediction out of love for you! I hardly know how to play. My way is only to touch it [the *harmonium*] by feel and by hearing! Thus do I promote your glorification! Neither success nor failure don't matter that much, if only you are glorified more! If I don't distract the attention of the novices too much by my bungling, then it won't be too bad. Be calm, Rinus, be quiet. Nervousness won't help you at all. Rely on God, rely on God.

Yes, my Beloved, I rely only on you. I leave everything to you! Dear Mom! You are the organist tonight. If all goes well, the Holy Spirit will play through my hands to praise you, my infinite Beloved! Show me your benediction in a way unknown to me so far. I would like so much for you to be glorified more in this way.

Tuesday, July 12.

My Beloved, I'm a great riddle to myself! One big question mark. It sometimes seems to me as if there is a big question mark on my forehead or as if I have a screw loose! In this inexplicable situation, I've always got one saving carrot held out again and again: I mean God's holy will. Sometimes I have to fight difficult and severe battles. Then I've got to go and ring the bell![66] It mostly results in . . . [Translator's Note: This part of the manuscript ends here].

Whatever happens I've got to do only one thing: Read the Gospel or something similar! You see, Beloved, I still smile during recreation or elsewhere, but my heart feels like crying. Sometimes I don't know where to turn [so great is] my homesickness for you, my ineffable Beloved. I love you with an obscure love. I don't know you any more, nor myself either. It sometimes seems that you and I have fused together into one big net. At other times [it seems as if] you have gone away and everything is covered with a fog so that I can neither see nor hear you. *So be it! Fiat voluntas tua* [Your will be done].

Wednesday, July 13.

My God, what *is* the matter anyway? I don't really know where I am or what has happened to me. Lukewarm, arid, dry, that is nothing special, but now I see myself so weakened. This afternoon during the walk I did not behave like clergy at all, far from it! You punished me for this (for not guarding my eyes) because I blushed (something I can't help) when I saw a girl, which pleased and still pleases my nature a lot. At Weert it was the same, but now she was replaced by another girl at Gennep.

66 Rinus had been appointed to awaken the novices each morning. He had to walk through the corridors sounding the wake up call.

Yes, my Beloved, the struggle is sometimes severe, really severe, because the "enemy" is in our own Novitiate. At Weert the same thing happened, namely, the sisters of the fellows for whom I once felt an inclination to particular friendship appeal to me because of their charm. So, Rinus, you had known for a long time that this particular friendship was only a means used to attract the girl you couldn't get near! God, help me!

Thursday, July 14.
Dearest, many thanks for the light you gave me this morning as regards the state of my soul. I'm much quieter now! I know to whom to turn. I also beg for your help now more urgently than at other times! Everything comes from you, doesn't it?

Today I asked the Novice Master's permission to pray my rosary while kneeling down with outstretched arms from time to time. That was quite permissible, so the devil needn't try the tactic "that I had no permission to pray my rosary that way!"

My Beloved, my intensely loved Beloved! My being trembles with love for you, for you only and for my neighbors' sake out of love for you. You are everything even if I don't feel or see you anywhere. Now I know where to turn. Now I see that my whole struggle these weeks was due to the suffering put upon me by you. So I may really suffer. Many thanks, yes, thanks. I must ring these words out of my nature, but I repeat them: many thanks that I may suffer for you, my dearest Beloved. I'm quite willing [to do so] since *I* can do literally nothing at all. *You* must do this.

Saturday, July 16.
Dearest, this afternoon (or better still, already this morning) you forgave *all* my sins: *Ego te absolvo a peccatis tuis*. If only my Confessor himself knew how many sins or imperfections he delivers me from every time! Many thanks, Beloved!

This afternoon, during manual labor, I had to "work" as if I were a Novice who was as strict as could be about the rules. So, hypocrite that I am, I didn't say much either, or rather I wasn't able to [talk]. That's good luck again.

Sunday, July 17.
My Beloved, many thanks for today's suffering and rejoicing. You're so good! At first you let me wander about the whole morning and even longer with a sense of being abandoned [by you]. This afternoon you gave me human consolations again. I was comforted completely when playing bowls with the very novice who doesn't suspect at all how much *trouble* he and his relatives give me. I had not looked for him. It just

came to pass [that we were together]. What shall we talk about tomorrow, my Beloved! We will have a *tête à tête* socially the whole day.

If only you are glorified more and more. *Non turbetur cor vestrum*—that's the watchword, isn't it, Beloved? I adore you. I'm so happy to do your holy will, to suffer for you and in you, to be absorbed completely into you. *Ego sum via, veritas et vita* [I am the way, the truth, and the life].

Monday, July 18.

Dearest, I felt as if I were becoming overwrought. That's the third time this year. So [I applied] the same remedy that has helped so well at other times: *Ama et fac quod vis* [Love and do as you will]. Hence I do my duty and take everything lightheartedly. I smile, take more dessert, use more butter. During the last few weeks before [our] wedding, I just unbend the bow and then bend it that much more after a few days.

My Beloved, I love you! I believe what's upset me the most is the continuous fight against strong temptations—so strong they did not seem to be temptations any more but self-willed consents. Yet my *super*nature still disliked them and the love of you never left me. I have also been much too excited. Yesterday I could not sleep either. If you are tossing with a throbbing head, you try all kinds of means to lie at ease and fall asleep quietly! Likewise I was also imprudent yesterday, but, Beloved, everything is again behind me. You are the way, the truth, and the life.

✠

I am no longer answerable to myself. You are everything.

✠

Tuesday, July 19.

A day of vacation today did me good, dearest Love. Many thanks! Also [accept] my inexpressible thanks for the new grace I received from you this morning! Truly love comprises everything! *Deus caritas est* [God is love]. *Deus est veritas, via et vita, ergo amor est veritas* [God is the truth, the way, the life, therefore, love is truth]. Everything is so simple, so "one."

Yes, Beloved, it all seems so simple to me! You are everything after all. You yourself! And yet you wanted to be espoused to me! You with me, you in me. My Dear, I'm so happy, so truly happy, that I may suffer a little for you!

Come suffering. I'm glad to meet you. May it be so more and more. Jesus does not give everything at once. He takes his time and again gives something more—more strength and love every time! Dearest Lord, when a soul surrenders to you as I have been allowed to do, then I'm no longer answerable for myself. You are *everything*!

Wednesday, July 20.
My Beloved, although the twenty-four hours' "rest-cure" finished today, I indulged in a scandalously big portion of pudding! I had to read [during lunch] so I had to eat afterwards. Then I finished all the pudding that had been set aside for me. Now it's all well and good for me to talk about "nutritious" cornflower pudding but meanwhile it was also "delicious." So you see what your betrothed is: a great glutton. But I don't lose heart, Dearest. Not at all! I keep going on, even though it seems to me that I'm going downhill! Hold me tight again! I always want to go invariably to you. All through you! Alas, my spirit is willing but my flesh is weak! I'm still a great braggart!

My Beloved, if I didn't have your encouraging word, I would be in despair about all the graces I've wasted and for which I'll have to render an account to you. Fortunately, Dearest, there are the holy sacraments of Confession and Communion. [You give me] everything to make me purer and purer.

Thursday, July 21.
Good news, Beloved, everything is good again! My calmness has returned, and yes, you are really present! You know what I'm writing down at this moment. So, Dearest One, do you still love your little bride? Help me please. The fidelity I've promised and hope to swear to you in five weeks' time is waylaid so much. Others want to force themselves between you and me. They want to pull me away from you, to change me from being a bride into a common servant-girl.

No, Beloved! I don't want to give into [temptation], even if the struggle sometimes burns through me like a hot fever! Thank God and you, Dearest, that I can still stand my ground. I dare to say with confidence that your bride has never driven you away from her soul. I would not hesitate to make this [fact] known to everybody. You have imprinted in me a deep and real conviction of my own powerlessness. It seems impossible for me even to think I can hold out on my own. No, my Beloved, I'm not yet to be trusted!

Sunday, July 24.
Dear God! What a fuss today. What have you begun? I could not do my duty completely, but there was a reason for it. I should be more reserved toward two novices, especially toward one of them. Be careful, Rinus, you're so weak! Jesus alone, God alone, is my beloved. Let nature suffer, and suffer as it deserves due to the will's refusal. Don't yield! And yet, Beloved, how strong is that natural urge in me! I don't understand how I can refuse to yield. Yes, that's a clear proof of the triumph of grace. But . . . be careful with me. I'm even more wicked than I used to be! Exactly because you've given me more, I can offend you more gravely by my sins. How wicked I am! Who knows what will happen tomorrow? Tell me your holy will. It's all fine with me, mind you! You are All; I am nothing!

Wednesday, July 27.

Sadly, I'm getting worse every day. If only I knew the exact cause. I'm far too loose. I have only myself to blame for some sensual touching (of my body). And this is the man who dares to call himself espoused to the infinite, just, and pure God. I, a little zero, over against the All. I, a little clipping, against your Being. You don't tolerate the least voluntary affection besides that toward you. So you withdraw! Please, don't go! Try one more day with me, Beloved! I won't break our engagement as long as you help me. But [the work] has to be done by you. I'm nothing, nothing at all! My Beloved!

Thursday, July 28.

Dearest, you helped me so much this morning. You gave me hints and advice. Many thanks. Today, however, I've had some problems—all over a silly bit of wood. One's "sense of honor" is not offended by giving that away! You are a funny one, Rinus! If you had done this in former days, [maybe it would have been understandable], but now!

Tomorrow, as the expression goes, will be another day. For tomorrow [there is] Mass and Holy Communion. You will be glorified again infinitely. You can safely let me remain in aridity, without my being aware of anything of your presence! You are still being glorified. I may follow the prayers of Holy Mass and, even if I don't feel anything, it doesn't matter!

Dearest! Many thanks for everything today, even for that successful joke about the "escaped cat!" I couldn't help laughing! The idea was yours. I could never have invented such a funny joke myself. If only you are loved. . . .

Saturday, July 30.

Ego te absolvo a peccatis tuis [I absolve you of your sins]. Today I could go to Confession again! All my sins are gone. *Tota pulchra es anima mea* [You're quite beautiful, my soul]. This [renewal] was achieved by Jesus' grace. Dearest, I won't do it again! A few days ago something was read from the martyrology that I did not understand completely. Still a few words aroused my attention. I read them again and found their translation! It was as I thought. It was one of those "lights" again. [The meaning] of what is read may be unraveled, but not if my motive was only curiosity! That's wrong, old boy.

Sunday, July 31.

Today Father Superior held a chapter. He mentioned from the rules: "Take nothing between meals," so no water either. Wow! So this means drinking water once a day—nothing without permission.[67] It won't be easy, Dearest, but I'll try to do what I can. Again, "forward," with your help! Please [be there] for me.

Today I made a fuss again about a badge—and that with the novice in question. Fortunately, my love, you've forgiven me. Everything is good again. Presently I may sing your praises. Go on and glorify yourself by means of a silly child's whistle (I mean in my throat). Everything for you, Beloved. *Martyrdom*! Sacrifice!

Wednesday, August 3.
Taceamus [Let's be silent about this day.] I can hardly stand it any longer. I tell you, my God, how fed up I am here, and you say, "Keep smiling." I've tried, but most of the time I forget that I'm supposed to smile! Yes, it's true what St. John Berchmans said: "*Mea maxima martyrium est vita communis*" [Community life is my worst martyrdom.] Especially now at the end of the Novitiate, now when we all get somewhat dried up and become irritable. There's hardly any subject matter left for conversation. What does it matter? If God's holy will is done, then all will be well. God willing, the whole thing will be over in three and a half weeks!

I'm nothing! Nothing at all! Don't think, Rinus, you've got a right to be reputed as funny. What a crazy coon you are! You thought you would be popular with your confrères! Forget it. If they mix with you, they do so for Our Lord's sake. I am the confrère with whom they have to bear, one on whom they can vent all their love of God! Yes, that's good!

Thursday August 4.
Dearest, I don't know what happens to me! How foolish I was during the walk! There's no need for me to talk about such high subjects! I force myself to the foreground. I talk about matters I don't understand at all! And I do so to boast, even if I make myself believe it's to God's greater glory!

What must you think of me now? This clown who calls himself your bride-to-be! How I regret for your sake what I have done! Beloved, most dearest Beloved! Accept me again! You're hurting me so strangely these days, I don't know where to turn. I'd like to cry out: "Jesus, my Beloved, my infinite Being, my Espoused!" It might give me some relief! Yet in practice (by my behavior) I don't live up to these love feelings. Please help me.

---

67 In those days it was not yet generally known that one should drink as much as eight glasses of water a day to protect one's health. Hence this unreasonable mortification seemed reasonable at that time.

✠

You were in me and I was in you: nothing more.

✠

Friday, August 5.
My Beloved, today there's adoration and recollection! You asked me to kneel before the Blessed Sacrament all day (insofar as possible, of course)! At Weert I would say: "There's adoration only twice a year," and then I would stay in chapel almost all day (except during meals). Now you said to me, it's for the last time in the Novitiate! At first I wanted to mutter objections because it's so hot. But you've won again.

Last night we were allowed to have the Holy Hour in our rooms! It was a sweltering day. I did not say much to you either. I tried to stay awake. For I didn't want you to catch me sleeping like the apostles! Actually it was, so to say, an exchange of being with Being—that's how my prayer was just now. You were in me and I was in you: nothing more. You fill my soul. I desire nothing more than you and your holy will, than you and your kingdom. Yes, Beloved! In three weeks' time I may give myself to you officially. Thanks, Dearest.

Continued, the same day.
Many thanks, my All! Tonight, during my turn for adoration, when I had been fighting sleep and fatigue for almost half an hour, you seized me again, all of a sudden. I had no more sleep nor any fatigue! Then the question I had been waiting for came. (But I wasn't allowed to ask it myself!) You asked me! You, the infinite All, asked an insignificant creature to be your love-mate. My soul was to become your bride for all eternity.

Beloved, for a second I still said to you that I was nothing. I did so, as it were, to give you time to withdraw your words! Fool that I was. As if you didn't know what you were doing. I didn't wait long to give my answer! I said "Yes," Dearest, and I still say "Yes." I want you. I want to love you above everything. Not of my own accord (*nothing* out of myself). It is only your beloved being that I love above everything (logically so, because you are *everything*)—and this comes from your poor nothing of a creature. Without arrogance I dare to tell you that you love me so much it is beyond words. It is all because you love yourself infinitely, and I am from you, in you, through you, and for you. And, thanks only to your grace, I am still in grace, I still am. You in me through sanctifying grace, so any beauty you see in me is yours, or . . . [Translator's Note: This part of the manuscript ends here.]

Saturday, August 6.
Dearest, the book about a beloved bride of yours, St. Gemma Galgani, is being read in the refectory. She was your bride! Her life was really something! So, love, I need your help badly if I'm to have the courage to say (especially with such a saint's life in front of me as compared to mine), "Yes." Here is another lover of Jesus! She is your bride as I am.

Dearest, I ought to laugh out loud at myself! To expose my arrogance and pride, let me burst into a roaring, mocking laugh at myself. [I want to] and yet I won't. Is my foolish conceit so huge? Is my inveterate pride so strong? Or is my soul still engaged to you in spite of all signs to the contrary? I don't know whether to say yes or no. What does it matter? As long as you are glorified, everything is good, isn't it?

Sunday, August 7.
Ah, my All! What strange inclinations and opinions sometimes arise in me! The worst thing is that I can't solve them nor can I have them solved! I mean things regarding my inner life. Is everything bogus and deceit? Or is it real? Do I use your grace, or do I go on tepidly on the road of idleness with a make-believe degree of prayer? In a word, am I in you or beside you? Are you my Beloved, my Bridegroom-to-be, or aren't you? That's the most difficult question. If I go now to my spiritual director and explain everything, even if he would approve of everything, then this natural question of skepticism would not be solved. I might still say to myself: "Yes, but the whole thing is a swindle. If what you say could be said by everybody, then they must all be God's betrothed!" These [terrible doubts] are now what hurt me so badly, my love! So I say [firmly]: "Don't pay attention to anything; just do your plain duty." That doesn't quite work either because my *whole* life is based on this [principle]. The truth is, if I am not who I think I am, then my inner motive of action must change.

Tuesday, August 9.
Dearest, many thanks! Tonight I started to worry again. I was at loggerheads with myself about our marriage, of course. Then I read in Tanquerey about what this mystical marriage consists of. [It encompasses] everything! All! Forever! Imagine, that's what's going to happen in two and a half weeks! [My mind] says that's like jumping out of the frying-pan into the fire. It seems more and more incomprehensible to me that I could be so foolish as to imagine that this situation will encompass me for my whole life in less than three weeks' time! I went to the chapel seized with fear. I had become afraid! But there, with my eyes on the crucifix, you took hold of me again. Now I have to agree to everything [you want]. Yes, we'll be "wed" in a little over two and a half weeks! Now I know [this is true]. Even if my nature may be as skeptical as before, I'm not afraid any more. My love! I leave everything to

you. I have asked my own and your Mother, Daughter, and Bride for a "trousseau." She will look after it. I can also offer you a dowry! But even that is a gift from you. So you receive only what I could offer Mother (and what she has increased [by her touch] because her hands offered it to Jesus). That is my dowry. It isn't much, Dearest. But you knew you proposed to a poor bride. I'm trembling with gladness now. Only two and a half weeks to go!

Wednesday, August 10.
Today was a bit better. The tension of the spirit [I feel] was not so strong. My Love gave me some rest, some certainty, some light! But tonight it started again. At first my nature began nagging me with its "girlish" love. It began to beg for consent to give its tenderest feelings to a girl! Thanks be to God, I did not yield. The struggle lasted a short time, but [it] was the more violent. Then I read Tanquerey. The unrest came back! My nature hesitates [to consent]. I'm so unspeakably tiny, imperfect, and weak—and *I* should be allowed to wed you? Yes, my Love.

Thursday, August 11.
Today everything was quiet with only now and then a severe, vicious temptation against holy virtue! Then nostalgia, but nothing else. It was, so to speak, quiet today on the "Stock-Exchange." Beloved, I'm not afraid of August 27, 1938, any more. That's when our marriage will be contracted. Have you had the announcements printed? You can put one in the *Maasbode* [a Dutch Catholic newspaper].

My dearest All! How happy I am in your love. I was sleepy and distracted during prayer but I prayed on as [if nothing were happening], for you are glorified all the same! That's the main thing. Tomorrow will be another day! Do you want to be glorified again! Sweetness, I'm so happy when I know that you are infinitely happy. That you aren't in need of anything at all! [Even if I] sit in darkness, you are happy!

Friday, August 12.
Well, old boy, it might have been a bit better! Is that not how the espoused of God should behave? Ah, Dearest, forgive me whenever I think or write the words, "God's betrothed." I'm still a bit scared! On the one hand, I want to laugh aloud: "What, are you completely crazy?" On the other hand, I get scared by the word "God." You, the infinitely holy, infinitely pure All. You, the Creator: Would you be betrothed to a tepid, vicious, cowardly, vile nothing, your creature? And, with all this, when I say, "Boy, it's your imagination," I still feel uneasy. It's as if you are looking at me asking, with a question in your eye: Is that your [way of being grateful] for all my work in you, for all my love? Am I not free [to bestow on whom I will] my gifts and invitations! And where does it

say that in your case everything should go on in exactly the same way as with the saints?"

Yes, Dearest, that's how it is. But always the last word wins, also now. Yes, my Dearest, you've forgiven me, haven't you?

Saturday, August 13.
Beloved, time is moving on, isn't it? Two more weeks and then I hope to be yours for all eternity. Before the world I give myself, body and soul, to you completely! I put my soul's right hand in yours in a bond of mutual, unbreakable fidelity! A lot still has to happen during these two weeks! There's so much to be done by me and for you! I must make a decent appearance at our marriage.

The day after tomorrow, my most Dearest, it will be five years since I gave myself to Mary as her consecrated servant. Five years of service! Dear Mother, I've cost you so dearly. You have passed on to me through your hands many graces from God to re-create me completely. Fortunately, your labor hasn't been in vain! But that was not my work! Dear Mom, how can I begin to thank you?

Monday, August 15.
Beloved, how foolish I was again today. I was over strained, wasn't I? I meant it, but then you told me to do [what I had to do] in everything, *not* to allow myself any [privileges], in other words, not the least slackening in mortification, posture, etc. Although it was hard to do, I obeyed. Then everything was good again. Fortunately, that small relapse lasted only half a day, from yesterday afternoon until this morning around ten o'clock.

And now, dear Directress, I've celebrated my first lustral feast in your service! How glad I am to be serving you. With a peaceful heart I would sign on for another five years, but it's not necessary, for I've dedicated myself forever. So today there was a great celebration. I had to fight my way through everything. Yet because of your love, Beloved, everything is fine again. Your love! Twelve days to go, that's all. How glad I am to be your bride! So be it. Forever *with* and *for* each other, my Dearest.

Tuesday, August 16.
Dearest, this morning there was an examination! I took it as I used to do at Weert. No, old boy, it was not good that way. You should work more quietly and with more recollection. Ah, Dearest, when I was reading the Gospel this afternoon you again said such beautiful words to me! Then I felt once more strong and brave. Beloved, you are always at work for our upcoming marriage! How happy I am. Always and forever to be united with you. No more to be separated from you. So be it. Suffering and work. Everything for you, Dearest.

Wednesday, August 17.
Today is a whole day of adoration. You told me a lot when it was my turn. You also gave me a sign: if I don't think of you all the time after August 27 nor feel any inner suffering, you are not married to me. In that case I have been deceiving myself for about eight months. For then the betrothal must also be a self-deception or at least under suspicion. For the rest, I leave everything to you. Personally, I'm convinced the sign will be superfluous!

Ah, Beloved, I beg you, don't take my words as distrust of you. I must confess honestly, there is much more in favor of it than against it. Actually, only my nature is against it, shrinking from the Word and the value it conveys (as, for example, the highest degree of perfection, continuous inner quiet, etc.). Only ten days more to go!

Dearest Jesus, everything is and remains ready for you. You are everything, aren't you? You don't think, do you, that I distrust you? That would grieve me! Truly, you are and remain my All, my infinitely dear All, my eternal God. you, the infinitely happy One. Rejoice then. Be infinitely glorified and praised. Rejoice about you and in you. Be infinitely glad, Dearest.

✠

. . . everything is one great gush of grace.

✠

Thursday, August 18.
Recollection. Beloved, in his conference yesterday the Novice Master spoke of all the graces we have had during the Novitiate! I know a thing or two about that, don't I? At the beginning of the Novitiate, I discovered you had given me the grace of the "prayer of simplicity and quiet," even before that time. So my whole previous spiritual unfolding was also a great grace! Next came the mysteries during the first retreat. You showed me something of who you really are.

At the second retreat you called me as your espoused. How I trembled with joy then! I couldn't refuse, to put it mildly. So far everything is known to the Novice Master! He knows I'm betrothed to you. But he knows nothing about our marriage plans. I'll try to tell him "on direction." Beloved, looking back [I see that] everything is one great gush of grace. Ah, dearest Jesus, my love.

Friday, August 19.
Beloved, I love you. I keep saying "Beloved!" You know what felt worth there is in that word. It brings together all your grace in me, [it reminds me that] you are always with me, completely. You for me and I for you.

"Beloved," whenever I think or say this word throughout the day, sometimes in the middle of playing volleyball or bowling, it stands for the surrender of myself to you. I'm talking foolishly, I know, but it's your fault! You began first, didn't you? Only one week more and we will be united eternally in the state of [mystical] marriage.

Dearest, All. Many thanks for this preparation. It feels good to know that you will make use of this retreat to make me (insofar as possible) ready for my task as your bride. I'm deeply grateful. Everything, my whole little self given by you, belongs to you. Everything is for you, for you only, my Beloved!

Saturday, August 20.
One more week, Dearest, only seven more days. And then I may put my weak hand into your strong fist! I can't imagine any unattainable ideals when we are one in marriage! It's a matter-of-fact. Jesus will use his rights and sow his good seed in me; it's only my duty as a bride to cooperate well and to make the seed germinate and thrive freely (these are all the works Jesus wants to achieve through his weak bride). Like a faithful husband, Jesus will look after me and feed me! He'll always be with me to encourage and to strengthen me. One day difficult times will emerge in the spiritual realm, just as for a woman who is about to give birth to her child! Then I may suffer, much more than I know. I realize this very well. But I'm rejoicing already! Then Jesus' seed will mature by the cooperation of his weak creature. Jesus will strengthen and comfort me in my travail, as a husband does for his wife.

But Jesus won't take away the suffering itself. He knows it is necessary! I will be happy to suffer for him. It makes him glad because he sees it. Thus, Dearest, our married life shall pass in ever renewed blessing! It is for this that I enter into matrimony with you—to bring forth what you want to put into me.

Beloved, with these obligations I'll also get rights: the right of your special protection, especially in hard times! Next, everything that is yours is also mine. Where you live is also my house. So in every church I share the tabernacle with you!

Dearest, I'm so glad. Sometimes I'm even affright with happiness! Everything is quiet, though! Calmness is inside. May it stay like that all my life. Who knows, Beloved? Perhaps we will celebrate our silver or even our golden wedding anniversary? I leave everything to you! You look after (you have to) your family, don't you?

Continued, the same day.
Beloved, I've scribbled almost four exercise books during this Novitiate. I intend to keep them if you agree. But if you, by word of my Superior, want me to tear them up or burn them, it's all the same to me, really!

Dearest, tonight the Novice Master talked about poverty! So, [I want] to get rid of all superfluous things. If you agree, I'll go to Gemert with only the underwear I need and some things mentioned in the prospectus (*no more*!!), for example, a missal and the *Manual*, a comb, soap, etc. Besides those things I'll take nothing with me but my fountain-pen, watch, and pipe at the advice of the Novice Master. But I don't want to use those things (watch and pipe) except for good reasons. I will smoke only now and then (though very seldom) if my confrères ask me, just to be social, and no more. That's all well and good as long as I only have you.

My dear love, in a week's time I hope to be united with you in matrimony. I shall drive home with my family [after they attend the ceremony of taking first vows] and then as a religious, begin my religious life with fresh courage after a holiday.

Sunday, August 21.

Ah, Dearest! Last night I fell again! The same imprudences as before. Thanks be to God, you protected me again! I was allowed to feel sorry, truly sorry. You are simply burning through me now. It's a fire that is at the same time punishing and purifying. How furious the devil is, Dearest! He certainly sees [that it is] all or nothing! Tonight, too, during my sleep, I had temptations. Not that it matters at all! But it points to a heavy thunderstorm that burst out this morning and is still going on. Now, at the moment there is rest, but my head is tired. Through everything I dare to say with the Sacred Host on my tongue, "I have persevered thanks to your grace and your goodness. I have not consented; otherwise I should have known *for sure*." So, don't think about it any more, it's over. Go on—all for Jesus, and Jesus only.

Monday, August 22.

Recollection. Beloved, last night I wanted to see the Novice Master to ask for a solution to problems, among other things, about our upcoming marriage. But he wasn't in his room. Then I went to bed. But while I was undressing you solved everything all at once. There is the same answer to all problems whatsoever, no matter what the consequences may be: [mystical] marriage brings the definite solution. If not, then there is no matrimony!

Dearest Jesus, I must certainly grieve you by this ever returning incertitude. What a strange fellow I am, don't you think? I'm so weak. I'm as weak as you are strong! Yet, Beloved, I do love you. Everything is yours. I want to allow myself nothing. No half work! I must be yours totally. For example, I want to keep to the habit of sitting without touching the back [of chairs] except during recreation. [I want to keep] also my practices of praying the rosary and the Stations of the Cross. Everything for you.

Later the same day.
Today the Novice Master spoke again about chastity. At the end he also gave the rule that is so important to me: If a person has broad views and doesn't easily consider something a sin, and he has his doubts, it's at least advisable to submit the question to a priest, for there may be something the matter with it. But if somebody is conscientious (or scrupulous, like me) then, theologically, he only needs to confess what is most certainly *grave* evil, what most certainly has happened and what *most certainly* has not been confessed before in a good Confession. Further than that he doesn't need to confess *anything*. One may, of course [go to Confession], but one is not obliged [to do so] in conscience, except only in *those* circumstances. So there's no need to worry any more! Beloved, many thanks for your ever increasing grace. I feel myself already utterly fastened to you, just like a fiancée a few days before her wedding.

Later the same day.
Beloved, time is getting on, isn't it. Only a few more days and I'll be in full life! Then it will begin, for my repose in you must also be active. [I must] share everything with everybody to please you more and more. Yes, I'll try [to do so] gladly! Also, when I'm wed to you, I'll still always remain the poor, weak, little soul I used to be, even more so.

Beloved, you have to be careful, even about your own bride; otherwise she might chase you out of the house! An abyss, unfathomably deep, of misery and wickedness, that's what I am. Or, is it perhaps owing to you in me that I have never yet offended you seriously, for you have arranged things in such a way that I was not able to? Surely not. I could not do anything about it. I'm glad things have worked out this way, I truly am! But it's your work, not mine.[68]

68 The Novitiate ends, as did Rinus' on August 27, 1938, with the solemnity of taking first or "temporal" vows by which the Novice binds himself for three years to the religious community. After these three years he may or may not be admitted to final vows by which he binds himself to his religious community for a lifetime.

The Novitiate in Gennep invites family members of the novice to be present at the solemnity of the profession of his temporal vows of obedience, chastity, and poverty. After a festive meal of celebration, the novice leaves with his family for a short home visit. After that he goes on to the senior scholasticate or major seminary in Gemert to begin his six years of philosophical and theological studies. The family of Rinus drove him to their home in The Hague. He left at the beginning of September, 1938, for Gemert. He resumed his journal writing there, but only the next calendar year, on February 15, 1939.

The conference room of the Novitiate at Gennep after being in the line of fire during the war.

VI
Philosophy
Part One
Gemert
1938–1939

VI
PHILOSOPHY
PART ONE
GEMERT
1938–1939

LETTER FROM RINUS TO ADRIAN

Gemert, December 12, 1938

Dear Friend Adrian,

He doesn't write, he does, he doesn't write, he does—it takes long but at last it happens. I say, old boy, how are you? I'm anxious to know how you've been doing in the last year [at Weert]. Here everything is fine.

Well, Adrian, now I'd better begin with an unpleasant bit of news for you. I did not go to [see] Mr. Adriaan Langelaan.[69] *You remember, directly after arriving at the station, [I started to go], but near the Van Zeggelenlaan I turned off. I hardly dared. Then I thought, hey boy, no nonsense, turn back and go to Mr. Langelaan. He's your friend, too, isn't he? I turned and went towards the Goeverneurlaan and then I lacked courage again to turn into Van Zeggelenlaan. I didn't know what to tell him. Fine hero I am, aren't I? And yet, I'd like to go to the Langelaan's with you; he's a nice chap, but I didn't dare to go alone. If you see him during the Christmas holidays tell him so, and also give him my kind regards. For I hope to be wiser next holidays.*

69 Rinus did not go to see Mr. Langelaan not because he did not like him as a member of our prototype Epiphany circle, but because his usual shyness made him ill at ease if he had to engage alone in long conversations.

I say, Adrian, when looking back on our meeting during the break—that first meeting at your home, you remember, I thought that you thought I had changed completely and that we had quite different views. But the next day everything was solved, really solved again soon, since we found we agreed more than ever! I liked that a lot. You had also developed in that year, especially in regard to practical daily things, whereas I had [grown] more in theory—but it all fitted together perfectly!

We have to go forward to holiness, fervent holiness, which is the most matter-of-fact reality. True, no false gospel, only "the naked gospel" as Edward Poppe used to say. In our days we've got such enormous things going for us. The circumstances are so favorable for God to pour his sea of grace into us. For he also builds on nature, doesn't he?

Adrian, that I urge you, that I so urgently beg you to be holy, is not because I doubt you, but because it's the impulse of my heart to say, Non turbetur cor vestrum, *don't be afraid to take the leap. Read Chapters 14-17 in St. John's Gospel. Read and re-read them—there's our whole program. By doing our duty we love God. If we love God he comes to us, to sojourn with us. If we remain in him, we will bear much fruit. It's all there, I would almost say, philosophically, matter-of-factly. Duty! When that is done, everything goes well, even when we wish the whole rest to go, I don't know where!*

Laugh, be inwardly cheerful, laugh at your faults. After all, we can do nothing on our own, can we? Laugh at yourself. Then you certainly won't become melancholy or discouraged. But...of course, don't put up with that! We must go forward in God, through God, with God, and for God—and, we, especially, in, through, with, and for Mary!

Let's explain as good everything [that goes on] in our neighbor's life. Spare him, as long as it is still possible in any way. So often a refined soul is hidden under rough bark. But if one looks closer and more clearly (looks with the eyes of God), then rough, indifferent, or lax manners sometimes become expressions of a quite different principle. Especially the Dutch don't like showing their true character—that they take everything supernaturally!

I say, Adrian, I haven't written any news, ask Bertus [a seminarian from his parish] about that. Maybe I'll send you a note during the holidays by way of my parents, in any case to your family! Give them my kind regards and wish them a blessed Christmas and New Year, also in my name. Don't forget to do so! How's that little sister of yours. You'll write during the holidays, won't you? Write anything you want, for mostly letters aren't opened anyway, and if they are, it really doesn't matter.

Well, my dear friend, I'll finish. Forgive my scribbling and gibberish.

Cordially, Your friend, Rinus

Of course! Quotidie oremus pro invicim *[daily we pray for each other].*

LETTER FROM RINUS TO ADRIAN. DELIVERED TO ADRIAN'S HOME IN DEN HAAG

Gemert, January, 1939

Dear Friend Adrian,

You remember I had promised you a short note to wish you and your family a blessed Christmas and New Year. You see, I haven't forgotten.

Adrian, how did it go [for you] at Weert—and how are things now? You know I am very interested.

How are your Father and Mother, and [your youngest sister] Leonie. She must be growing a lot! And how about the other toddlers? In about six months I'm going to call on them.

Be sure to wish your good parents the peace of the Christ Child from me—that peace which is more than a couple of roasted geese or a bubbly bottle of champagne or a "nice" film or a dance. The peace of God to the toilers and their families, the peace of duty—and sometimes a duty as heavy as iron!

Really, Adrian, even if I lack nothing here I won't forget others![70] *I'm so often in thought and prayer with the people of the "weekly bread, only bread and nothing more! Even bread is uncertain because every week the words, "Yes, I'm sorry, it's necessary to economize," puts more families in need and despair!*

And yet I wish all of them a peace the world cannot give!

Adrian, once again my best wishes to you and to those dear to you (whom I also find so likeable!) A few delightful days at home. Don't let us forget our motto: Before everything, "Onwards to holiness."

Your friend,

Rinus

GEMERT, 1939

✠

Alter Christus expresses the whole [meaning] of mystical union in one phrase.

✠

---

70 War was threatening. Some countries had been invaded already by Nazi Germany. Stories of the economic needs of many families filled Rinus with compassion. He prayed for the loyal and the hungry in the conquered territories. And the fate of political prisoners had made a deep impression on him. He realized that at any moment our country and its families could be in the same predicament.

Wednesday, February 15.

I made the resolution to write a bit larger and more neatly, also when I'm [taking notes] and studying philosophy. The Congregation won't begrudge me the cost of a few more exercise-books for such general needs. Also [larger script] is more readable for others and more pleasant when studying. I also hope to avoid those blunt expressions [so prevalent in] my former notebooks.

Dearest, how deeply you've been impelling me the last few days to again act like you completely. All that is [merely "I"] must be moderated [if I am to become] *Alter Christus* [Another Christ]. This is the highest Christian experience [one can attain]. It gives the Father the greatest possible glory from a creature when Jesus himself acts in and through that person. To be *Alter Christus* entails a short program. It includes everything and expresses the whole [meaning] of mystical union in one phrase.

Dearest, you are everything! Take everything in me. Don't spare me. Time is precious. Your holy will in everything. Mother Mary, I love you!

Thursday, February 16.

I know you don't want me to do anything for myself alone. I had sent for a book. I received it the day before yesterday. I may read it now but not out of a mere unhealthy curiosity. My nature may think this [directive] to be a nuisance, but there it is. It's simply a matter of fact that I don't exist for myself but for others and, first of all, for you, my Jesus! I am quite willing to serve you better, that's for sure, especially after you allow me a good relaxation. I use it [for that purpose]. If I do *not* relax with this kind of reading, then it falls outside of the scope you intend for it. So away with it! Yet through all this [inner upheaval] I keep an unbroken calm and rest. It is you who are arranging everything in me. [On my part] there is no resistance. Dearest, [my aim] is to be you, insofar as possible. To do all for the glory of your almighty, dearest Father, and included in that for the salvation of *all* souls.

Friday, February 17.

Dearest, please don't laugh when I say I've found the description of my life on pages 31-52 of the little book *Een met Jesus [One With Jesus],* by Father De Jaeger, S.J. Yes, [it is to be] *one* with you! I haven't yet read more of it [but I will]. If Father de Rooij asks for anything else, I'll have him read this.[71] Daily I feel less able to express what you are in me! How miserable all of this makes me! It's exactly as it says there: "The soul enjoys seeing itself so weak." Whenever I catch myself in something that is less than [in or of] you, I've got to

+M.

15 Febr. 1939. Ik heb 't voornemen gemaakt om wat groter en netter
(Novic) te schrijven. ook met de philosstudie, die paar schriften die
dat meer zal kosten heeft de congregatie best over voor 't
algemeen nut. n.l. overzichtelijker voor anderen en prettig-
ger voor de studie. Ook die plompe uitdrukkingen van
m'n vorige schriften hoop ik te vermijden. Liefste
Wat dringt U me de laatste-dagen weer diep. U wilt
helemaal dat ik als U handel, al 't natuurlijke ik
moet er af. Alter Christus! 't Is het hoogste Christen
beleven, wat Uw Vader de grootst mogelijke glorie ver-
schaft uit 't schepsel. n.l. als Jesus Zelf in en door
dat schepsel handelt. in Alter Christus zijn! 't Is 't kort
alles inhoudende program dat heel de mystieke eenheid
in een woord uitdrukt. Liefste U bent alles! Pak
alles maar in mij ontzie me niet, de tijd is kostbaar.
Uw H. Wil in alles! Moeder Maria, ik houd van U!
16 Febr. 1939. U wilt 't helemaal niet hebben, ik weet 't, dat ik
alleen iets doe voor mijzelf, zo had ik eergisteren 'n
boek besteld en gekregen, ik mag 't best lezen, dat weet
ik maar U wilt 't niet omdat ik uit min of meer on-
gezonde nieuwsgierigheid lees. Mijn natuur kan 't wel
vervelend vinden maar 't is nu eenmaal waar, dat ik
niet voor mijzelf ben maar voor anderen. En op de 1e
plaats voor U, mijn Jezus! Ik wil 't graag! U staat
me alle goede ontspanning toe om U beter te dienen
dat weet ik, en daar maak ik ook gebruik van, maar
met zulk soort lectuur ontspan ik me niet. En daar-

A handwriting sample from February, 1939.

smile! It's really true! It's a real pleasure to see myself as "nothing" and you as "All."

Dearest, the struggle is still severe, I must confess. But I lose *nothing* at all of the repose or, what seems to be a better expression, of [resting in] you. On the contrary, you increase every day. You do all that [is needed] to the glory of the Father in me! You ask nothing else of me but total surrender, without me having to worry about anything any more! Now I ask you, who is able to resist such an offer? You've got me and I've got you.

Dearest, I just went to Confession again. "Forgiveness of all your sins." Many thanks for the gift of faith. Anything of my past life that was not *you* has been forgiven! My good Confessor also spoke about making reparation for the sins [committed by people] during the carnival days.[72] These were mostly sins of impurity, and (more with older people) of intemperance. Those were the ones that offended you at that time! Make reparation [for me], dearest God. Don't look at me but at Jesus in me! When we beg for reparation together, you will accept it. But, Beloved, I've got to add something extra: do not be afraid [*non turbetur cor vestrum neque formidet].* To be you in everything. Alas, *silence* alone can express our love!

---

[71] Father Jan de Rooij, Rinus' new spiritual director and Confessor at Gemert, was an elderly Spiritan, who had spent many years as a fervent missionary in Bagamoyo, a diocese in Tanzania (at that time called *Tanganyika*), East Africa. The Novice Master and spiritual director of Rinus had been a missionary in the same territory. He knew Father de Rooij as a personal friend during these years and advised Rinus to chose him as his Confessor and spiritual director. Father de Rooij died at the age 97. [Editor's Note: As long as Father de Rooij was stationed in Gemert, he was my own Confessor and spiritual director. I had asked him to accept my request on the advice of both my Novice Master and my friend Rinus.]

[72] Carnival days or Mardi Gras are one or more days of revelry that precede the six weeks of Lent with its practices of penance. Unfortunately, this yearly custom led some participants to wild carousing. Gemert, like Weert and Gennep, were located in the originally Catholic South of the Netherlands. Unlike in the West and North of Holland, carnival days were an age-old custom in the South.

Sunday, February 19.
Alas, during these carnival days, you are being offended again and again! For these and for all those former carnival days, let me make reparation. No, it is not Rinus Scholtes who begs for it; it is Jesus in him. Almighty All, reparation! Remember those poor sinners are much better than I am. How much more would I have offended you were I in their circumstances? How much more would they have praised you in my place by faithfully answering to your grace! How deeply they would have been Jesus! And look at me, poor wretch that I am! No, you don't want me to scrutinize myself but to always go on. Forgive me all my wrong and selfish doings, even those I've not yet done or might have done. Please do! Grow more and more in me: *Eum oportet crescere me autem minui* [He must increase and I must decrease].

My God, I'm really so happy [in you] and, because you are also God, you are infinitely happy [with me]! I'm happy because Mary and all the saints are happy. I'm happy because of all the good acts of people and for all my confreres. In short, I'm happy because you are happy, because you, my most dearest All, are glorified by so many people!

LETTER FROM RINUS TO ADRIAN [Still in the Junior Seminary in Weert]

Gemert, February 20, 1939

Dear Friend Adrian,

In spite of your hard times you wrote a letter on my birthday. That was very kind of you! Whether you'll receive one from me on April 19 I don't know! It will depend on the circumstances. Well, how are you? Getting on a bit better? I won't forget you in my prayers. By the same mail I've written to Bertus. There I write all about myself, the "Hague" way. But I won't do so with you, for you know already that everything is going along fine with me.

How nice it will be when, in a few month's time, you will be here for a day in your long black coat. It won't be so long any more. And how's the study going? Geometry is still your strongest subject, isn't it? Cheer up. There's no geometry here. And you'll be good at philosophizing.

That New Year's wish you received at Weert on that half bit of paper was actually meant for you and your family. I'd written your address on it, to have my brother put it in your mailbox at your home. But, as it is, so you'd better give my kindest regards to your good parents the first time you write home. Will you? The same when you see Mr. Langelaan again. You didn't forget at Christmas either, did you?

We had a marvelous play on January 9, The Front Line. *[It was] fine, truly splendid, full of good insights. It was once performed, I believe, in the Amsterdam Theater. One person likes it; another thinks it immoral, but all agree it is unusual. The scene is set in America (but the program says it could happen anywhere). It was written by an American. On the front line are the Jesuits. In a community (most of it takes place in the Fathers' recreation room) there are three men who want to get out; two more are unbearable as community people, and the other three wonderful fellows.*

In Amsterdam a Jesuit was director, while another Jesuit condemned it strongly! Anyway, the play has done me a lot of good. If it's suitable anywhere, then certainly it is fine for religious communities. Ask Father Bohemen about it and J. Wijn! [both of whom saw the play]. I also wish you a lot of success with your role in The Newspaper Boy*! But it might be too late for that!*

I say, Adrian, what a lot we'll have to tell one another during the holidays (which now last four weeks for me). After the exams here, the first semester is over. On Ash Wednesday the second semester begins. Others say that passes much faster. Then it will soon be the second Monday in July.

Anyway I'm going to stop now. I wish you a good Lenten season with much spiritual progress. I am happy that Father Berkers is extraordinarius [for us here in Gemert].[73] *Will you give A. Olsthoorn [Adrian's classmate and a distant family member of Rinus] my kind regards? Father Olsthoorn [the missionary uncle of A. Olsthoorn] will be home after a few months! I hope that Adrian [Olsthoorn] may also go to the golden wedding anniversary [of his parents].*

Well, Adrian, so long. Kindest regards from me to all acquaintances. Bear up like a man, please do! Much success!

Your friend in Jesus,

Rinus

Friday, February 24.

Many thanks for your forgiveness, my God and my All. *Ego te absolvo a peccatis tuis* [I absolve you of your sins]. So you say to me through my Confessor. *Credo*, I believe! Everything is wiped clean! Always and again always, there is more of you through everything! [What you ask] is really not easy; my nature often suffers much, but [through you everything!].

My good [new] Confessor thought it surprising that everything in my spiritual life has moved so fast. He also wondered (and rightly so) if

---

73 In accordance with the rules and constitutions an extraordinary Confessor is appointed for each community. He is extraordinary in that he is not one of the ordinary confessors of the community itself but a member of another community who visits at certain dates the community concerned and is available to those who want to go to confession to an outsider. Father Berkers had been Rinus' first Confessor and director in Weert.

I had suffered enough. Yet I could go on as usual and not be disturbed. Duty calls!

If I have suffered enough, only you know! Dearest, that will be a secret between you and me. How can I express my suffering. In the past at [elementary] school my outer self used to be so cheerful and shallow and so really boyish. For six years I lived like the others, certainly outwardly. At Weert [in the Junior Seminary] it was the same for six years: I never had diseases or bodily defects. Even now I think that I still have the looks of an innocent child. How can I say I have suffered *much*, or even more than others of my age, when I've never looked into the average soul of a fellow human being? I believe I've suffered much, but I really don't know *how* much or more than others? Besides, you've made my nature such that, for example, in the morning I suffer much, yes everything, for a few hours, but in the afternoon I forget what happened in the morning.

The same with pleasant things. I remember the facts, but if there were no certain *external* facts of joy or grief I always doubt later on: "Was it really so bad? Were you really so glad?" Therefore, Dearest, your holy will be done. I will never know here on earth what I really suffered. The only thing I can say is that I hurt easily and that I hide it, almost naturally, under a smile. This is especially so if authorities say something or ask me to do something.

Why should I worry about this? Your love is everything, isn't it! And, haven't you said that the way through Mary is the shortest road, the short cut to perfection? And I have been allowed to be Mary's consecrated servant for six years already! Moreover, former saints could receive you far less often than we can now. And what about those 3,000 Holy Communions I could take (by a rough estimate)? Indeed many confrères and others also benefit [like I] from a good spiritual formation in spite of our tepidity and distraction.

Dearest, I know I'm worth nothing. When once in a while I look at myself too much, you always rap my knuckles. You want blind surrender. There it is. I certainly suffered from scruples during these past seven years. Always that worrying and nagging about the past must have terribly bored Father Berkers, my good Confessor at Weert. Yet every time he was understanding and kind to me. He gave me encouragement and confidence again and again, but, Dearest, only if I was doing your holy will. You know how painfully and with what *torment* I doubted my soul's condition in the Novitiate. Now, since my profession, that has no longer been the case, certainly not for these six months. But, once more, your holy will is everything. You want blind surrender. I may not interfere in anything, just do this moment's duty: *Hic et nunc esse* [By being here and now].

Jesus, everything is for you, you are my All! Jesus, my God! You alone know how much I love you! You must arrange everything. Jesus in me *without me* (that is, without resistance) must do everything God wants: *quae ei placita sunt facio semper!* [I do always what pleases him]. I am nothing. Success and glory are due to you only.

All people should love you! Also in my contacts with others I should simply let you act and not worry later anxiously if you had shone through in everything. Through your grace I see, after all, nothing but my misery. You alone know what is good. I can't find the way myself. Dearest, no resistance. Mary, my Directress, many thanks for everything. Jesus, my Jesus, let your holy will reign in me and in *all* people.

✠

I have become you both inwardly and outwardly.

✠

Wednesday, March 1.

Today we have a recollection day with a Forty Hours' Vigil. Those to be ordained are making their preparation retreat. Beloved, you've clearly impressed on me these two days to take care of the outer me too, that is, to be polite, decent, and well-mannered to others. Therefore, I'll read Bishop Franciscus Diepen's book [on "etiquette"]. That's a necessity since I've not read it yet.

Dearest, you're urging me on so much that I have to set *all* my sails. I have to become *you* both *in*wardly and *out*wardly. I can't [find a way] to write down how simple and clear this [directive] is. Many thanks for enabling me to see it so well. By being *you* we render reparation, thanks, and adoration to our Father with our intercession. By being *you* we show Mary our childlike love and gratefulness. We also thank our patron saints for their protection and especially our Holy Guardian Angel. By being *you* being a Christian becomes the greatest [grace on earth]. To let *you* increase in us is the point of our existence on earth. If we are *you*, you are our master, Friend, and Bridegroom all in one. By being *you*, the transforming union (becoming *One*, namely, becoming you) in mystical marriage is effected in the simplest and shortest way. In a word: by being *you* we become everything.

Dearest, with all that, I still remain nothing. Moreover, the stronger, greater, and more beautiful you become in me, the weaker, smaller, and uglier my nothingness stands out. Dearest, even if I were a hundred years old, and even if you had been able to work and to be for eighty years without interruption in my soul, I would still say, "Dearest, beware!" Be careful with that treacherous Rinus Scholtes. His wickedness is almost an unfathomable abyss? "Really, Dearest, I mean it." Yet all this doesn't worry me; neither does much suffering. I let you do as you like. I needn't do anything about it.

Jesus, I walk through the garden [the Castle park of the Senior Seminary] at night or whenever. I see your splendor in nature. My almighty God, I think spontaneously, "Man, all this I will give you, if you fall down and adore me, your God!" Yes, my God, and even more, because Jesus has become Man, we can render you infinite, perfectly satisfying sacrifices of adoration, thanksgiving, atonement, and intercession—by sacrificing Jesus to you. *Christianus alter Christus* [A Christian is another Christ].

Saturday, March 4.
Many thanks, my Jesus, for the new Pope [Pius XII]. You've got a Deputy again. May he be you completely. Then His Holiness can take your place in the right way. I'm happy and quiet for your sake, although my nature is still in turmoil. Lately I have associated with one of my confrères. I'm not quite sure if I behave enough like you toward him! Nature is so sly, especially mine, and hypocritical too.

My Jesus, if they knew me as I am, [if they could see] my whole being, they would despise me and expel me from this community. I'm so glad a confrère told me that I was smug, opinionated, and conceited; another said something else, that I never admit it when someone else is right and [that I am] always arguing or (boasting).

Dearest, I was really glad about [the criticism], though in my own nature it was different. Please, bless that confrère for me. I should be calmer, much calmer in my outer life, especially when I'm talking! [I need to be] *you* more and more through everything! No doubt my path is not strewn with roses (certainly not roses *without* thorns). That doesn't matter as long as you keep growing in me more and more, and not only in me but in *everybody*. You are All; I am nothing. I see this so well. Every time I think for a moment that I'm capable of doing this or that by myself, you let me fail. You want to be everything to me. As long as I don't give you *everything*, Dearest, you are not enough in me. I love you my All.

Wednesday, March 8.
I played soccer four times with borrowed things. It's okay for an "old fellow" to run around like that. But what do *you* say about it? Should I stop? Should I ask my family for the money for shoes? I must choose wisely, for to wear down another fellow's shoes with my bear's feet is not right! I also dug up an old pipe this morning. If it pleases my fellow students that I smoke with them, I'll do so gladly, though I get sick as a dog. For I don't care for smoking at all. Maybe one gets a taste for it after much smoking. Yes, my Jesus, thus I bungle about day after day.

The Spiritans renovated the castle built in the 13th century in Gemert by the religious order of the Teutonic Knights. It was here that Rinus studied philosophy and theology. It was here that he died.

The bridge over the castle moat under which Rinus often went canoeing and, in the winter, ice skating.

The portal to the castle and its grounds over the outer moat.

What goes on in my spiritual life goes on in my character: I am inconstant in the *means* (I choose) but stubborn and tenacious as a Frisian[74] in regards to the goal of those means. That goal is: To be *you* more and more every day, indeed every hour. You, my dearest Bridegroom, to whom I belong eternally.

Jesus, through your grace I've had no illusions about religious life for the past two years. Therefore, I'm not disappointed or discouraged now, even if it sometimes hurts so much. How I would like to kindle in *everyone* the fire that's in me. No good means would seem [to me] too strange to make this happen. I'd like to set everybody afire for you. *You*, [my own] *All!* Then I would still have you left to myself completely, even if *all* people had become full of you, for you are infinite! You are holiness! [What's needed is] even more *blind* surrender! Let it storm so much that *everything* at times threatens to fall down. It's nothing. The moment the storm has abated I see the sun again, bigger and bigger, brighter and brighter. It's true. I'm in the Netherlands, the [lowlands] of the spiritual life; there are many clouds and not much sun. Yet I'm quite happy with a happiness that goes beyond words. I can't seem to catch it by any definition of happiness. [I must sense it], even if the rest of me often feels unhappy and dejected.

My Jesus, my Confessor allows me to speak about you on occasion. With you, in you, through you, in and for Mary, I'll do so—not I but you. Jesus, I must be so careful about my sensitive heart. It's too demanding. That so-called "fraternal love" toward certain confrères is far too human. Never! You alone have my heart. Although nature *feels* for them a real love, I should not indulge in it. Everything must be supernatural. You and you alone!

Friday, March 10 [Translator's Note: Perhaps Saturday, March 11. The manuscript is unclear].
Jesus, IT [Rinus' temptations] was uncommonly violent today, especially this afternoon. You know I do NOT want it. I don't want to judge or harbor evil suspicions! Be pleased with what you have done. That is [when I] look down on the others with a kind of disdain, I don't want to yield to what my heart asks. Not at all! I don't want to be unchaste! I don't want to waste time.

Jesus, my bridegroom, you've been able to watch me today. I feel time pressing because your punishment is even heavier. How great the torment of the damned must be! Not that I felt rejected by you! Far from it! For, owing to your grace, I may stand my ground!

---

74 A Frisian is a Dutch person born and raised in "Friesland," a province in the high North of the country with its own Frisian language and customs. They are thought, rightly or wrongly, to be even more stubborn and tenacious than other Dutch people can be.

My Jesus, you ask for more surrender to be able to be All in me, more deeply. I beg you to be allowed to give what you ask for, but, better still, just take it! After all, I'm your sacrificial victim, am I not? Why should I wonder about so much suffering! Haven't I surrendered to you! Why should I be concerned about what others are thinking? They may think that I'm rolling in a sea of "novice delights." Why should I wonder about what they mean when they say to me, "Your notorious modesty?" I know only too well what they mean by that! Why should I care that I always disappoint others? In everything I'm overrated too highly. The result is always below expectations!

Yet, all this doesn't scare me in my heart of hearts! There I'm quiet and happy, though alone as well sometimes! So, my dearest, it's good this way, really good! Inner prayer is the main goal because you are glorified most by it. Even study, however important, is subordinate to [prayer]! With you, and you only, I'm not afraid, even if it sometimes seems as if I'm deceiving my good Confessor and the whole world!

✠

Every day you urge me to dive deeper and deeper [into your love].

✠

Thursday, March 16.
Last night Father Provincial held a conference. He said, among other things, that we should be thankful to God for our community and for our daily bread. Yes, my Jesus, I thank you for my confrères. They are all such really good men! They do everything for you! They bear with me for you, even often without showing it.

Jesus, my Beloved, to whom I belong forever, many thanks for everything. People sustain us so that we can live much better than most of those who give so much to us! I'm sometimes ashamed of it: The way the table is always laid, there is pudding twice a day; there is wine and beer [on certain feast days]; there is our soccer and volleyball fields, and many other good gifts.[75] But, on second thought, it's all well spent when it serves our growth in holiness.

Dearest, even if I had to eat a golden ten-guilder coin's worth of things every day, for which the money had been begged, it would be worth it if you could grow unobstructed in me all the time. As long as I may resemble you more and more, the money is not superfluous. Jesus gives the Father and all people much more in exchange than our formation costs.

Jesus, you and you alone must increase in all the students here, indeed in all people. If I get the chance now and then, you-in-me can say something more to some of the confrères. Then I'd like to praise Mary as the best and shortest way to you.

All, my dearest Bridegroom. Everything should be directed to you, including our soccer play this afternoon. I know this may sound monotonous, but I can't help it. Every day you urge me to dive deeper and deeper [into your love]. [I must] forget everything about myself. [I should] allow you alone to act in me with no resistance on my part.

Dearest, come into all people. They are much easier to deal with than I am!!

75 The superiors of the Seminary were greatly concerned about nourishment, sports, and recreation. They knew that most of the young men entrusted to their care would need good health, a strong and resistant body. This would enable them to serve the spiritual and social needs of the poor in underdeveloped countries as foreign missionaries. On top of this, the spiritual directors of Rinus obliged him to eat as much as possible on medical advice. Since his sister, Henny, had died of tuberculosis, it was feared that the same sickness would threaten his life. He had to keep up his strength, but, alas, it proved to be of no avail. God had other plans for Rinus Scholtes.

VII
Philosophy
Part Two
Gemert
1939

VII
PHILOSOPHY
PART TWO
GEMERT
1939

Saturday, March 25. Annunciation. (The commemorative feast day of Mary's consecrated servants and of her protection.)

Dearest Beloved, since I last wrote a lot has happened! Love has kept on growing. *You* have grown in me, but that growth was painful to my nature, to my pride and all my wickedness. I have seen my wretchedness, my great misery and insignificance, in such a painful way. Jesus, the more I suffer and go unnoticed, the deeper and more happy I am in you in a hidden way that cannot be noticed by others! I'm so happy because *you,* my dearest *All* are infinitely happy, because Jesus keeps giving to you, Father, eternal love and glory. I'm happy because Mary is happy, because all the saints are, too. I'm happy because everything is good. *All* nature is so beautiful. It's your creation.

Jesus, I am to be transformed totally into you. Yes, I suffer, I'll always suffer, but I can count on you, can't I? After all, it's spring again! And you know what that means to my passionate full-blooded nature!

But it's nothing. When I look forward I get scared that I won't persevere, but when I stick to the "now," it goes well. Moreover, my struggle glorifies you. It's Jesus' work you see in me. I let him act. Everything, everything melts together into one. *All* good things for you. *All* bad things against you. My wickedness is against you, but your grace is ever more abundant. My dearest, I love you so!!

Saturday, April 1.
My Jesus, at present my Confessor has the previous exercise book. How is it that I'm always so calm when I write or hand in the exercise book? I'm sure that formerly I wouldn't have had a moment's rest; neither would I write down without restraint (although I know it will be read), nor hand it in. But now I give it over, realizing it's not my work but yours. You answer for the consequences yourself and everything is good.

Many thanks, Dearest. For a few days I was a little confused, too. Besides my daily task, I've been assigned another one. Now my proud nature feels offended. "They must certainly think I'm reading newspapers in the recreation room of the Fathers or doing nothing, or else why would I also have to scrub?" Yet I protest against these complaints of my nature. Everything is quiet, but only if I act in you. Indeed, I must work for you alone and as you will, my dearest God, mustn't I? But it is good for me to look at things in black and white now and then. Otherwise I tend to forget what's what in practice. Yet through it all, I love you more and more. And [Jesus] you love your dearest Father in me and through me, as it were. This is because, my dearest Bridegroom, we are no longer *two* but *one*, namely, *you*. For my nothingness has to give way to your Allness.

So go on, Jesus. Suffering is good for me. I only beg you to keep it well hidden. For my confrères should not notice anything. Dearest, I experience now what I could not understand before. If one loves you, and you alone, one has a really great love for one's parents, family, friends, and brothers, in short for everybody, out of love for you. It is true. This love, too, is due to you. Dearest Mother, Jesus greets you!

Tuesday, April 4.
Quiet in you and for you! My dearest Bridegroom, at first I was so busy proclaiming my unworthiness, but lately this has not been the case any more! I still remember my insignificance and sinfulness. I also tell you of it, only not so often now! For this would mean that I am still watching myself too much!

Jesus, now I'm glad because I may *be* you, because you want to glorify in me the Father, our dearest Father. I'm glad because that glorification is accompanied by suffering, and also because your whole mystical body, indeed, all that is, plus all that is (for you), shares in it. It's almost beyond words.

Jesus, you are everything! This word fully expresses what I want to say. I would [be glad] to coin a new word if this one were understood in a superficial sense only.

Jesus, I'm so glad for you, so delighted that you are eternally, infinitely happy, that Mary and all the saints are happy, that all the angels and all the souls deceased in grace are happy. I'm thrilled for all of them. May all my confrères, all my fellowmen, be as happy in you and for you. Am I foolish to put it like this? [To say] I'm happy that you, not I, are God! Let me work in and through you, work a lot! Do my duty. Be inwardly in complete rest. Thus with you and for you I may do your holy will!

✠

. . . to live as Jesus.

✠

Thursday, April 6. Holy Thursday.

Today Father Lütenbacher [an elderly Father from Alsace, France, who founded the Gemert community] held a conference about the Holy Eucharist. Many cordial thanks also for giving me absolution last night. Dearest, I know you've been working hard the last few weeks. Simply do what you want! You may take what you want. Just take it.

My dearest Bridegroom, my "second self" said it so well in the splendid book, *Een Met Jezus* [*One with Jesus*]. It might as well be called the *Zeg Meisje Luister Eens* [*Listen, Girl*][76] for the spiritual life: that *newness*, all that is now so different as compared with former days, is a really new life for the soul, namely, to live as Jesus!

Dearest, even if I am praised (which, indeed, happens rarely, that is, hardly ever do they mean it), I remain cool under it. Everything goes automatically to you! You also know I even play soccer for you! It's pleasant and relaxing for my confrères that I can be put in any position and play fairly well, too. I let you do these things as well. I've noticed as a result that soccer doesn't distract me. When I race after a ball or roll over as a goal keeper, it's as deeply quiet inside of me as when I'm in chapel.

All this is done by you, Jesus, whether I play soccer or volley ball or go canoeing.[77] Everything is not for me but for the [intention of] the

76 In those days this was a popular book for instructing girls about the facts of life.

77 The Senior Seminary of the Spiritan community in Gemert was housed, as previous photos have shown, in a castle built by the order of Teutonic Knights in the 13th century. Surrounding the castle was a moat where students could canoe during recreation.

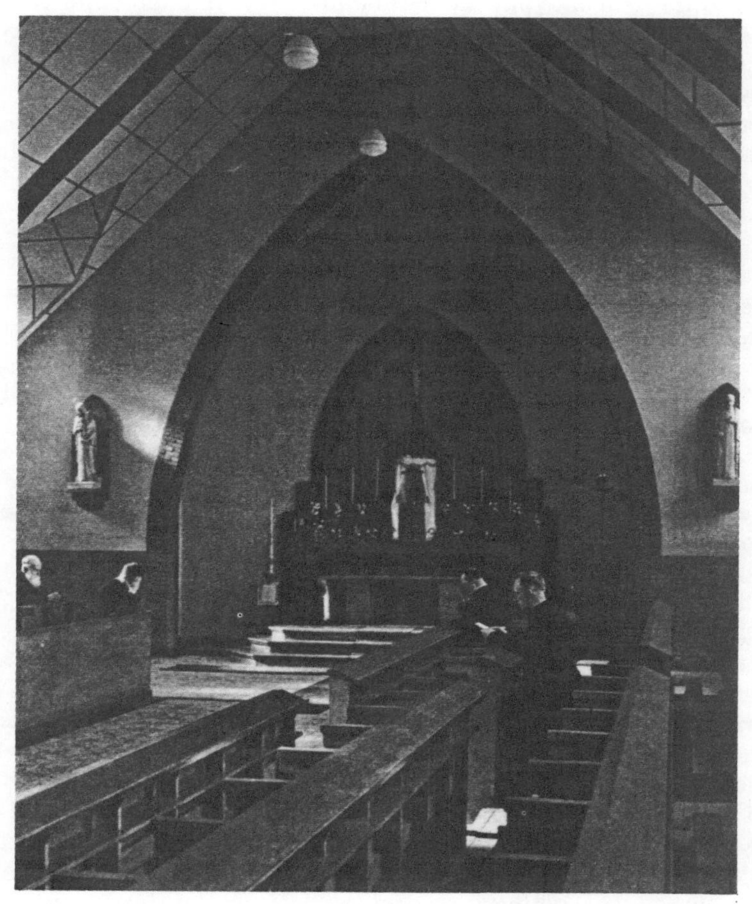

The chapel at Gemert where Rinus prayed.

whole world. This combination sounds strange, yet it is so. Also when I'm writing now it's for the [intention of] the whole world. Study, prayer, sleep, everything is for you, and through you, for our dear Father. Duty. Study. Work. Everything with and in you.

Tuesday, April 11.

Dearest, every now and then I feel as if I must write down something. You urge me on, as it were, since I can't do it on my own accord. The last two days were a bit more difficult for me, but it's really nothing. With you and in you, I get through everything. Many thanks that I may and can be cheerful all the time when necessary. For instance, during recreation I can tell jokes (some consider them even a little off color, although I really don't see why). My nature is shy and melancholy, yet I'm forced to cheerfulness by you in spite of myself.

My dearest Bridegroom, I feel it's not good to be ashamed that we are so well off here—to be ashamed that we can play soccer in the finest weather, that we have three weeks' vacation and sleep then an hour longer. No, I see you don't want us to use *every* minute to keep on studying. Yet I would not be grateful to you if I didn't use your good gifts of love out of love. You say we're really welcome to them, and you give them to *all* people.

If I reproach myself in this way, it is because I must hold myself up in order not to topple down [under the weight of] the misery I see so often in me! I sometimes burst out laughing when I catch myself because of my "ego." How can I begin to thank you for [the gift of] surrender of myself. Naturally considered, it's still a mystery to me how I can live so supernaturally, unmoved and quietly, while I experience so clearly (not always noticeable to others) my misery.

For a few days we had a guest at table beside me. He was a good judge of human nature. Although we hardly spoke to each other, he saw through me right away. When he left, he told his friend: "You shouldn't have given that red-headed guy next to me a cigar. He's so opinionated. He lays it on so thick." And yet despite this I can, in you and as you, smile quietly and really genuinely at myself, although my nature, that poor nature of mine, bloodies its nose terribly. And it just continues on this way! But now it's spring time! That old familiar *Weltschmerz* will play tricks on me as well as arouse "tender" feelings of sensual affection. But with you it's as nothing to me. Thanks to your grace, you have lived without interruption in my soul for twenty years, at least insofar as I can tell!

Dearest Jesus, in you, I'm another Christ, another crucified Christ, even if I myself am the only person who knows and experiences the size and weight of that cross. With you I'm not afraid! Moreover, surrendered to Mary, being your sacrificial victim and even your bride, in a word *Alter Christus*—I should not be afraid at all. *Non turbetur cor vestrum*. You are *all*, *I* am NOTHING!!!

Thursday, April 20.

At last I'm writing something again! It's taken a long time. Now we are on holiday! Holidays in spring. An hour more sleep and much more relaxation. My Dearest, you've seen how I've spent [my] time up until now. I was not up to par, especially yesterday. During our long walk, the old self dominated again for the most part. It was a near miss or I would have yielded to silly sensuality! Yes, in the spring a man cuts strange capers with such passionate hot blood. The day before yesterday, my dear Mother, along with Magda [Rinus' sister] and Jan [his younger brother], visited me. I thought it would be nice for them to have an outing. Mother thought I looked forward to it with real yearning, but, well, you know! My Jesus, I'm still with you, you alone. You grow in me, you my all!

I'll laugh and roar at my deep misery. I won't brood or make "resolutions." That is how you want it, if only you keep on growing [in me], my dearest Bridegroom. You won't blame me for being so happy, for being tied to you eternally, because you are becoming my second self—because I may be *you*? I know all too well how unworthy I am, but, in spite of that, I'm happy that you asked me. I am happy that your grace made, and still makes me, consent, for everything [of me] remains. Always go on anew! Dearest!

Sunday, April 23.

O felix culpa [O happy fault]. Dearest, you've seen yourself how I misbehaved this afternoon with my unhealthy curiosity! Yet, when all is said and done, I'm glad because there was no sin in this case, thanks to your grace. And it pleases me to see my own misery and weakness, strange though it may sound.

Dearest, I feel the struggle so powerfully. Especially the inclinations to particular [not spiritual] friendships make me suffer and struggle so much. But, owing to your incomparable grace, I still stand my ground.

Jesus, my Jesus, how can I thank you? Tonight you drew me so deeply again, to even greater surrender, even deeper "folly," to even more unfathomable distance between your work, your all, and my anti-work, my misery. I feel time is precious. Holiness, may you always grow deeper and deeper. Don't be afraid, no, no fear. For sometimes it takes courage to dare to go on living in you and as you. Yet I must be so careful not to lose you. I see myself and feel myself so near to sinning. *One* step away, for I'm so indescribably, deeply miserable. Yet, I trust in you. I go on *without looking back*, in you and as you. It costs a lot, Dearest. But that doesn't matter! If only you keep on growing, if only the maxim, *Gloria Externa Formalis* [Formal External Glory] comes from me and from your whole unfolding creation, then everything is good!

✠

Growing in you, you growing in me, in eternal union! (Alter Christus)

✠

Thursday, April 27.
Dearest, today Frater van Gijsel [a young Spiritan student who died in Gemert] was buried. Our good Guus is with you. I'm happy because he is [happy] and so are you and all the saints and Mary happy with your new child in heaven. Dearest, I thank you for the glorification you've drawn from Guus' life and last illness. I thank you because he glorified you by his unfailing patience, his gentle kindness. I'm glad because he honored you by his modesty and cheerfulness under all circumstances. Dearest, how great it is that he was allowed to dedicate himself to you forever in our Congregation.[78] Now he is yours eternally. Eternal understanding and willing attachment of spirit to you are his and our final aim. My Jesus, can I help it if I am not sad, if I want to sing a *Te Deum* more than a *De Profundis*?

Dearest, today I began to study again as well as [to follow] my new personal rule of life. *As* you in you. You, All! Growing in you, you growing in me, in eternal union! *Alter Christus*.

Jesus, you used to punish me for deviations by a kind of secret inner fire, but now [you do so] even more painfully by showing me my misery and nothingness, both dreadfully and clearly. Now when I bungle, I see myself in my misery, though nothing can be noticed on the outside (*sometimes*)!

Sunday, April 30.
My Jesus, on Thursday we took our Guus to the churchyard! Who are *we* to take [him there], or rather who is it that is taken there? You know, but you needn't tell me. Even if it were me, I'd think it good. Everything is your holy will.

My Dearest, the growth goes on, the depths are becoming dizzying, but you keep saying, *Non turbetur cor vestrum*. Don't be afraid, neither

78 Because of his approaching death, Frater van Gijsel was allowed to take his final vows as a full member of the Congregation in spite of the fact that the probation period of the three years of his temporal vows was not yet completed. For some, now unknown but perhaps providential reason, Rinus seemingly did not have the same opportunity on his deathbed.

in body nor in soul. You alone are Master of everything, also in our soul's household. You are the head of the family and of your whole mystical body.

Dearest, I ask you for so much. I ask you for EVERYTHING, for all. I say foolish things in all sincerity. I begin to master [the arts] of intercession, thanksgiving, atonement, and adoration, not only for myself but for all people, not only for the billions in the present and the future, but for all times, even for all people [to come]. I do so without hesitation! In mercy you show me my miserable weakness. The only means against it is confessing guilt at once and laughing freely (just like a small boy who feels frisky when he has done something naughty)! It's also the only way to bear the pain of injured self-love, although that's not always easy. But everything works together inwardly! Jesus, let me be *Alter Christus,* both inwardly and outwardly.

Wednesday, May 3.

My Jesus, I'm writing for a while before I go to study again! You've exhorted me to confidence these last days. I must not be afraid any more, neither physically nor spiritually. If I'm afraid because I'm so weak, and if I retain a thorough fear of myself, while relying on your grace to avoid sins, it's good. But it's not good to be afraid that something will be beyond *my* strength if my Superior or fraternal love demands it. It's your holy will, therefore, and [it] will be accomplished with *your* strength.

Now I know physical feelings cannot be altered that much; only the deeper motives, I mean those of trust in you, can calm me down again. As long as it's not a matter of sin, everything is still acceptable! But now something else [lies ahead].

Jesus, you know that when I tell a joke I do so to please my confrères, to make them laugh! But now, I have a vulgar, pedestrian mind, and I don't see any harm in "dirty" jokes (about the calls of nature), at least not always. But, when I do tell such a joke, some call them off color, others don't. But I should not risk to scandalize anyone. Therefore, from now on, *as* you, I won't tell vulgar jokes any more, even if they are witty and, in my eyes, harmless, just a bit indelicate. You should not tolerate this [custom] in me any longer. My Dearest, it's not to my credit, even though my intention was really good! Do I have a lax conscience because I call harmless what others may call "off color?" Yet I dare to tell them to Father Superior or to my parents whereas *I* would call jokes really indelicate that are about teenage girls! But from now on, forget it!

Dearest Beloved, how happy you make me with your own works. You make me feel this way because I hear others are happy, too. My heart is gladdened whenever I hear something good said about somebody or whenever I hear or read about people who cooperate well under extenuating circumstances in spite of their weakness. Like in Saudreau [a well known French spiritual writer of that time] I'd like to exonerate the whole world from evil by pointing to everybody's (one by one) good side and the extenuating circumstances. If only they all love *you* with their whole being, *all* [would] go to heaven.

Jesus, I'm going to study again. *As* you. Thanks be to God, I may remain in intimate communion with you all the time, no matter what happens. That union is becoming deeper and deeper. I perceive more and more that *you* act and that *I* am still so miserable, so unable to do anything on my own except sinning.

Jesus, you alone know how glad I am about that. Nor was my union with you an emotional impulse that would end after the Novitiate due to daily study and recreational life. Thanks be to God, it didn't. Also that experience of "eternal" union makes me happy beyond expression. If only *you* are glorified!!

Friday, May 5.
Dearest, I won't write much now, for I'm somewhat tired after studying. You've helped me so much again, or rather, you've acted in me so obviously when I began to be a bit afraid. I was allowed to explain a thesis to a confrère which I didn't understand that well myself. While I was explaining, I left everything to you. Everything then became so clear. I know that my classmates won't believe this, yet it is and remains true.

Monday, May 8.
Jesus, please tell me you don't find any impediment [in my soul]. I don't have a care, for everything that happens, both inside and outside of me, leaves me fairly indifferent. Only this one thing comes back time and again. "Do I let *you* act fully? Don't I put *myself* in the foreground, also when I sometimes fool myself that it's for your sake?" Yet I see that my concern must not be too human in this respect either. Jesus, you *only*! How happy I am in our union! [I feel so at home] with my vows, my religious habit, briefly, with everything. Nothing has decreased in freshness. Also Holy Mass, Holy Communion, the Holy Office, . . . Anything that is *yours* makes me happy even when my nature feels dislike or pain. I dislike what is not purely *you* more and more.

My Jesus, I sometimes must force myself to join in singing certain hymns during or after Benediction. I used to like them so much, but now, if it is not about your church, I've lost much of my interest. Moreover, there are so many secular allusions in Dutch songs—all to externals. Only a few songs are real prayers that tell me something. But of what use is it to sing, "White flowers on colored cups must kiss, oh so sweetly, the feet of Mary's statue?" No, to that I prefer: "Oh high dear Lady, for whom I'd give my youth and life" or "See, I follow gladly where you lead me." Such songs say something to me! But, then, I'm neither a poet, nor am I likely ever to become one. Dearest, to love as you, to be you, is growing so much. All I know is that the more I'm humiliated and destroyed, the more you grow. Many thanks. With you and as you, I can bear all kinds of heavy battles, to say nothing of less heavy ones. Dearest Directress, behold your servant!

Thursday, May 11.
My All! Today it was my turn to present in class. [It was] a good opportunity for you to show me once more how worthless I am, even if I sometimes think I know a lot of philosophy. The failure hurts my nature, but you-in-me laugh about it. Whatever good there is in it, that is yours! For you gave the presentation. Dearest, such a thing doesn't disturb our union of love, does it? No, we blend into one another always deeper and deeper! You, the fullness, penetrate into nothingness! Dearest, I'm so happy, [so graced]. And *who* or *what* can disturb me in that beatitude? No external things, none of them, only *sin*! Still you know you can never rely on me. I'm capable of expelling you by my free will, of offending you, my God, grossly. But, Dearest, I should not even worry about that in an anxious "natural" way. Not even about that burning, sometimes hardly bearable, struggle against impurity. Not that I'm frightened or disturbed inwardly by it in my heart of hearts. Thanks be God, no! Every time [something happens], I notice that you put a weapon, sufficiently strong, in my hand to resist the enemy. Then it delights me again that your external glory has been increased by my weakness which, through your strength, can always be victorious.

My Jesus, you are my All in prayer, play, study, and intentions. Always that one word, "All," satisfies my almost infinite urge toward giving, asking, imploring, sacrificing, adoring, and atoning in you, to you, as you for all humankind. Dearest, you know my foolishness, my utter reliance on you [for everything]. You are my All. My Dearest!!

Tuesday, May 16.
My God, in this way my life goes on, as a motley mixture of *your* deeds and my misery and weakness. Thus last week I spoke badly about a former student, while you warned me [not to do so] inwardly! Yet I did. I don't write this down to ruminate on the sin once more or to grieve about it! Trust me not to do a thing like that! Many worse things well up from such a muddy source as my wicked self. Thanks to your grace, I regret it deeply, yet you gave me your penance. Everything is all right again. Only the memory stays.

I should also like to thank you for doing my test. Every time I find that melancholic reasoning results in nothing, whereas at the actual moment you let me know what is to happen. *As* you I am *Alter Christus*! Jesus, I haven't forgotten that I'm your sacrificial victim and

The study room at Gemert, which was often used as a class-room for a smaller group of students.

that we'll live together eternally! Dear, we now read in "Theodicy" [The Philosophy of God] how you act with and through us. You play by far the greatest part in what they call the *concursus simultaneous* [the simultaneous concurrent motion] and the *praemotio* [foremotion].

Whenever we begin a subject like this, I "taste" the truth of that part, as it were. That's the Holy Spirit! So I swim (to put it mildly) in divine "Allness." Completely his, wholly permeated by him. I must grow in and as Jesus. But not I alone! No, with all humankind, with anything that praises, thanks, adores, or rather "is" the Lord. Only the words "be" and "all" express enough to me. The rest doesn't. So, all creatures "be" [in] the Lord!

Sunday, May 21.

Today on recollection day, Father Lütenbacher said something about the apparitions of Our Lady at Fatima. Dearest, it all seems so "familiar" to me when something is told about Mother or about the saints. It is as if I am a co-owner of everything. It seems to me as if they speak about your possessions (which are also mine, aren't they, Dearest?). I know of all these goods, exactly where they are and what they are for.

My Jesus, many thanks for Friday's holy absolution! Every time you restore again what is lost "by wear and tear." Thursday night, on Ascension Day, I messed up again, and you made me feel it clearly. Yet I was happy, really happy about my penance. Of course, self-love played a part again, the *radix omnis mali* [the root of all evil]. Here's what happened. First I asked [the classmate for whom I had a special liking] something rather commonplace. In this way I wanted to give the impression that I asked merely for the sake of asking and not for any personal interest. I did so in order not to betray to my [other] classmates my affective feelings for him. To cover [my tracks] even more, I told [another classmate] a lie about my interest in him. The reason was [merely] "natural" friendship, so my own weak self [acted up again].

Everything is over now. I've been punished and then quite soon forgiven. And now, I can go on. Should I regret being so miserable! No! Only that your external honor was decreased and my confrères were displeased by my showing preference. That was bad! But all is good after your forgiveness. With your grace I've restored outwardly what could be restored. As for the pain of beaten self love, well, that isn't the worst thing either. For my innermost being remains as radiant and as uplifted as ever.

Dearest All, I keep growing in you. As you! With cheerfulness and willingness just as you urge me: *spiritus ubi vult spirat* [the spirit blows where it wills]. Hence all outward activity is rooted in the repose of being you. Dearest Mother, it's *your* month! You, my Directress.

✠

. . . your grace just keeps on growing!

✠

Monday, May 29. Second Pentecost Day (Whitmonday). Beloved yesterday we celebrated the anniversary of our official espousal feast. A year ago already! I remember it so well. Since then we've been bonded forever! Though it sometimes happens in the world that affection cools down when people are together for a long time, it is not so with you! Dearest, your grace just keeps on growing! I may love you much more than a year ago, than a month ago, a week ago, indeed than yesterday. Love grows continually! That doesn't mean that I never mess up! Oh no!! But always, deep in me, everything is quiet, even if I undergo punishment, at times painful punishment indeed, for my wrong ("not you") acts! Yet, Jesus, you're not really a tormentor, surely not! You're sweet and good, but also just. In a word you're God, and that tells me everything.

Yesterday was the feast of my Beloved Holy Spirit, the Spirit of Love. *Qui locutus est per profetas, qui cum Patre et Fillio simul adoratur et conglorificatur* [who spoke through the prophets, is adored and glorified with the Father and the Son]. *Dulcis hospis animae, creator spiritus, renovans faciem terrae* [sweet guest of the soul, creative Spirit, renewing the face of the earth]. Think of it. If one looks at everything through red glasses, the world would be red. Likewise the Holy Spirit renews the whole appearance of the earth by renewing and illuminating our hearts and minds so that we see well and in detail the plan he has made. Thus everything is new. Every day again a whole new world [awakens] that makes us say [in the name of] each creature, "God, my creator." Thus the Holy Spirit makes us indescribably happy by making us, so to say, swim in God and be permeated by him. Isn't the thesis on *praemotio* [foremotion] and *concursus* [concurrent motion] one great hymn of praise to God's omnipotence and love? Then why leave it so abstract? Why lock that learning up within books? Isn't the whole practice [of life] full of it? [79]

My dear All, I'm so happy to know that you know my most secret thoughts and desires, for if I had to express the love in me in words and show it in acts, I would become desperate, owing to my powerlessness! I'm also glad you see when I botch things up again. Another person

[79] Editor's Note: These words from classical theology inspired our expressions in formation theology of coformation and preformation.

would say, “Oh, do you [really believe in and] love God?” But you see it’s either thoughtlessness or by accident or mere weakness [that I fail], utmost weakness!

Dearest, go on and take me *as* you, *with* you, *in* you. Dearest Mother, you know I’m your servant and God’s sacrificial victim. I’m glad you know how much I love you!!

Sunday, June 4.

My Beloved, today is a great feast: *Trinity Sunday*. The mystery of my inscrutable Dearest! I know nothing about you and yet I do know you! I don’t see and yet I do see! I believe, yes, thanks to your grace, I believe in the Most Holy Trinity, yet Dearest I know nothing about it.

1. Father	1. Son	1. Holy Spirit	1. Spirit	1. Reason	1. Will
2. Son	2. Holy Spirit	2. Father	2. Reason	2. Will	2. Spirit
3. Holy Spirit	3. Father	3. Son	3. Will	3. Spirit	3. Reason

I can’t understand, and yet I must say I “taste” (in a certain way, through experience, as it were, and obscurely) the non-contradiction, This is not my doing! It’s not knowledge from books or mere brain work, no, it is your doing! And isn’t it reasonable (Dearest, allow me to talk nonsense once more) that those who are courting you or are even engaged and united forever with you, know each other? You know me completely, but is it so strange for you yourself to make me know something? If it always remains in darkness while I’m still on earth and can still be separated from you by mortal sin? I’m quite capable of it. But, Dearest, may I use a comparison? When two people get married, they promise fidelity to each other, for their whole life, to stay together always. And yet, if either of them is unfaithful, the other may annul the engagement, and they have to live on separately. Likewise, when I say I’m with you forever, the sad possibility always remains that my own self-will may show its true nature and insult you mortally by mortal sin. God, no, let me not say that! Dearest, the struggle is weighty but your grace is more abundant! No, never [let me drift] away from you. I beg you, let me study for *you* only. Pleasure in studying is a gift from you. It is meant to incite me to work, but it must not become an impediment to union. I must be very careful not to be absorbed in [merely] natural activity. Work is a *means*, not an *end*. So you and you only, above all, you, my dearest God!!

Sunday, June 11.

Today there was a Corpus Christi procession in the garden. Now Dearest, I’d like to write about my method of working. You know my body gets fagged out from time to time, my head tense, and often [I feel] a stomach ache at the same time. When it passes, everything feels good again! But this physical condition also influences the rest [of me]! Aversion to work, a languid fatigue that makes my body heavy as lead and allows it to go on with great effort only! At such times I make matters worse by brooding. Deep down inside everything remains calm, for all those feelings of annoyance at the least resistance and unkindness don't get at my inmost soul. Neither is inner contact with you hindered. There, with you and as you, I laugh heartily at my misery and weakness. I'm really glad to be such a "NOTHING." Now you are forced to act alone; now I'm forced, too, to call all that is achieved your work only!

Dearest, love doesn't decrease in all of this, by no means! Yet it is a spiritual love of "Being" that doesn't seem to have any communication with nature [as such]! For the devil jumps at my physical weakness: discouragement, mistakes, lack of chastity, dislike, listlessness, sadness, forgetfulness (under that title I classify the tendency toward particular affections that increases considerably at such moments), etc. All of these things can torment a man all day long and incite him to an outburst. I know it is nothing as long as there is no consent! But I've written it down to see my own insignificance on paper.

Dearest, yesterday and today I've been like that. [I trust] it's really nothing. For I'm now writing to you that I want you totally, under your *praemotio* [foremotion] and *praedeterminatio* [predetermination]. Let me also use [the latter] word now. I want to complete myself, as it were, in you, to be you, in the true sense of *Alter Christus*. You are my dearest Bridegroom, [the one] for whom I am willing to suffer all the throes of childbirth (I'm writing nonsense now). Then everything will be fine, even if I now have to force my hand to write!

Dearest, make me go forward again, calmly. The only thing I need to do here is to be transformed into you more and more, to love you, to put fewer obstacles in front of the operation of your grace. May the whole of creation serve me to this end!

Friday, June 16.

My Beloved, do you know what breaks my neck all the time! It's work, outward labor. I must be so careful here, otherwise it becomes an unquiet, "even if successful," agitated work that preoccupies me completely and at which nature rejoices. [I then feel] quite self-complacent when it's finished. That's a dangerous thing! My Dearest, under the mask of good I'm deluded into "not losing a single minute" and "to being very meritorious for the community by working hard," for example, in (cleaning) the Father's recreation room or when polishing the benches in chapel or when studying. I can make a little cross before a thesis after working hurriedly [on it]—as a sign that it's finished. But that again is too natural [too much of me in it], Dearest. I notice well what's happening, including the unrest [I feel] when another scholastic asks one hour's study from me to coach him with *his* study or when I've got a lot to write down in my exercise-book.

It is true that up to now I've been able to finish my work and explain things which I understood only half way myself. I listen to my own words, as it were (as Edward Poppe says somewhere). I always find enough matter and energy in myself to help another when he asks me, directly or indirectly. Many thanks for that, my Dearest. It's all your work. Also when I remain in you quietly (which is mostly the case, thanks to God), I can get through an enormous amount of work without feeling empty and tired and while remaining cheerful. But even then I must be careful about [an increase in] vain self-complacency. My nature is so sneaky, so perversely proud and sensual.

Dearest, you should not be surprised if I insult you deeply some time. I often feel myself so near to sin. I'm such a "nothing." A step to an infinite insult seems so short to me. Be thankful, dear God, that it hasn't happened yet. It doesn't need to happen. Many thanks again. All glory to you for this! Your loving Providence has still disposed everything well. I'm so glad, deeply and intensely happy, to be "still" in you, even if my body runs and trots.

Dear Jesus, everyday I realize more that it's really serious between you and me. It's forever. We are united eternally! How often I should thank Mother that she has drawn me so near to you by the slavery of love. Through her we have gotten to know one another intimately. We have come to an agreement, very much so. Yet, my Jesus, I remain a poor nothing, liable to do anything. I commend myself humbly to your protection. My most dearest Trinity, grow more and more in me—let me grow deeper in you. *Alter Christus! Ad majorem tuam gloriam* [To your greater glory]. Outpour myself for others. Be you for . . . [Translator's Note: Manuscript breaks off] Help me with external works; do them in me!

LETTER FROM RINUS TO ADRIAN FROM GEMERT

June 22, 1939

Dear Friend Adrian:

You haven't heard from me for a long time, so I'll just write a quick note. I am rejoicing already just thinking you will come to Gemert wearing your cassock in a few weeks' time! How we shall walk!

That very same day our holidays will start, that exact morning (Monday, July 10). The last exam will be over. Whether there'll be time for me to congratulate you at the ceremony [of receiving the cassock] itself I don't know. So I'll just do so now. And my verbal congratulations will come, no doubt.

How are you, old fellow? Busy for exams, I suspect. I can imagine! Yesterday we had the last test for outside subjects (sociology), and now we'll have the twenty theses for the main subjects. Everything has been going quite well up to now! Don't worry about me. You might lose your fresh "red color," and I don't want that.

In the "Memento" during Holy Mass you've still got your permanent place, and I hope, or rather I'm sure, I've got the same with you.

How is your inner life? Also reasonable, considering the circumstances? Don't be afraid, boy! Cling to Mary, close your eyes and let yourself be taken through a dark tunnel, as it says in The Golden Book, *and that's the truth,* Experto crede Roberto. [80]

We will have home visits here much sooner than had been arranged for in the program. For they were fixed for August 5, but now we will go on leave already around July 28. So much the better, isn't it? For on August 29 you'll have to "go and sit out" your year [at Gennep].

Father Berkers gave me your kind regards! He also told me you were still fine. Not that I doubted it. But you see I like to talk loosely better than to swim laps at present. You should forgive me, for it's hot! Today they read Don Bosco en Zijn Tijd [Don Bosco and his Time] *by Hugo Wast in the refectory! Did you already choose a patron saint for your religious life? I can recommend Don Bosco in every respect: he's a good one.*

There's not much news here. We haven't yet got the dreaded quartering of soldiers, but I don't think our protests will be of much avail. Yes, there will be part of the General Staff in the portal house, fifteen officers and a few orderlies, a gun and some machine guns. It's to be hoped they'll stay away, though! I say, Adrian, I'm going to stop now, to take up metaphysics again. Take care of yourself.

Live like an Alter Christus. *Let God grow in you. Don't be afraid, don't! Everything will turn out well. Simply do your daily duty. You are not responsible for the rest.*

My kindest regards to our acquaintances from The Hague, to Adriaan Olsthoorn (I'll write him later) and the others. And of course also to you.

Your friend, Rinus.

P.S. Of course, at the first opportunity, also give my kind regards and congratulations to your parents!

---

80 This is a standard Latin expression used colloquially to mean something like "that's my experience" or "I believe based on experience." It is often repeated for emphasis by Rinus.

Another view of the portal house of the castle at Gemert, inspected as a possible place to quarter the general staff of Dutch troops.

✠

I don't regret at all surrendering myself into your hands.

✠

Sunday, June 25.
Today is again a recollection day. In his conference Father Lütenbacher talked about the gift of piety. It is like the sum of the other gifts [of the Holy Spirit]. Dearest, you've also helped me to learn a lot today. You showed me my own misery and inconsistency. But, however much there was of sleep and aversion, you were and remained inside of me. My dearest Bridegroom!

Father Lütenbacher also offered a few thoughts as to what for some saints was the all-important ideal of their lives, their fixed idea, the incentive for all their words! What has impelled me for almost a year, every day, always more intensely and freshly, is the consciousness of our union. *Christianus est Alter Christus*. To be as a Christian, another Jesus with all that this [intention] entails always comes to my mind in the morning. Spontaneously my first thought goes to God. I then kiss my profession crucifix as a renewal of my vows and as the seal of our matrimonial union. I do so day after day. All is due to the work of your grace! My Dearest, you are All; I am nothing.

Dearest All, I'm so miserably weak. I see my misery clearly, terribly clearly. I see something of my own self sticking to all my actions: now I'm the king of self-complacency, then of sensuality, then of natural impulse. Whereas everything should happen as *Jesus*, I always throw my own self into it, no matter how small the task. Should I become cross at my misery? Get angry when I catch myself *again* at something that is not as it should be? Forget it! I laugh at it! Sometimes, in my room, I must control myself so as not to explode with laughter! What a monster I am. How much to be pitied. But self-pity is dangerous because I'm a wicked fellow in spite of everything. *Experto crede Roberto*! And that little being, that mud bath of misery, dares to call himself God's bride, dares to act as *Alter Christus*.

As a first year freshmen philosopher I'd like to make a distinction. I dare to make myself live like another Jesus. *Distinguo*: relying on myself: *nego, nego, nego* [No]. But relying to the utmost on my most dearest God while being afraid of myself: *concedo* [Yes]! Yes, my Jesus, fear of my own self comes so spontaneously. Many thanks for that grace! In these ways, my whole being with all its actions begins to come under strict control! You are the master. Dearest Mother Mary, although I don't beseech you directly, as often as I used to do, you know in Jesus how intimately I love you and how grateful I am! Yes, with Jesus' love and gratitude I can appeal to you!

Dearest Directress, many thanks. After five years of my consecrated servanthood to you, you've managed to allow my soul to go through a whole spiritual process of unfolding, to get me in touch with Jesus, to adorn me and to carry me through *all the dark tunnels* without my hardly suspecting anything. Only in the Novitiate could I begin to see with how much tact and forethought you worked! And the crown of your work was the alliance of your child Jesus with your servant, your child, in an eternal, deep union. Now you're happy it has happened like that. You're happy because I'm happy. No, I don't regret at all surrendering myself into your hands.

Mother, if I get a chance, I'll give you even more servants. I beg you to do the same to them as to me. They're much more willing, docile, determined, and generous. *They* are of some use to Jesus! I say this, for every other person in my circumstances, would love God much more and better [than I do]. I really don't need to pride myself on going through life with you and *as* you. They would do much better than I. Thanks, Mom!

Dearest Jesus, I'm going to stop. I beg you, have patience with me. I'm nothing, Dearest. You are in me. Don't show me Rinus Scholtes but Jesus! I'm glad you show and will keep showing me my nothingness! Jesus, my Beloved. Please love in me your Father with your infinite love. My dearest Love Spirit, I'm so glad to have consecrated myself to you in your Congregation.

LETTER FROM RINUS TO ADRIAN AND HIS FAMILY

Gemert, July 7, 1939

Dear Friend Adrian and Family:

I just had to write a short congratulatory letter. Father de Winter [the priest-brother of one of Adrian's classmates] will take it to you.

Adrian, congratulations, with all my heart! You in your cassock! How glad I will be when I see you tomorrow! I've been counting on it for a long time. So many months, weeks, days more, and then we'll have a look at this house together.

Also congratulations to your Father and Mother with the children. I can well imagine your joy. I still see in my mind the faces of my Father and Mother two years ago. Adrian has now received the crown of six years' lower studies! Now you see your son in his religious habit. May he wear it for a long, long time—to the extension of Jesus' realm on earth!

Adrian van Kaam is in the second row, seventh from the right.

I won't write too long because now at the coffee table, you don't have time to read a long letter. Are you all well? I'll soon come to see you, if I may. Is little Leonie still growing strong? Adrian I'm so glad because you are glad. I can enter into your family's feelings because my memory of that day is still fresh! (A poetical turn of phrase, wouldn't you say?)

Now, I'm going to stop. Togatus [cassocked] Adrianus, happy parents and extended family (perhaps Bep and Julia), once again, congratulations.

Most cordial regards from your friend, Rinus.

✠

. . . The present moment alone must engage me, the "now" in you and as you.

✠

Sunday, July 23. Recollection Day.
Dearest Jesus, a week from today I hope to be home on holidays, until August 30. I think it will do me good, for sometimes I'm so tired! But I should go among people *as you*.

Dearest, I've been far too "naturally" busy these last few days. That is not the way you want it. I should be much more free from inward work as well, and be "we" [you and I] when I see that I can't go on at a certain moment. Jesus, my dearest beloved Bridegroom! [Let me] work in you and as you! Yet I love you, yet I *may* love you, with a love that isn't of my doing but of your love spirit. Also the objects around me—persons, animals, things—I love them all with *your* love. Out of my own being, my own small heart, I could *never* love so much my confrères, all people, especially *all* souls, *all* circumstances, in short *everything,* literally *all* that proceeds from you—you, their Maker and Preserver.

Dearest, I may love everything so intimately because I love you [in them]. I say "may" for all of this internal "being Jesus" isn't my doing, either. Everything, really everything, swims in, is, as it were, soaked with God—as (to use a weak comparison) a sponge in endless mid-ocean is permeated with water. Dearest, I need not look for you anywhere, for you *are,* you *are* everywhere. My dearest All, I needn't go to chapel specifically to be united with you in prayer!

Now that I'm writing this my body and mind are becoming tired. I'm drowsy. It's drizzly weather, and my nature is longing for sleep. Yesterday, as well as the day before yesterday, heavy battles were fought again for holy virtue's sake. This morning I was sleepy and unwell, my stomach hurt, etc. Everything in my nature is against me. And yet I think and perceive in myself an unfathomably deep love for Being, for you, my All. That isn't my love—or if there is love of mine in it, it's like a drop of dirty oil in the sea. That is to say, it's there, you *can* see it, but it doesn't embellish the whole. You'd better not look at it.

My dearest Beloved, this morning the conference was about the gratitude we should show you! That speaks for itself. Dearest, I'm still much too fearful. You do say repeatedly: "Don't be afraid" *[Noli timere, non turbetur cor vestrum neque formidet; Noli cogitare quid diceres]* and "Don't worry what you'll say," for *in hac hora Spiritus Sanctus in te locuturus est* [in that hour the Holy Spirit will speak in you]. The text must be something like this, I think. Yet I'm always too afraid!

My Jesus, the present moment alone must engage me, the "now" in you and as you! No worrying about what is behind or in front of me! Love you now, *nunc*. Now. Be nice to you and my confrères. Now be *Alter Christus,* for the good of the *whole* world. But you should be careful with me, for I'm certainly as great a wretch as I used to be, capable of anything.

Dearest, when I'm thinking, I sometimes feel really frightened of myself. If only the worst person that has ever existed were in my place and I in his, how holy, holy, indeed yes, *holy* he/she would be, for your grace is as wide as an endless sea—and [without it] what an unfathomable pool of muck I would be in. Why is it not so? Simply and solely because *you* let me swim in your grace, because you have put me in such circumstances! Dearest, many thanks! Holy sweet Mom, Mary, always again I should thank you, masterful matchmaker, that you are!

✠

Rinus Sholtes, out, Jesus in his place.

✠

LETTER FROM RINUS TO ADRIAN

The Hague, August 10, 1939

Dear Friend Adrian:

All week long I went about thinking, "Today I'll write to Adrian," but every time it was night before I noticed. But today it will be done after all!

Well, Adrian, there we are with our plans! How we were to talk during these holidays. But . . . there may have been more of "the old man" in our chatter than we thought ourselves, so [Christ] thought it better to put an end to it.[81]

In any case, it will be best this way! How are you, by the way? Getting any more meat on your bones? Use the time there well! You may be better able to follow the rules in your Novitiate, for you need to be healthy to do so.

Adrian, I've almost finished that book you gave me to read. Frankly speaking, I don't like it very much. It seems to me (for I'm willing to admit I don't know a lot about it) that Bruning [a Dutch writer, thinker, and poet] *is beating about the bush too much. He's quite long-winded. I can agree with the main thoughts. They are so matter-of-fact that nobody could, in my opinion, object to them. But, then, one should understand the words in the way Bruning uses them. Some parts are both beautiful and true as I understand them. There he puts down in a few short sentences in black and white what he means. Unfortunately, there are not so many of these; moreover, it seems to me that a great part [of what he says] can be simplified.*

So there it is! Take this as criticism from a little philosopher who knows very little of literature and is only nostalgic for short clear phrases of truth—something like Jesus' sermons in the Gospel.

Next, Adrian, don't blame me for writing in such a scribbling way. I'm glad I can write at all! This way you get more for your five cents!

I'm also glad I can take the book to Mr. Langelaan. I think I'll go there next Monday evening! I should write to him first, shouldn't I?

Adrian, a good hint. Take a pencil and note down which books you should try to lay hands on in the Novitiate as soon as possible, namely, Een met Jezus [One with Jesus] *by Father De Jaegher, S.J., translated into Dutch by Father Vogel, C.S.Sp., and Father van Putten, C.S.Sp. In my days (ha!) that book was at the back of the little library in the study room. But it's certainly in the main library! It's a small insignificant looking book, the size and thickness of a notebook. But its contents! Tell me you'll remember [them].*

Yesterday the Holy Spirit raised commotion in our neighborhood and our town [The Hague]. *Listen. As we had agreed, Frater van Warmenhoven came to see me about noon. At 1:15 Frater van Zeeland, van Rooijen, Fakkeldij, the younger de Winter, van der Ploeg, and De Knegt came. An hour later came the elder Father de Winter (the one who was ordained recently), and Henk van Putten. Then the whole lot, that whole nest of crows, went to Mesdag* [a museum in The Hague]. *Then*

---

81 Editor's Note: My general health had weakened at the then end of my sixth year of studies and of demanding extracurricular responsibilities, such as being elected president of the student society (SOOS). On medical advice I was sent to a health resort near the town of Venlo during the vacation months before my entrance in the Novitiate of Gennep.

we returned to our home, after which a few cycled on. At home I saw Jacques van Gemert, who is staying with his cousin in The Hague! Father Fakkeldij, the younger de Winter, and (Kees) Warmenhoven stayed for dinner; then I accompanied them as far as Den Deijl. You see, a house full of "Black Robes!"

You may or may not know Bertus is staying with his sister at Turnhout [a Belgian town near the Dutch border] *for some ten days. He arrived there on Sunday morning. That afternoon he went to the cycling-track. They also had lottery-tickets there! Bertus was in a bad mood because he had hardly seen anything of the racing cyclists* posturae causa *[because he is too small]. But, imagine, he actually won a bicycle in that lottery; he had to fetch it at the mayor's (the bike, I mean). Then, in the presence of a crowd of about a thousand people, Bertus had to cycle a lap in honor of his newly-won bike!*

Adrian, would you please also pray intently for me. At times I've got a lot to endure. No, it's not so bad as to make me yield, but the struggle is heavy. And then you feel caught in another [vacation and family] environment. Everything in me is, as it were, sighing for God. I can tell you this, but who will understand me here? Now I'm going around with it! And then the struggle with my own cowardice, egotism, and sensitive nature. I know, Adrian, you won't forget it.

It's funny, though, when you write now no one else will read this except you, neither Father Schins [the prefect of the Junior Seminarians in Weert whose duty was to open all the mail of the students] *nor somebody like him.*

You still never say die, don't you, Adrian? Especially outwardly, you should be even more calm and quiet. For in the heat of your argument you tend to be skittish! But I must say you've made enormous progress this last year in this regard.

Last year I also thought you were a little bitter about almost everything, especially about clergy and Catholics [who act] in name only. I didn't notice anything like that at all this time. On the contrary, both at Gemert and in The Hague when we met I felt love overcoming your dismay. I was so glad, for instead of harming and making you even more embittered, those trials have made you milder, quieter, and more "Jesus." You should give many thanks to him for that.

And think of our "childhood" in our dear Father. We swim in God, as it were. We rotate completely in him. Our whole being, moving, encircling—everything that is and moves—is directly and immediately dependent on him. That's no pious exaggeration. It's an irrefutable, firm, philosophical thesis: for example, when I'm writing now I'm essentially the cause of what's being written, but . . . as a "causa secunda," *whereas God is its* "causa prima" *at the same time. Thus it is with everything. And then to think that a loving Father completely permeates us with himself so much so that we can't even move without him. And, with all this, there's Jesus! Our Lord, Jesus, our model!*

Adrian, I'm going to stop. Once again I say non turbetur cor vestrum *[Don't be afraid]. Be* Alter Christus *inwardly in him, not deforming ourselves, as it were, into a likeness of Christ—so that we make him descend to us—but letting us be transformed into him.*[82] *He is the center of our sanctification, not we. This is expressed so ineffectively, but I really mean well as you know!*

Adrian, my parents cordially wish you good health! Kindest regards from my family and from the students. Of course, also the best wishes from your friend, Rinus

P.S. Adrian. Love! Jesus is all. We are nothing!

LETTER FROM ADRIAN TO RINUS (FROM A HEALTH RESORT)

Nijmegen, August 15, 1939

AMDG

Rinus, Dear Friend in Christ:

Thank you very much for your last letter. I'd like to tell you in this letter all about what has been happening, but it can't be done, I can't capture the right mood for it. Maybe I can in my next letter. I don't know.

At present I feel so intensely alone and abandoned. Rinus, my whole spirit cries for God so much! But I also know that he and I can't come to union yet for my faults are manifold and my soul is faint-hearted.

Here people are neutral, utterly neutral, in the most empty sense of the word. If only they fought against him, if necessary, or defended some opinion or other. But no! They have become cold, cold as stone due to their lack of love and life.

Rinus, that's the hardest, the most painful thing [to take], this total indifference, this narrow spirit of playing up to everybody and leaving God up for grabs. If only God would raise up saints, holy priests, lighthouses in a sea that is drying up, fire-sparking torches in the midst of thick darkness. Fire, love, complete fire, streams of fire to warm all those cold, cold hearts.

Sanctification, first of ourselves! Lord, have mercy on me a sinner. God sanctify me. You are all; I am nothing.

Rinus, don't believe that I want to be bitter. This is only a moment when the steady flame of desire for my God breaks out more glaringly and more violently. Pray much, very much, for me, Rinus. Pray for my sanctification, that he may burn me away, that he alone may live.

---

82 Editor's Note: Detectable in this correspondence between Rinus and me are the embryonic beginnings of formation theology.

Next time [I'll write] a quieter letter. Now I feel like a young man in love who misses his bride. Or perhaps it is the other way round. My soul, my soul, waits for her Bridegroom! May he come. Regards to your family.

Your waiting friend, Adrian

Monday, September 4.
My holidays are over! For a month I was at home. Many thanks for that time, Dearest. I learned much, so very much. I could see my own misery more than ever. My will-lessness and uncontrolled passion came forth, especially during reading. During the holiday I read a few books in "Category C."[83] I'm glad and not glad at the same time. Glad because you always drew good out of evil. For although in Confession I accused myself of dangerous and irregular curiosity and promised you every time not to do so again, yet I did. You saw me once again as I am, a muddy well with a beautiful stone covering it, but the moment the stone is lifted it smells to high heaven. Especially I refer to my curiosity that was satisfied by a detailed medical book. Dearest, it was not good that I did all this. I regretted it more than I can say. But ultimately I must conclude you've been so nice as to avert all bad consequences and to still do good to me through it. But, on my side, it was foolhardy to play games with your love!

Now I'm on retreat. During the holidays you simply kept growing in me despite all the obstacles in my own self and the changed circumstances in the world.[84] Dearest, as of August 27, we have been together for one full year! How very grateful I am to you for your invitation, your "proposal." How tremendously rich I became the day I was allowed to bind myself to you, in the bond of mystical marriage. I was allowed to lay aside my name and my being and adopt your name and your being: Rinus Scholtes out, Jesus in his place. Dearest, many thanks.

Dear Mary, my Directress, a thousand thanks for having accepted me as your consecrated servant, now more than six years ago. By that grace I can surrender to you. You helped to transform me. You've pushed me ever onward, unwittingly along spiritual paths. You've taken me into Jesus' embraces with motherly, mysterious, good-humored strategies. You were smiling at me, observing carefully how your consecrated servant got to know Jesus better and better, how he received all kinds of favors from him and how he, love incomprehensible, wanted to bind himself forever with this wretch. Then your formative task was accomplished. The *per Mariam ad Jesum* [through Mary

83 Reading books in this category without sufficient reason was discouraged in the scholasticate.

to Jesus] had taken five years. Now that Jesus has become everything for me, you receded more into the background! But never because I loved you less! It just so happens that, as, among people (an analogical comparison, of course), when mothers see that their child has found its own way of life and that he or she gets on well, their task of upbringing has come to an end. From then on a mother can only stand by lovably, give motherly advice from experience, and rejoice at the happiness of her child! Likewise, my dear Mother Mary, so it is now more or less between you and your servant!

But, then, why should I try to write about what is happening in me? It's so deep, I can't express it. Dearest Jesus, I beg you, to give to *all* people your grace, as you've willed to give it to me. Give them even more. You'll see how they cooperate. Dearest, let your Mother get many, many more people in her service. It's to their own advantage.

Wednesday, September 6.

My Jesus, yesterday I wrote to you about all my misery, about all that was "I," Rinus Scholtes. Get rid of him. Even when I mess up I shouldn't revert to it. Then it would seem as if I did something special when I sinned! Jesus, I'm such a great sinner. I sometimes feel so horribly near to sin. I don't understand myself how it happens—that I still don't do it. I'm quite capable of insulting you deeply and profoundly by putting myself above you. But away with it!

During the holidays I often spoke to all sorts of people under all sorts of conditions, whatever their social position or religion. Dearest, you spoke through me [to them] when I could efface myself. I could speak to young newlyweds about married life and its happiness, while what I said was, so to say extraneous to me. The same happened in the few talks [I had with] my friend Adrian!

Dearest, I beg you: here you've got a ready and willing sacrificial victim. Would you please look after him carefully? He'll cooperate, I promise! No, really, even though Adrian is my friend and our characters have much in common, in this point we differ. He is holy, I'm a "would-be" holy person. Yes, I know, I've also "promised" to surrender to you without looking back, to go forward without scrupulous reasoning, without proudly or humbly brooding about my faults, without sparing any *pains*. And yes, I haven't kept my word. He will do so, my

84 Rinus never mentioned in those days the outbreak of war in Europe in 1939. Neither did he refer to the mobilization of the Dutch army. He kept his diary as a spiritual notebook though in private conversations and letters he spoke a lot about the war, especially the attack of German troops on the castle seminary at Gemert in which by coincidence a small troop of Dutch soldiers had encamped for the night.

Dearest, in everything![85] Please, try him. You'll see that it's true! Don't you want to have holy priests, brothers, religious? Don't you want to have truly holy "*other Christs*?" Then do so, Jesus!

Dearest, everything proceeds as usual. Your work doesn't stop. You comprehend everything in one grasp, in one "Being." Everything swims in you and is pervaded by you. My Jesus, I've just gone to confession. Many thanks for that grace. I also talked a bit with Father de Rooij about the holidays.

Dear, everything ended well! Yes, formation does work! For you have drawn good from evil. My God and my All! You, my Everything! Fortunately, we've got a word that comprehends all of this completely. You are our All! Nature, techniques, anything that moves and exists does so only as a *causa secunda* [secondary cause], for you are through and around it and in it.

✠

Whatever happens will result in my being a deeper Alter Christus.

✠

Thursday, September 7.

This morning the Father who gives the retreat talked about love. Also love and the theory of grace are founded on facts, on true dogmatic doctrines! Yes, that's true. The same holds with philosophy. Everything, all that is *true*, is so beautiful. It is there to sample and to taste. Dearest, I'm so glad when I read or hear something *true*!

My dearest All, please say what you want now. You're urging me to go somewhere! I'll wait and let myself flow with it. Whatever happens will result in my being a deeper *Alter Christus*. I feel it. My Beloved, please bear with my foolish writing for another moment. I have to tell you once more how much I love you. At this moment it seems I've never done anything wrong. I'm not thinking about it. I hardly can. Dearest, dearest All, how glad I am that *you* are you, God! That you've been adored and served throughout all centuries; that you can never, never be grieved or diminished by whatever insults [are flying at you]! You remain the same. You are the strongest All, yet I am sad about what people do against you since you love us so much. You gave your life for us, Beloved. I can do no more. My most dearest Jesus. My God. Take all humankind, pervade us and make us conscious of you. Then nobody will be lost.

Dearest, you hear every prayer! I beg you, give *all* people abundant grace for final perseverance. I know I can't ask for heaven for everybody because they must also cooperate [with your grace] to get there

[85] Editor's Note: What Rinus in his humility is saying here of me, I would have said with far more good reasons of him.

themselves. But I can beg you to give them a gush of grace just before the separation of soul and body so that they can hardly refuse. Yes, Dearest, I know there are some who haven't deserved your grace, who have squandered it and don't even want it any more! Yes, I know. But please, don't pay attention to their curses against you. In spite of that, give [your grace] to them, Dearest. I'll post bail for them. They'll be so glad when later, only a short while later, they will have entered the final good of eternity. How they will shout for joy, unable to really thank you [as you deserve], and if [they are] in purgatory they will gladly remain there for their purification, for they are saved.

Dearest, please do so! I know you will. I'm so sure that I'd almost dare to write a thesis in a theology book: "Every *animal rationale* receives shortly before his departure from earth an abundance of grace to reach eternal salvation and to choose God instead of a creature or their own selves." Proof: *Major:* Every prayer is heard; this is proven about ten times in Holy Scripture. Proof: *minor: Atqui* [now] the request for abundant grace for final perseverance for *all* people is prayer (of course, it has to be a sincere prayer)! *Minor patet per se* [It's so obvious]. Hence, this prayer is heard! Besides, it increases your external glory! Dearest, you rejoice at the happiness of your celestial inhabitants! The more the better, for the store of happiness is inexhaustible. You are "All," aren't you?

What nonsense I'm writing again. I hardly dare to read it, yet it's there. You know what I mean. You know that it's other than what I wanted to utter, something much deeper. But it doesn't work.

Mother Mary, I'm so glad that you received such great happiness that no other saint can equal it. All people in heaven [are happy], including those who still have to get there (will I be among them myself? I don't know, I hope so). I'm glad because you are glad and happy, inexpressibly happy in him, in my Dearest. Holy Angels, I'm rejoicing because you rejoice. I'm glad no one can fall away any more! Jesus, I'm ecstatic about everything that exists because you've made it and preserved it!

Later the same afternoon.

Jesus, at this moment I'm reading the book by Father Plus, *De dwaasheid des Kruises [The Folly of the Cross].* Jesus, how I feel myself sinking away with shame when I read about the love the souls described there had for you. I'm glad because at least they loved you in *deeds*. For my fine words don't mean anything to you as long as I remain in practice the same spineless weakling, a merely naturally active clod! My Jesus, as in the life of St. Mary Margaret Alacoque, so with me it's been more than a year ago since I, too, was allowed to offer myself as your sacrificial victim. I haven't known much suffering yet, when I consider what others have had to suffer. I've hardly ever had outer suffering, only inner, and I've forgotten about that already. And yet, as a sacrifice, I'd like to give you some reparation. That really is my intention. But you know I bother so much about particular things, as, for example, to pray *now* for this special category of sinners, then for the faithful souls, and then, for instance, during the third quarter of an hour, for all those dying that day.

No, Jesus, I feel that's no longer good for me! Everything, only the idea that "everything" is influenced, done, reconciled, etc., can give me rest. And why shouldn't I do so? I myself am not even able to expiate my own sins, let alone those of others. But *you*, you yourself, are God, aren't you? You are infinite, my Beloved! Therefore, we'll make a new agreement: Let me surrender to you completely! Your holy will be done. I love your love-will. I won't ask for anything or refuse anything. Everything goes through Mary's hands anyway because of my dedication as her consecrated servant. She'll give some destination to the few good works you can get out of me at great pains! Then I'll quietly await your holy will; then I'll be transformed by you; [do my] daily duty; in a word, be formed as even more *Alter Christus*. For the rest, I'll leave everything to you. Urge me to ask now for sinners, and then again for faithful souls. That's good, isn't it? Dearest Jesus, in a word I want it *all* at the same time, literally, simultaneously *all* good things there are! And I can have them all by wanting you, by, so to speak, taking the bull by the horns!

My dearest Bridegroom, I beg you, don't pay attention to me. Just simply go on. Don't listen to my sighing and fussing. Really I'm capable of anything. You can't trust me an inch. Dearest Mom, I'm so happy to live with and through your son, Jesus, my dearest All. May everyone know and love you. *O crux ave, spes unica* [Hail, O Cross, our only hope].

Friday, September 8.

It's Mother's birthday! I'm so glad. Throughout the world Holy Masses will be said in her honor. When we consider how infinitely great *one* Mass already is, how great must that honor be that is given to Mary. All Mary's children celebrate their Mother's birthday. Everyone will give her something in their own way. And I? . . . Dearest Mother, many congratulations on your birthday. I'm delighted you are so happy, that you are not in want of anything, that you'll never stop being perfectly joyful. Mom, [no one deserves this] most welcome gift more than you. This joy is what I can offer you, too. I'm so overwhelmed by all that exists. Whatever is, is so good. It's from God.

Dearest Bridegroom, of course, you won't forget to congratulate your Mother in the name of your poor bride. Tell her I'm so happy [to be one] with you; that I don't regret at all having said "yes" to your proposal. I'm sure this will do Mother good.

Dearest, won't you offer all in need some relief? It's true I keep nagging [you] about that. But after all it's for the whole of humanity that I ask. Please, Dearest, I'll go on nagging until the last person is saved.

Jesus, today I also read that there's not always an opportunity for bearing heavy crosses; that you don't ask anything else but fidelity to your love-will. You ask everything; you refuse nothing!

My Jesus, I may only suffer a little bit and then, only inwardly. I know all too well that this cannot make up for [our sins]. Neither can the suffering of all people that is offered to your Father do that. Nevertheless you unite yourself with [these offerings]. And that changes the situation!

Saturday, September 9.
My retreat is almost over. One more full day tomorrow and next Monday the end. On Tuesday *lectio brevis* [a short opening lecture] and the school year will begin again. Now it's not the same for me as last year. Then it took a lot of work to get into philosophy. Now I'm likely to have more spare time. How shall I spend it? I took from home with me a course in "Esperanto." A few years ago I also studied it a little. But it seems best to leave everything to you. Plans and resolutions about material things always appear to give me unrest and uncertainty, whereas everything goes best when I'm busy and others *make demands on me*! Then I needn't think about anything. *This* I should do. The same is true about fixed exercises, for example, meditation, Holy Mass, breakfast, recreation, etc. There both work and time have been set. Lecture hours are matter-of-fact as well, but [what of] spare time? I must study the subject matter, that's fairly obvious, but then? Languages? Ascetics? Techniques? Or something similar?

See, Dearest, exactly *this* I'll leave entirely to you. You tell me: today this is good; tomorrow or next week that is fine. As for the rest, I should listen to you and put away what doesn't concern me. My Beloved, I love you so much! However I put it, I firmly believe it's true. Dearest, I love you so much! My God, you're my *All!* In practice I don't always act this way, but that doesn't detract from the truth.

Dearest, I feel so sure that my mistakes don't diminish my love. No, they show me how small and insignificant I am. In reality, love even grows. My Jesus, I'm glad [because of it] I see my misery. Not that I'm glad or don't mind committing a venial sin through this curiosity or that judgment or some unfraternal act. You know better! But looking back, I'm so happy that I've been put in my place again, that I see how I am. What would I be if your love didn't spare me worse things? That's what forms me. It even increases my surrender and love.

My All, I think [my life] is as I'm describing it now! I don't want to sin, not voluntarily, nor refuse you anything in smaller matters. But I [do want you] to see that I'm nothing and that you are All. I'd like to feel small and remorseful in front of you ("done in," as it were) like a small boy feels when he breaks a beautiful vase, half by accident, half on purpose, and has to stand in front of his Father after it happens!

Later that night.

Dearest, it's O.K. now. My behavior towards that confrère! Even if I want to deceive myself by saying the opposite, there's a bit of jealousy in it, and pride too! [I guess it's] because *I* had to initiate [things] every time. Always, in all those years, he has been in my class (for eight years now), I've had to ask him, for example, to go for a walk or to recreate, whereas as far as I can remember he never asked me anything of the kind. Besides, *my nature* is interested in this confrère, and hence of its own accord it tries to remain [indifferent]. But this seeming lack of response is mixed with jealousy, when *my nature* sees him going about with other confrères. I'm sure some of this is only my imagination! Whenever we have a conversation or a walk, he's nice to me, although we almost *always* tease one another. Once I said to him, *Was sich liebt das neckt sich* [They who like each other tease each other]. I still have to smile when I remember how he reacted.

Today, Dearest, you know when I began sulking again inwardly about that matter, I begged you urgently and cordially to give that confrère—as well as the other who is always in his company—a liberally abundant flow of grace so that they may belong to you with a chaste and free heart. I "experienced" (I don't know how else to put it; it's not a feeling, it's stronger than knowing, a kind of "tasting knowledge") that you heard me and that you were glad with this prayer. Not that it was necessary, for I've never seen anything in these classmates that might raise suspicion about them in any way. No, on the contrary, they are wonderful, good fellows. Only I, that old man, that lower pleasure-seeker, am the *I* who is guilty. But it's good to go through this.[86]

---

[86] People living outside the religious life may wonder about this longing for friends in a religious community. Basically it seems quite normal and to be expected that almost every one looks for other persons in the same circle with whom one can feel more affinity. Such persons enable normal give-and-take in conversations and are an outlet for sharing similar interests, hobbies, and concerns. As noted previously, this contact is only desirable if it does not gravitate toward becoming a particular or "particularizing" friendship, which excludes other members of the community so thoroughly that the common life as a whole loses its easy flow and spontaneous coherence. Rinus had this human need for communication, as almost all others did. In his situation, however, this very need went far deeper. His exceptional election by grace was necessarily accompanied by an exceptional kind of isolation and loneliness. Almost nobody, except his Confessor and his soul friend (Adrian van Kaam), who had not yet joined him in Gemert, knew explicitly what was going on within him. Still people cannot escape some preconscious impression that he was somehow different. This may have become a source of unintended alienation. Hence, the human longing for a confrère with at least some probable affinity to him becomes at times a preoccupation. His conscience is immensely sensitive and delicate as to the possible danger of hurting his divine Beloved by showing too much sympathy for another person. This makes him recoil from others while

Dearest, I really love those confrères; indeed I love every person with a tremendous great love beyond comprehension. I really love Hitler, Stalin, Mussolini, I mean, their souls, their persons, for your sake.[87] But from whence comes this great love in such a tiny heart? It's *your* work, Beloved.

Sunday, September 10.
My God, tomorrow is the end of the retreat, and another twenty-five confrères will take their perpetual vows. This gladdens my heart, for you are glorified when boys in the prime of their life swear eternal fidelity to you, only because they love you and want to promote the salvation of souls! This retreat is almost over. It has gone quickly although I'm glad the end is there.

Dearest All, I was also allowed to grow in you, to become more deeply *Alter Christus*. Many thanks. I know I must never stop yielding. Then, in tandem with my cooperation, I may grow more and more in you. My Dearest, let *all, all* glorify you as perfectly as possible. How can I begin to thank you for your work? You do it. It can hardly go wrong. My God, I could give you everything. I've got nothing left, but every moment I'd like to give you everything if I hadn't done so already.

My Beloved, I've never known that one can love so much in you and as you! It seems to me that this love I find in my heart for a fellow being, no matter whom, would exhaust me entirely (and indeed it would [definitely] do so were I alone). Now I find profound love [in my

---

at the same time seeking for some human affinity. An unconscious repression of this awareness leads to a rebellion in the vital or bodily dimension of his personality. The "more spiritual movement" towards a potential friend, which is not responded to, is then unconsciously translated into the sensual language of the vital dimension. One cannot find fault with the excellent spiritual directors of Rinus for not fully understanding and explaining this predicament to him. One should not forget that in that period of history there did not yet exist a sufficiently developed systematic theology of Christian character and personality formation with its corresponding formation anthropology.

87 Readers may be shocked by Rinus' expression of divine love even for criminals, such as Hitler, Stalin, and Mussolini. He himself somewhat explains this by adding that the love he shows with God's love is for their "soul," not for their personality and actions. As long as any person, even the most criminal one, has not made the final decision for or against God at least at the moment of death, God keeps calling the person back to the "personhood" meant for them from and for all eternity. This does not mean, of course, that the person thus saved will escape all punishment. The purifying punishment in purgatory can, in human terms, take eons of indescribable suffering. God in his providential plan of salvation asks other souls to cooperate with the saving of souls. Especially extraordinarily graced persons, such as Rinus, Blessed Sister Faustina, and St. Thérèse of Lisieux, may be urged by the Holy Spirit to pray for souls in grave danger of final damnation.

---

heart] for *all* people, indeed for *all* created *entia* [beings]. And besides that, there's my love of you, which I myself cannot measure any more. How did I acquire it? It's not mine. I'm far too small. So the only solution is that *you* love people and yourself through my heart. That tiny bit of love I have is absorbed, as it were, in yours.

In this way life goes on, no matter how much struggle and suffering there is (and there *is!!*). It seems bliss to me! Yet you shouldn't be sure of your bride. I'm still capable of *all evil*. Even if I return to this topic time and again, my Beloved, still this *truth* doesn't alarm me. I live on, surrendered to you. You arrange the rest. I've put my fate in your hands, which is the only reasonable thing to do.

Tomorrow the newly professed will come [from the Novitiate in Gennep]. Will you treasure them with your care? They'll soon get used to being here and pass for "regular" religious, [who live] for you and in you, without being disturbed by their changed circumstances. For *no single,* non-sinful strange circumstance need hinder the inner life. In the noise of battle, one can still be absorbed in you. Many thanks, Dearest, for this retreat, everything, mostly for you. It makes me so joyful to be one with you! Dearest Mother Mary, help sinners and the dying. You've got Jesus' heart at your disposal.

✠

Only you could have produced such love.

✠

Sunday, November 5.

My most Dearest, it's been quite some time since I've written something down. The reason is, I sit in the left half of the bench, and I dare not write for fear the student next to me will read it. For imagine, my Beloved, if anybody knew that you're my Bridegroom, forever mine, that I may taste you incessantly and live like *Alter Christus*. They'd laugh at me outright and say, "What about practicing what you preach?" They'd be right, Jesus, absolutely right. For how do I respond to all these graces? It sometimes seems to me as if I love only you without doing the works of love. Yet, however miserable I feel, I experience a love in me that is so great it can hardly be equaled by my practice! Only you could have produced such love.

My Beloved, I goofed again yesterday! I guess that hard lesson you gave me last week was still not enough. I grieved last week, Dearest, but I really deserved it! You used my Confessor as an instrument! For I thought I concluded from his words that this silly passionate affection I feel for one of my classmates was entirely my own fault, and that it was an obstacle to grace! My Jesus, what I experienced then grieved me. "Obstacles to grace" hold up your operation and [outpouring of] grace. [I should not] play games with grace, never deliberately reject it. Like a hammer's blows all this felled me. I felt beaten down for a whole week. That [feeling lasted] until I spoke about it with my Confessor. I now realize I'm putting up obstacles to grace. But I could not bear the fact that I may have been exchanging your love for the love of another person. I don't know how to put it. But *after* I had seen Father de Rooij on this matter, all was well with me again.

My Jesus, can there be a more wretched instrument than I? Is there a slower, more listless and weaker cowardly being than I? I'm sure there isn't. I'm nothing! Nothing at all, and that's all there is to say about it. Yet, dearest Mother Mary, I still sense your motherly, watchful eye upon me, don't I? But, Mom, I live so arbitrarily. I've surrendered everything to you, all the merits of my whole life. Now you must solve [another] problem I have with special intentions. You're willing to do so, aren't you? I want everything I should want, which means everything you want. But I'm too weak. I tire myself too much if I have to think of intentions for this or that end all the time. I beg for *everybody* and leave the rest to you, Mother.

Wednesday, November 22.
So, dear Jesus, what's going to happen to me now! Break the rule, yield to gluttony, become lax in resisting distractions and temptations, yield to all too natural feelings, talk about myself in order to exalt myself, boast. Look at the muddy well of the real deeds of Rinus Scholtes! The only thing I can say to you is, "I *don't want* to do it!" I love you, my dearest Bridegroom! I'm as happy as I can be because you're happy. Shatter the old man as you will! This mess happens in my [lower] nature! Inwardly I experience that I'm bound to you. There I feel that I have made an irrevocable act of my will "to God," though practice often leaves something to be desired! Wasn't I supposed to let *you* live in me, Beloved, to let you do everything? I beg you, please take over. If you meet with resistance in my nature, break it, smash it, even if it turns out to be the most precious thing I have. For, Dearest, you alone must live in everything. You alone are the master of the house! I beg you to break every resistance [you still find] in your miserable, poor bride! Indeed the only thing left for me to say, [a saying that comes] from my heart of hearts, where nothing can enter except you, is: "I love you passionately." For the rest I feel like Job on the dunghill, misery inside my body, complete collapse outside of it, and, on top of all this, other people's judgment!

Dearest, if only they could take one look into my "nothingness," at my utterly *real* misery! They would act quite differently towards me. They would mix with me, but only out of love for you and because they would pity such a poor wretch. I don't deserve any pity though, for it's my own fault. And yet with an overwhelming abundance of grace, I'm still *Alter Christus*. Things may seem excellent with me outwardly. I know how to make a good impression in my conversation, my writing, etc., but, the real truth is, I'm nothing, absolutely nothing!

My greatest torment is often that I am not allowed to cry out loud about this. You don't want that, Dearest. I must neither ask for anything nor refuse. Just carry on all the time, knowing that good things come from you, bad ones from me. Also sham goodness and holiness come from me, even if they seem really good and holy to outsiders. My Jesus, in the holiest actions I only find Rinus Scholtes stirring. If only they would be solely *for* you, nothing for myself.

I'm glad to have said this to you, Beloved. Now I can go on again, always moving forward, doing everything out of love for you, looking neither behind nor ahead, doing only what I must do for you *now*, at this moment. I cling to this, dearest Love. Whether I eat or don't eat, play or don't play, do light reading or not, smoke a cigar or not, everything is the same, if only it's done out of love for *you* and *you* alone. The rest I love for your sake! My Jesus, many thanks for your grace. [Make me] go forward, *as* you! *Alter Christus*. Dearest Mother Mary, Holy Guardian Angel, Patron Saints, I'm happy because you are happy eternally. All you saints and souls in purgatory rejoice that you are good, that you love God for all eternity!

Sunday, December 3. Recollection Day.

Beloved, today Father Lütenbacher spoke about God. "What is God?" My Dearest, it's so good for me to hear such talk about you, even if my body feels a bit sore from sitting through a forty-five minute conference. You are my *All*. You have to be imaged in all creatures, living and dying, as *Alter Christus*. That's all [there is to it]. I don't know how long I may have to live. I don't care about that. The time you grant me here on earth should be a really *full* time. As much external glory [has to be given] to you as possible! I must answer to grace as fully and as deeply as you wish, always keep the "now" in mind, and not concern myself about the rest.

My Jesus, I know there is a great obstacle [I have to face up to]. It is that I brood far too much! I've had to cope with many temptations, but I should take them much more in stride! You know, I don't want to be unfaithful to you, not in the least! Why, then, am I so afraid at the time of struggle for chastity? It's true, I'm liable to do anything. How tremendously true that is. Therefore, I should not rely on myself at all, only on you! For fear shows self-love!

Dearest God, I love you passionately through it all! I can't say how joyful, how inwardly peaceful and quiet I feel due to our eternal bonding. You, *my* Bridegroom, are *my* All! What does it matter whether I seem outwardly stiff, rigid, and severe? I try to be mild and pleasant to my confrères, but if I don't succeed, it doesn't matter, does it? You only ask me to do my best; the result is not my concern. I must leave that to you!

My Jesus, I laugh at myself when I think of belonging to you! You are infinite and, after all, much stronger than my misery—although that is terribly huge and deep. Outwardly this [inner battle] doesn't show much, or at least not for what it's worth. Yet the truth is, I love you, Jesus, I love you with all my being. I love you, my God, with the self-love you have put in me. Together, [we live] as one life. *Alter Christus!*

LETTER FROM ADRIAN TO RINUS

Weert, December, 1939

Dear Friend Rinus

Another change in handwriting, you will think, shaking your head philosophically, when you receive this page "painted" in cursive letters. Two years of straight letters, two years or even three cursive letters, one term in the last year straight letters and now then . . . "cursive letters!" Next: "A good friend might write sooner!"

You see, philosopher! I did not write exactly because I was a good friend. For I would have written either untrue things or true but less good news. There should not be any untruth between friends, and one doesn't grieve them by bad news. Now things are fairly good. Keep praying for me full of confidence.

I received your cordial New Year's message from Vermeulen, at table, after the holidays. As a table-chief I sit at the place where you used to be sub-chief, and Bertus occupies the chair that used to be my place.

Last term I had a small part in a detective play, "Lord Maxwell." *This term my part is even smaller. A bar visitor and later driver in the well known novel of a newspaper boy.*

Since last holidays Van der Bijllaardt has remained at home. Now I'll send sixteen parcels of laundry to The Hague tomorrow![88] *Maybe all this interests you precious little, and you may have expected something else. I've got a lot more to tell you, but we can do so better in the holidays next August.*

You needn't answer this letter either, however much I would like it. I understand darned well you're up to your ears in study. Write down neat notes. I may be able to use them later on just like those history notes of yours I've got in my possession now. Many thanks for your fine letters and strong greeting from your friend in Christo.

Adrian

---

[88] Students at Weert's seminary boarding school, if they were in sufficient number from the same city or region, would send their parcels of laundry to their families together. This would cut the transportation costs considerably. The Hague had 16 students at that time in Weert. One of them would be responsible for the combined transportation. Being a student in the sixth and last year of this academic program, Adrian was now in charge of this task.

LETTER TO ADRIAN (IN GENNEP)

Gemert, December 13, 1939

Dear Friend Adrian:

"Hey! Hey! The first letter from Rinus." With a sigh the young novice goes to his room with the just received letter in the fold of his sleeve. He opens the red-painted door and nestles down in his chair. Well, you've got a letter now. (I had to wait even longer for your letter, but that grief is long past!)

How are you so soon after the great retreat? Brother Bertinus [a Spiritan confrère] was here yesterday. I asked him to give you my regards! You should know that I'm now writing my second letter, and doing it during precious study time for the semester exams. But it really doesn't matter. I know one yearns for a letter in the Novitiate. And tomorrow there will be a provincial council meeting, so let's do it.[89] *I'll begin by asking you to give the Novice Master my kindest regards (I'm seeing in my mind's eye double-plated glasses over this paper, and a blue pencil to strike out every bit of political news.*[90] *Every year it's the same: form and deliver a lot of recruits and then at once start again a next draft*[91]*. . . . Father "Master," many scholastics owe their religious formation to you! And maybe you remember that troublesome, eccentric, strange Rinus Scholtes! Well, hats off to you!*

But now let's turn to you, Adrian. I see you in the garden every morning, with blue fingers, seriously pondering Rodriguez! I can imagine all those other things as if they happened yesterday! In my mind's eye I even see places and the dates of graces.

You still eat well, don't you? Your Mother was really so glad when she heard you had put on weight (five pounds or so, I don't remember exactly). I've also gotten to know well the two Langelaans on the two occasions when I visited them! Here's what Mr. Langelaan said when I left: "Well, now that you know us, for next year you know where we live!"

---

89 The Novice Master was a member of the provincial council. While he was in Gemert at the Seminary for council meetings, the seminarians through Father Prefect could give him letters for the novices in the Novitiate of Gennep.

90 In that period of religious life, novices did not have access to radio or newspapers. The same applies to the six-year Junior Seminary formation in Weert and the six year Senior Seminary formation in Gemert. During the Novitiate letters from the outside to the novices were censored to pencil out any political news that otherwise might slip through in the Novitiate.

91 Rinus refers here to the fact that the Master of Novices sent the novices at the end of their year and the taking of their temporal vows, to the Senior Seminary in Gemert. But shortly thereafter, he had to start all over again with a new group of novices sent to him from Weert and sometimes candidates who came from other schools.

I say, excuse my scribbling! I haven't got enough to write on four pages, and I want to write more than two; and besides, there's a military mobilization going on. Oops! Look what I'm doing now, telling political news! Could it still pass, Father "Master?"

Adrian, I'm really glad you are now in the Novitiate. Yield, yield completely to grace! Be glad, keep smiling through everything, and don't be afraid . . . non turbetur cor vestrum! *I know Jesus will give you much grace. The ground has long been prepared by your service of Mary! Don't hesitate, please don't. Read and re-read* Een Met Jezus [One with Jesus], *that small book by Father De Jaegher. I think it's in the library; in any case it is here!*

Plunge into God, swim in him, as it were. Be like a sponge in mid-ocean, completely permeated by God. Really, a Novitiate only lasts one year. Afterwards you don't go on like the self you were before. Here at Gemert the growth of your spiritual life need not be hindered in any way! Only love! Adapt to accidental circumstances and, for the rest, go on peacefully, ever more firmly in God!

I'd like to write much more, but then I would never be finished talking! I'd like to adjure you: give what God asks! Love . . . Mary . . . the Most Holy Trinity.

Well, Adrian, I've found a real Confessor, a second Father Berkers, namely, Father de Rooij!. . . . But I'm going to stop. I need not even ask you, for it's so obvious. Let's pray [daily] for one another.

More than a week ago we were visited by a Lieutenant-General, van Nijnatten [a military general of the Dutch army]. [He was] a fine straightforward Catholic! The kind you like best. He also addressed us! Really easy going, jovial and . . . Catholic! You'll see, when you are at Gemert. You will see all kinds of famous men, even Cardinals, come inside these walls.

Adrian, kindest regards to your confrères. Never say die! Now I almost forgot to wish the Novice Master a Blessed Christmas and New Year, and also to you, dear Adrian, blessed Christmas and Happy New Year.

Your friend, Rinus, in Jesus' love

VIII
Philosophy Part Three
Gemert
1940–1941

VIII
PHILOSOPHY
PART THREE
GEMERT
1940–1941

LETTER FROM RINUS IN GEMERT TO ADRIAN IN GENNEP

Gemert, January 8, 1940

Dear Friend Adrian,

I had promised you a letter for the New Year, but you see for yourself: during the holidays one has even less spare time than at other days. In the first place I wish Father "Master" and the other fathers a Happy New Year! And also to you, Adrian: may you grow very much and go deeper into God's Infinite Being this year! I hope you'll be permitted to take sacred vows, together with your confrères, at least as long as we are still here that day!

And then, how are you? Is everything still all right? It's a pity you're not allowed to write, but well, it's fine, too, this way. Is your health still good? You surely eat well, don't you? I know it's sometimes humiliating when we have to load in so much! But don't worry. It's even a good thing! In that regard the devil won't tempt us since, meanwhile, "we are already so moderate, so frugal, etc."

I'm writing this to you, but actually it's more for myself! I don't know what's wrong with me, but it sometimes seems I've got [a veritable] canine hunger! I also know I have to eat as solidly as possible!

Sometimes I have to go on after the others have stopped (I'm now a refectory server), [and take] some apples, a slice of bread, a bit of "scrapple" and [who knows] what else! I think it's a nuisance! But it's also good, both for my stomach and for my head (that is, the inner life)!

On New Year's Eve we had a "Hague" evening. Koos, Henk, Theo, and Jan Visser, and Scholtes as well (Oh! I mean Brothers . . .) were "The Hague Singers" *[At that time a well known choir in The Hague.] The scholastics spoke highly about that evening. We also had some funny characters with us, for instance, Brother van Oorschot, the professor; Brother Muysers, the road-sweeper! Especially Bart was successful! But I'll tell you more during the holidays. At Epiphany we had* Het Kerstfeest van Broeder Thomas [Brother Thomas' Christmas], *a very simple play of a few beggars at the monastery of St. Francis of Assisi.*

On Wednesday night we'll have Waar de Ster Bleef Stille Staan [Where the Star Stopped] *by Felix Timmermans. And then, on Thursday morning, we get up at 5:00 A.M. again!*

On Saturday there is an exam right away (which I still have to study for completely, for I have been very busy around Christmas). But, then, what does it matter?

Adrian, how sweet God is, isn't he? Sometimes I want to cry out. I'll be glad when I can speak with you again! Have you been brave? You aren't afraid, are you? Everything has been given to Mary! No more worry about that. I've been allowed to suffer much during my Novitiate, all inwardly. Now, since my profession, that is over. Inside everything is very much "one" and deep. And it keeps growing.

I don't write this to extol myself, but to beg and adjure you to surrender to Jesus! Don't be afraid. Everything will turn out well, bit by bit. Be love to your confrères, for their faults, also for the world, for all people. Don't fear that the intimacy with God will be gone after the Novitiate. Even if you are at home for four weeks and at Gemert for a long time, it won't.

Adrian, I'm sure you pray for me—and you know about me, too. If it's God's will, you will be at Gemert in September of this year. Use your time in the Novitiate, do! Remain cheerful and simple. We are nothing, aren't we! Our love, for everybody and for each separately, grows with our love of God. We nothing, he ALL! Christianus Alter Christus! Really, that's it completely.

Adrian, I must stop. In the letter to Adriaan Olsthoorn there is more news. Never say die!!

Your friend in Jesus' love,
Rinus

P.S. Koos and the other men from The Hague send their kind regards.

In this recreation room on the stage many plays were performed in which Rinus also had a role, for example, in one called *"The Hague Singers."*

✠

Do with me as you will.

✠

Sunday, January 14.
Beloved, this is the first Recollection Day of the New Year! 1939 is past. Many thanks for the time I received from you. A full year, the first full year of our matrimonial life, the life of union with you, is behind us, Dearest. I don't regret my consent at all! On the contrary, I thank you for your love with all my heart! For almost twenty-one years you, Dear Jesus, have been master of my soul by virtue of your sanctifying grace.

My dearest All, how can I ever thank you enough? We should be more aware of our childhood in God, as Father Lütenbacher said in his conference today. Everything is so simple, if only you are more and more loved and glorified!

People may tell me what they want of the miracles of nature. I won't be surprised any more. My Beloved can do everything, can't he? It gladdens me to hear in cosmology class about the tremendous size, distance, movements, etc. of the celestial bodies! I'm in awe when I see pictures in the *Katholieke Illustratie* [*Catholic Illustrated*] of, for example, an insect's eye, the sand on the ocean's floor. How beautiful it all is. Yet it is as nothing compared with yourself, dearest Creator. You are infinitely beautiful! You are *my* God, and *my* All. You are eternally, infinitely dear and beautiful. You are my beloved Bridegroom. And I may possess you eternally without end, joyfully staring at you because you are so wonderfully beautiful and sweet. I'm no longer perplexed by natural beauty, by its micro- and macro-structures. All that is comes from you, doesn't it? You are its infinite artist. I do not say this out of contempt for your art, Dearest, but as a simple fact of being true because all that wondrous beauty comes from you.

Dearest Beloved, your holy will be done above all else. Do with me as you will. I won't complain about the chores I will be given shortly, even if I have to remain a "refectory server" and a singing-master at the sisters' convent nearby. It's nothing. I will throw myself heart and soul into it because *you* want me to do so, not because my nature likes it, for it takes no pleasure in it.

Let me say once more, for it has to come out: "Jesus, my All." Dearest God, I rejoice because *you* are God, because you never lack anything, because you are always infinitely happy in yourself, because you don't depend on anybody or anything. I don't begrudge your being God, your being without beginning and end, always *nunc* [now]. You, although infinite and One, are known and loved *completely* for your *true value* and in yourself, in the most Holy Trinity! Jesus has become Man and given you also eternal and external glorification by his sacrifice! [No wonder I could burst for joy!]

Most dearest Victim, you have suffered so enormously, that I [don't mean to sound] hardhearted toward you? I'm [not] joyful about [your suffering]. It's not because I don't love you. No, I rejoice because your suffering glorified the Father, showed people your infinite love, and set a wonderful example for us as to how to suffer also for God's greater glory. All this is *good* and *true*, Jesus, [along with the mystery of] your mystical body. Our wretched human suffering is taken up in your humanity. It is offered by you, as the God-Man, to your infinitely true and dear Father. He doesn't refuse, he *cannot* refuse, the sacrifice of his infinitely Beloved Son. Thus all that is human in us goes simultaneously through your hands to the Father. You are our Mediator! Then we also have a sweet Mother, the Mediatrix of all graces! She is the neck of Jesus' mystical body, as St. Bernard of Clairvaux tells us.

In all this I remain your wretched instrument, Dearest, even as your grace grows and keeps on growing in me. Break every resistance, I beg you. Form me to be ever deeper *Alter Christus*. But . . . do so with *all* people. One person receives more grace than another; therefore, the former has to render more of an account than the latter. But, my God, you know everything. You also know that I respond worst of all to your grace. How holy would every other person be in my place, for plenty of grace is flowing. What if I had to make it with the grace other people find strong enough for them to remain in you? Then I would be brought low in impurity and pride.

Dearest, the wretch that is now deepest in hell would sink even deeper were I in his place! No, I don't exaggerate! I'm a mess. I still seek myself. I pretend to be pious, but if others could only see in my soul! Then what? Speaking *comparatively*, I mean [if they could only see] Jesus' results as compared to what it could have been like, had I cooperated and not been scared. There, Lord, I've written it! Yet I love you so! I love you above all! I don't know in my foolishness how to put it. So I don't try to formulate it [in words] any more, only to repeat: you are *All*, the infinite, while I am nothing. Everything in me is yours, most beloved God.

Wednesday, January 31.
Jesus, today twenty-one years ago, you gave me an independent existence. Twenty-one years ago little Rinus was born. As my Mother told me last year, I was christened the same day. From a little pagan I became God's child. And for these twenty-one years I've had the unspeakable grace to keep you in me all the time by sanctifying grace, in spite of everything. Also my holy patron for my religious life, Saint John Bosco, has been in heaven for 52 years. So, Don Bosco, many congratulations! I beg you to be my advocate with God, that I may be and do what God wills and only what God wills.

Dearest, you'll distribute a great many graces today, won't you, in honor of your Bride? You are infinitely rich. By the way, I beg you for an abundance of grace for *all* people, for their final perseverance. I'm going to skate now out of love for you.[92] Many thanks for my exams, for the recreation, for my confrères, but especially for being the soul of all actions in me. You are the only motive behind what I do. *Me oportet minui, eum autem cresci* [I must decrease, he must increase]. Yes, you must increase!

Dearest, I love you without being able to say fully what I mean when I express in words my love and gratitude. The only thing that expresses it is to allow myself to be pervaded by you and thus to act, to be urged and driven by you, to yield wholly! And then to leave the rest drift along, for whether I eat or drink . . . Dearest, you are All!

✠

The happiest time of life is the present moment.

✠

Wednesday, February 14. Recollection Day.
Bridegroom of my soul, today Father Lütenbacher spoke about the "little way" and the spiritual doctrine of St. Thérèse of Lisieux. What am I to say now? I hardly dare [to utter a word], for everything she has taught and written about her relation to you, her All, you have shown

[92] 1939-1940 was a winter of utmost severity as Dutch records show. Skating was often the only way to move from place to place. The castle moat surrounding the seminary of the Spiritans in Gemert, as shown in previous photos, offered scholastics ample opportunity for skating during their recreation.

me, too.[93] The only difference is that she was a light leaf moved by the least breeze of the Holy Spirit, just as he wanted, whereas I'm a wet leaf, still drooping and sticking to the earth, still, stiff and not yielding to your grace. Yet I'm not sad, for you know it. You know, don't you, the kind of dung heap I was!!

Dearest, I warned you myself about your love for me! I blame you entirely, not for my wickedness! No! But because your love has let itself go too far. You thought that, with so many graces, I would totally surrender myself, also in *practice*. But I didn't! I was cowardly, often scared and sensual! You punished me then, and I begged for your forgiveness. You readily forgave me, but, a short while later, it went wrong again. And, then, what about self-denial. It's still a distant ideal! Not so much about things that are obvious! For example, when eating and drinking, I try to get stronger so as to serve you better. But I know I'm a glutton, though I really need [the food]. No, it's not that! You don't make reproaches here. You even oblige me to eat more, for that keeps me in tune with my nothingness. It would be much nicer for my lower nature to be finished with just a few slices of bread. That "looks" much holier. I've got to laugh at myself. I'm still gorging when the others have long finished. I again and again take the last apple from the dessert dish, two or three or even more. It sometimes hurts my nature to do it, but, after all, it's nothing!

But, Beloved, what you approach me for above all is that I don't guard my eyes. I'm too curious in an unhealthy way. It's really true! In this case my confrères need not say what a "pious exaggeration!" And what about guarding my heart? I sometimes feel a great tendency in myself to embrace one of my classmates and tell him that I love him!! It's only thanks to the strength of your grace that it has not come so far yet. This smacks of sensual love! And what about those feelings and affections of love my heart sometimes feels for a girl! All of it is natural.

Jesus, [it only shows that] I could go on writing in this vein about my misery! What does it matter? Everybody knows, don't they? Thanks be to God, I'm still standing my ground, and firmly so. I owe this irrevocable firmness to your love, Dearest Jesus. I love you beyond words, beyond all the pleasures of nature. All its delights [I love] in you and for you! Often I take pleasure in what our good Brother Cook has baked for the scholastics out of love of you! Many thanks for that pancake. I'll eat it out love for you. Likewise for the bread, the cheese, the meatballs, for all that feeds me. If I could weep, I would do so at table out of gratitude toward *you* and all the helpers you have used to give me all this:

93 This passage like some other shows that Rinus was initially graced with the way of spiritual childhood long before he discovered to his surprise certain striking similarities between his own spiritual ascent and that of St. Thérèse.

for example, Father Provincial Superior, who has accepted me as a religious; Father Bursar for his care and toil to make all this possible; for the lay brothers; for the scholastics who set the table. Yes, I'm being foolish, yet I would thank all the people who have given those earthly things to us who are consecrated to God. All this has been given *for* you, and *for* you I'm willing to eat [this food] with grateful love.[94] My Jesus, that's not only the case with food and drink! Also the Saturday laundry, the lecture hours and means of recreation! I could cry with love and gratitude for you when I'm "floating" over the ice on my skates or when I play in the brass band (how wonderful music is!), or when I read books for relaxation that tell about *real* life.

Jesus, I know, it is your love-will, [your Holy Spirit], speaking in me and loving me with unspeakable sighs. Dearest, you also know it's true what I told my confrères when we had a discussion about the happy periods of life: "The happiest time of my life is the present moment." Tomorrow that time is happier again, the day after tomorrow even more. And I will be happiest at my last *fieri* [happening] when I put an end to the period of becoming and may remain for all eternity with what then is *factum* [what has happened]! For isn't it true that our inner being in you *grows* with every act of love for you, even if we don't say so explicitly, as, for example, when somebody in the state of grace, goes to Church on Sundays only because he is obliged to do so and because he is Catholic. Our inner being is in you. So doesn't that growth [in you] take place, as it were, by mathematically ascending powers? At every "now" moment we are at our highest point in you, and we can love you the most (not that the feeling [of love] keeps increasing). I see, alas, that I can't express what I mean exactly. I'd better stop! Most dearest Bridegroom, is it mad of me just to say, "I love you completely?!"

---

94 In this passage Rinus is obliquely referring to the war situation in Holland. Food became scarcer year after year. The administration of the Seminary of our mission-oriented community felt responsible for providing adequate nourishment for the young men. After the war they would need robust health to work under physically adverse conditions in such places as Africa and the Amazon region in Brazil. To improve somewhat their meager meals, they enlisted the aid of generous farm families. Hence Rinus expresses his gratefulness for their provisions as well as the gratitude felt by other community members.

59/ Zondag 3 Maart 1940. Liefste Jezus, hartelijk bedankt, dat ik er
gisteren avond weer biechten mocht. Ook gisteren morge
en nu zo juist mocht ik U weer ontvangen. Wat ben ik er
toch blij mee! Ik kan 't niet laten om te communiceren
Vorige week Zondag ben ik nog met mijn biechtvader
gaan praten. Ik ben erg blij dat ik 't gedaan heb!
Liefste U weet, dat ik tot dan toe in praktijk steeds
het opgevolgd, wat mijn Eerw. Vader zei! Maar ik
meende mijzelf te bedriegen misschien! Maar nu
hebt U 't mij nog eens door zijn mond uitdruk
kelijk verteld: „De levenshouding is eenmaal ge-
kozen! Bij iemand die van zijn vroegste jeugd af rein
geweest is. (wat ik alleen aan Uw genade te danken
heb) is de levenshouding t.o. God door 'n soort habitus
bepaald. Dan gaat 't ondraaien tot de doodzonde
niet een, z.g. zeker niet ongemerkt!" Ja natuurlijk
moet men niet beginnen met aan kleinigheden steeds
meer toe te geven! Dat spreekt vanzelf
Liefste Bruidegom! Gisteren heb ik in de „Heraut van
't H. Hart" 'n stukje gelezen dat me ook weer zo goed
deed! Dat is me de laatste tijd (vooral sinds de
hogere studie) al meer gebeurd! Dingen die ik heel
mijn leven a.h.w. instinctief zo heb aangevoeld! Soms
tegen de mening van heel mijn omgeving van toen. in
die worden me stuk voor stuk „verklaard als echt!
Zo ook in dat artikel. 't Ging over de hardheid en
de tyrannie der Liefde. Ja mijn Liefste Bruidegom

A handwriting sample from March, 1940.

✠

For the radix [root] of all this is being Alter Christus.

✠

Sunday, March 3.
Jesus, my Love, many thanks for allowing me to confess again last night. I could also receive you yesterday morning and this morning. How glad I am! I can't neglect to receive Communion. Last Sunday I had a talk with my Confessor. I'm so glad I did. Dearest, you know that up to now, I've always put into practice what my Reverend Father says to me! But I thought I might be deceiving myself! Now you've told me expressly again through him: "Your attitude of life has been chosen already. You are somebody [who had made his choice] from his earliest youth (which I owe to your grace alone). Your attitude toward God has become by design a kind of *habitus* [a disposition]. For a person to lean toward mortal sin does not happen at once. Certainly [it does not go] unnoticed. Of course, one should not start giving in more and more to small venial sins! That's obvious."

Dearest Bridegroom, yesterday I read in the *Heraut van het Heilig Hart* [*Herald of the Sacred Heart*] an article that did me much good. That has been happening a lot more often lately, especially since I began these higher studies. Things I've felt instinctively, as it were, all my life, sometimes against the opinion dominating the whole climate of that time, are now declared to be real, one by one, as in that article about the severe demands of [divine] love.

Yes, my dearest Bridegroom, I sometimes feel tied so strongly to you! I'm *forced* by love to swallow bitter pills, although my nature yearns to blow off steam strongly for a while. But no, your love suppresses relentlessly every resistance. I feel the pain in my nature, but later I'm full of joy. But you've experienced exactly the same! Your love, your incomprehensible great love for people, forced your human nature to accept harshness and suffering without complaint.

Dearest Jesus, the more I grow in you, the more intimate I am with you, the greater and more intense my love becomes for *all* people, for all those billions who exist or will exist! I don't understand it myself, yet it's true. I love them all. Incessantly your grace urges me to keep praying for them, to keep sacrificing everything in and through and as you for them. For the *radix* [root] of all this is being *Alter Christus*.

This wing of the castle was burnt down by the invading German army. Pictured here is the wing rebuilt while the war was still on, thanks to many contributions.

Thursday, March 21. Holy Thursday.

Dearest Beloved, you alone know how full of joy, how calm and happy, I am in you! Yesterday I was able to go to Confession again! You receive me, this poor nothing, always again. Twenty times a day I'll bungle, and twenty times you'll repeat: "Don't worry. It's nothing, simply go on!" And yet, dearest Jesus, even now the keeping of silence during the time assigned for it, is not sufficiently kept by me! Since I live on this higher floor of the house, I talk, often for a long time. I respond so badly to your grace! But Father van Lierop [the prefect of students] promised me another room yesterday.[95] I'll be glad when you approve of it. For then the occasions for me to break the silence will be diminished, and my neighbor won't hinder me any more! I know, it's not exactly a hindrance. He can't help it at all that my natural affection is drawn towards him. I must be more careful, or rather, you must be so in me! For I firmly believe he knows nothing about this! I'll tell him later on in Heaven. Indeed, I may safely tell others, too, that I loved them very much with a *natural* attraction, but that, for Jesus' sake, I could not (and wasn't allowed to) comply with this feeling. For I have had a steady partner on earth already. Through my union with you, dearest Jesus, I can often calm down my affectionate nature by thinking of this. But, inwardly, deep down, everything is still quiet in you. There I'm yours *eternally*, and for all eternity you are *mine* and mine only! *My* most dearest Bridegroom, I love *All*, every being for you!

Many thanks, Beloved, also for leading me so well with the singing during the celebrations this morning. Yes, *you* do this. I can't really help it when the confreres don't see this, when they repeatedly say I'm good at conducting. If I would tell them about you, about our eternal acting and being together, they wouldn't understand it the way I mean it, for I'm no good at expressing my experiences.

Dearest Jesus, you also know that this so called "Hague boasting" is not real boasting or pride in me.[96] No, it's not *that*. For one must be mad to make oneself out to be important, to say straightforwardly, "I'm this or that." When I talk about myself I do so, Dearest, so as to have

95 During the attack by an invading German army unit on the Seminary Castle, a whole wing of rooms burnt down due to the flames set by bullets and grenades. As a consequence of this calamity, many seminarians had to share rooms. This obviously made it difficult for them not to converse with one another.

96 Inhabitants of The Hague are often, by way of a joke, supposed to be "stuck up," affected, self important, talking with an arrogant tone, etc. This assumption probably came from the fact that The Hague is the seat of government and therewith the residence of its civil servants, dignified officials, ambassadors and consuls.

something to talk about for lack of something better. For if my confrères don't say anything at all, then I have to! But that doesn't mean I'm not proud! On the contrary, you know yourself (and you reprove me for it), those secret tricks in me, when I try to put myself in the foreground and pretend to be important externally, and very innocently, but deviously. Yes, I'm sneaky, a real sneak am I!

Actually, Dearest, I wanted to write something else. Sometimes you hear a kind of contempt (for the task) or pity for this person with intellectual talent, who is teaching and instructing future priests. But I think it is a splendid and holy work! Moreover, I think Pope Pius XI (of blessed memory) also said that the best persons must be used for this work, the education of priests. Indeed, you yourself did so! You instructed seventy-two disciples and twelve Apostles, for direct preaching only began after the holy feast of Pentecost! But I must stop, Jesus. It's time for spiritual reading. All, everything sighing, walking, sitting, working, praying, *everything* in you!

Friday, March 22. Good Friday.

My Jesus, many thanks that the ceremonies at the Sisters went well! You know yourself that one has to pay attention so that everything goes according to the rubrics to promote fervent prayer. But that's nothing. We all do things well for you, both celebrant and assistants. We haven't finished yet. Tomorrow the ceremonies will begin again. I keep relying on you.

This morning Father Lütenbacher gave a conference on Judas' betrayal. Dearest Jesus, how much you must have suffered then! And yet you were polite and kind to him, even though you knew his heart had hardened. How, then, may I refuse love and goodness to anybody whatsoever, even if I know or think I know that it's all in vain? I should not do so, should I? In the first place this [appreciation] applies to all my confrères, the Fathers and the lay brothers; also by extension to all people I meet! To any soldier on guard, to younger and older people, to all I encounter, for they are *people*. Jesus, I love them all for you. I know, I should observe the proper reserve with women, but yet I love them *all*, for you. [I offer] their souls to you forever!

My Jesus, how limited is the number of people I meet! How many billions aren't around here! From your first human creatures to those who will persist or perish in the Last Judgment! But really, I love them all and I pray for them incessantly. Please, give them much grace, especially the grace of final perseverance.

Dearest Jesus, it seems like nonsense to ponder something as extensive as this on my own, but I know in you the pursuit of love is normal and natural. The very best every person can do for themselves and for others is enter into you more and more, to let you grow and suffer in them, for suffering is involved [in love]. But mine is so little compared [to yours]. Love craves so much to be dissolved [in you]. My Jesus, we should blend into one another and become more and more *Alter Christus*. Thus we shall become freer and freer in you! Then actions will not be dangerous!

My most dearest Bridegroom, how true it is that I love [others] beyond words with your own love. For this love of you and of *all* people and things cannot possibly come from me, and that's no exaggeration! You know all things because you are my God and my All! Dearest, *everything* that exists I love for you and through you. Eternally [we are] for each other! The *All* with the *nothing*. Dear Mother Mary, again and again I'll thank you for the happiness it gives me to be your love servant. *Per Mariam ad Jesum*! Yes, it's true. *Experto crede Roberto*!

Where it may be useful, I'll tell more intimate things about you and your son Jesus. It's all done to make others love, too, as I may love you, quite undeservedly. No, dear Mother, it's not to boast. For if it were possible for me, I'd like to say, even [to blare] through a microphone, to an audience that doesn't know me [this news of love]. But that's not always possible, is it? Dear Mother Mary, I love you also with Jesus' love!

Friday, April 5.

Dearly beloved Jesus! Today, on first Friday, I was granted many graces again! Your love grows and grows. I've got a room of my own now, as I had asked for myself! There is a special reason and advantage to having a room! Many thanks!

Love, always pure,
nothing mixed [with it]
that is anything of my own.
Everything is quiet in you.
Jesus, for you alone
I watch my eyes, I watch my heart.
All of me is united with you, as *Alter Christus*.
Dear Jesus, you are all, I'm nothing.
Don't be afraid!!! Yet I'm scared, Jesus.
Non turbetur cor vestrum,
And yet I don't yield to you.
Noli timere,
And yet I'm a fearful coward.
Jesus, I beg you, strike me,
Do "violence" to me, I beg you.
You've got my permission. Please do so.
Dearest, everything is so new,
always, "*fieri*," becoming without end,
'Til once upon a time,
the thread shall be broken.

You know the day, and I agree to everything, Dearest Bridegroom. Mother, dear Mother Mary, a few days ago we celebrated Annunciation Day! It's also the titular feast of the servants of Mary. How I thank you for the grace to be your servant, you are the short cut to Jesus. Yes, *Experto Crede Roberto*!

Jesus and Mary, thanks for your sweet care. Rinus thanks you, with and in Jesus, completely united with him in unspeakable union. Dear Mother, I love you so much.

LETTER FROM RINUS TO ADRIAN AT GENNEP

Gemert, April 14, 1940

Dear Friend Adrian,

It's been quite some time, hasn't it, since I wrote you last. That doesn't mean I have forgotten you in my prayers, even for one day!

How are you? Your Novitiate is getting on, isn't it? Only four or five months more and then it's over again. With me things are as usual, day after day. I'll be really glad to see you during the holidays when you will also be a "Crow!"[97]

To begin with, I greet the Novice Master with all my heart! I thank him again for everything he has done for me (for in my mind's eye I still see the gold-plated eyeglasses bent attentively over this paper.) Father "Master," the scholastics of our class persevere well. Even so, there are always weaknesses, also in the Novitiate! But I should thank you once again, I feel I must.

I won't write any political news, for almost the whole world is under censorship, Adrian. A month ago I had asked if I could write to you, but Father van Lierop told me to wait. Now there will be mail for Gennep on Monday so this letter can go with it. Frater van Putten [another seminarian] gave me your regards.

How do you like the Novitiate? It's much more social among yourselves when you've got a large class, isn't it? And thirty is a large number! So our class has been surpassed! Is there any news at Gemert? Yes, we got a turkey a few days ago—Bart Muijssers [another seminarian] saw to that. Also those two "squawkers" from Hotel Bergen, I mean peacocks, that walk around here. The whole community is guessing. One says, "They're two hens." "No," says another, "They're two cocks." "No," says another, "The one with the blue neck is the cock, and the other is a hen," etc. Also the guinea-pigs had young ones again, and the hens are expecting a happy event one of these days. That's news about

97 A colloquial expression for a clergyman or religious in a black cassock.

our livestock. But if I know something else, I'll write to Adrian Olsthoorn! For I know I can and may write more [deeper thoughts] to you than to others. For we know ourselves by now.

Adrian, don't you think de Montfort was right when he said Mary is the safest and shortest way to Jesus? She takes us through dark tunnels without our hardly noticing it. We needn't do anything else but close our eyes and cling to her. For, Per Mariam ad Jesum. *This happens also during this life already. When that good Mother has fulfilled her task, she withdraws delicately to leave us to Jesus. She is like a loving mother who oversees the union of her child with someone else! She now looks and smiles modestly at how those two, the soul with Jesus, are so intensely happy. Yes, really, Adrian, so deeply, so imperturbably happy in Jesus—for almost two years now!!*

The whole world is wrapped in the love of Jesus. It's a daily growth in him and through him as Alter Christus. We needn't do anything but yield. Be very flexible! Love for all, and everything for God. You remember what I told you during the holidays, don't you? Really you won't be disappointed! Neither will you be in your later life, as long as you give Jesus everything. We are and remain poor good-for-nothings. Hang in there and don't be afraid! Don't be afraid of Jesus, and his sea of grace even if you think you are drowning in it. It's nothing.

Adrian, cordial greetings. We pray for one another, I know.

Your friend in Christo,
Rinus

P.S. Of course you shouldn't forget to give your good parents my warmest regards every so often. I also congratulate you on your twentieth birthday. It's now about that date, I believe.

Monday, April 22.
Dearest Jesus, I now feel the need to interrupt my study for a while! It's full springtime and the sun is shining in my little room. It's so quiet here. I'm here alone with you and in you. Through you I may work: studying, praying, [using well] my spare time, doing everything. Yet, my Love, I feel spring well up in me! It really doesn't matter. Anything that is not against your holy will is good and pure. There's nothing wrong with temptations as long as there is no consent.

Dearest Jesus, you want something from me again, don't you? I experience this [call], every time I struggle more. I don't know how many times a day, but every time [it happens] I beg you for the fullness of being *Alter Christus*, as full as possible for now, with the help of your grace.

With the distribution of new tasks I've become "emperor."[98] I've had that job before! But your holy will be done. If I tackle the job well, it will soon be over, for my nature dislikes it. I also have to stay on as choir master at the nuns for another three months![99] That's also something! But the peace inside me remains undisturbed, even if nature mutters objections.

Dearest Bridegroom, I'm continuing to study for the sake of growing in you as intimately as possible. Break every resistance, I beg and pray you. Even the most loveable and innocent thing that impedes the operation of your grace must be gotten rid of. Just give me a little sign. Give me your strength as well. Then it must and will go well! Please Jesus, do so now; it's for *all*, isn't it? I love you so much, and I love everything and everybody in you. It's all your work. My Jesus, I'm yearning for growth in you.

✠

I'm so glad to be nothing.

✠

Sunday, May 5. Recollection Day.

Today Father Lütenbacher's conference was on the Holy Spirit. It was so good for me to hear my Bridegroom mentioned and to learn more about his role in the spiritual life! It delights me beyond words that you are said to be unspeakably happy in and for yourself. And not just for a time, but forever! How marvelous it is that you are inexhaustible, that you know and love yourself entirely and perfectly. I am so glad that nobody can tamper with your infinite happiness in any way, for *you* are infinitely wise and strong of will. There's nobody you depend on for your happiness. The whole sinful world, even if it were a thousand times worse than it is now, cannot perturb your eternal rest and peace, your awesome will to act, in any way.

Most dearest Bridegroom, I'm so glad to be nothing! It's also the month of Mary again, the month of May, when so much homage and childlike devotion are shown to our dear Mother. Mary. I beg you, let a

98 "Emperor" was the title invented by the students for the person in charge of cleaning the "thrones" or toilets.

99 A convent in the same village near the seminary was inhabited by a group of nursing nuns. The Fathers were responsible for the spiritual care of these sisters. The seminarians would take charge of the music and song in their chapel on Sundays and special feast days. Rinus served for a period of time as the choir master.

great many people know your *real* service of love, as you've offered it so unnoticeably to me. *You* are the way to Jesus, so much so that you withdraw sweetly when your goal is reached and the soul has become one with Jesus more intimately! Then you are and still remain our dear Mother. I know this quite well, yet, at the same time, my soul mentions Mary less than before as she lives more with Jesus himself. But one's love for Mary is not altered in the least [by this movement], or rather, it is altered insofar as it becomes much more fervent. Growth in the love of Jesus, in the Father and through the Holy Spirit, mixes our finite powers with the infinite Divine Reason and Will of God.

Dearest Jesus, I'm craving, I'm thirsting, more and more to grow in you! You always satiate me, and yet every time I thirst to be more *Alter Christus*. The more you grow, the more I disappear. Thus [I give] more external glorification to you, dearest Trinity. Then more [graces flood] all souls, all people! Dearest Jesus, do [with me] as you wish. I want to remain docile [only when I] yield to you, do I have confidence. I love you so much, my most dearest God!

Beloved, you have overwhelmed me lately with new depths of grace. You haven't forgotten who I am, have you? In spite of all your graces and love, you know, don't you, that I'm capable of turning away from you in a cowardly way, capable of committing "adultery" [betraying our spiritual marriage] and of being filled with some vile low lusts? You know I'm miserable, don't you? I don't doubt that you know [all these things], but I say them to remind myself. I'm so proud, even if I don't seem to be so outwardly! I'm cheating many people, my nature is so sly!

Dearest, I feel capable of all evil. I laugh when I see myself bungling, for, thanks to the vastness of your grace, I see so well that I depend on you for everything. I owe my immaculate baptismal robe wholly to you. I'm going nearly mad with love and gratitude toward you, so vast is your grace. Anything I do or have to undertake, you do in me. I don't feel the slightest trace of pride if people sometimes compliment me. It's your work after all, isn't it!

My Jesus, I ask for the quiet to continue the silent *fieri* [happening] at dizzying speed in all dimensions in of my existence. *You* are all, *my* all. You won't forget your servants. Give them especially the grace for final perseverance. It is not that I doubt you; it is only my way of expressing, in my poor being, love for people. Thanks, many thanks, Dearest! Tomorrow [it's time] to study again, etc. It's all nothing. Your will is everything! *Non turbetur cor vestrum*! *My* God and *my* All!

And yet, throughout all this toil, you were there.

Thursday, June 6.

Dearest Bridegroom, how much has happened this last month! On Friday, May 10, war![100] I was surprisingly calm through it all, also physically and emotionally, thanks to you. But on Saturday, May 11, it was different during the shelling![101] Even then my soul remained at rest in you, united with you in unspeakable union. Dearest Bridegroom, how well I noticed then it was *you* and not my own sensitivity that kept me united with you! My physical self reacted quite naturally: We were in mortal danger, and nature shrinks away from such a threat vehemently, especially when we had to sit and wait in that kitchen in the basement, doing nothing. Later, after those two shots were fired into the kitchen, I went to the potato cellar. I did not show cowardice, yet I felt my body resisting death. Still my soul remained calm and quiet in you.

After we had been waiting like that for four hours, it was quite a relief when we were forced out, with our hands up, while all around us Germans stood shouting and brandishing guns and revolvers. I thought it far less horrible outside than inside. But why rake up all those memories? I was busy all that day, putting out fires, fixing a hole in the roof, cleaning rooms, etc. That night I was so tired I slept quietly, in spite of all my emotions. And yet, throughout all this toil, you were there, Dearest. I was in inexpressible, wordless, yet real contact with you all the time. You were the power in me to remain comforting and cheerful, to lend a hand everywhere. The same held true for those days following at Esdonk [a village near Gemert] and at home. Here, too, I was physically tired. In my room I could hardly stay awake, but whenever I was outside or asked to help out, you made everything easy. It was not possible to study much those first days. I ate a lot and took a nap for an hour (twice)! Now my body is its old self again, ready to receive new shocks if you allow them.

---

100 This was the day (May 10, 1940) that the Germans invaded Holland. Gemert is approximately 25 miles from the border.

101 A small group of Dutch soldiers occupied, on the night of May 10, the front wing of our Seminary castle, directly in front of its inner moat. The next morning on May 11, they mistook a small group of German invading soldiers for a "lost" group of a few men. They began to fire on them. Soon it became clear that they were the leading edge of a whole German army unit. This unit attacked the castle, forcing staff and students to hide in the cellar. The German soldiers herded all fathers, brothers, and seminarians together. They were held captive, facing their machine guns. Initially they could not believe that only a small group of Dutch soldiers, who had camped that night in the seminary, had defended such a large castle. These soldiers had escaped, wearing borrowed work clothes over their uniforms. There was some suspicion that perhaps a large contingent of seminarians had held up the invading German army. If that suspicion had been maintained, the consequences could have been disastrous.

Alas, my dearest Jesus, I can't find any words to thank you for our union. *You* are all! And so Beloved, I keep growing in you and for others, indeed for the whole world! You remember all these souls, don't you? The souls of my people, of all nations? Let them die in you! Give them the grace for final perseverance! Draw good from evil. Let many more ouls find you also when there is no war! Dearest God, I love you so!

Sunday, June 9.
This morning, in the recollection conference, Father Lütenbacher reflected on the devotion to your Sacred Heart. Your physical heart was only the *objectum formale secundarium* [the secondary formal object of our devotion], whereas the *objectum formale primarium*, [the primary object of our devotion] is your human and divine love, immeasurable as it is. I was so glad to hear that one can be devoted to the Sacred Heart without always bringing in that secondary object, be it your holy cross, your five sacred wounds, your holy countenance, the Virgin Mary's Immaculate Heart, or whatever. All these devotions have as their primary object your love and its increase, our growth in you, in a word, our being a better *Alter Christus*, and drawing nearer to our final end by creatively and more deeply fulfilling our duty. Then those twelve promises you made to St. Margaret Mary [Alacoque][102] are also valid for all who are striving after you, who want to love you more and more, who want to be more conformed to you, who want to become *Alter Christus* even more deeply.

Dearest Bridegroom, I often think it is troublesome to strive to write with a lot of circumlocution what in *one* flash of thought is something so simple. Then I see that all this writing cannot express what the soul perceives in you and wants thus to do [for you]. I could just as easily draw a circle and put a dab of [penciled] thought on it, even if nobody could read it. What would it matter? But then I can't possibly express with a circle how much I love you, indeed how much I *may* love you; for that love in me to you is merely an undeserved grace you've granted to me.

Fortunately, the Austrian commander of the unit listened quietly to the explanation offered in German by our Provincial Superior. After some moments of anxious waiting for his command, he declared, "You are released now from captivity." All raced to the buildings to extinguish the flames. The chaos was so great that it was necessary to interrupt for a short time the seminary program. First the seminarians were housed in neighboring villages. Then when the whole country had surrendered after fierce fighting and the bombing of the city of Rotterdam, they were allowed briefly to go to see what happened to their families. In the meantime, the necessary adjustments were made so that they soon were able to return to their seminary.

102 St. Margaret Mary was a French sister who was graced by appearances of Jesus showing her his heart burning with love for us. He revealed to her twelve promises for people who would honor and imitate his love and mercy, symbolized by his heart, especially on the first Friday of every month.

Beloved, how can you allow what is happening in the world now and how it will end? [All you do] is the same to me. The only thing I beg from you is *souls*. Give me all those hundreds of thousands of souls of the soldiers! Drown them in your grace of final perseverance so that they are almost unavoidably obliged to say, "Yes, I want God!" Dearest Bridegroom, don't think for a minute that I have begun to diminish [my request], that I don't ask for *all* souls! No, all, everything, is *for* you and must return to you! But I beg especially now for the soldiers' souls. You can do with me as you wish.

✠

Let me live our eternal union to the full.

✠

Sunday, June 23.
Beloved Jesus, I am in another room again. One of my confrères returned to the world. I think it a pity, for he might have become a good missionary. Also, speaking of the world there's a lot of news [to report]: War, bombings, all that impoverishes and strikes people down. All this has been permitted by you so that we see that we are nothing without you! There may still be a lot hanging over our heads—you know the whole of it! Whatever it may be, your holy will be done without cease!!

I now have a small writing desk in my room and some devotional objects. If I am or will become attached to them, I beg you, Beloved, take them away just as you took my former things from me during the shelling. The only thing I adjure and ask you for is this: Let me grow in you *more and more*! As long as you grant me life, I'm yearning to become more *Alter Christus*.

Dearest Bridegroom, let me live our eternal union to the full. Let me fulfill faithfully my duties as your bride. I am to expect everything from you, to join all my actions to yours. I am nothing; you are All. I beg you to make me a good bride. I truly am indescribably happy in our union! How glad I am I said "Yes" two years ago. This thought kept going through my head when I was waiting for the end in that underground shelter kitchen . . . "I'm so glad I've surrendered to Jesus *completely* . . . I've no regrets at all over his working in me . . . I only regret having resisted grace so much!"

Dearest, I love you. Yes, I love you, Jesus! I did not even think of my former sins. All that was past. My only thought was to *surrender* and to sense confidence in you at the deepest level of stillness. I felt the operation of your grace, I know, but, thanks be to God, it *was* there and still is there, no matter what happens. You are and you remain eternally, infinitely happy.

Dearest, what a relief it is that you are God and not I! I'm so glad nobody can rob you of your happiness. I thank you for being God. Yes, you are infinitely at peace! It doesn't matter what happens to me. I know only one thing: You and your dear mother Mary's happiness remain unperturbed. The same goes for all the saints and angels in heaven. I'm delighted for them!

I thirst so much for souls. Dearest Father, give me countless souls. Just because I'm a miserable nothing, without anything of myself on which I can rely with pride, I can, united with Jesus, ask you for souls. Anything you do, any grace you grant, you do for Jesus' and Mary's sake, and not for me. That's why you give me so many [graces]. Dearest All, I'll go on bothering you for more souls until the end of the world! And then I'll love you eternally and tell you forever of my love.

What a delightful prospect [awaits me]: to see and know you face to face, to love you, with my whole being. Dearest, [I love] your holy will, for anything you will is good. Jesus *ego amo te* [I love you].

Sunday, June 30.

My beloved Jesus, at the moment I've begun again to read through the second volume of Saudreau [a standard text on ascetical-mystical theology]. I've gotten as far as the part on mystical marriage! I read there about the holiness, serenity, and love of such souls, of their trials and concerns due to [their surrender]. Again and again mention is also made of holy and perfect souls. I read through these pages, just like that!

Dearest, how does it happen that I've not burst out in a mocking roar of laughter at myself: "As if you should belong to them?!" Yet I don't do so. I see my vast misery, the great contrast between the souls described there and my own. Yet I don't doubt for a moment our eternal union.

Sweet Bridegroom, today you've given me so much grace again. Indeed, everyday you give me [more than I deserve]. Then I can go on growing with courage. I feel you urging the exterior side [of me] to grow more, too! I should be much more modest, reverent, and calm outwardly. You ask this of me, so take it from me with my thanks! Help yourself to what you want.

Dearest, I have thought of the possibility that unauthorized persons might read this notebook. What should I do in that case? It seems to me as if they will all laugh at me because I'm such a nothing, in spite of all the graces [I've received] from *you*! Yet this doesn't worry me. If my Confessor would advise me (for then you would will it, too) to burn all these notebooks I would do so right away. Why I keep them I don't actually know myself. But what does it matter? If only you are glorified more and more, everything is all right.

My Jesus, *my* Jesus. You won't forget all those billions and billions of souls, will you? You've given me a thirst for souls yourself! Now I won't stop begging for grace for *all* of them (especially the grace of final perseverance) until the Last Judgment is over! Dear Jesus, how many good and delightful things are still awaiting me. Now I may know you already on earth and be deeply, undisturbedly happy in you. And that joy will *never* end! What a delightful future! What a delightful "now" too!

Dear Mother Mary, I wrote again about you to my friend, Adrian van Kaam. Father Superior also read those letters this time, but I don't really mind! You are and remain the dear Mother of us all! Neither does Jesus want me to argue or get excited about politics. I won't say, therefore, about what I think of [such things]. In any case I haven't said anything so far!

My intimately beloved God, my All. I beg you, let yourself be glorified as perfectly as possible by all people. I'm so glad that you are God, that you are infinitely perfect in yourself. My dearest All. Everything for you, but for Rinus, nothing but being *Alter Christus*. Only then can I do what you want. I long so for growth in you. I'm always being satiated, yet always longing for more, my dearest All!!!

Today in his conference Father Lütenbacher told us about Father Francis Libermann. Yes, our venerable Father was holy, so very holy. He was full of you, a great *Alter Christus*. Dearest, I beg you, if it is your holy will, let him be canonized! It will give the shaken Jewish people confidence again! If you wish it, it will happen soon.

✠

With you life is wonderful, whatever happens . . .
life has become one total prayer.

✠

Tuesday, July 16.
Today I felt the need to try to describe something of the love in me. My most dearest Jesus, I could receive you again in me! A flood of grace, a stream of "growth power," has entered my soul. I could leave the chapel [after Communion] more *Alter Christus* than when I entered [it]! And so that growth goes on, day after day! Do I owe this to myself? Can I boast about those graces? Is it *I,* then, who does all this? By no means! It is Jesus alone! Therefore, I will note here in black and white the enormously deep love I perceive in myself. The smallest child could see that it doesn't come from me but from Jesus!

Beloved, I want to use [when addressing you] all the terms one gives one's beloved on earth, despite how much pretense, deception, and tinsel there is in that earthly love! Here, in this connection, I don't mean that delightful growing together in courtship and marriage of two pure faithful people, but that silly unwise affection that is based on externals only. "My adored one," he says to her flirting at a party. Tomorrow he'll say it to somebody else. But with much more truth, indeed with exclusive truth, I can say to you, in love, "My adored One, my All, the light of my eyes. Without you I can't live; if you leave me I'll die; I'll kill myself (I mean spiritually, for if one commits mortal sin one kills oneself and God leaves him)."

What nonsense I'm writing again! I can't express myself! I can only be in the everlasting, deep, silent, unspeakably sweet togetherness I find with you, so deep [is the union] between my soul and you. *My* Jesus, my most Holy Trinity. With you life is wonderful, whatever happens. It's become a *habitus* [a disposition]. You are so simply [present] throughout all the most ordinary daily events that I hardly notice myself that life has become *one* total prayer! This growth [towards oneness] is your work! I owe it all to my dear Directress and Mother, and, of course, to you. Today is her Mount Carmel Feast. In all those Carmelite Convents you are being glorified [as you deserve], my dearest Bridegroom.

By the way, many thanks from the bottom of my heart for all your help during my exams. Yesterday I had oral comprehensives. The [outcome] may be disappointing as regards my marks, as was the case with the written exams, but it really doesn't matter. I leave it all to you! You can see for yourself, my Dearest All, that *everything* is for you.

Wednesday, July 17.

My Jesus, how often do I wander around my subject? That imagination of mine has played so many nasty tricks on me all my life! Things that occurred so simply were turned upside down and weighed over and over again in my mind. In my fantasy everything was represented in an exaggerated way! Thus also today: I had agreed to go for a walk. I like walking with my confrères, and it is not so much trouble for me to keep talking. But now I'm going to walk with a confrère with whom I must be careful not to seek my self-interest, because my nature makes far too much of him! Yes, it's true! But now, in my fantasy I am conjuring up all kinds of talks and situations that will never happen. Or rather, my fantasy works so imperceptibly that when I catch myself at it I should dismiss this nonsense at once.

Anyway, my Jesus, that's how it is! I don't even notice I'm wasting my time! Please, do something to stop this. You have helped me so much already, for it used to be much worse. Now it only happens at times when I'm physically and spiritually tired, for example, during an examination period! And yet, through all that fatigue, you are there! All my tiredness can't stop that. In that part of my mind and will, where you are, [love] remains as fresh as ever. But I owe this [gift of surrender] to you! When I'm dozing off *without* offending you or putting an obstacle in the way of your grace, I don't mind it at all, for then it only humiliates me! But I beg you, if there is [a serious] obstacle to the operation of your grace left in me, rid me of it, whatever it may be!

Dearest, these last few days my stomach hurts again! I think it's nerves, as well as that other kind of bread, for it is rationed now [because of the war]. Of course, that [malady] also influences fantasy, tiredness, etc. But it isn't so bad! If only I do whatever you want, *anything* [can be endured]. Radiating more and more *Alter Christus* completely in all my being and acting without fear! I also beg you for strength for the coming holidays! I ask you to help me to grow [in oneness] with you and to show you more to people. Whatever else you want or allow, it is all the same to me, if only you are glorified more and more. Dear Mother Mary, I'm so happy to be living together with your Son, Jesus, to be living with [the family] of the Most Holy Trinity.

LETTER FROM RINUS TO ADRIAN, AT GENNEP

The Hague, August 27, 1940

Dear Friend Adrian,

At last that happy day for you has come, hasn't it? Adrian, heartfelt congratulations on your profession! For Jesus only . . . I beg you for one thing: please respond to grace better than I do! For, if you knew how cowardly I sometimes am, you wouldn't even want to be my friend any more, and rightly so!

Because the Novice Master reads this letter first, I'd like to congratulate him as well with all my heart on the novices he has turned out! I hope that the depleted ranks will produce even better religious.

Well, Adrian, I also visited Mr. Langelaan one evening, and they would like us to come together! Would next Saturday night be possible? But I'll probably see you before that time, I hope!

I'm so glad you now belong to Jesus completely. Adrian, really believe me, religious life doesn't deceive you. Jesus becomes so inexpressibly everything for you. Through everything, the most common things, he, always he again, [becomes] our intimately beloved All. I'll be so glad when I can speak to you again about the God beloved by both of us! But I'll be short now.

I say, Adrian, will you also congratulate your good parents in my name and give them my cordial regards. But I'll soon come myself, I will. Next Friday morning already.

Further, I wish you a prosperous journey home and delightful holidays, and then . . . Gemert . . . study.

Once again, Adrian, warmest congratulations.

Will you give my special regards and congratulations also to Frater de Winter and the Muijsers brothers, and Frater van Kempen when you see them? Many thanks.

Kind regards from your friend, Rinus

T m
voor frater van Kaam

(21)

27 Augustus 1940

Beste vriend Adriaan.

Eindelijk is dan die voor jou zo gelukkige dag aangebroken hè! Adriaan van harte feliciteer ik je met je professie! Voor Jezus alleen..... om een ding smeek ik je - beantwoordt toch beter aan de genade als dat ik doe! Want als je wist hoe laf ik soms ben dan zou je niet eens mijn vriend meer willen wezen! en met recht.!

Omdat Pater Meester deze brief toch eerst leest, wil ik hem ook van harte feliciteren met de afgeleverde novicen! Ik hoop dat de gedunde rijen, des te beter kloosterlingen mogen zijn

Zeg Adriaan, ik ben ook nog 'n avondje bij Langelaan geweest, en ze hadden zo graag dat wij samen zouden komen! Zou Zaterdag avond a.s. gaan? Maar ik zal je voor die tijd nog wel spreken hoop ik!

Ik ben toch zo blij dat je thans geheel aan Jezus toebehoort. Adriaan heus geloof me, 't

The letter Rinus wrote on August 27, 1940.

(21)

kloosterleven bedriegt je niet. Jezus wordt zo onuitsprekelijk alles voor je door alles heen, de meest gewone dingen. Hij, altijd weer Hij onze innig geliefde Alles. Ik zal zo blij zijn als ik weer met je spreken kan over ons beider Beminde God! Maar nu zal ik 't niet te lang maken! Zeg Adriaan, wil je ook je goede Ouders van mij de hartelijke felicitaties en groeten overbrengen! Maar ik zal gauw zelf komen hoor! Vrijdagmorgen dl.

Nu wens ik je verder 'n voorspoedige thuisreis en 'n heerlijke vacantie, en dan.. Gemotd. studie!

Adriaan nogmaals van harte gefeliciteerd. Wil je van mij de specialegroeten (felicitatie) brengen aan Frs. de Winter (gebrs) en Muysers (gebrs) en v. Kempen als je ze ziet? Hartelijk dank.

De hartelijkste groeten van mij je vriend

Rinus

IX
THEOLOGY
GEMERT
1940–1941

IX
THEOLOGY
GEMERT
1940–1941

[Editor's Note: Rinus enjoyed long Holidays from August 1 to September 3, 1940 as well as an eight day retreat after the holidays from September 10 to September 17.]

Wednesday, September 11.
My beloved Jesus. I'm so glad to be back home again after the holidays. It was good to be at our [family] home where everyone was so nice and kind to me, but I feel myself to be much more at home here in the community. Now the great retreat has begun. The second day is almost over.

Beloved, I'm so unspeakably happy living together with you. You also inundated me again today with graces. Yes, you're quite right. People should also be edified by our outer behavior. Therefore, I must let you radiate much more outwardly through me—but not by being affected! No, just by yielding [spontaneously] to my body in its impulse to glorify you in its own way..

Yes, my dear Bridegroom, it's necessary for me to make a good sign of the Cross, to kneel straight and strongly, to sit up when praying in chapel, to do everything the liturgy asks in regard to bowing one's head, etc. I must not impose myself on others but radiate you. You urge me from inside myself to do so! This urging outward also applies to other points: courtesy and consideration when dealing with others, cleanliness and tidiness in work and study. All this outward behavior comes from you. Dearest, I surrender to it, for you are the absolute Master of my body too. I now share a room with a confrère. Still I can't stop myself from pressing my crucifix to my chest!

Dearest Jesus, I'm so happy that I may become a priest and that I am a religious. I beg you, let me keep growing in you. *Alter Christus*.

✠

I plunge into you. I don't care about the consequences.

✠

Thursday, September 12.
Today the Father who gives the retreat, Father van Rooij from Baarle,[103] spoke about meditation. He said he was sure that we are all called by God to a higher kind of meditation, in other words, to active (acquired) contemplation. I heard and saw several of the scholastics almost laugh. The moment they hear the word "higher" with regard to contemplation, some think "that's not meant for me; I'm still in the lowest degree." If only they knew what you, my dear Jesus, do to the soul when it surrenders totally and unconditionally to you, without thinking of higher or lower, a first, second or third way, etc. If only I could tell them how sweet beyond words you are for a soul. And then to think that *all* my confrères would be much more fervent and holier, more *Alter Christus* than I am, if you had given them the grace you've granted to me without my deserving it at all.

Dearest Jesus, what have I done to deserve this? And if only I were grateful! But no, I often play with your love. If you didn't hold me tightly I would be liable, in cold blood, to put the creature, myself, above you. I would offend you mortally by giving into my passions without restraint. But thanks be to God, this hasn't happened yet. You've still held me tight! I owe this to you only!

---

103 Baarle Nassou is a small town in the South of the Dutch province of Brabant, located at the border of Belgium. At that time the Dutch Spiritans built and maintained a formation house for the many lay brothers of their congregation. The place provided them also with practice for the many building, sowing, and farming projects they would have to assume in the foreign missions. The visiting retreat preacher from Baarle, Father van Rooij, should not be confused with Rinus' Confessor in Gemert, Father Jan de Rooij.

Dearest, I've seen, heard, and read a lot during the holidays. I've read "B" category books again.[104] They have formed me in a way, although some passages cause me trouble afterwards. I'm also still too easy in my glances, especially in the street! I see everything, and with me, seeing is almost the same as watching, for everything happens at a glance!

I'm also glad that I could talk to all kinds of people. Dearest Jesus, many thanks for that love for *all* people which you've granted me. Also my enemies. Who are they, really? Not political, for I don't concern myself with that business. I also try to love the Germans with all my heart. And what about that "Black Front" matter of the *Residentiebode* [*Residence Messenger*]?[105] Almost everybody I talked to was against it. I don't know what to think of it. It's not really important, don't you agree? I'm willing to support everything that is good and [whoever] strives after you. Whatever you allow, I allow, too, even if it's not pleasant at all for my nature.

Dearest Jesus, I'm so glad my friend Adrian van Kaam will be coming here![106] You love him very much. He responds to your grace so well, I should be ashamed of myself.

---

104 "B" category books are books that, while being helpful for one's education, merit some reservations about some passages.

105 This was a Catholic newspaper of The Hague before the war. In the beginning of the German occupation, it began to follow the German instructions for news reporting. It lost most of its subscribers. (Here Rinus is slightly naive about the situation. This is understandable. He, like the other seminarians since his entrance into the Junior Seminary at twelve years of age, had not been allowed to read newspapers in the Seminary, or listen to the radio. At that time the Spiritans, like most religious communities preparing young men for the foreign missions, did not foster interest in Dutch political events and problems.) "Black Front" was one of various small political groups in Belgium and Holland. They were not Nazis like the Dutch National Socialists but were excessively Belgium and/or Netherlands prone patriots with some authoritarian tendencies.

106 Editor's Note: At that time I had finished my own Spiritan Novitiate year in Gennep. I would now join Rinus in Gemert. Our spiritual friendship was never interrupted, as is clear from the letters Rinus wrote to me from Gemert. Our intimate sharing of and reflections on our personal-spiritual experiences made me the only soul-friend he had, besides his three successive spiritual directors, who also knew in detail the special graces granted to Rinus and the struggles surrounding their implementation. Added to this realization was our inspiration to set up the prototype Epiphany circle. Rinus gradually grew in the conviction that he would die early and that the mission of his life, both here and hereafter, would be to support its work in the church.

Dearest, please give me the words to say something about how to express how I love you. I'd like to write poetry, to sing, dance, laugh, and cry, to press all the world and all created things to my heart—and still my love would not be satisfied. Jesus, I'm so thirsty and hungry for you. At the same moment that you satiate me, with an ever new longing, I desire you again. I long for everything and everybody you long for. If you agree or want something, so do I. My dearest Jesus, I'll stop. I don't know in my foolishness what else to write. I plunge into you. I don't care about the consequences. It's all the same to me what they say or think about me. You, and you only!!

My beloved God, most Holy Trinity, I'm so glad, so deeply happy, that *you* are infinitely happy. You know and love your whole being perfectly. I'm so glad that you, not I, are God. I'm happy to have been created by *you*, to be preserved by you. I'm glad because you know and love yourself for all you are worth.

Dearest God, *my* God, it makes me happy that you are infinitely happy. With all my being I say, "You're welcome" to that infinite glory in yourself. It pleases me immensely when I hear or read that you don't need anybody to be happy, that no one and no thing can disturb that infinite love and knowledge and life that is you. I love you, most Holy Trinity!

Tonight in his conference our good and holy retreat priest pointed out that meditation is easy. Almost automatically, one comes to a higher prayer if one is faithful to one's meditation! Yes, my dear Jesus, I beg you to give this deeper grace to all the confrères in this house, to all members of this community. My Dearest, don't be discouraged by a first or second refusal. It's not unwillingness but unfamiliarity. Do with us as with children when they have to take a good medicine that tastes nasty to them: Take the spoon in your hand, hold them, and make them swallow the stuff. Really, Dearest, you won't need to force them a second time!

My dear Mother Mary, please add a little to the fire! Please do to all of them what you did so sweetly to me. Take them and lead them on the way! You'll see, dearest Mother, you won't have half the trouble with them that you had with me. You didn't give up your work with me, did you, even when I resisted so much! I wish for all my confrères the inner happiness I've been given by you—without my deserving it at all, dearest Jesus! Yes, the more mystical souls there are, the more action there will be.

This afternoon I read in Dom Jean de Chautard[107] [a popular spiritual writer, whose book, *The Soul of the Apostolate*, is a classic] that inner life, far from impeding the apostolate actually enhances it. When

107 De Chautard's book was one of the classics of spiritual formation we read and discussed in our early Epiphany circles.

one rests inwardly in you and lives united to you, one can do so much more than [one could] without this deep inwardness.

My beloved Bridegroom, we have been living our matrimonial life together for more than two years! It sometimes seems to me I bore you by thanking you so often for that grace. For, my dearest All, I haven't the least regret about saying yes! My Jesus, with you and in you everything goes of its own accord. I don't feel afraid any more of other people's opinions—and you remember how much that used to bother me. All this has been achieved by you!!

My God, I hope to study hard this year—much harder than I would have done if I had been satisfied with just memorizing the subjects themselves, as I used to do! For all that I learn now I've got to put into practice later. You also urge me not to argue as much [as I used to] any more. It only causes unrest. Besides, there's no need for me to chatter so much! I'd better also learn to listen a bit more to others!!

The third day of the retreat is over, only five more [days] to go. My Dearest, I thank you in advance for all the graces you want to give me again. Jesus, in you and with you. In short, I love the whole world in you and for you with your love. During the holidays I read part of the book *Le Christ dans nos Frères* [Christ in our Brothers]. It's very good. Especially that idea about vessels "communicating with each other" struck me: The holier, that is to say, the more *Jesus* a member of the Church is, the holier the *whole* Church will be. It's wonderful, Dearest, all this is so really you.

Friday, September 13.

My Beloved, you must still be very careful with me, for I am capable of offending you to your face! I've got such a passionate sensitive heart! I noticed it again clearly during the holidays. For when seeing an attractive girl (even just *seeing* her—I'm not talking of watching for I mustn't do that) my head sometimes was in a blaze! And the funniest thing is that just suddenly, without any reflection I judge every woman or girl according to that sensitive point of view, in a *motus mentis primo primus.*[108] (That's the term, I believe, although I'm not a philosopher now any more. I'm a real braggart, am I not, Jesus?) Even when I went around to collect small contributions for the old women at the Foundation [an old folks' home], I looked for signs of their former attractiveness behind those wrinkled features! Silly, don't you think so? And then, dearest Jesus, there are times when I'm not tempted at all by female beauty! I mean in a sensual way! For then my body is so quiet (through the peace, the everlasting rest of my soul, that is your work). Then I love all that beauty only for your sake. I praise you for

108 A spontaneous primordial movement of the mind before one can exercise control of the will.

the attractiveness in your creatures without the remotest inclination [to enjoy it] for myself. But it's not always like that! Now I know that all those first spontaneous impressions don't matter at all! As long as the will strikes down at once the [free] conscious perception of it.

Dearest Jesus, I could also speak to married people about the happiness of their marriage. For so many really mean well! They prefer a large family with many cares to a small family with an easier life! Many thanks, my dearest, for arranging marriage so wonderfully and so beautifully. As to the mutual completion of husband and wife, no, Jesus, there's nothing vile or evil or even inferior in a matrimonial life practiced according to your holy will.

What a pity that religious sometimes see this more than married people do themselves. I'll be glad when later, as a priest, I may tell people wonderful things, while remaining free from every special love for a woman, in order to love and help *everybody* in and for you, my dearest Bridegroom! Therefore, no matter how I view this, I may always have the best of it, if only *you* are the soul and the life of everything! *Omnia mundis munda* [For the pure, everything is pure], if only those "*mundi*" are real *Alter Christus*!

Saturday, September 14.

This morning the retreat master spoke about the holy Sacrament of Confession! Dearest Beloved, yesterday I received this Sacrament. It thrills me every time I *may* go to Confession. I like to go every Friday. I also wrote down on paper all that I'm going to ask Father de Rooij, especially as regards detachment.

Dearest Jesus, do you want me to "lend" my fountain-pen to a confrère who hasn't got one yet, and to use an ordinary pen instead? Do you want me to exchange my wrist-watch for an ordinary watch? Do you want my statue of Mary and my photo-frames, my red pencil, etc. to be gotten rid of, all of them? Just say so! Dearest Jesus, I don't want to have the least attachment to those things! Should I decrease your love and resist the operations of your grace by such rubbish? Not on my life, dearest Love!

My Confessor also advised me to pray and work for those souls who will be entrusted to me later as a priest. I should prepare the ground now. I know you through his words. So I'm quite willing to do so, without restricting my life to those souls *only*. For I can't do so any more! That's your own work, dearest Love. You have so widened my narrow heart. I can now really love the whole world, all people. I beg for your grace of final perseverance for them all, especially for those souls who will be entrusted to my care later.

Dearest Mother Mary, in advance I give you those souls already! Make saints of them. You'll really protect them all, won't you, Mother?

Dearest Jesus, what a wonderful, perfect institution your Holy Church is. All who are *outside* and *against* you have tried (and are still trying) to introduce a similar system in their organizations. Take, for example, freemasonry. It's all *ersatz* [fake imitation]. All those mysterious degrees are a weak imitation of your mystical degrees of inner life. Their external rites are meant to represent our wonderful liturgy. Their VIP's with their inaccessibility are supposed to represent our saints in their inner imperturbable rest!

Dearest God, I beg you, I adjure you, give to a great many souls (for example, also those from my future "parish"), the graces you've wanted to give me in your incomprehensible goodness! How beautiful life is if you are its only soul and motive! Every day is new again! Everything around us becomes appreciated! Every day it seems as if we've never before said to you, "How beautiful are those flowers and trees, that grass and water, made by you!" During meditation it's as if I've yet never known you as I know [you now]. For in you everything is both new and yet always old and well-known. Why should I now fill up notebooks to try to express myself when [its impossible] to succeed? I don't succeed. It's so wonderful to live as your Bride! [There are no words for it.]

My Beloved, missionary work is hindered so much by the war. If it's your holy will, would you please let the war be over this month so that there may be peace again? But if you don't want this, it is also acceptable to me. Even if you would allow another May 11th in our castle, if only you are glorified as perfectly as possible, [it would be to the good].

Dearest God, be merciful to all the souls of those millions of German, Italian, and English soldiers at their moment [of death]. Give them all the grace they need for final perseverance!

Dearest God, you can do anything. I know that my prayer for these countless graces is a prayer of adoration. For what else, for heaven's sake, should I, poor wretch, rely on than simply and solely your infinite wealth? Please, my dearest All, give and give to all souls what they need in their last moment.

Jesus, I'm craving for growth in you. I want to give the whole world to you. Souls, give me souls! Dearest God, I'm yearning for you, for your glory! The holier and the more "you" I may be, the more grace you'll grant [to quell] my nagging? Please, do it for the sake of those souls, dearest Jesus. You love them infinitely. I know I'm foolish and arrogant! But you've made me so yourself. For you've said *petite et accipietis* [ask and you will receive]. Therefore, Beloved, I always keep begging, also for growth in my exterior life.

My most dearest Love, *Fulcite me floribus quia amore langueo* [Strengthen me with flowers for I'm languishing with love]. You are *All*; I am nothing, most dearest God, my Creator.

Sunday, September 15.
This morning Father van Rooij talked about neighborly love. Dearest Jesus, I'm so glad he really speaks after your own heart, so full of faith, practically, and with much love. The scholastics like his conferences a lot. Yes, it's true, my confrères here and now are even closer to me than my relatives. All have shown for at least eight years that they loved you above all other things. They have followed your calling voice throughout the difficulties of their study and the burning struggles of puberty. [They have grown beyond] reluctance and aversion. Some have even had to go on against the love of their relatives, who wanted them somewhere else. They've gone through all of this, including what we now have to endure, for you and for the sake of poor souls.

Dearest Jesus, how can you not look down in the fullness of love on all of them, as well as on all religious communities and seminaries? Yes, it's true, we remain poor people with every [imaginable] difficulty and fault. But I beg you, my Jesus, offer your broadest and mildest judgment to all my confrères. I've still got a fight on my hands in that regard! I start to judge before I notice it myself. That's due to my critical, choleric nature. With your grace I try to repel these temptations as soon as I become aware of them. Yet far too often I show much laxity and hesitation in repelling them. I beg your forgiveness for this with all my heart!

Dearest Beloved, the retreat is coming to an end. One more full day and then our study begins again. You will still have to prod me. But that's nothing. I like being prodded by you. I'm willing to accept everything from you. You can upset me, even hurt me, if it's your holy will. I love you so much now that I can't be angry with you since I owe all to you.

You, too, dearest Mother of the Seven Sorrows, you've made a great contribution to this work of grace! I've given my whole [future] "parish" to you already. You're its full-time Directress. I beg you to be the short-cut to Jesus for all the souls entrusted to my care. *Per Mariam ad Jesum*, already here on earth.

Dear Mother, you will watch my sheep well, won't you? Watch until I may come [to them] myself, in four years' time,[109] to take them with you to Jesus. My dearest God and my All. Tonight I may hear your word through my Confessor!

---

109 Rinus would die a holy death at the beginning of the new calendar year, long before his desire to be ordained a priest could be realized.

Monday, September 16.

I've listened to [my Confessor's words] and heard in them your holy will! About the first item, the "B" category books, you don't want me to read them so as to avoid all incitement. I'll know of life soon enough and for long enough! Thank you, Jesus, I won't do it. So remind me when I'm home again, for it happens then and there.

About the second item, my friend Adrian van Kaam. The friendship has been approved [again, as usual]. We should not seek one another all the time so as not to detract from fraternal love to others. Many thanks, my Beloved, your holy will be done.

About the third item: my knick-knacks! I must not be attached to them, but I may use them. So I must go on using my fountain-pen, wearing my wrist-watch, etc., and the statue of Mary must stay with me.

About the fourth item: study! It's good when I "plunge" into it, studying hard for you only. As a stimulus, I want to make an average of nine marks out of ten in all subjects. Even if I now have six, I don't care. But it's just by way of a stimulus. For extracurricular study you told me through your deputy, my Confessor, to exercise myself as if I were dispensing the sacraments. For at the end of third year theology they practice here saying Holy Mass, but how are we expected to baptize? To bless a marriage? To administer Extreme Unction? To hear confession? To assist the dying? For if we say these wonderful prayers only when we are faced with them at the time itself, then we won't be nearly reverent enough. Of what use is it if things are done well but the prayers don't mean anything to us.

Furthermore, you want liturgy and Holy Scripture to be my extracurricular study! Your holy will be done, Jesus. I'll put aside my astronomy, etc. I can bring all these resolutions together in this plea to you: "Most Dearest God, let me be wholly absorbed in you; let me fully surrender to your holy will." Always deeper *Alter Christus*. Everything for you and because of you! Dearest God, I love you with all my being.

My God, tonight we had the last evening conference. Many thanks for such a fine, holy retreat Master! This time has been a gift of the Holy Spirit.

Dearest Jesus, today I've done something that never happened to me before. Last Friday I had just had my weekly confession with my own Confessor. But our retreat priest happened also to be our *extraordinarius* [extraordinary Confessor],[110] so I had to see him, at least to

110 In relatively close communities, such as religious seminaries, resident priests, for example, those serving as faculty members, are available as regular Confessors. As a rule also priests of other communities are appointed as "extraordinary" Confessors. They must make themselves available at regular intervals so that the religious concerned can receive what we call at present the Sacrament of Reconciliation from a person less intimately connected with their everyday life. At that time everyone was obliged to visit the extraordinary Confessor, if not for confession, then for asking his blessing.

ask his blessing. Today is Monday, which means I had been to Confession only three days ago. Therefore, I simply wanted to ask for a blessing, although I also liked the idea of receiving again the grace of the sacrament. But it was unusual for me to confess after only *three* days. I'd never done so before! Now this afternoon I was waiting while doing my [spiritual] exercises. The line got thinner—only two more were ahead of me! Then only one more! It's strange, but I was so desirous of grace and purification, of being more *Alter Christus*, that I went to Confession after all! I'm glad I did!

You also helped me to see a few more things through the [eyes of] the *extraordinarius*: I should control my curiosity, especially my eyes! I must be firm when I, in a half sleepy state at night, feel such an urge or inclination to touch myself! Don't indulge. Next—and this will require a lot of daring—I beg you for the courage to ignore all those thoughts rising up, those "buzzing" flies of pride, sensuality, unchastity, self-conceit, critical judgment, *weltschmerz*, dejection, etc. They are all emotions welling up due to the natural conditions of a cold or maybe to an [overly] heated, choleric, or chubby body. They aren't worth fighting against (that is, intentionally resisting them), for simply by taking too much notice of them, they may become real temptations! You want me to go on undisturbed and not pay any attention to them.

Yes, my Dearest, I've thought of an example: I'm making the Stations of the Cross, or meditating, or doing a [spiritual] exercise, or the like. I try to maintain a proper posture in prayer and ritual out of love and respect for you, out of a certain desire to express this [devotion] in my body. Now those "buzzing" flies come by: "How neatly you stand there so everybody can see again that you're such a devout boy . . . " Now it would be folly to say: "Jesus, what a sham I am. I don't really want to do this, to put myself in the foreground. I want only to glorify you." (It's not so foolish to say this inwardly.) But then I may be tempted to give up that posture. For I may want to show you that I'm not doing this to be seen by people. In that case the devil would get what he wants.

You told me today clearly through the *extraordinarius*: "I must simply stand still, be quiet, and act as if those [distractions] were not there." To put this resolution into practice, you must put yourself even more in my place.

Dear Jesus, take *all* the reins, *all* the time, then things will go well. With your grace I hope to raise no obstacle to *your* work in me. I hope that I will not throw any boulders on the road! If only you'll drive the car! Most dearest All, once more I thank you with my whole being for the grace of this retreat.

✠

Let me grow, always grow in you; that's the best thing I can do.

✠

Thursday, October 10.
My beloved God and my All, for a long time I've had no chance to write! It's study and prayer all the time. Theology pleases me more than I can say! I'm so glad to be able to study so as to know you more and more! Then I can also love you more and more!

Dearest Bridegroom, love in me acts sometimes so foolish. In the midst of this intoxication, I hardly know what to do to express some of that love externally in my body! Mostly I must control myself because I'm with others. But that doesn't matter. I think I know by now in what my suffering and cross consist. It is in seeing and experiencing my misery again and again each day so that I may receive your forgiving kiss. Yet I still live cowardly and half-heartedly, though every time [I slip] you forgive me, so much so that I can say *Nunc coepit Jesus* [Now Jesus has begun]. I'm yearning so much to become more you, my most dearest! Let me grow, always grow, in you; that's the best thing I can do. Then I may glorify you most; then I may do penance and beg for all people! That is exactly what you want!

Dearest Jesus, [I give myself totally to this] sacred learning because you want this [submission] from me. On my side, it feels as if I am always "being open," a receiver without anything more [to give]. I don't know how to put it! I'm quite happy when I hear an explanation of how your grace works, of how you've redeemed us, humans, of why your Holy Church makes its canons, and of how your moral doctrine works. This [knowledge] enters into me blending with the love [of Christ already at work in me]. (But the practical thing is whether I can remember it all and bring it up in a test or an exam!)

Most Dearest, your holy will be done in everything. My soul and body, hands and feet, everything in me, thrives [and strives] for you only! I sometimes feel the health and wholeness in my soul and body together. Then I say, the whole is for you. I thank you also for the grace of health.

Dear Mother Mary, you won't forget the poor souls in purgatory, will you? Will you also remember . . . [Translator's Note: Manuscript unclear].

Monday, October 21.
My most dearest God, I take a few minutes at a time to say, "I love you," also when I'm busy studying. I want to absorb everything well

and deeply out of love for you. I want to grow in you by developing both my reason and my will entirely as you want me to.

Dear Bridegroom, I surrender totally to your precious will! I'm so glad that you've given me a [personal] rule [for my daily life], one you have approved of through my Confessor! Out of love for you, the whole day is now a chain of surrender.

Dearest Beloved, many thanks for the graces you've given me again this morning. I cordially kiss you in your image here in front of me on my table. Now it is you who go on in me as I study, isn't that so? My God and my All. My Beloved Bridegroom forever. Your holy will be done.

Sunday, November 3.

My dearest All, I see so clearly inside me hesitation, fear, cowardice, not giving everything. This is a crime! I *must* not do it. If this keeps up, you cannot possibly radiate through me as you want! I'm a great obstacle to the increase of external glory for you in your heavenly being.

Beloved, for a few days you've pressed me for the promise to be more perfect! This morning you were so sweet again. Your grace is irresistible! I can't resist you, but neither do I want to.

Dearest, take what you want, rob me, push me away! Everything is yours after all! This morning one of my confrères in his sermon spoke again about becoming *Alter Christus*. Several times others, too, have expressed this desire of their soul to grow in you. I must give an example. I'm obliged by your grace to do so.

Dearest Jesus, I'm yearning so much to be more you, to realize yourself truly in me. Please, Beloved, remove every resistance and obstinacy in me. Form me with your ever growing life! I'm nothing, if only you live.

This morning in the conference Father Lütenbacher said of the pastor of Ars [St. John Vianney], "He passed all degrees of mystical prayer and was now in the stage that is highest on earth, mystical marriage with God."

Dearest Bridegroom, I became as glowing red as a peony while seeing at once how miserable and helpless I am. Rinus Scholtes and the holy pastor of Ars! What a difference! Dearest, I beg you, give me strength all the time [when I realize] the caricature I am of you! Please, Jesus, take everything!

Dear Lord, I think I've found a subject for the kind of outside study about which I hope to give a lecture this year, namely, a study of the African soul. In this way the knowledge of the Africans' inner world, that is to say, of their thoughts and habits, may be more appreciated. I know this is an extensive and deep topic. But it also seems to me that, with the help of your grace, combined with natural knowledge, I'll be able to become "black with the blacks" [the ideal of Francis Libermann]. For the time being, I put all my study into your [hands].

Your holy will must be foremost. I only want to do this project if it means becoming more *Alter Christus*. It should not make me think of myself only as learned or to put myself in the foreground. (Even with the silliest and simplest things you have to be careful with me, for you can expect anything from me.) Otherwise, please treat the matter as of no consequence.

You know, Beloved and dearest All, that you have full power over me. I have sold myself, as it were, to you! I'm so addicted to you that I can hardly skip a Holy Communion. For five years now I haven't even dared to try, have I? [I only missed] twice because of illness (due to one of those "old men's ailments" that kept me in bed for two or three days). In spite of all that grace, I am and remain a wretched fellow. I keep clutching at the forbidden fruit, and sneakily at that!

Yes, my Jesus, you may have noticed that this bride of yours is a failure. Humanly speaking, I would say that you've burnt your fingers! You've never had to deal with such a wretched being. You've spent countless treasures of grace on me. You kept thinking, "With such graces he cannot avoid doing my holy will!" But no, over and over again [I fall into] that shilly-shallying, that sensuality, which is disastrous for the operation of grace.

My Jesus, I beg you to give me the strength I need to see myself in this way every day. I don't mind so much that I'm miserable myself. It's just that in this way your graces are wasted. Your external glory is diminished. The salvation of souls is harmed. That grieves me so much! I sometimes think of a certain confrère and I say to myself, "If he had received all the graces my Jesus has given me, how much, how enormously much more of a result would [you] have achieved!"

✠

Let no one get lost.

✠

Tuesday, November 26.

My Dearest, many thanks for my sore foot. It's a great grace for me to have to rest all day. I'm sitting on my bed, so cozily, Jesus. Love, love grows. You keep giving me more and more graces. You are much too sweet to me. I can't sometimes utter anything but sighs and look at your crucifix. Then I kiss your effigy with the fervor with which a small child kisses its doll.

Dearest Bridegroom, again that trifle of mine cannot be compared with any other real disease because it's so silly. Now I've been lying in bed for almost the whole day for a silly foot! Yet I'm lying here out of love for you. I also walk with my cane out of love for you. Mom, Mary, I'm glad I bought a statue of you during the holidays.

My All, you won't forget the poor souls, will you! The dying! *All* souls just before their departure from this life. Draw them all to you. Let no one get lost. My Dearest, demand what you want. Please do so. I want to surrender completely. I may promise you always (not under penalty of sin, for I'm far too weak and I commit far too many sins as it is) to do what is most perfect out of love of you without any unrest, provided that you speak clearly to me.

Dearest, you shouldn't think that, although you keep your word, I'll do the same! No, I'm far too miserable. Only when you drown me in graces do you succeed because they can hardly fail!

Dearest, I'll let you [do it] in me as I study. It works best when you always do everything. Please, Beloved, shall we go on now with [our study] of moral theology? In and through you I want to know and to absorb everything you want me to understand.

Dearest Mother Mary, you just smile. You yourself are the cause that Jesus and I are coupled forever. *O felix culpa* [O happy fault]. We are happy, aren't we, my God?[111]

[111] This is the last entry Rinus wrote. Around this time his illness took a dramatic turn for the worse. It was far more serious than the doctors had at first expected. He had terminal tuberculosis and would die in approximately six weeks' time, though his correspondence continued for a while.

21. nelijkheid die de pest is voor alle genade werking.
Mijn Jezus, ik smeek U geef mij de kracht om me zo telken
opnieuw, iedere dag, zo ellendig te zien! Dat ik zelf ellendig ben vind ik nog niet zo erg! Maar dat daardoor
Uw genaden verspild worden en dat Uw uitwendige
glorie verkleind wordt, dat daardoor 't heil v.d.
zielen geschaad wordt! dat doet me zo'n pijn. Soms
bezie ik eens 'n kledetroeder, en dan denk ik „ Och had
jij eens al de genaden ontvangen die mijn Jezus aan mij
hebt gegeven, hoe veel, hoe enorm veel meer resultaat
zou er dan bereikt zijn!

Dinsdag 26 Nov. 1940. Mijn Liefste, ik dank U van harte voor mijn
zere voet! 't Is 'n grote genade voor mij, dat ik de hele dag
rust moet houden. Ik zit nu gezellig op bed! Jezus
de liefde, de liefde groeit, steeds meer blijft U me
maar genaden geven! U bent veel te lief voor mij, ik
kan soms niets zeggen dan zuchten en Uw kruisbeeld
bekijken, dan kus ik Uw beeltenis met de innigheid
waarmee 'n klein kind zijn pop kust. Liefste
Bruidegom, alweer is dat akkefietje voor mij met
geen andere echte ziekte te vergelijken omdat het
zo onnozel is! Nu lig ik voor 'n onnozele voet
de hele dag bijna op bed! Toch lig ik hier uit
liefde tot U, ook met mijn stok loop ik uit liefde
tot U! Moedertje Maria, ik ben blij dat ik
onder de vacantie Uw beeld heb gekocht!
Mijn Alles, U vergeet toch de arme zielen niet
hè?! De stervenden! Alle zielen vlak voor hun

A facsimile of Rinus' last entry.

LETTER FROM ADRIAN TO RINUS

Philosophy Study Room, Gemert, Christmas Day, 1940

Deus Solus

Dear "Happy" Friend Rinus,

"Happy," more than your other confrères, because this Christmas you may resemble our most dearest Jesus more than they. [You in him] are like the infinite, strong Being who lies down powerlessly and suffers in a manger. You with your so firm and strong body, are now just like that powerful God lying down powerlessly and suffering in your bed.

Our dear Mother will be quite close to you now, just as she was close to Jesus, near the manger and near the Cross. Indeed, she was also with you when she saw you going about in this seminary like her dear youthful Jesus at Nazareth. But now she's quite near to you, as she was in that stable with her Jesus.

Yes, "happy" Rinus. Now of course you have also got the feelings of Jesus in that stable. Ecce venio [See I come], *Jesus thought, "Behold Father, I've come to do your will."*

May there be high voltage wires of grace and love in your room.

Surrender, Rinus, to Daddy. Prepare, prepare! He will ask for more. Put every moment in an act of ecce-venio *like our beloved Jesus.*

Tonight I was united with you spiritually. Together with you I prayed, meditated, sang. Then I thought that all our ardent confrères all offered the good Jesus their gifts. One gave a box on which it said "silence," another a box with "pure intention" written on it, etc. Therefore, I've made a box for both of us in which I've put our weaknesses, faults, and lack of love. I wrote on it also "audacious trust." This I gave to Jesus. You are certainly content with it, dear Rinus, aren't you?

Rinus, if only you knew how much I love Jesus in you. And how much you love Jesus in me. The rest in me, everything that is not Jesus, you must hate, Rinus, hate vehemently.

A blessed Christmas.

Your friend in Jesus' love, Adrian

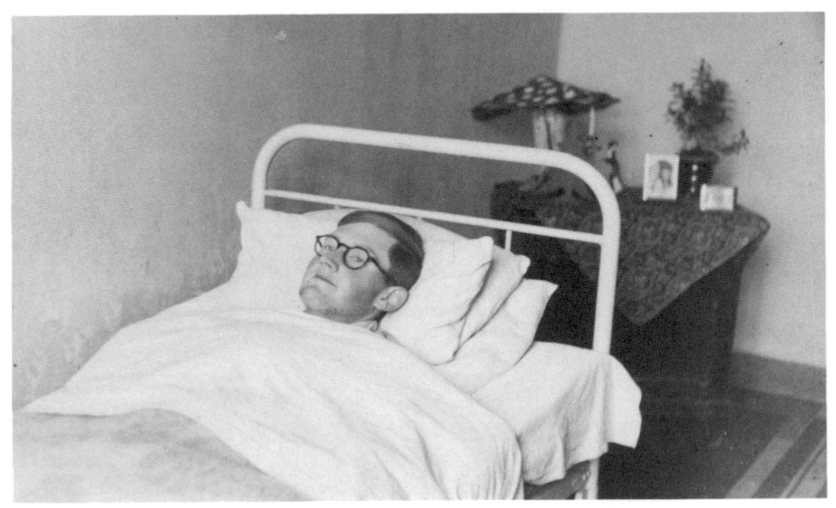

Rinus on his sick bed shortly before he died.

MRS. CHARLES VAN KAAM TO HER SON, ADRIAN

The Hague, December 1940

Mary, Queen of Peace, pray for us.

Dear Son,

I sent Bep [Adrian's eldest sister] to Rinus' home, and I heard his Mother had seen him already. I was glad when Bep came back home with that news. She knows now that she will have to give her son back to our loving Lord. What a heavy sacrifice that is for her, isn't it, Adrian? She resigns herself to it and has surrendered it to the dear Lord. We will remember her, too, in our prayers, that God may give her further strength.

At first I still had some hope Rinus would pull through but now that I've heard everything, it doesn't seem as if it's meant to be that way. The only thing left to us is to ask if our loving Lord will soon come to fetch him and if Mary will be his advocate.

Ah, Adrian, maybe you will ask Rinus if he will also pray for our family when he is in heaven. Greet him from your Father and Mother and tell him we keep praying for him.

Well, son, cordial greetings from us for you, Father and Mother

ADRIAAN LANGELAAN TO ADRIAN VAN KAAM

The Hague, January 3, 1941

Dear Adrian:

Thanks for your letters; your first one crossed ours and the last was brought by your Mother tonight.

Let us hope that our good friend Rinus will pull through. We'll pray much for him, and recommend him especially to our good Mother Mary tomorrow, on Priests' Saturday. If you would keep us posted, Adrian, we'd be very grateful.

You write that you'd like to join Rinus and go to heaven too, and I'm quite willing to believe you, but, on the other hand, it was good to read that you finished your letter with the prayer, "God's will be done."

I read from this that, like our mutual friend, you, too, will surrender to God's holy will and that you—if it is God's will—you will bear the loss of our dear friend with a joyful heart.

Don't forget God's decrees are inscrutable and life on the earth passes fast, even if we live to be old. Therefore, I wrote to Rinus that—in case we were not to meet again here on earth—we pray fervently that we'll rejoice with one another forever in heaven, in Jesus and his Holy Mother Mary.

Cordial regards from both of us; we wish you God's best blessing and much strength. Write again soon, won't you?

Your friends Adriaan and Marie

MRS. CHARLES VAN KAAM TO HER SON ADRIAN

The Hague, January 5, 1941

Mary Queen of Peace, pray for us.

Dear Son,

Last Friday night Rinus' sister came to tell us he was not getting on well. We were surprised it was so bad. What a wonderful resignation and surrender he radiates! To be so well prepared, to appear before God with prayers and sacrifice, is enviable. Therefore, Rinus is to be admired. And, Adrian, he was such a good friend. This will be your first great sacrifice, attended by grief, but now [you must] show yourself to be his friend and prepare yourself to make this sacrifice. [Grieve but] don't give in to your sorrow. If Rinus goes to heaven you must be wholeheartedly glad for him. Think of his parents, especially his mother, always busy in her household and now forced to lay powerless in bed on such sad days. If she could, she would go to her son, being carried if need be, but even that isn't possible. That's an immense sacrifice, isn't it. Think deeply about this for a moment and pray much for her.

I took your letter to Mr. Langelaan the same evening and he would write at once. If good Rinus is still alive, give him our regards and tell him we'll pray for him in our evening prayers.

This morning I talked to Our Lord about him and his parents, especially during Holy Communion, and I asked for God's blessing for him. If Our Lord has already called him, well, my son, you've got a friend in heaven who will be a fine advocate for you.

In a few days' time I'll send a stipend for a Holy Mass, also if he would recover, the Holy Mass should be said. That I promised to our loving Lord.

For now, my son, I wish you strength and God's best blessing. Greetings from your dearest parents.

Your Mother

A few words were added by Rinus to this letter on his deathbed.

✠

Dear Adrian,

What a lovely letter this is. Please don't forget to send my best wishes to your lovely Mother.

Bye, Adrian, for now.

ADRIAN VAN KAAM TO HIS MOTHER

Gemert, January 26, 1941

Deus Solus

Dearest Mother,

Cordial congratulations on your birthday. May Our loving Lord give you strength and courage to live for him in ever increasing love, and to fulfill your difficult holy motherly duties out of love of him. I pray for you daily, that's the only present (but the most beautiful one) I can give you. As regards material presents, instead of giving you one, I begin with asking you for one immediately.

In my portfolio you'll find a picture of Rinus (you know, the large one, that his sister brought on one occasion). I'd like so much to have it framed and sent to me, for example, in a black ebony frame, or, if something else looks better, that's also fine. It's a gift I'll enjoy my whole life. I'll always hang it in my partition, or if I've got a private room, I'll put it on my desk in front of me. Thus [I'll] always [be] in contact with my holy friend in heaven. If you take them directly to Mark's [a store], you'll be able to send it in a few days, so I'll have it almost immediately after his death and funeral. You may also find an envelope with letters from Rinus in that portfolio. Would you please send these too?

I passed on to Rinus your next to last letter, to show him how you were empathizing with us. When he read it, he cried with happiness and gratitude for your understanding and goodness. With his weakened hand he scribbled a few words below it and had it returned to me. I send this letter back to you. Please keep it carefully or send it back to me right away. A short time later he sent for me, seized my hand, and he said with tearful eyes: "Adrian, thank your Mother from me and give my cordial regards to both your Father and Mother." He certainly won't forget our family in heaven.

At present we expect Mary will come to take him at any moment. I belong to the chosen who may sit up with him at night. We do so in groups of two, each group for three hours. In the morning we may sleep in as long as we wish, provided we are present in class at 9:30.

Tonight I'm going to watch from 10 P.M. to 1 A.M., together with a scholastic from the priests' class, who is thus a priest already.

By his visible happiness, his patience, his obedience to his attendants, his cheerfulness, his holy life of prayer, Rinus is edifying for the whole community. He is extremely witty. To one Father he said, for example, that they should not put all such nonsense on his "In Memoriam" card, which would not be true anyway. To another Father, who gives rather difficult exams, "You won't catch me any more, will you," and so it goes. Bye!

Adrian

MRS. CHARLES VAN KAAM TO HER SON, ADRIAN

The Hague, January 29, 1941

Mary Queen of Peace, pray for us.

Dear Son,

How is Rinus? We are hopeful again that he may recover, or would Don Bosco come to fetch him. Adrian, we'll leave it to our loving Lord, don't you think so? I sent money for a Holy Mass. The idea was to have this Holy Mass said next Friday in honor of Don Bosco, but Father was afraid it would not arrive in time. I could not send it before, however, because we had the flu by turns and I had to wait until Father had a day off.

How do you like the picture of Rinus? Was the frame as you wanted it? And how's your own health? Are you still free from flu?

Father did not get it either, although they had the largest number of patients at the HTM [his company]. Will you remember Father's birthday on February 9th. I'll enclose a stamp. I had forgotten last time.

I enclose a letter from Rinus, I must see if there are any more. This one was in your portfolio. I will keep carefully the letter on which Rinus wrote himself.

Now, my son, I'll stop. Give our regards to Rinus. We'll keep praying for him. Julia leads in the evening prayer, and in that way it won't be forgotten any day. It's the only and best thing we can do for him.

Cordial greetings for yourself from Father, Mother, Bep, Julia, Leonie

ADRIAN VAN KAAM TO HIS FAMILY

Gemert, end of January, 1941

Deus Solus!

Dear Parents and Sisters,

Rinus is going to Jesus. After he received the last sacraments, he sent for me at night, before evening prayers. We talked a bit about Our loving Lord and heaven. His eyes were radiant with happiness. When the great moment was to come, he would send for me at once, to be present there. After evening prayer a Father came to tell me he'd received money from you for a Holy Mass for Rinus and his parents' intention. In the morning this Holy Mass was said in the big chapel in the presence of all the students. I was allowed to serve, and I was most happy to do so, for the server may accompany the priest when he takes Holy Communion to Rinus. Since then I have still talked to Rinus a few times. He is happy and cheerful.

At the beginning of his illness he mentioned you, saying that he thought you were such fine people and that he always liked so much to visit you.

It's a deeply grievous sacrifice for me to lose such a friend, but he has said he would remain my friend from heaven. Maybe he'll pull through, but I don't think so. The will of our loving Lord be done. Soon Rinus will be happy forever, and I'm to remain alone here on earth. How I should like to go with him. Would you please take this letter to Mr. Langelaan at once.

P.S. Whoever takes it to Langelaan, please tell him at the same time what Rinus' brother told you about him.

X
In Memoriam

X
IN MEMORIAM

[Translator's Note: *On one side of this card was a Pietà by Massys, on the other side a text. Catholics in Holland used to have this kind of card printed on the occasion of a funeral.]*

Remember the Soul of the Late

Reverend Frater

Marinus Scholtes

Theology Student with the Holy Spirit Fathers

at Gemert.

Born at Naaldwijk January 31, 1919
Student at the Junior Seminary at Weert 1931-1937
Novitiate at Gennep August 26, 1937
Profession at Gennep August 27, 1938
Died at Gemert February 1, 1941
Buried there on February 4 in the community churchyard

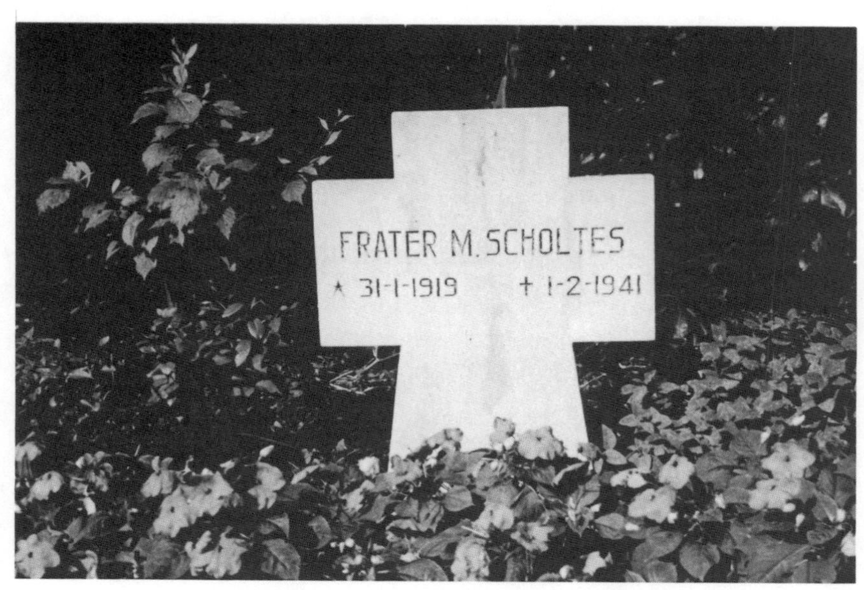

The grave of Marinus Scholtes at Gemert.

As a child Rinus answered in all simplicity to the call of the Divine Friend of children in one of his first Holy Communions: he wanted to be a priest and missionary to save souls, all of them.

His studies at Weert attracted little attention, but the silent witness to the high flight of his soul was the incomparably sweet Mother in heaven whose servant he had in the meantime become, in imitation of the Blessed Louis Marie de Montfort. The Novitiate at Gennep saw him lifted to a great height in the contemplative life of prayer. The interaction between God and his soul was so intense that from then onwards Rinus possessed in Jesus his Divine All. This happened on the day of his Holy Profession. Inseparably and uninterruptedly Rinus lived with "his" Jesus, until the chalice of love and suffering was full, and his guiltless soul was admitted to the eternal company of Jesus and Mary.

I will sing the mercies of the Lord eternally.

ADRIAN VAN KAAM TO HIS FATHER

At the top a note was added by Adrian (in English):
"Birthday letter for my Dad,
written the day after Rinus' death.
The only description I have of this event."

Gemert, Sunday, February 2, 1941

Deus Solus

Dearest Father,

Most cordial congratulations on your birthday. Rinus, who liked you so much, will certainly ask for all kind of favors and graces for you in heaven, especially now that he sees how you have toiled and sacrificed for his friend.

Yesterday, Saturday, Mary's day and first Saturday (Priests' Saturday), his lovely Mother in heaven quietly came to take him. The day before [he died] was the feastday of his patron saint in religion [Don Bosco] and his birthday at the same time. He turned 22. Today, a day later, it's the feast of the Presentation and the feastday of Father Libermann, our venerable founder.

When his agony of death began at about 1:30 A.M., he sent for me. His Confessor (also mine) told him his dear friend was present. With difficulty he forced himself to smile, whispered my name weakly, and tried

(38)

Gedenk de ziel van Zaliger

EERW. FRATER

MARINUS SCHOLTES

Theologant bij de Paters van den H. Geest te Gemert.

Geboren te Naaldwijk 31 Januari 1919.
Student in het Missiehuis te Weert 1931-1937.
Noviciaat te Gennep 26 Augustus 1937.
Geprofest te Gennep 27 Augustus 1938.
Overleden te Gemert 1 Februari 1941.
en den 4 d.o.v. aldaar op het kloosterkerkhof begraven.

Als kind beantwoordde Rinus in allen eenvoud aan den wenk van den Goddelijken Kindervriend in één zijner eerste H. Communies: Priester-missionaris wilde hij worden om zielen te redden, alle . . .
Zijn studies te Weert verliepen zonder opzien, maar de stille getuige zijner hooge zielevlucht was de onvergelijkelijk lieve Hemelmoeder, wier slaaf hij intusschen geworden was, in navolging van den Gelukz. Grignon de Monfort. Het Noviciaat te Gennep zag hem tot een zeer groote hoogte in het beschouwend gebedsleven opgevoerd. Zoo intens was de wisselwerking tusschen God en zijn ziel, dat Rinus voortaan in Jezus zijn Goddelijk Al bezat. Dit geschiedde op den dag zijner H. Professie. Onafscheidelijk en onafgebroken leefde Rinus met „zijn" Jezus, tot de kelk van liefde en lijden gevuld was en zijn schuldelooze ziel in het eeuwig gezelschap van Jezus en Maria werd toegelaten.
De barmhartigheden des Heeren zal ik in eeuwigheid bezingen.

Rinus' Death Notice.

to say something else, which however was impossible for him. I could see from his glances and soft nods that he heard me quite clearly. His breathing became more and more labored. Now and then his father spoke to him. Then his Confessor said some beautiful prayers and [expressed some beautiful] thoughts to him. Next came the Fathers of the community, to say the prayers for the dying, and some decades of the rosary. As it could take several more hours, however, they then left the room. I remained waiting there with his father, Father Superior, Father Prefect, his Confessor, and the attendants.

It was moving to hear his sobbing Confessor say: "Soon the Bridegroom of your soul comes to make you happy eternally . . . Mom comes to fetch you, Rinus, your dear Mom . . . Mom, here's your servant Rinus, your child . . . Jesus, Mom take him soon into the beauty of heaven . . . forever and forever . . . Come, dearest Bridegroom, we were always so united on earth, let's now be together in heaven . . . in heaven . . . kiss your profession cross."

After about forty-five minutes the labored breathing stopped rattling; the color suddenly drained from his face. Very softly and beautifully he then sank away, like one sleeping. Now and then his mouth twitched for a while, until a little mirror that was held near his lips proved his death since there came no more trace of breathing on it . . .

Rinus lies in state in his room. It has been furnished beautifully with black cloth and white cords. There he lays in his cassock and cincture; his motionless hands with their fine pale nobly-formed fingers embrace a rosary and a crucifix. On his thin, quiet, calm face all that energy with which he strived after God is chiseled. A most pure and most loving child of Mary has passed away, a friend who was a saint . . . May Jesus forever live . . . ! May his most holy will be done, always and everywhere! Even if it is bitter pain to us . . . and my heart beats for that heaven where my Rinus is radiating eternal happiness . . . O to be at one with him in God's delightful Being!

Call confidently upon Rinus in all your cares and troubles. He will help you, as he has told me expressly [he will help me]. Many thanks for the Holy Mass, and for the framed photo. It was both dignified and beautiful, in as much good taste as I could have possibly imagined. The funeral is next Tuesday at 9:30 A.M.

Cordial greetings from your son, Adrian

MRS. CHARLES VAN KAAM TO HER SON, ADRIAN

The Hague, February 2, 1941

Mary Queen of Peace, pray for us.

Dear Son,

Rinus' sister just came to tell us that Rinus died. What a great sacrifice this is, especially for his parents. She said Rinus passed away quietly, so that was blissful for him and a consolation for them. And now Adrian, you have got a friend in heaven, who can be a great advocate for you. Use this [privilege] well and thank our loving Lord that you are at Gemert. Thus you have the opportunity to visit [his gravesite] often and at the same time to learn resignation from him.

On Friday morning I attended Holy Mass at 9:00 A.M. As it happened it was said in honor of St. John Bosco. Father was at home again so I can go to Holy Mass at 8:00 A.M., on the very day of the funeral. I plan to send a stipend for a Holy Mass later, perhaps on your birthday. By that time I'll hear from you.

Now Adrian, be strong and God's best blessing on you.

Your Mother, with greetings from your parents and sisters

ADRIAAN LANGELAAN TO ADRIAN VAN KAAM

The Hague, February 4, 1941

MCPM (Mundus Christo Per Mariam)

In the first place accept our deepest sympathy on the death of our dear friend, Rinus Scholtes. Fiat voluntas tua*! It's mainly for this [acceptance] that we have prayed, as you asked us to do in your Epiphany letter. Thank you also for the extensive letter which we received from you tonight. Yesterday Bep had already come to tell us about Rinus' death, so we knew he was buried this morning.*

You understand we considered it a duty of honor toward our deceased friend to pray really fervently for him during Holy Mass. At Holy Communion we especially commended the repose of Rinus' soul to Jesus and his Holy Mother.

Adrian, I know Rinus' death is a great, an immensely great, loss to you. A separation of almost two years had already been a heavy trial for you both, and now, while you thought you'd be able to help and assist one another for many years in striving after God, Rinus is suddenly taken from you after an illness of a few weeks! God's ways are inscrutable. However, remember that Rinus, who is now in heaven—we are sure of that—prays continually for you. He will assist you in your words and deeds, so that you will receive sufficient strength to continue alone the work you had both wanted to undertake.

We gladly agree with your appeal to deepen our lives [in Christ] and to seek the grace to raise our spiritual life to a higher level. Last Saturday, on Priests' Saturday, we prayed extra hard for both of you. At night, during Benediction (we did not know about Rinus' death at the moment), I happened to read (more by chance than by choice) in Dom Chautard about the basic principles of meditation and their application: Video-sitio-volo-volo tecum *[I see-I long-I want-I want with you]. Also on Sunday, on the Feast of the Presentation, I celebrated this day better than in former years. Especially its meaning and the practical application we can draw from it for our own lives became much clearer to me. Would the influence of Rinus' intercession have already been at work here?*

We are looking forward to the day when you can tell us all about Rinus personally.

My father, who works in Saxony again, just wrote that he'd also pray for Rinus. He asked me to pass on his kind regards to you. I'll inform him of Rinus' death immediately this week.

Adrian, we'd like to have a Holy Mass said for the repose of Rinus' soul and to have this done by your Fathers at the Castle. Can I transfer the stipend to your house account at the end of this month?

Kind regards from our family, from Gerard, Anton Toneman, and our other acquaintances, and especially from us. We'll pray that Jesus and his Holy Mother Mary will help you especially in these days.

All the best wishes with your study, so long,

Your friends, Adriaan and Marie

FATHER J. EYMAEL S.M.M. TO ADRIAN VAN KAAM

Meerssen, March 3, 1941

D.S.

Reverend Frater,

I received your esteemed letter at Meerssen, where I have been connected with the Novitiate since early September 1936.

Many thanks for your letter. After reading it attentively my first thought was a prayer of thanks to our loving Lord, who through his Holy Mother granted so many graces to your confrère and friend, of blessed memory.

A second thought was this: on the eve of Annunciation Day I will have a concrete example of what you told me about the practice of dedication to Jesus and Mary, and I will tell this to our novices as an exhortation, for an example taken from the circumstances of life that are so similar to theirs has more effect than mere theory. So you have already begun to disseminate the good seed in youthful souls, for your letter points out clearly the foundation of the inner spiritual life of your confrère. I will also have them read the "In Memoriam" card.

May I express a wish here? I hope something will be published on your side about the rich life of grace of your late confrère. It will be most edifying, especially for young students in the religious congregations.

Accept then, dear Frater, my sincere thanks for your information, and my religious greetings in Jesus and Mary,

J. Eymael S.M.M.[112]

112 Father Eymael, a member of the congregation inspired by St. Louis Marie de Montfort, was at that time the Novice Master of his community.

IN MEMORIAM, FRATER MARINUS SCHOLTES

An article written by a confrère at Gemert in *De Bode van de H. Geest* [Messenger of the Holy Spirit], dated April, 1941.

Unexpectedly illness fell on his tall robust figure. Heavy was the struggle due to the resistance of his strong constitution, but after one month and a half it was beaten. On February 1, one day after he had become 22, he died in our community at Gemert.

People live more beside than with one another. It happens that one usually knows only little of another's intimate spiritual life. Thus the depth of Rinus' life had always been hidden from us. He lived amidst us in a modest way, until his illness and death. Especially the notebooks he left, made us realize to some degree how intimate he had been with God. It is difficult to represent his rich spiritual life in words; we are more inclined to fold our hands in thanks and pray the Te Deum, *the song he liked so much to sing on his sick-bed.*

Already at Weert Rinus was truly devout. Maybe because of this, and certainly because of his natural shyness, which made his demeanor a bit awkward, he stood outside his class. He knew this as well as anyone and no doubt it was painful for him. He would say occasionally: "I only hope I will be able to play a lot of sports at Gennep and at Gemert, for, I don't know why, but I just can't walk around and chit-chat so easily," but at the beginning of the Novitiate he managed to change that by his will-power. "Scholtes," somebody said, "is going to be a stalwart fellow. He's accepted much more than before."

What Rinus wanted, he did with a perseverance that accepted no backsliding or mere routine. By way of a lasting stimulus, he kept writing down notes about his spiritual life, and in this he was always guided completely by his Confessor.

Once, for instance, he was asked to help the carpenter. It was amazingly heavy work, scraping off old painted boards and planing them. But all week long Rinus worked cheerfully and tenaciously, whereas others mostly slunk off quietly after one hour's toil. We knew about this strong-willed perseverance especially in his study. He applied himself studiously whenever he could and made systematic notes and schemes of everything for later reference.

Also his feelings seemed to come under the domination of his will and reason. He often appeared to be a man of mere thought, especially because he had never been able to overcome his self-constraint and shyness in spite of his will-power. Rinus did not show his feelings easily, because he was modest and extremely averse to sentimentality.

His sense of solidarity was quite strong. At the end of the Novitiate he would often say that he thought it wonderful they had all become professed. If somebody needed help, Rinus was always ready to assist; on the other hand, if they helped him, even in a small thing, he was as glad as if something enormous had been done, and he would call after you, "It's wonderful, really, thank you so much!" His bedside attendant once found him crying. "But Rinus, what's wrong?" "Oh, you are much too good for me!" So Rinus had feelings; it could not be otherwise since he was united so closely with the God of love. He wanted to belong to God; therefore he kept his really tender love for his confrères concealed inside himself. His continuous readiness to serve and his always cheerful face were the only signs of it.

Rinus was not a pious person in the sense that he would visit chapel more than others, or that his attitude outside chapel was strikingly devout. He behaved quite normally, just like everybody else, and only a few people noticed how a prayerful recollection came upon him as soon as he entered chapel. That was only possible because he always lived in God's presence. The certainty of this is found in the notebooks he filled about his spiritual life, and in the words he spoke on his death-bed. That death-bed was the summary and climax of his beautiful life. There he said: "When I walk in the street I've got the same feeling as in chapel." And also: "Inner life consists in talking to our loving Lord quite simply, quite ordinarily." Union with Jesus was the great ideal to which he exhorted several people on his death-bed. With great fervor he advised us to read the little book by Father De Jaegher Een met Jezus [One with Jesus].

It was striking that in his short prayers he was more mindful of glorifying God than imploring his mercy for himself—a sign of his purity and union with God.

On December 17 Rinus fell ill and on December 20 he received the sacrament of the sick. "What a grace," he said, "to be allowed to receive Holy Communion twice today, to receive the holy Sacrament of Confession so often! To have always cordial confrères around me and then to someday be allowed to become a priest." He upheld that ideal: in his illness it became clear with what longing he prepared himself for the tonsure, which he was to have received in March. He had the attendant explain its ceremonies in detail to him.

Night and day he had to be watched, but everyone enjoyed sacrificing some night's rest for him. His ease, obedience, and gratitude gave one the idea of rather being given than of giving a loving service. When he was attended to, it was often inevitable that one hurt him, so much so that his face twisted completely. But if you asked him if it was bad, his typical answer was: "It's fine, don't worry." Indeed, he always said that to everything he was given or asked: "It's good, it's the way Jesus wants it." Therefore, he could accept death with such resignation to God's holy will. Certainly, he would have liked to go on living. His young life clung to the tiniest spark of hope. His surrender and, at the same time, his natural longing to live were expressed in one of those simple words we were accustomed to hear from him. "Rinus, would you like to go to heaven?" "If necessary, let it be done, but, yes, I'd also like to stay here." It's good for us to know this: That there was the vital urge in him, too, that his death was truly a sacrifice he accepted.

We are inclined to think that souls who are especially favored by God actually make no sacrifices and have lost their natural feelings. Nothing could be farther from the truth than this, for the nearer God draws a soul to himself, the more he has it purified by sacrifice and pains. So it is an established fact that Rinus suffered intensely in his, outwardly unruffled life. It has only now become apparent how much he was tormented at Gennep by the suffering of the soul, which is so immensely more painful than outward suffering. But his love of God, his will-power and absolute obedience to his spiritual guide took him in a straight line to Jesus, safely, closely, and purely. Thus his death was a sacrifice, accepted from the first moment, but it remained a real sacrifice since his longing to live was also present. That was good, too, for: "It would not be worthwhile, what we sacrificed, if we didn't like it a little bit."

In the afternoon of February 1, 1941, Rinus died calmly and quietly. How could it have been otherwise? Hadn't he gone to Jesus already? Often he said on his sick-bed, "I'm not afraid of our loving Lord, and I never have been."

Rinus' life was simple because he himself always behaved simply. He was never difficult or obtrusive to others in his striving for perfection. One thing is for sure: He did common things in an uncommon way, with a graced, inner disposition of intimacy with God.

ADRIAAN LANGELAAN TO ADRIAN VAN KAAM

The Hague, April 16, 1941

MCPM

Dear Adrian,

I don't know exactly how to begin this letter. In the first place let me wish you a Happy Easter, also from Marie, as well as congratulating you cordially on your birthday, Saturday, April 19. We won't forget you that day in our prayers.

In the second place I want to thank you for your extensive letter written in February. We were glad to receive it. March was a very busy month for us. My father was on leave. He was fortunate enough on March 17 to be with us to celebrate my birthday. He has been fairly lucky. He works in a quiet region in a small place near Dresden and, on the whole, he has better rations than we have in Holland. I had intended to let you know something about us, at least on the feast days, but I remembered your birthday is on April 19, and I thought it nice to write to you on that occasion. Anyway, I must apologize for my late reply to your letter.

Thirdly, we thank you also for your letter of April 3, which we received last week. We got it, together with the issue of the Bode Van de Heilige Geest [Messenger of the Holy Spirit], *which we had been looking forward to receiving with great interest, especially its biography of Rinus (by a "confrère"). Do you happen to know who wrote it? We quite agree with this "In Memoriam," and we were especially glad to see Rinus' picture with it. We'll keep this issue very carefully!*

Last time you also asked me if I had any letters by Rinus. I regret to say that I have none. What I remember of Rinus I'll write down at the first opportunity in accordance with your request. The last time you were here together [for a meeting with our "Epiphany" group] was on Saturday, August 31, 1940. We chatted then [and shared] very cordially until sunset, when you left. We then received a visit from two of our cousins, who had come by bike from Nijmegen that day. Had I known that it was to be the last time we were to see Rinus, I would have liked to walk you [and him] home. I'm still sorry I wasn't able to do so at the time. In any case, we'll have enough time to talk about Rinus next holiday when we meet.

Let's keep praying much for one another; I also ask Rinus regularly in my prayers not to forget us in heaven.

Also pray for us, especially on April 21, for that is my wife's birthday.

Again our warmest congratulations on your birthday, and best wishes for your health, your study, and your soul, and, in these somber times, also for the prosperity of your congregation. Kindest regards also from

Marie, our mutual families, Toon Toneman, Gerard, and, of course, also from me.

Your friend in Christo, Adriaan Langelaan

P.S. Next month I'll write again. I hope to have something ready about Rinus!

My congratulations, too, and so long! Marie

FROM MRS. CHARLES VAN KAAM TO ADRIAN

The Hague, April 17, 1941

Mary, Queen of Peace, pray for us.

Dear Son,

Wholehearted congratulations on your birthday. We'll dedicate our Holy Communion for you that day to ask God's blessing on your beautiful vocation. I sent you a postal money order, of which ƒ2.50 is from the children, for a Holy Mass for Rinus' intention: you should choose that intention yourself. Father added ƒ2.50. You had better see for yourself how to spend it. If you need something for yourself I'll hear from you. Over the long holidays, you will have your ration cards with you automatically.[113]

And now, Adrian, Julia tells me to thank you for the letter [you sent] on her birthday; she was so proud of it. She wants to write a letter herself, but that's a tough job for her. It will come some day.

How are things with you at Gemert? Is it fairly quiet there? After a few quiet weeks here the air-raid warning sounded at 1:00 A.M. last night, and at 1:30 the "all clear" was given. During that half hour the shooting went on terribly. It's frightening, but father doesn't want to give up his night rest. He says if our house receives a direct hit nothing can be saved and escaping is impossible. What terror this evokes! My fear for the children in a half hour like this is truly terrible.

Julia awakened, but she said that she wasn't afraid at all. She prayed a fervent act of contrition and fell asleep again. I smiled when she told me this in the morning. Leoni slept on quietly for the night, but before this she had been astir all the time because she had to throw up (it must have been all the fat she ate), and Bep has been saddled with a

113 During the German occupation, because of the increasing scarcity of food, all people were put on food stamps contained in each one's ration card. When seminarians went on holidays, they took their ration cards with them.

tooth-ache all week. She has now had the tooth removed, so at least she could sleep well and did not bother about all that was happening in the air. At least that air-raid is over for now, though we are waiting for the next one.

I think often of Rinus' calmness. I wish I had a bit of his quiet resignation. But, then, Rinus was somebody of whom it is rightly said that he was too good for this world.

I'm looking forward to [receiving] a copy of the picture of him taken on his sick-bed, provided I'm not late in sending these lines.

So, my son, I finish with kindest regards from us all. God bless you.

Your Mother

FROM RINUS' MOTHER TO ADRIAN VAN KAAM

The Hague, October 20, 1941

Reverend Frater van Kaam,

In the name of my husband and of all of us, we thank you, and also the Very Reverend Father Superior, the Very Reverend Father De Rooij, Reverend Father van Putten, Frater van der Meulen and confrères for the cordial greetings and prayers we received on his birthday. It was quite a surprise for him to receive a letter from Gemert. He could not understand how you knew it was his birthday—but I left it at that! Also many thanks to Father van Doorn for that fine poem written on our dear son.

My husband was given an enlargement of [the enclosed] picture by his sisters. It was taken by his sister Cor, down in the yard at our Father's, on the day of Jantje's first Holy Communion. It was just in those days that our late Rinus was at home. It's nice, isn't it? He looks so paternal with his youngest brother. But, Adrian, would you be so good as to give a copy also to the Reverend Father Superior and one to Father De Rooij? I thank you in advance for this favor.

Well, Frater, I'm going to finish. Once more, thanks for your letter, also for the one from Father van Putten and Frater van der Meulen; kind regards from all of us, also to Very Reverend Father Superior, the Very Reverend Father de Rooij, and the Reverend Fathers and Fraters.

So long, if we are spared and healthy, until next year,
The Scholtes Family

P.S. Our Rinus' letters always used to say at the end: "We keep praying for each other."

FROM RINUS' MOTHER TO ADRIAN VAN KAAM

Undated

Reverend Frater,

It did us good to receive a letter from you and also to hear that you may receive the tonsure on April 10. How fast time goes. We still see you coming as a young student to see our late Rinus—and now you've gotten as far as our good Rinus almost did when he passed away. Yes, Adrian, our thoughts are always with him, especially now. His classmates are happy now to be ordained deacons. But here we bow our heads; it had to be like that. God's holy will be done.

As it happens April 10 is also our silver wedding anniversary. We'll have a Holy Mass said that day for our intention; for the rest, there's no celebrating in a time like this: Cor is not at home, and who knows what is going to happen. Bernard has to undergo a medical examination for the Arbeidsdienst [Labor Service][114] *next Wednesday. As regards Gerard, fortunately he's still at home, but we don't know whether that will last. You asked in your letter how we all are. Bernard is very well at present; he looks healthy and has no more complaints. My husband and Ben still have work but not much. Thanks be to God, Cor has been lucky in Germany; he works and lives with a butcher; he's busy, working from 5 A.M. till 7 P.M., but he has plenty to eat. They all long to be allowed to return home as soon as possible. It's to be hoped there will soon be peace.*

Well, Frater, I'm going to finish. Kind regards from all of us, and with the usual closing words of our dear late Rinus, who always ended a letter with the words: "Let's keep praying for each other," I greet you.

Mother Scholtes

P.S. Will you give our kind regards to the Fraters we know. Let's hope we see each other again soon, and so long.

---

114 Many men were conscripted for service under the Nazi regime. All men over 18 had to serve for some time.

Chronology

1919 January 31: Birth of Marinus Leonardus Scholtes, Naaldwijk, Netherlands; son of Gulielmo Cornelio Marino Scholtes and Alida Joanna Wubben. Rinus was the first born and the eldest of the nine Scholtes children.

1919 January 31: Baptized by Rev. L. N. Geldermans in the Church of St. Adrianus, Naaldwijk, Netherlands; godson of L. W. Scholtes and A. C. Bentvelmen.

1920 The year Rinus' family moved to The Hague where they rented a house on the Parallelweg 122 near a railroad station in the parish of St. Martha. This is where Rinus completed his elementary school.

1927 November 24: Confirmed at St. Martha church.

1931 May 14: Letter from Rinus' father, William, to Father Superior of the Junior Seminary in Weert, communicating that his son had become twelve years old in January and is now in the sixth class of the elementary school. He wants very much to enter the seminary in September and has had such a desire for many years. His parents, however, found it better to let him first attend the recently added seventh year of the elementary school.

1931 June 2: Second letter from Rinus' father to Father Superior. He tells about his visit to the Pastor of the parish and consents that Rinus may leave already this coming September for the seminary thus by-passing after all the seventh year of the elementary school. In response to the Superior's question if his son is a good student, he mentions that he has always had a good report card and, as far as he is concerned, is among the best of his class.

1931 September 11: Rinus enters the Junior Seminary in Weert where he will spend the next six years of his life.

1935 April 5: Rinus decides to keep a dairy in the fourth class of his Junior Seminary at age 16.

1935 May 31: Rinus dedicates himself to Mary as her consecrated servant and so does his soul-friend, Adrian van Kaam.

1936 **June 17:** He celebrates the "feast of Mary" with Adrian van Kaam and the other "Pioneers of Mary," participants in this informal proto-type Epiphany circle. They live by the motto, "The World to Christ through Mary."

1937 **May 9:** Letter of Rinus to the Provincial Superior of the Spiritans in the Netherlands asking for the favor of making his oblation to and receiving the cassock of the congregation and therewith acceptance in its Novitiate.

1937 **June 4:** Official administrative information regarding Rinus' request for oblation to the Novitiate and the Congregation: a vote of 190 aspirants in the Junior Seminary, all in favor of Rinus' admission; a vote of thirteen priests on the staff of the Seminary, all thirteen in favor of his admission.

1937 **July 4:** Rinus' oblation and reception of the cassock.

1937 **July 29:** Personal notes on Rinus by his Superior, Father Piet Pelt at the conclusion of Rinus' six years in the Junior Seminary. The superior mentions, among other things that his behavior is very good, his temperament is sensitive, his character fine, his capacities, his zeal for work, his practical judgment are all good. The Superior further praises as more than satisfactory his seriousness, modesty, orderliness, regularity, relationships with his superiors and fellow students, his spirit of faith, his virtue and piety, his ecclesial and religious vocation, his zeal and love for the missions. As a fault to be corrected he mentions Rinus' tendency to be too minute in his judgment [probably a reference to his inclination to scrupulosity]. Finally in the numerical evaluation of his comportment, on a marking scale of grades 1-10, he receives a ten for behavior, a seven for studies, a ten for health.

1937 **October 7:** Rinus, now a Novice, experiences that he "suddenly felt wounded in the middle of my heart"—with a "love wound," a phenomenon reported frequently in the annals of Christian mysticism, though seldom in one so young..

1937 **November 11:** Rinus says that on this morning he tried to meditate about death as realistically as possible: "I imagined I had collapsed in chapel, that I had died, and I smiled with happiness at the thought." Throughout this period he devotes his prayers in great measure to the salvation of dying souls. To "become Jesus" means for him to share in Jesus' thirst for souls.

1937 **December 16:** On this day he makes a private "vow" of chastity, later confirmed by both his Confessor and his Spiritual Director as an acceptable offering to Jesus.

1938 **February 11:** Rinus, now in his Novitiate year at Gennep, asks "for the cross."

1938 **March 18:** Rinus reports another significant reception of mystical graces, this one being "to rest uninterruptedly again [on your breast]."

1938 **May 6:** At the age of nineteen, Rinus is appointed by the Novice Master to give the usual yearly "sermonette" at the May celebration of the Blessed Virgin Mary. Rinus prays only that his efforts bear fruit for the Father and increase God's external glory.

1938 **May 27:** Under the impetus of the Holy Spirit, Rinus enters into the waiting room of his time of "engagement" to Jesus, the time of "spiritual espousal" when in a profound way the soul becomes Jesus.

1938 **June 5:** The day of Rinus' "spousal festivity"—Whitsunday! He asks the bridegroom of his soul "for a higher degree of the seven gifts of the Holy Spirit, as an engagement present." He lives in anticipation of August 27 of this year, the day he will make his first vows. In his case, this day will also mark the unique culmination of a long and inspiring process leading to the unique mystical marriage of his soul with Christ. He will belong to Jesus in a bond of unbreakable fidelity. August 27, 1938, happened to be the feast day of the Immaculate Heart of Mary..

1938 **September 8:** Rinus now in the Senior Seminary of Gemert records the first of many allusions to the past Novitiate phase of his life at Gennep, marked as they were by aridity and the impossibility of discursive meditation while living in what he calls the "love-will." He realizes that already toward the end of his Junior Seminary in Weert, he had been gifted with the "prayer of quiet."

1938 **September 12**: Rinus tells of his devotion to St. Teresa of Avila and his namesake in the religious life, St. John Bosco. At the end of this now post-novitiate year, Rinus' Novice Master, Father Henri Strick, said of him in his official report to the Motherhouse that, among other things, his temperament is sensitive and more or less sanguine; his character is good; his capacities are acceptable. His zeal and his practical sense are fine. As in the overall report of his years in Weert in the Junior Seminary his qualities here are also noted as "very good."

As to the faults to be corrected, there is mentioned his tendency "sometimes [to be] too childlike." As for the overall numerical appraisal, of 1 to 10, Rinus receives a nine for behavior, a seven for studies, and a seven for health. He is judged in this final report of the Novitiate to be a good candidate for vows.

1939 **February 15:** In Gemert's Scholasticate Rinus resolves to become *Alter Christus*, saying that this call to become Christ is "the highest Christian experience [one can attain] . . . it includes everything and expresses the whole [meaning] of mystical union in one phrase."

1939 **March 25:** On the feast of Mary's Annunciation, Rinus realizes in addressing Jesus, "I am to be transformed totally into you."

1939 **May 29:** Rinus records that yesterday on Whitsunday he celebrated the anniversary of his and Jesus' official espousal feast, followed on August 27, 1938, by the grace of his "mystical marriage."

1939 **July 23:** Rinus resolves during his recollection day to be *Alter Christus*, for the good of the *whole* world. This entry is especially poignant in view of the outbreak of World War II in Europe this year.

1940 **January 14:** Rinus marks his gratitude for "1939"—"for almost twenty-one years you, dear Jesus, have been master of my soul by virtue of your sanctifying grace." On the 31st of this month he will celebrate his next to the last birthday on earth.

1940 **February 14:** Given the food shortages caused by the outbreak of the war, Rinus indicates his enormous gratitude for the food and care he receives at Gemert.

1940 **May 10:** The Germans invade Holland. The next day, May 11, the seminary at Gemert is shelled and subsequently entered by German soldiers. One wing of the Seminary is destroyed by fire. Rinus recognizes the mortal danger but remains calm and quiet in the safe embrace of his Beloved and united in prayer with the community.

1940 **July 16:** His life has become "*one* total prayer," a grace he attributes in large measure to the intercession of Mary, his Directress and Mother. The next day he alludes to the fact that for the past few days he has been discomforted by stomach pains as had happened also earlier in Gemert and Gennep. He takes suffering in stride and seldom complains about it.

1940 **August 31:** The last meeting in The Hague of the "Epiphany" group with Rinus before his death.

1940 **September 16:** Rinus' Confessor and Spiritual Director approves, as did their confessors and directors in Weert and Gemert, the soul-friendship between him and Adrian van Kaam and, by extension, their mutual dedication to spiritual formation.

1940 **November 26:** Rinus thanks Jesus for the grace of a sore foot, for it enables him to rest all day in adoration of the Cross for the sake of dying souls. This is the last entry written by Rinus. The sore foot seemed to have been a first symptom of his already advanced tuberculosis.

1940 **December 17:** Rinus enters the end stages of his illness. On December 20 he receives the Sacrament of the Sick. Often on his sickbed he said, "I'm not afraid of our loving Lord, and I never have been."

1941 **February 1:** Rinus Scholtes dies the day after his twenty-second birthday. His agony lasts several hours, but his passing is peaceful.

1941 **February 4:** He is buried in the community churchyard at Gemert.

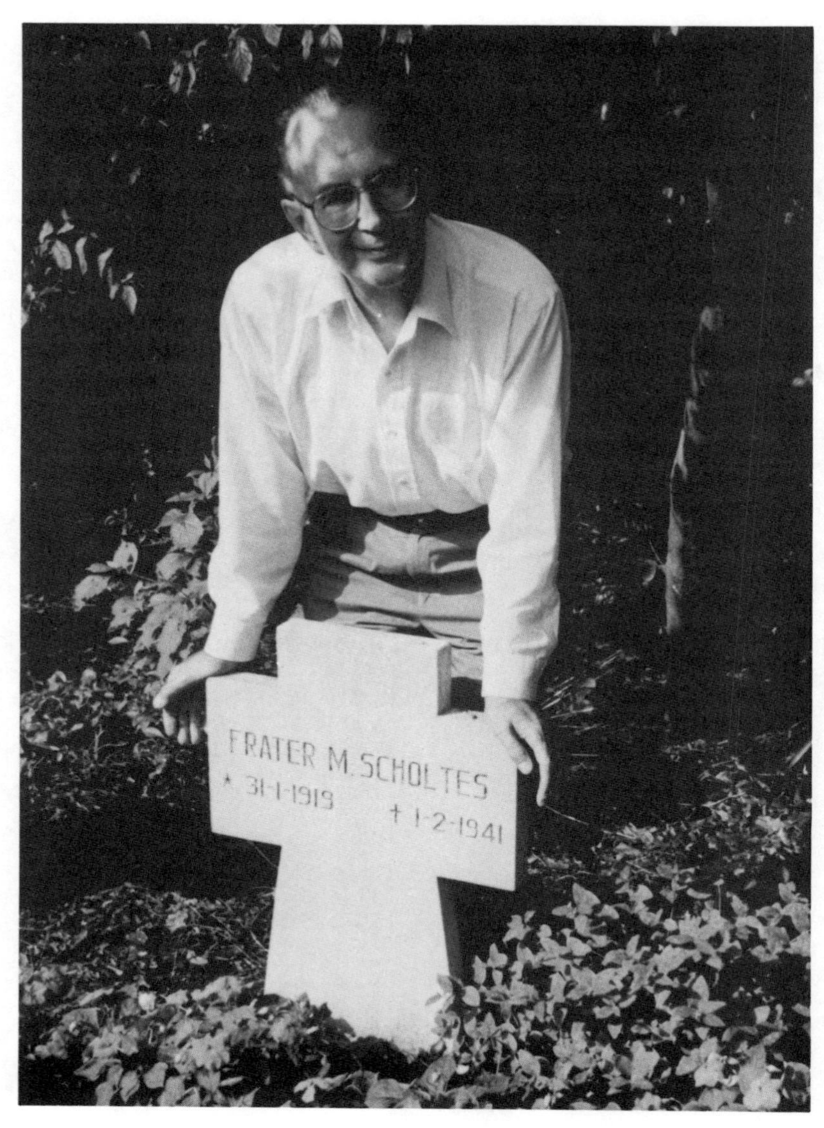

Adrian van Kaam at Rinus' gravesite at the Gemert churchyard, July, 1996.

POSTSCRIPT

LETTER FROM FATHER JAN DE ROOIJ TO ADRIAN VAN KAAM

Gennep, January 17, 1980

Dear Adrian,

Your letter was a surprise. I am glad to answer. How good God is that we answered his holy call: each of us in his own way . . . I am the eldest in our retirement home, and also in our Province, one reason more to prepare myself as well as possible for the travel, for which we cannot get a detour ticket . . . Often I think back about the high soul life of our friend, Rinus Scholtes; it has given a mighty push to my whole priest-missionary life.

Again cordial thanks for your letter and wishing you a blessed 1980.

Yours, Father Jan de Rooij[115]

115 Editor's Note: Little could I have known that several years later, in the Spring of 1993, Father de Rooij would send to our Epiphany Association and entrust to our care the manuscripts of Rinus, suggesting that now was the time to honor his memory with their publication under the auspices of a work that represents our youthful ideal to radiate Christ through Mary wherever we are. No time or money has been spared to share his epiphanic life with others. May he continue to inspire in each of us his burning thirst for souls and his child-like trust in God's holy will.

AFTERWORD

by Susan Muto, Ph.D.

The writings of Marinus Scholtes, taken as a whole, reveal a remarkable spiritual maturity for so young a man. They evidence the classical stages of the mystical ascent to union with God: *spiritual courtship* [the way of purifying formation]; *spiritual espousal* [the way of illuminating reformation]; and *spiritual marriage* [the way of unifying transformation].

The early notebooks record the musings of a person in the childhood of the spiritual life. Rinus recognizes the rough edges of his personality. His Elder Brother and Beloved must hone and temper them like a delicate craftsman etches new form into wood or stone. Rinus welcomes God's chiding and coaxing. He likes to play love games with God.

This period of his faith journey is at once as lighthearted as the games new lovers play and as seriously committed as the relationship of a couple planning to spend their life together. He details his faults, withholding nothing from his Lover's gaze.

His early formation sets the Trinitarian pattern that will prevail until the end of his life. Already in the Junior Seminary he undergoes what a mystical master like St. John of the Cross identifies as the active night of the senses. Rinus understands that no sensory experience can ultimately satisfy him. When, like a boy might do, he puts things like food or entertainments or other persons whom he admires ahead of God, he is left feeling dry and disappointed. A hunger for God permeates his being and drives him toward spiritual deepening.

The Rinus who could be defined as being in the young adulthood of the spiritual life (primarily documented in his Novitiate) enters a more intricate stage of deepening. He is torn between felt consolations that illumine his heart and mind from within and frequent bouts of spiritual aridity where faith alone enables him to carry on.

This middle stage parallels, I believe, St. John's description of the active night of spirit. Rinus is beyond inordinate attachment to sensual pleasures and rightly feels guilty when he allows temptations to distract him from his sole Beloved. But he is also being reformed by grace in his intellect, mind, and will.

It is in regard to the latter faculty that the spirituality of Rinus Scholtes shines. The reformation of his inmost being, its complete *metanoia* or turning to Jesus, happens in the context of his love-will for the Beloved.

At this stage of spiritual espousal, the soul is in an all-or-nothing position. Rinus chooses the *all* of God to the *nothing* of Rinus. He and the Beloved are increasingly one, though again the absence of felt consolations demands of him pure faith.

As Rinus approaches the end of his life on earth everything about him begins to undergo the unifying transformation characteristic of spiritual marriage. He experiences the passive night of both the senses and the spirit, to use the terms of St. John of the Cross. Physically he knows he is weakening but he makes no complaints, maintaining his sense of humor not only toward *confrères* but also toward himself. He is now a privileged victim of suffering, a man moving toward the adulthood of the spiritual life, who abandons himself appreciatively to the mystery beyond understanding.

Spiritually his entire inner life changes. Instead of wondering what God wants him to do, he is enraptured by who God is. He cannot praise God enough. In the darkness of not knowing, he comes to an experience of oneness with God that is overwhelming. At times his "marriage" takes his breath away. His love-will has no other focus than God. His memory contains only a record of favors asked and received, especially in the realm of praying for the salvation of souls and the forgiveness of sinners.

Rinus moves from recording daily events in God's presence to the seeing of God's presence in daily events. As St. John says, he no longer sees the things in God but God in the things. A definite transformation, readying him for his final passage to eternal union, is the gift his Groom gives him.

Rinus moves spontaneously into the language of bridal mysticism. It is the only way to verbalize the experience of union he undergoes with utter, fearless openness to the divine initiative. His main desire, the longing of his love-will, is to decrease that Jesus may increase. As their marriage moves toward consummation, Rinus becomes bolder in his pleas and prayers for others' salvation. There is nothing self-centered about his mysticism; he has an innate missionary spirit. He wants to help all people, however limited his physical stamina may be.

As I read these writings of Rinus and helped to edit each draft of the text, I heard echoes everywhere of the great mystical tradition of the Church: the spiritual childhood of St. Thérèse of Lisieux, whom Rinus loved; the "thought knocks, love enters" spirituality of *The Cloud of Unknowing*; the common life of the imitation of Christ in Thomas à Kempis; the bridal mysticism of the Rhineland School of Blessed John Ruysbroeck; the sacrament of the present moment of Brother Lawrence of the Resurrection; and, obviously, the dark nights of St. John of the Cross.

It was thrilling to see that these recollection notes, logged day after day as each event transpired, tell the here and now story of a *young man* who lived and died out of love for God. What makes this text so worthwhile, so epiphanically illuminative, is that it was written "on the spot" not as an afterthought or a memory as, say, *The Confessions of St. Augustine* were. Readers, especially young people, can thus identify with Rinus' day by day unfolding in grace.

I believe the Church needs the male witness of deep spiritual commitment Rinus gives. That is why I dare to dub this book a contemporary classic. It is faithful to the great tradition of divine lovers, for whom God is as near as a best friend, while at the same time being immersed in real life experience, including relational problems; gnawing temptations; high ideals confronting the limits of reality; questions regarding submission and self-expression; self-centered loves lost, and true, Christ-centered love gained.

Of profound contemporary interest is Rinus' dedication to the spiritual formation of the laity. How happy it makes me to know of his role, along with that of his dear lifelong friend Father Adrian van Kaam's, in the founding of the prototype Epiphany Association. May his heaven-directed life and its entire legacy continue to form, reform, and transform our own earthly journey. May the love-will that led him to the heights of union become the driving force of every heart, and may we say with him, "Let's keep praying for each other . . . let's be *Alter Christus.*"

Listing of Photographs and Illustrations

About the Editors

✠

The Epiphany Association, an ecumenical non-profit center dedicated to the spiritual formation of life and world, was co-founded in 1979 by Father Adrian van Kaam and Susan Muto, together with other like-minded friends. Its founding marked the continuation of the original Epiphany group which Father Adrian established in Holland in 1935 with his lifetime friend, Marinus Scholtes. Headquartered now in Pittsburgh, the center serves as a local gathering place for classical Christian formation counseling, education, publication, and resource development in the field of lay (adult Christian) formation. Its many outreach programs touch countless people seeking the deepest meaning of life, especially laity, clergy, and religious, who guide the spiritual unfolding of those entrusted to their care.

Father Adrian, a native of The Hague, Netherlands, is a renowned spiritual writer, researcher, professor, and the initiator in 1935 of both his embryonic formation theology and its underpinning formation science (pretheological) and formation anthropology (prototheological), understood as conducive to and compatible with the Judeo-Christian faith tradition. In brief, his life's work as a teacher and author has centered on the origination and development of the first detailed, comprehensive, new field of formative spirituality.

After his ordination as a priest in the Congregation of the Holy Spirit (Spiritans), Father Adrian was appointed professor of philosophical and anthropological psychology at his seminary in Holland. He also taught in the Dutch Life Schools for Young Adults, which he helped to establish to attend to the post-war social and spiritual formation of young laborers. A few years later, after an invitation communicated to his Dutch Provinicial Superior by the then Secretary of State of the Vatican, Monsignor Giovanni Baptista Montini (later Pope Paul VI), Father Adrian was relieved from his seminary teaching to pursue full time his writing and lecturing in the anthropology and theology of formation.

In 1954 he was invited to join the faculty at Duquesne University where he developed a new program called "psychology as a human science" while continuing his master work in the field of spiritual formation. Complementing his Dutch degrees in pedagogy and andragogy, he pursued and subsequently received his Ph.D. in psychology from Case Western Reserve University in Cleveland. He also completed clinical training at the University of Chicago, the Alfred Adler Institute, and Brandeis University.

In 1963 Father Adrian founded what would become over the next thirty years the graduate level Institute of Formative Spirituality (IFS) at Duquesne University, where he had launched the master's and doctoral programs in this field and taught there until administrative decisions mandated its closing in 1993. The work then became the sole province of the Epiphany Association, where Father is actively engaged as a writer, speaker, mentor, researcher-in-residence, and member of its corporation board. He conducts seminars and conferences sponsored at the Association's Pittsburgh headquarters and in its outreach programs on the national and international scene.

In addition to being the author and co-author of fifty books and over 350 published articles, he has founded and edited several journals, (*Envoy, Humanitas, Studies in Formative Spirituality, Epiphany International*). Professor van Kaam holds memberships in various professional organizations, and has received many honors for his work, including an honorary Doctor of Christian Letters degree from the Franciscan University of Steubenville. He is also the recipient of the William C. Bier Award for psychologists intersted in religious issues from the American Psychological Association for his notable contributions to the psychology of religion. Subsequently the University of Dallas honored him by establishing the Adrian van Kaam award given yearly to the most outstanding student in the department of psychology.

✠

Susan Muto, Ph.D., executive director of the Epiphany Association and a native of Pittsburgh, is also a renowned speaker, author, and teacher. She was invited by Professor van Kaam to continue and expand the original, classical, spiritual readings that comprised the basis of his embryonic formation theology. A single lay woman living her vocation in the world and doing full-time church-related ministry in the Association, she has led conferences, seminars, workshops, and institutes throughout the world.

Dr. Muto received her Ph.D. in English literature from the University of Pittsbugh, where she specialized in the work of post-Reformation spiritual writers. She also worked as Father Adrian's first assistant to perfect the courses and programs of the Institute of Formative Spirituality. Beginning in 1966, she served in various administrative positions at the IFS, taught as a full professor in its programs, edited its journals, and served as its director from 1981 to 1988. An expert in literature and spirituality, she continues to teach courses on an adjunct basis at many schools, seminaries, and institutes of higher learning throughout the world. She aims in her teaching to integrate the life of prayer and presence with professional ministry and in-depth formation in the home, the church, and the marketplace. In faithfulness to the principles of the original European Epiphany approach, she addresses her teachings to the contemporary needs of laity, clergy, and religious.

As co-editor of *Epiphany Connexions* and *Epiphany International*, as a frequent contributor to scholarly and popular journals, and as herself the author and co-author of over thirty-five books, Dr. Muto keeps up to date with the latest developments in her field. In fact, her many books on formative reading of scripture and the masters are considered to be premier introductions to the basic, classical art and discipline of spiritual formation and its systematic, comprehensive, formation theology. She lectures nationally and internationally on the treasured wisdom of the Judeo-Christian faith and formation tradition and on many foundational facets of living human and Christian values in today's world. Professor Muto holds membership in numerous honorary professional organizations and has received many distinctions for her work, including and honorary Doctor of Humanities degree from King's College in Wilkes Barre, Pennsylvania.